ISDN Systems

Architecture, Technology, and Applications

EDITOR

Pramode K. Verma
AT&T Bell Laboratories

CONTRIBUTORS

Burton R. Saltzberg
Pramode K. Verma
Ryoichi Komiya
Sadahiko Kano
Anthony M. Rutkowski
Gustav Laub
Edward K. Bower
Stephen B. Weinstein
Gottfried W. R. Luderer

PRENTICE HALL, Englewood Cliffs, New Jersey 07632

Library of Congress Cataloging-in-Publication Data

ISDN systems : architecture, technology, and applications / editor,
  Pramode K. Verma ; contributors, Burton R. Saltzberg . . . [et al.].
      p.   cm.
    Includes bibliographical references.
    ISBN 0-13-505736-1
    1. Integrated services digital networks.   I. Verma, Pramode K.
  II. Saltzberg, Burton R.
  TK5103.7.I84   1990
  004.6—dc20   89-27754
                                                          CIP

Editorial/production supervision: *Raeia Maes*
Cover design: *Debra Watson*
Manufacturing buyer: *Robert Anderson*

© 1990 by Prentice-Hall, Inc.
A Division of Simon & Schuster
Englewood Cliffs, New Jersey 07632

The publisher offers discounts on this book when ordered
in bulk quantities. For more information, write:

> Special Sales/College Marketing
> Prentice Hall
> College Technical and Reference Division
> Englewood Cliffs, NJ 07632

Printed in the United States of America

10 9 8 7 6 5 4 3 2 1

ISBN   0-13-505736-1

Prentice-Hall International (UK) Limited, *London*
Prentice-Hall of Australia Pty. Limited, *Sydney*
Prentice-Hall Canada Inc., *Toronto*
Prentice-Hall Hispanoamericana, S.A., *Mexico*
Prentice-Hall of India Private Limited, *New Delhi*
Prentice-Hall of Japan, Inc., *Tokyo*
Simon & Schuster Asia Pte. Ltd., *Singapore*
Editora Prentice-Hall do Brasil, Ltda., *Rio de Janeiro*

Contents

2 ISDN: A Pragmatic Approach 49

PRAMODE K. VERMA

3 ISDN Physical Interfaces 75

RYOICHI KOMIYA

Contents

4   ISDN Signaling Protocols   119

SADAHIKO KANO

5   ISDN Standardization Process   156

ANTHONY M. RUTKOWSKI

6   Components for ISDN: Partitioning, Definition, and Realization Abstract   185

GUSTAV LAUB

Preface

The term Integrated Services Digital Network came into existence more than a decade ago to represent the evolution of the telecommunications network toward a single integrated structure to accommodate a wide variety of services. The concept of ISDN came about as a response to the then practice of creating application-specific networks, usually mutually exclusive, from a services perspective. With the emergence of the Information Society and progression toward an era where new applications are identified at a rapid rate, the need for an integrated structure that could offer flexibility and ease in terms of new services provisioning became apparent. In addition, there are at least two other factors that are responsible for the impressive progress ISDN has made in terms of standardizing the user–network interfaces and in terms of actually delivering ISDN services in limited geographical areas. First, ISDN recognizes and allows for a highly functional coupling between the user-owned, premises-based devices, such as PCs, intelligent terminals, and host computers, and a common user network. The ISDN's framework thus exploits the potential synergy between the premises-based systems and the network in delivering end to end service. The second factor has to do with the commercial aspects of providing ISDN service. After at least a couple of decades of experience with proprietary protocols, a growing number of communications products and services vendors now recognizes that standardized and open interfaces benefit not only the user community but the vendor community as well. Open interfaces resulting in multivendor solutions are important in terms of providing the flexibility needed by the user community and the ability to create general as well as niche markets of ISDN products by the vendor community.

It is important to realize that the concept of ISDN started emerging at about the same time, during which a profound transition of the industrial society to an information society was taking place. The realization that the movement and management of information are no longer just ancillary aspects of doing business or running a government or an educational institution, but that they bear an integral relationship to the survival and growth of modern business, has fueled the development of the ISDN technology at an unprecedented rate in the entire history of the development of communications. This development is not localized. It is for the first time that one can clearly observe a truly international effort to define standards that will facilitate global communications services.

All this, of course, makes the task of writing a book on ISDN truly challenging. The fact that the authors of this book began this effort more than a year ago is based on their belief that the technical advancement associated with ISDN has reached a point where a book on the subject is warranted. In other words, it reflected their collective thinking that, even though the advances of technology for ISDN will continue at a rapid rate, there is, at this time, a sufficient body of knowledge associated with the subject that will likely remain intact for the foreseeable future. With the philosophy of ISDN being to provide a common infrastructure for the entire range of communications services, it naturally encompasses almost all major specialities in communications. The decision to have this book as an edited volume from a number of specialists in ISDN is again a result of our collective belief that progress on ISDN is taking place at a rate that is somewhat beyond the capabilities of a single individual to keep up with all of it.

This book is fundamentally aimed at the practicing communications engineer. To a specialist in a particular area, it will provide the appropriate background in other areas. To someone beginning to work in the field of ISDN or the general area of communications, it will provide in one single place an overview of almost the entire ISDN technology base. The book should also prove valuable to consultants and systems engineers in providing an overall framework for ISDN. The book can also be used as a one-semester graduate course in communications at universities where communications is emphasized.

The book is organized into nine chapters. While the chapters are generally self-contained, studying them in the sequence presented will allow the reader to progress from the concept and tools of technology to the actual services it can provide at the present time and in the future.

Digital technology is the backbone of ISDN. Chapter 1 reviews the concepts of digital technology for the reader. It emphasizes the basic principles of transmitting and receiving digital signals over various communication channels. This opening chapter can be used as a condensed review of digital technology and serve as a link between a mature subject and the rapidly evolving ISDN technology.

Chapter 2 introduces ISDN as a single integrated network that will offer a variety of services. The technological building blocks of ISDN are reviewed, and it is demonstrated that the ISDN vision is technologically realizable today, at least over limited geographical areas of the world.

All common user networks function on the basis of well-defined physical, electrical, and signaling interfaces. Chapter 3 discusses the physical and electrical interfaces of ISDN, covering both the basic and primary rate interfaces. The ISDN signaling mechanism constitutes a fundamental departure from most of the existing signaling procedures, where user information and signaling information traverse the same paths together. Mandating the out-of-band signaling procedures gives ISDN a range of flexibilities not possible otherwise. The ISDN signaling protocols are reviewed in Chapter 4.

ISDN is the first communications technology that is truly globally driven. (We often tend to forget that communications, by definition, are of global interest.) Developing standards procedures that are acceptable to a diverse set of needs existing in different countries with radically different technological infrastructures is a challenging task. Chapter 5 reviews the functions and jurisdictions of the international bodies that are responsible for developing the standard interfaces for ISDN and the means for interworking among ISDNs. Chapter 6 discusses the components of ISDN, how they are partitioned, defined, and realized.

Applications determine whether a particular technology will be successful in the marketplace. Chapter 7 is focused on the near-term applications of ISDN, while Chapter 8 emphasizes more sophisticated services of the future. Finally, Chapter 9 conjectures on the future evolution of ISDN from a technologist's perspective.

Wherever possible, we have attempted to create a balance of viewpoints on ISDN. The extremely rich but diverse backgrounds and professional affiliations of the authors of this book bear ample testimony to this fact. In closing, I would like to thank the contributing authors of this book, whose efforts have resulted in what I expect will become a milestone in the continuing progress of ISDN. I would also like to acknowledge the help and understanding of my wife, Gita, during the editing process.

Finally, it is important to note that all the views expressed in this book are solely those of the individual contributors and should not be construed as necessarily reflecting those of the editor or the organizations with whom they are affiliated.

Pramode K. Verma, Editor

CHAPTER 1

Theoretical Foundations
of Digital Communication

BURTON R. SALTZBERG

AT&T Bell Laboratories

ABSTRACT

The main purpose of this opening chapter is to present the basic principles of transmitting and receiving digital signals over various communication channels. The effects of various channel impairments are described, as are the techniques for achieving good performance in their presence. The impairments most heavily dealt with are additive noise and linear distortion. Methods of converting analog sources to digital signals, and the converse reconstruction are also presented.

1.1 WHAT IS DIGITAL COMMUNICATION?

There is much confusion as to what constitutes digital communication. No clear-cut definition exists, and none will be given here. Digital and analog transmissions are not the dichotomy that is frequently presented. Analog techniques are essential components of any digital transmission system. Before exploring the characteristics that distinguish digital communication, we must first separate the nature of the communication from that of the source information to be transmitted.

1.1.1 Analog and Digital Sources

Analog sources are those that can be represented as a continuous function of time. The signal is continuous both in that it is defined over a continuous range of time and in that it can assume a continuous range of values. Speech is the most common example. Others include scanned images with continuous shades of gray or color and analog instrument readings. At the receiver, it is desired to reconstruct the continuous time function with some fidelity criterion.

A digital source generates a sequence of symbols, where each symbol is chosen

1

from a finite set, or *alphabet*, and the symbols are typically presented to the communication system at discrete instants of time. The goal of the receiver is to recover the sequence of symbols with as few errors as possible. Examples of digital sources are text and computer data.

Sources exist that are intermediate between analog and digital. A signal may have only a finite number of levels, but be defined over a continuum of time, with transitions between levels allowed at any point in time. Examples are scanned black-and-white images and the classic random telegraph signal. These sources are sometimes referred to as *asynchronous data*. Conversely, a source may consist of sampled data values, which take on values over a continuous range but occur at discrete points in time. These intermediate forms of sources are not very important for modern communication systems, but are mentioned to illustrate the difficulty in characterizing information sources as either analog or digital.

It is extremely important to distinguish between the analog or digital nature of an information source with that of a communication system. As will be discussed in detail in this chapter, an analog source can be converted to digital format and conversely in order to match the requirements of the communication channel. Such conversions can take place not only at the origination and destination points, but internally within the communication network as well. The entire concept of ISDN arises from the ability to perform such conversions.

1.1.2 Amplification and Regeneration

All communication channels introduce loss together with other impairments to a carried signal. Depending on the transmission medium and the type of signal, beyond some distance the signal becomes too weak to be reliably received. Some form of repeater function must be introduced at appropriate distance intervals to restore the signal amplitude.

In conventional analog transmission systems, the repeater function is primarily that of amplification. Each repeater boosts the signal amplitude to that of the output of the previous repeater and therefore compensates for the loss of the span. However, any noise that was introduced over the span will also be amplified and passed on to the next span. An amplifier cannot increase the ratio of signal power to noise power, which is a critical determinant of performance. In fact, to the extent that the amplifier introduces noise itself, the ratio is degraded. The noise introduced over a long analog communication channel will therefore accumulate and lead to steadily decreasing signal-to-noise ratio.

Other impairments, particularly linear distortion (amplitude and phase variations), are also introduced by each span between repeaters. To a large extent these can be compensated by the repeaters by a process known as *equalization*. The equalization process is never perfect, however, and the residual impairments will also accumulate over the length of an analog channel.

If the signal to be transmitted is generated by a digital source or has been converted to a digital format, then the repeater can *regenerate* the signal rather than amplify it. A regenerator acts as a receiver followed by a transmitter. The incoming signal is detected, decisions are made as to the symbols, and a new signal based on those symbols is transmitted over the next span.   No noise or other impairments are present in the output.   Unless the regenerator makes errors in detecting the symbols or introduces timing perturbations, there is no accumulation of impairment.

The presence of regenerators as opposed to amplifiers is the only difference between digital transmission and analog.   Each regenerator span is in fact an analog channel, in that a continuous signal is transmitted, subjected to loss, noise, and other impairments, and detected.   It is meaningless to classify a channel without repeaters as either analog or digital.

The use of regeneration can lead to enormous improvement in performance and capacity.   It is only necessary to design the spacing between regenerators such that the error probability is sufficiently low.   Fortunately, improvements in technology over the past few decades have permitted the design of low-cost speech digitization and regeneration.   Digital transmission, via the T1 system, has been the preferred technology for medium-distance voice transmission for the past 20 years or so.   When inherently digital information is carried in addition to voice, the advantages of digital communication are further increased substantially.

1.1.3 Multiplexing

A communication channel in general terms can be considered to have an inherent information-carrying capacity.   For analog sources, the quantity of interest is the bandwidth in hertz (Hz), while for digital sources we are interested in the number of bits per second (bps) that can be carried.   As we shall see, the two measures are intimately related.

It is usual that the capacity of a channel is considerably greater than that required by a source of interest.   For economic reasons, channels are shared by many sources by some technique known as *multiplexing*.   Far less common is the practice of *diviplexing*, in which a high-rate source uses more than one low-capacity channel, and the information is reconstructed at the receiving end.

1.1.3.1 Frequency division multiplexing.   For analog sources, the usual form of multiplexing is *frequency division multiplexing*, or FDM.   Each source must first be sharply band limited to a fixed frequency interval.   A set of different carrier frequencies then enables single-sideband modulation to transmit the sources over nonoverlapping frequency bands over the same channel.   At the receiving end, the same set of carrier frequencies is used to separately demodulate each information source.

The best-known application of FDM is in radio or television broadcasting. Each station or channel in a geographic area has a unique carrier frequency.   These frequencies are spaced so as to efficiently use the available radio spectrum, while maintaining a certain program bandwidth, or quality.   By setting the receiver dial, the user chooses the demodulation frequency, which in turn determines the program to be received.

Standard hierarchies of FDM have evolved for transmission of voice over national and international telephone networks.   The multiplexing hierarchy, at least at the lower levels, is independent of the actual transmission medium used, allowing tandem transmission of large ensembles of voice circuits over different facilities, such as coaxial cable and microwave radio, without full demodulation and remodulation at intermediate points.

Different standard hierarchies have evolved in North America and in Europe. In both cases, the voice band is restricted to less than 4 kHz, and voice channels are spaced 4 kHz apart. While far from audiophile quality, this bandwidth provides excellent voice intelligibility and economical use of transmission facilities.

In North America, the first stage of FDM consists of modulating twelve voice circuits into an entity called a *group*, which occupies 48 kHz of bandwidth. At the next stage, each group is treated as a unit, and five such entities are modulated into a *supergroup*. The process continues in stages to the *mastergroup* (ten supergroups) and higher levels whenever the transmission facility can support such bandwidth. This hierarchy is shown in Fig. 1.1. Demodulation is performed in identical stages. The hierarchy permits cross-connection at group or higher levels as previously mentioned. It also provides units of bandwidth that can be used for purposes other than voice or voiceband services. For example, a group band can be dedicated to the transmission of a single high-speed data stream instead of twelve voiceband circuits.

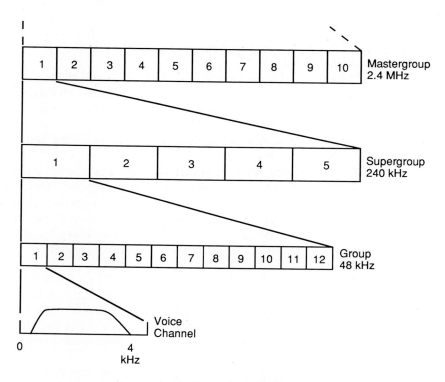

Figure 1.1   North American FDM hierarchy.

1.1.3.2 Time division multiplexing. In digital communication systems, multiple signals are transmitted over a channel by *time division multiplexing*, or TDM. Here bits or small clumps of bits from different sources are interleaved to form a faster bit stream. Some means of *framing* is needed to identify which bits belong to which original source so that the signals can be separated at the receiving end.

As in the case of FDM, hierarchies of TDM multiplexing have evolved differently in North America and in Europe. In North America, the first level in the multiplex hierarchy is the DS-1, 1544 kbps, which is the signal carried by the very widely deployed T1 carrier system. In the most common application, the signal carries 24 digitized voice channels. As will be described later, a voice channel is digitized by sampling 8000 times per second and representing each sample by a binary number of up to 8 bits, for an aggregate bit rate of 64 kbps.

The DS-1 signal consists of frames 193 bits in length, generated 8000 times per second, to produce the 1544-kbps total bit rate. Each frame contains a single framing bit, followed by 8 bits in sequence for each of the 24 constituent channels. The framing bits from successive frames follow a unique sequence that is unlikely to be generated by any of the bits in the information channels. As the demultiplexer, this particular sequence is searched for to establish framing and therefore to permit separation of the 24 subchannels. It should be stressed that this frame synchronization process can only be accomplished after bit synchronization has been established; that is, a local clock has been adjusted to agree with the timing of the incoming bit stream.

In earlier versions of the T1 system, 1 bit of each 8 channel bits was used for signaling and network administration, so that only 7 bits were used to encode each speech sample. In more recent systems, a bit is "robbed" from an 8-bit sample only on a fraction of the samples. The European system has evolved in a different manner. Here a 2048-kbps bit stream is used to carry only thirty 64-kbps channels, with the remaining 128 kbps used not only for framing, but also for the signaling and administration associated with the constituent channels.

The basic 64-kbps channel is often referred to as the DS-0 level. It can readily be used for the transmission of digital information in place of digitized voice. In such an application, the DS-0 channel can itself be used to carry several multiplexed lower-speed digital signals. Various transmission constraints and the possible need for signaling and administrative information frequently do not permit the free use of the entire 64 kbps in the DS-0 channel, so user information is restricted to a slightly lower rate, such as 56 kbps. The migration to the ISDN environment, however, envisions the availability of 64-kbps "clear channels," which are fully available for user data.

As in the case of FDM, lower levels in the TDM hierarchy are interleaved to form higher levels, as illustrated in Fig. 1.2. Four DS-1 bits stream are interleaved and framing and other overhead bits are added to produce the 6.312-Mbps DS-2 level in the North American hierarchy. Similarly, seven DS-2 signals plus overhead bits form the DS-3 level of 44.736 Mbps, and the 274.176-Mbps DS-4 level is formed from six DS-3 level bit streams. In constructing a digital network, high-speed bit streams need only be partially demultiplexed at nodes within the

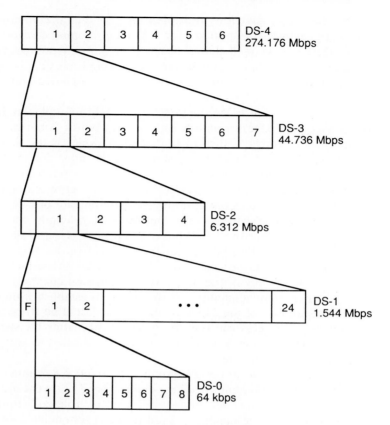

Figure 1.2   North American TDM hierarchy.

network for cross-connection at any DS level. In fact, it is even possible to efficiently cross-connect digital and analog transmission systems by converting TDM signals directly to and from FDM signals of the appropriate level by means of a *transmultiplexer.*

Any level of the TDM hierarchy can be used to carry a single-user data stream in place of multiplexed signals of lower levels. For example, the DS-3 level can carry a digitized video signal. As in the case of DS-0, various constraints may preclude the use of the entire bit stream, without restrictions, for user data.

Multiplexing of digital streams is straightforward if they have the exact same bit rate or exactly related rates. Several schemes have been proposed and implemented for synchronizing widespread networks so that all clock rates are tied together. Modern digital networks are tending to evolve in this direction. However, the usual practice to date does not include such synchronization, and DS-1 and higher-level bit streams are timed by independent clocks of specified accuracy.

Digital bit streams that may be generated by independent clocks can be multiplexed by means of a process known as *pulse stuffing.* Consider four independent DS-1 streams being multiplexed to a DS-2 signal. The DS-2 clock must be fast enough to accommodate the fastest allowable DS-1 clock.   Each DS-1 stream that is clocked at a rate slower than maximum is brought up to the maximum by stuffing extra bits into the stream at a fixed point in the frame and adding overhead bits that denote the presence or absence of such bits.   This brings the four DS-1 streams into synchronism so that they can be multiplexed.   During demultiplexing, the overhead bits are examined to determine if stuffed bits exist that must be dropped.   A new clock is generated to smoothly reproduce the original DS-1 signal.   Even in a synchronous system, this technique may be desirable in the presence of significant variation in the propagation time of the transmission facilities.   Alternate approaches for removing the effects of variable delay involve the use of long buffer stores and introduce appreciable additional delay.

The most important characteristic of the TDM digital hierarchy is that no matter what multiplexed level is being carried by a digital transmission facility that signal is transmitted digitally with all the benefits of the regeneration process.

1.2 CHANNEL IMPAIRMENTS

All communication channels have a set of impairments that place ultimate limits on the channel's capabilities for carrying digital signals.   The limits show up as constraints on the bit rate and error probability that can be achieved.   Within wide ranges, one of these constraints can be traded for the other.   Another limitation that is of importance in some applications is the delay of the channel.

To describe the impairments that are present on various types of communication channels, it is first necessary to present a very brief review of Fourier analysis.

1.2.1 Brief Review of Fourier Analysis

In analyzing communication channels and their effects on signals, it is convenient to represent a signal as a superposition of sinusoidal functions.   This convenience arises primarily from the fact that most communication channels can be approximated as linear time-invariant systems.

A linear system is one in which, if an input $x(t)$ produces an output $y(t)$,

$$x(t) \rightarrow y(t)$$

then

$$ax(t) \rightarrow ay(t)$$

for any constant a, and

$$x_1(t) + x_2(t) \rightarrow y_1(t) + y_2(t)$$

for any allowable x_1 and x_2.

A time-invariant system is one in which

$$x(t + \tau) \rightarrow y(t + \tau)$$

for any τ.

In particular, if the input to a linear time-invariant system consists of a sum of sinusoids, then the output will consist of only sinusoids of the same frequency. A linear time-invariant system can therefore be fully described by its treatment (amplitude multiplier and phase shift) of any sine-wave input.

Decomposition of a signal into sinusoids is most easily understood for the case of periodic signals. If $f(t)$ repeats for all time, positive and negative, with period T, then under very general conditions it can be expressed by the *Fourier series*

$$f(t) = \sum_{n=0}^{\infty} a_n \cos \omega nt + \sum_{n=1}^{\infty} b_n \sin \omega nt$$

where

$$\omega = \frac{2\pi}{T}$$

and the series converge in the mean; that is, the mean square error approaches zero as the number of terms grow large. The signal is thus expressed as a sum of sinusoids whose frequencies are integral multiples of the repetition rate of the periodic signal.

It is mathematically desirable to introduce complex notation, using the identity

$$e^{i\theta} = \cos \theta + i \sin \theta$$

The Fourier series then becomes

$$f(t) = \sum_{n=-\infty}^{\infty} c_n e^{i\omega nt}$$

where the c_n's are found from

$$c_n = \frac{1}{T} \int_{-T/2}^{T/2} f(t) e^{-i\omega nt}\, dt$$

If $f(t)$ is real, then c_n and c_{-n} are complex conjugates.

While not as intuitively clear, under certain conditions a nonperiodic signal can be expressed by its *Fourier integral* or *Fourier transform* [10]:

$$f(t) = \frac{1}{2\pi} \int_{-\infty}^{\infty} F(\omega) e^{i\omega t}\, d\omega$$

where

$$F(\omega) = \int_{-\infty}^{\infty} f(t) e^{-i\omega t}\, dt$$

If one is willing to take liberties with mathematical niceties, then the Fourier integral can be thought of as the limit of a Fourier series as the period of the time function become infinite. The discrete, equally spaced frequency components then become a continuum of infinitesimal frequency components.

The similarity between the Fourier transform and its inverse should be noted.

If the transform of a time function is known, then the inverse transform of a frequency function of that shape can easily be found.

Two functions are of particular interest in communication theory, the impulse and the square pulse. The impulse, or *Dirac delta function*, $\delta(t)$, may be thought of as the limit of an even, large-amplitude, narrow-width pulse, as the amplitude become infinite and the width goes to zero in a manner that maintains unit area. Because of mathematical difficulties, it is more precisely treated as a generalized function that is defined only within integrals. In particular, for any function $g(t)$ that is continuous at $t = 0$,

$$\int_{-\infty}^{\infty} g(t)\, \delta(t)\, dt = g(0)$$

The Fourier transform of the delta function is simply 1, a flat spectrum extending to infinity.

The square pulse

$$f(t) = 1, \qquad -\frac{T}{2} < t < \frac{T}{2}$$

$$= 0, \qquad \text{elsewhere}$$

has the transform

$$F(\omega) = T\, \frac{\sin \omega T/2}{\omega T/2}$$

This function is important enough to be given a name, *sinc*, where

$$\text{sinc}(x) = \frac{\sin \pi x}{\pi x}$$

[$\text{sinc}(0) = 1$ to maintain continuity]; so the preceding equation can be written as

$$F(\omega) = T \,\text{sinc}\left(\frac{\omega T}{2\pi}\right)$$

The sinc function has the important property that

$$\text{sinc}(0) = 1$$

$$\text{sinc}(n) = 0, \qquad n \text{ an integer} \neq 0$$

Similarly, the *ideal bandlimited function*

$$F(\omega) = 1, \qquad |\omega| \leq W$$

$$= 0, \qquad |\omega| > W$$

has inverse Fourier transform

$$f(t) = \frac{W}{\pi} \,\text{sinc}\left(\frac{Wt}{\pi}\right)$$

A sufficient, but not necessary, condition for the existence of the Fourier integral is that the signal have finite energy.

$$\int_{-\infty}^{\infty} [f(t)]^2 \, dt = E$$

In that case, the energy can also be found from the Fourier transform

$$E = \frac{1}{2\pi} \int_{-\infty}^{\infty} F(\omega)F^*(\omega) \, d\omega$$

where F^* denotes complex conjugation. $F(\omega)F^*(\omega) = |F(\omega)|^2$, a real quantity, which is called the *energy spectral density*. Since for real $f(t)$, $F^*(\omega) = F(-\omega)$, the energy spectral density is an even function. Here we have used the two-sided form of this function, rather than the less commonly used one-sided notation, which is defined for positive frequencies only.

A linear system can be defined by its frequency transfer function,

$$H(\omega) = A(\omega)e^{i\phi(\omega)}$$

where $A(\omega)$ is the amplitude function (gain or attenuation) and $\phi(\omega)$ is the phase shift. In particular, a simple constant delay τ can be represented by a phase shift proportional to frequency.

$$H(\omega) = e^{i\omega\tau}$$

If $X(\omega)$ is the Fourier transform of the input to a linear system $H(\omega)$, then the Fourier transform of the output is simply

$$Y(\omega) = H(\omega)X(\omega)$$

The inverse Fourier transform of $H(\omega)$ is the *impulse response*, which is the output of the system when the input is a delta function.

For signals of infinite duration, whose power rather than energy is finite, the Fourier integral is not defined. However, a *power spectral density*, analogous to the energy spectral density of finite energy signals, is defined by

$$P_f(\omega) = \lim_{T\to\infty} \frac{1}{2T} \left| \int_{-T}^{T} f(t)e^{i\omega t}dt \right|^2$$

It can be shown that

$$P_f(\omega) = \lim_{T\to\infty} \frac{1}{2T} \int_{-\infty}^{\infty} \int_{-T}^{T} f(t)f(t + \tau)e^{i\omega\tau} \, dt \, d\tau$$

so that the power spectral density is the Fourier transform of the *autocorrelation function*, defined by

$$R_f(\tau) = \lim_{T\to\infty} \frac{1}{2T} \int_{-T}^{T} f(t)f(t + \tau) \, dt$$

Both the power spectral density and the autocorrelation are real even functions.

The concept of power spectral density is also applied to random time func-

tions.   A stationary random process is one in which the statistics do not change
with time.   Its autocorrelation is defined as

$$R_f(\tau) = E[f(t)f(t + \tau)]$$

where E denotes expected value.   As before, the power spectral density is the
Fourier transform of the autocorrelation

$$P_f(\omega) = \int_{-\infty}^{\infty} R_f(\tau)e^{i\omega\tau}\, d\tau$$

N. Wiener and A. I. Khinchine have shown that the expected value of the power
in a frequency interval is the integral of the power spectral density over that interval,
and the variance of that power goes to zero as the measurement time interval
becomes infinite.

The total power of a signal, deterministic or random, is

$$P = R_f(0) = \frac{1}{2\pi} \int_{-\infty}^{\infty} P_f(\omega)\, d\omega$$

The input and output power spectral densities for a linear, time-invariant system
are related by

$$P_y(\omega) = H(\omega)H^*(\omega)P_x(\omega) = |H(\omega)|^2 P_x(\omega)$$

1.2.2 Noise

An undesired extraneous time function that corrupts the desired signal is referred
to as *noise*.   The most common form of noise is a random function that adds to
and is independent of the signal and is the only type that will be considered here.
It is referred to as *additive noise*, as distinguished from multiplicative noise, which
varies the amplitude of a signal in a random manner.

The sources of noise are myriad.   Other communication channels can crosstalk into the channel through a variety of mechanisms.   Electrical devices and
atmospheric disturbances generate noise that is picked up by electromagnetic propagation, inductive and capacitive coupling or through power lines or any of a host
of diverse paths.   More fundamentally, even in the most isolated possible environment, electrical noise is generated by all physical objects not at a temperature
of absolute zero.   This basic thermal noise power is proportional to absolute
temperature.   Even interstellar space contains noise that can be traced back to the
creation of the universe.   Therefore, while good engineering practice can eliminate
or minimize many sources of noise, some noise must remain, and its effects rather
than its presence are then to be minimized.

The most mathematically tractable model of noise, which in fact is an excellent
approximation for many noise sources such as thermal noise, is the Gaussian random process.   A Gaussian random process is a stationary one whose amplitude
follows a normal probability distribution.   More precisely, any set of time samples
must be jointly normal.   A zero mean normal probability distribution has the form

$$p(x) = \frac{1}{\sqrt{2\pi}\sigma} e^{-x^2/2\sigma^2}$$

The quantity σ^2 is the variance or, in our terminology, the power. The prevalence of the normal distribution arises from the central limit theorem, which states that under fairly general conditions the sum of a large number of random variables of arbitrary probability distribution approaches a normal random variable. The mathematical usefulness of the Gaussian model is the principle that any linear operation on a Gaussian process leads to another Gaussian process. A Gaussian random process is fully described by its autocorrelation function and therefore its power spectral density.

A special limiting case of a Gaussian process is *white noise*, which has a flat, constant power spectral density. The autocorrelation function is the delta function, which has infinite power. White noise is therefore physically impossible. However, it is a very useful approximation for noise whose spectrum is flat over the frequency range of interest. Gaussian noise that is not white is referred to as *colored*.

Another very common form of noise is the *impulsive* type. This consists of discrete sharp spikes with various probability distributions of amplitudes. The spacing between impulses also generally follows arbitrary probability distributions. These characteristics of impulsive noise lead to great difficulties in analyzing its effects. However, noise generated by electromechanical devices and atmospheric disturbance do tend to be of this type. A common measurement of impulse noise is the count of instances per unit time that the amplitude exceeds one or more given amplitude levels.

Interference from other channels of the same type is known as *crosstalk* and may be considered to be a form of noise, although it may not have the randomness properties usually associated with noise. If the interfering signal is sufficiently distorted or if a large number of different interfering sources combine, then the effect in the interfered channel will appear random and under certain conditions can be treated as Gaussian. An important consideration in studying crosstalk effects is whether the interfering signals are of the same type as the signal of interest. If not, the randomness assumption is usually an excellent one.

It is obvious in a radio system how crosstalk can result from other radio channels of the same or adjacent frequencies. The complex process of spectrum management, practiced by governmental and international agencies, serves the purpose of minimizing such interference while trying to satisfy demand for a limited resource, the radio spectrum.

For the purposes of this text, we will be particularly concerned with crosstalk in wire-pair cables.

1.2.3 Crosstalk in Wire-Pair Cables

Wire pairs are commonly provided in cables of many pairs, which are used by different users for different purposes. Even if not assembled in cables, wire pairs may physically be installed in proximity to each other. Inductive and capacitive coupling causes signals on one pair to interfere with those on another.

Crosstalk can be minimized by providing different twists to each pair and by carefully maintaining balance referenced to ground. At considerable expense, shielding greatly reduces crosstalk, particularly at higher frequencies. It should be noted that coaxial cable, in addition to providing excellent transmission characteristics, is also inherently shielded. For ordinary unshielded wires, however, crosstalk is the principal source of noise. The power that can be transmitted over a pair of wires, as a function of frequency, must be limited in order to constrain the possible crosstalk into other pairs.

Figure 1.3 illustrates two modes of crosstalk, near end and far end. In near-end crosstalk, the signal from a transmitter interferes with a nearby receiver. Because of the loss of the channel, transmitted signals are higher in level than received signals by the amount of the loss. For far-end crosstalk, the interfering signal is subjected to the same loss as the desired signal before it reaches the distant receiver. For this reason, when both modes of crosstalk are present, near-end crosstalk is usually much more severe. When different wire pairs are used for each direction of transmission, then near-end crosstalk can be virtually eliminated by using different cables or shielded groups in each direction.

Crosstalk is characterized by its power transfer function, $H_n(\omega)$, such that the power spectral density of the interference seen on the channel of interest is

$$P(\omega) \; = \; H_n(\omega)P_i(\omega)$$

where $P_i(\omega)$ is the power spectral density of the interfering signal.

For near-end crosstalk, $H_n(\omega)$ can be very well approximated by

$$H_n(\omega) \; = \; K_n\omega^{3/2}$$

particularly at higher frequencies. Note that this increases with frequency, at 15 decibels (dB) per decade. The transfer function is approximately independent of length, provided that the pairs are long enough to have a loss of at least 5 dB. The reason for this effect is that crosstalk that results from coupling at some distance

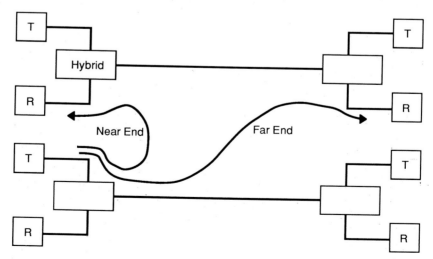

Figure 1.3 Crosstalk mechanisms. Two-wire paths are shown, but the mechanisms apply equally to four-wire transmission.

from the interfering transmitter and interfered receiver is subjected to round-trip loss.

When there are several interferers, crosstalk adds on a power basis. The different crosstalk coefficients, K_n, typically follow a probability distribution such that the resultant crosstalk powers have a log normal probability distribution. That is, the noise components in decibels are normally distributed. In any event, when many interferers are present, approximation of the total crosstalk as a Gaussian process is usually reasonable.

Far-end crosstalk is usually much less of a problem then near-end, for typical values of channel loss. As in the case of near-end crosstalk, we can express the interference power as

$$P(\omega) = H_f(\omega)P_i(\omega)$$

but the power transfer function is now of the form

$$H_f(\omega) = K_f\omega^2 l$$

This transfer function is proportional to distance and increases with frequency at 20 dB per decade. Far-end crosstalk can be appreciable relative to near-end at very high frequencies.

For most wire-pair channels, near-end crosstalk is the dominant noise impairment. If the system is designed to reduce this problem, then both far-end crosstalk and impulsive noise become important.

1.2.4 Linear Distortion

The predominant impairment introduced by any communication channel is the variable loss (or gain) and variable phase shift as a function of frequency. Such distortion is referred to as *linear* in that it can be expressed by a frequency response $H(\omega)$, and no frequency components not present in the input signal are introduced.

The channel frequency response is usually considered to be of the form

$$H(\omega) = A(\omega)e^{i\phi(\omega)}$$

where the real quantities $A(\omega)$ and $\phi(\omega)$ are the amplitude and phase response, respectively.

$A(\omega)$ is commonly plotted in decibels. If we wish to treat amplitude distortion as separable from flat loss, $A(\omega)$ may be given in terms relative to the value at some nominal frequency.

In considering the phase response, it should be remembered that a constant delay is represented by $\phi(\omega) = k\omega$. Since absolute delay, and in most cases a constant phase offset, have no distorting effect, any linear function can be subtracted from the phase function $\phi(\omega)$. Frequently, the *envelope delay*, $d\phi(\omega)/d\omega$, is specified and given relative to some nominal frequency. The term arises from the fact that it is the delay experienced by a very low frequency envelope modulating a carrier of the frequency of interest.

Two types of linear channels of special importance are the telephone network or radio channel and the wire-pair channel. Voiceband and higher-bandwidth channels in the telephone network are sharply bandlimited to avoid interfering with other channels in the frequency division multiplex system. Radio channels must be similarly bandlimited to avoid interferences with other channels with adjacent frequency assignment.

Although perfect bandlimiting is impossible, in practice the loss outside the band is extremely high and the approximation is an excellent one. To achieve this, the loss must have some significant roll-off region within the band. Phase distortion must also exist in these band-edge regions.

The wire-pair channel, on the other hand, does not have a sharply defined bandwidth. The loss increases steadily with frequency. A reasonable approximation for the transfer function of a wire pair, particularly for higher frequencies, is [2]

$$H\omega = K_1 e^{k_2 \sqrt{\omega} l} \, e^{ik_3 \sqrt{\omega} l} \, e^{ik_4 \omega l}$$

The last factor is a flat delay that can be ignored as far as distortion is concerned. The second factor is the phase distortion. This corresponds to a envelope delay that decreases with the square root of frequency. The first factor is the loss, which in decibels is proportional to length and to the square root of frequency. It is primarily this loss function that limits the bit rate and distance over which the wire pair can be used without regeneration.

The impulse response for the wire pair is of the form

$$h(t) = \frac{A_1 l}{t^3} \, e^{-a_2 l^2/t}, \qquad t > 0$$

The time spread of this function increases greatly with distance.

The most obvious effect of linear distortion is *intersymbol interference*, which is the spreading of signal pulses so that they overlap into the signal intervals devoted to previous and subsequent signal pulses. Both amplitude and phase distortion produce intersymbol interference. Conditions for the elimination of intersymbol interference are discussed in a subsequent section.

Equalization is the process of eliminating or reducing the intersymbol interference due to the linear distortion of the channel. In its simplest form, equalization consists of cascading the channel with a network of frequency response

$$\frac{K_1 e^{i(k_2\omega + \theta)}}{H(\omega)}$$

over the frequency band of interest. This amounts to inverting the channel, within a constant gain factor, delay, and phase shift. Automatic adaptive equalization, using tapped lines, is a field of great activity that will be discussed later in this chapter. The net effect may still be approximated as an inversion of the channel's frequency response.

An undesirable side effect of equalization is amplification of noise in the spectral regions in which the channel amplitude response is low. If the noise power spectrum present before equalization is $N(\omega)$, then after equalization it will be

$$\frac{K_1^2 N(\omega)}{[A(\omega)]^2}$$

The effect on the signal is such that the signal-to-noise ratio is generally degraded. Note that equalization of the phase function has no effect on noise power. The matched filter, which optimizes the signal-to-noise ratio subject to certain constraints, is again a subject that will be discussed later in this chapter.

1.2.5 Nonlinear Impairments

Nonlinear effects are introduced by amplifiers, frequency translators, and other active subsystems that are part of the channel. Purely passive channels such as the wire-pair, are free of such distortions.

The simplest form of nonlinearity can be expressed as a power series expansion of the signal waveform. More generally, the nonlinearity may have memory, in that multiplicative terms involving the signal amplitude at different times may be present. Fortunately, nonlinear distortions are usually much smaller than linear ones. However, they are much more difficult to correct.

The presence of carrier systems in telephone network voice channels may lead to frequency offset and jitter of the phase function. Other effects include sudden changes in the amplitude and phase function.

Fading on radio transmission paths leads to variation of the amplitude, in addition to linear multipath effects.

1.3 DIGITAL REPRESENTATION OF ANALOG SIGNALS

The key technology leading to the present widespread deployment of digital transmission is the economical conversion of analog signals, particularly speech, into digital bit streams by the process of *pulse-code modulation*, or PCM. The process consists of two steps: first sampling the analog signal at regularly spaced intervals of time, and then representing each sample by a finite number of bits, or *quantizing*. We will first consider the sampling operation.

1.3.1 Sampling Theorem

The justification for the sampling operation lies in a remarkable mathematical theorem in Fourier analysis. In its simplest form, the sampling theorem states that any continuous time function, whose frequency spectrum is confined to a band of less than $1/2T$ hertz, can be fully reconstructed from regularly spaced samples of that function separated by time intervals of T seconds [5], [10]. The theorem as used in practice is sketched next.

Sampling of a time function can be expressed as multiplying the function by a sequence of delta functions at the sampling instants.

$$f_s(t) = \sum_{n=-\infty}^{\infty} f(t)\, \delta(t - nT)$$

The Fourier transform of this sampled signal can be shown to be

$$F_s(\omega) = \frac{1}{T} \sum_{n=-\infty}^{\infty} F\left(\omega - \frac{2\pi n}{T}\right)$$

which, ignoring the scaling factor, is the periodic repetition of the spectrum of the original unsampled time function. This is illustrated in Fig. 1.4. It is interesting to note that, since the spectrum of the sampled signal is a periodic function, it can be expanded in a Fourier series, and the coefficients of that series turn out to be the sampled values of the time function.

In practice, the time function is sampled by finite narrow pulses rather than impossible delta functions. This leads to an overall spectrum that drops off at very high frequencies. As long as the sampling pulses are sufficiently narrow that their Fourier transform is essentially constant over the range $|\omega| \le \pi/T$, they can be treated as though they were delta functions.

If the original function were bandlimited to less than half the sampling frequency, that is,

$$F(\omega) = 0, \qquad |\omega| < \frac{\pi}{T}$$

then the periodic repetitions in $F_s(\omega)$ do not overlap. The original spectrum can then be recovered by a low-pass filter that selects the copy of the spectrum centered about zero frequency. The simplest such filter is

$$H(\omega) = 1, \qquad |\omega| < \frac{\pi}{T}$$

$$= 0, \qquad \text{elsewhere}$$

As discussed previously, the large linear phase shift that must in practice be associated with this filter is neglected here. Applying this filter to $F_s(\omega)$ is equivalent

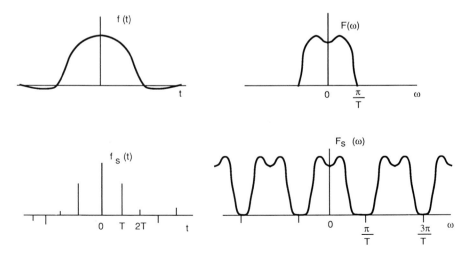

Figure 1.4   Sampled signal and its spectrum.

to selecting its $n = 0$ term, provided that contributions from other terms do not overlap that term, so that

$$F_s(\omega)H(\omega) = \frac{1}{T} F(\omega)$$

Ignoring the scale factor, the original spectrum, $F(\omega)$, is recovered.

The recovery of the original waveform from its sampled values can also be explained in the time domain. The inverse transform of the low-pass filter $H(\omega)$ is

$$h(\tau) = \frac{1}{T} \operatorname{sinc}\left(\frac{\tau}{T}\right)$$

If the input to this filter is the sequence of samples $f_s(t)$, then its output will be

$$\frac{1}{T} \sum_{n=-\infty}^{\infty} f(nT) \operatorname{sinc}\left(\frac{t - nT}{T}\right)$$

This is the original waveform, $f(t)$, scaled by the factor $1/T$. It can easily be seen that this is true at the sampling instants, because

$$\operatorname{sinc}\left(\frac{t - nT}{T}\right) = 1, \qquad t = nT$$

$$= 0, \qquad t = jT, j \text{ an integer} \neq n$$

The sinc function is sometimes referred to as the *interpolation function*, since it provides the unique interpolation of a function between periodic sample points, assuming the function is bandlimited to half the sampling frequency.

We have shown how, if samples of a bandlimited waveform are transmitted to a receiver, the receiver can recreate the waveform by passing the samples through a low-pass filter. If the waveform is not perfectly bandlimited to less than or equal to half the sampling frequency, then the component spectra in $F_s(\omega)$ will overlap. After filtering samples from such a waveform, the resultant spectrum will include the unwanted higher frequencies, "folded over" the frequency $1/2T$ so as to appear as lower-frequency components. This form of distortion is referred to as *aliasing*.

1.3.2 Quantization

To transmit the samples over a digital communication system, they must each be encoded into a finite number of bits from which the sample value can be reconstructed at the receiver, within some level of accuracy. The simplest form of quantization is uniform quantization, which will be described first.

Assume that the signal samples that are to be quantized are known to be confined to the range $[-V, V]$, and that n bits are available for representing the samples. Then 2^{n-1} positive levels and the same number of negative levels can be represented. If they are equally spaced, then the separation between adjacent levels is

$$\Delta = 2^{1-n}V$$

Each sample is encoded to the nearest level, and at the receiver a sample of that level is reconstructed from the received bits to be fed to the low-pass filter. An error is introduced that is equal to the difference between the true sample value and the level to which it has been quantized. The error is often called *quantizing noise*, which may be misleading since its effect can be very different from that of the usual signal-independent additive noise. As an example, consider a pictorial input that contains a gradual shading of gray from light to dark. If the levels are far enough apart to be visually distinguished, the result of quantization will be an image with step contours separating regions of equal intensity. This is quite different from the speckled look of a noisy image. However, if the quantization error is added to other impairments, its added degradation is usually similar to that of additive noise.

If the levels are reasonably closely spaced so that the signal can be treated as uniformly distributed within each interval, then the quantization noise is very well approximated by a uniform random variable that takes values between $-\Delta/2$ and $\Delta/2$. The mean-square error, or noise power, is

$$N_q = \frac{1}{\Delta} \int_{-\Delta/2}^{\Delta/2} x^2 \, dx = \frac{\Delta^2}{12} = \frac{V^2}{3(2^{2n})}$$

A reasonable measure of quality is the signal-to-quantization-noise ratio. The signal power depends on the probability distribution of the sample values. If the signal is uniformly distributed over the range $[-V, V]$, then its power is $V^2/3$, and

$$\frac{S}{N_q} = 2^{2n}$$

If the signal is a sine wave of peak V, its power is $V^2/2$, and

$$\frac{S}{N_q} = 3(2^{2n-1})$$

If $n = 7$, the signal-to-quantization ratio is 42 dB for the uniformly distributed signal and 43.8 dB for the sine wave. The ratio improves by 6 dB for each bit in the code used to represent the quantized sample.

The uniform quantization described here is inappropriate for speech signals for two reasons. It is suboptimum for handling a particular speaker with known volume, but more importantly it performs poorly in accommodating a universe of speakers with widely differing volumes.

First consider a particular speaker. The probability distribution of sample values will be higher for low amplitudes in order to accommodate the rarer loud peaks. Now the average quantizing noise for unequal quantizing intervals, Δ_i, is

$$N_q = \frac{1}{12} \sum_i p_i \Delta_i^2$$

where p_i is the probability that the signal lies within the range of Δ_i, and it is assumed that all Δ_i are small enough that the probability distribution within that range is uniform. It is clear that, for a fixed number of quantizing levels, N_q is minimized by choosing smaller intervals where the signal probability is high (at low amplitudes), and letting the intervals be wider at the lower-probability high amplitudes.

In addition the dynamic range problem of a given speaker, if uniform quantization were used to serve a population of speakers, then the low-volume speakers would suffer a much worse signal-to-quantization ratio than the louder speakers. If, on the other hand, quantization intervals were proportional to their central values, then signal-to-quantization ratios would be the same for all speakers and over the volume range of each speaker. This ideal cannot be achieved because the intervals near zero would have to be vanishingly small. However, practical systems do approximate this form of nonuniform quantization for moderate and large sample values.

Nonuniform quantization can be physically implemented in different ways, which are entirely equivalent. First, the quantizing levels can be unevenly spaced. Second, the signal can be uniformly quantized using a large number of bits, and that code is mapped onto a code of fewer bits so as to achieve the desired spacing. The final approach involves warping the input samples by a nonlinear operation, $y(x)$, uniformly quantizing the new samples y, and performing the inverse warping at the receiver. This last process is referred to as *companding*, a contraction of compression and expansion. Whichever technique is actually used, it is convenient to think of nonuniform quantization in terms of companding. Figure 1.5 illustrates the use of companding for nonuniform quantization.

A logarithmic compression function, $y(x) = k_1 \log(k_2 x)$, followed by uniform sampling, would provide quantization intervals proportional to sample values. However, the logarithmic function blows up in the vicinity of zero. The two

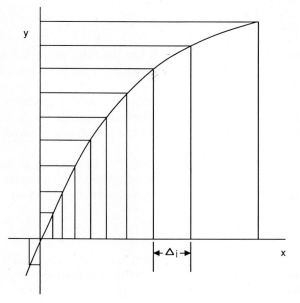

Figure 1.5 Companding for nonuniform quantization.

compression laws in widespread use attempt to approximiate a linear function for small values and a logarithmic function for moderate and large values.

In the North American and Japanese telephone systems, *mu-law* compression is used.

$$y(x) = V \, \text{sgn}(x) \, \frac{\ln(1 + \mu \, |x|/V)}{\ln(1 + \mu)}$$

with $\mu = 255$. For large signals, $\mu|x| \gg V$, the function becomes logarithmic and the signal-to-quantization ratio is independent of signal level. For $\mu|x| \ll V$,

$$\ln\left(\frac{(1 + \mu|x|)}{V}\right) \approx \frac{\mu|x|}{V}$$

and the mapping is linear.

In Europe, *A-law* compression is used

$$y(x) = \text{sgn}(x) \, \frac{A|x|}{1 + \ln A} \, , \qquad |x| \leq \frac{V}{A}$$

$$= V \, \text{sgn}(x) \, \frac{1 + \ln(A|x|/V)}{1 + \ln A} \, , \qquad |x| > \frac{V}{A}$$

with $A = 87.56$. This is linear for values below a threshold and logarithmic above.

In both of these standards, a piecewise linear approximation to the compression law is actually used. The sampling rate is 8 kHz, and 8 bits per sample are transmitted for a transmission rate of 64 kbps per voice channel.

A detailed treatment of quantization is given in [5].

1.3.3 Other Source-encoding Schemes

Numerous source-encoding schemes have been developed that provide much better performance than PCM, by either making use of the particular characteristics of the source or by adapting to those characteristics. The improved performance is usually realized by the requirement of a lower transmitted bit rate for the same quality of reproduction. The quality achieved can be measured either subjectively or objectively by a measure such as mean-square error.

A broad class of coding, known as *differential pulse-code modulation*, or DPCM, makes use of the property that signal samples are highly correlated for sources such as speech or images. This correlation allows a prediction of what the current sample will be based on past samples. The difference between the actual sample and the prediction will have a lower variance than the sample itself. This difference is then encoded and transmitted using fewer bits than would be used for PCM. An identical predictor is used in the receiver, and the received bits are used to construct corrections to that prediction. A block diagram of such a system is shown in Fig. 1.6.

The most common predictor is simply the previous reconstructed value multiplied by the correlation of adjacent samples. A more general linear predictor uses a weighted combination of several past predictions and several past input

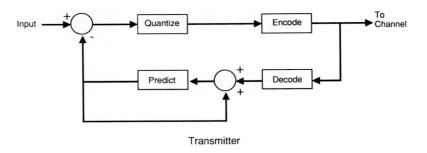

Transmitter

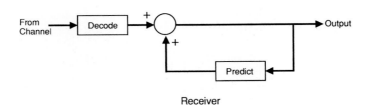

Receiver

Figure 1.6   Implementation of differential PCM.

samples. As a further refinement, the weighting factors can be made to adapt to the actual correlations of the input signal.

A particularly simple form of DPCM, which is very easy to implement, is *delta modulation*. Here the predictor is just the previous reconstructed value, and only 1 bit is used to encode the difference. In effect, what is transmitted is a binary signal instructing the receiver to either increase or decrease its previous reconstructed output by a fixed quantity. Unlike most DPCM schemes, a much higher sampling rate is employed than in PCM, but the net bit rate is comparable.

A further improvement that is usually incorporated in these schemes is to adaptively adjust the quantization mechanisms. As an example, in the case of delta modulation, assigning a fixed increment to each bit may cause difficulty in tracking a large, long slope in the input signal. A long string of bits of the same sign in the transmitted output is an indication of such slope overload. The encoder can adapt by increasing the amount of correction to be made by a bit after a given number of consecutive identical bits. The same algorithm must be followed by the decoder. Various forms of adaptive quantization can be used with all the encoding schemes. A particular form of adaptive DPCM, which can transmit high-quality speech at 32 kbps, has been adopted as an international standard as an alternative to 64-kbps PCM.

Source encoding is a very active field of research, and many very different schemes have been proposed and implemented. The reader is referred to [7] for an extensive treatment of the subject. The apparent complexity of these approaches is not much of a barrier with modern technology. An occasional concern is the robustness to transmission errors, since some of the schemes can lead to a

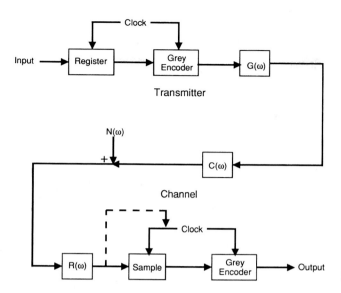

Figure 1.7 PAM system.

large, long-duration error in the reconstructed signal if 1 bit is received in error. This effect is not important in those ISDN implementations that include error control.

1.4 BASIC TRANSMISSION PRINCIPLES

The most basic technique for transmission of digital signals is *pulse-amplitude modulation* (PAM). PAM is also the basis for other transmission schemes, and its theoretical principles and design techniques are directly applicable.

The transmission system is shown in Fig. 1.7. The transmitter groups one or more information bits into a symbol that determines the amplitude and sign of a pulse of a given shape $g(t)$. The modulated pulses are then transmitted at intervals spaced in time by symbol or *baud* interval T. The reciprocal of T is the *baud rate*. The transmitted signal is thus of the form

$$s(t) = \sum_k a_k g(t - kT)$$

The information is carried by the values of the a_k's. In a binary system, each a_k is either $+A$ or $-A$. If n bits are carried by each symbol, then each a_k is chosen from the set of L values, $\{\pm A, \pm 3A, \ldots, \pm(L - 1)A\}$, where $L = 2^n$. It is assumed that $g(t)$ is normalized in amplitude such that $g(0) = 1$.

The mapping of input bits to levels is usually done such that adjacent levels differ by only one input bit: Grey coding is a scheme that accomplishes this. The reason for this encoding is to produce only single errors for the most likely error events.

A usual constraint is a limit on the allowed transmitted power. If the a_k's are independent and equally probable, then the average transmitted power is

$$P = \frac{\sigma_a^2}{T} \int_{-\infty}^{\infty} g^2(t) \, dt = \frac{\sigma_a^2}{2\pi T} \int_{-\infty}^{\infty} |G(\omega)|^2 \, d\omega,$$

where σ_a^2 is the variance of the set of levels:

$$\sigma_a^2 = \frac{2A^2}{L} [1^2 + 3^2 + \cdots + (L-1)^2]$$

$$= \frac{A^2}{3} (L^2 - 1)$$

Under the same conditions on a_k, the transmitted power spectrum is

$$P_s(\omega) = \frac{\sigma_a^2}{T} |G(\omega)|^2$$

The channel is considered to be linear with transfer function $C(\omega)$. The noise as seen at the output of the channel is Gaussian with power spectrum $N(\omega)$. $N(\omega)$ is often treated as white, that is, flat over the frequency band of interest.

The receiver first filters its input with a linear filter $R(\omega)$. Included in this transfer function is any automatic gain control that may be required to bring the signal up to a standard level. The output of the filter is then sampled at times spaced by T. The process of generating these sampling instants, known as *timing recovery*, is a very important consideration that will be discussed later in this section. For each sample, the nearest level a_k is determined, and the bits that correspond to that level are presented to the output.

1.4.1 Error Probability

The signal at the output of the receiver filter is of the form

$$y(t) = \sum_k a_k x(t - kT) + n(t)$$

where $x(t)$ is the inverse Fourier transform of $G(\omega)C(\omega)R(\omega)$, and $n(t)$ is a Gaussian noise with power spectrum $N(\omega)|R(\omega)|^2$ and variance σ_n^2 determined by integration of that spectrum.

Without loss of generality, choose the time origin so that it coincides with the sampling time for the symbol labeled $k = 0$. Further assume that the overall gain is such that the receiver levels coincide with those at the transmitter. The sample value at $t = 0$ can be written in the form

$$y(0) = a_0 x(0) + \sum_{k \neq 0} a_{-k} x(kT) + n(0)$$

The first term is the desired signal for recovering the value of a_0. The amplitude is assumed scaled such that $x(0) = g(0) = 1$, the height of the original transmitted pulse. The second term is the *intersymbol interference* caused by the overlap of pulses other than the one of interest. This term adds to the noise as an error-producing mechanism. As we shall discuss later, it is important to minimize or eliminate the intersymbol interference.

The levels are separated by the quantity $2A$. As long as the sum of the intersymbol interference and the noise is less than A in magnitude, the received sample will be closest to the correct level. For the most positive transmitted level, the sum must be more negative than $-A$ to produce an error, and conversely for the most negative level. For any other level, an error will result if the sum is greater than A in magnitude in either direction.

Since both the intersymbol interference and the noise are symmetrically distributed about zero, the probability of error for equally likely symbol values is

$$P_e = \frac{2(L-1)}{L} \, Pr\left[\sum_{k \neq 0} a_{-k} x(kT) + n(0) > A\right]$$

Evaluation of this expression is extremely difficult. Let us at this time look at two special cases.

First consider the noiseless case. The worst case of intersymbol interference occurs when the values of all interfering symbols a_{-k} are of maximum amplitude, $(L-1)A$, and of sign that agrees with the pulse sample $x(kT)$. Then

$$P_e = \frac{2(L-1)}{L} \, Pr\left[(L-1)A \sum_{k \neq 0} |x(kT)| > A\right]$$

This probability is zero if

$$\sum_{k \neq 0} |x(kT)| < \frac{1}{L-1}$$

The preceding criterion is important, since it is very desirable that the system be error free in the absence of noise.

Now let us take a preliminary look at the case where noise is the only degradation. Since the noise is normally distributed with zero mean and variance σ_n^2,

$$P_e = \frac{2(L-1)}{L} \, Q\left(\frac{A}{\sigma_n}\right)$$

where $Q(x)$ is the normal probability integral

$$Q(x) = \frac{1}{\sqrt{2\pi}} \int_x^\infty e^{-y^2/2} dy$$

1.4.2 Elimination of Intersymbol Interference

A converse of the sampling theorem, due to H. Nyquist, states that independent symbols can be transmitted at a rate $1/T$ using a bandwidth of $1/2T$ hertz. If the combination of the transmit pulse shape, the channel, and the receiver filter are such that

$$X(\omega) = T, \qquad |\omega| \le \frac{\pi}{T}$$

$$= 0, \qquad |\omega| > \frac{\pi}{T}$$

then

$$x(t) = \text{sinc}\left(\frac{t}{T}\right)$$

This function has the desired property

$$x(0) = 1$$

$$x(kT) = 0, \qquad \text{all integers } k \ne 0$$

which leads to no intersymbol interference.

The ideal bandlimited spectrum is undesirable both because of the difficulty of approximating it with real components and because of the slow decay of the resultant time function. Nyquist has shown that intersymbol interference can be eliminated with a class of spectral shapes of wider bandwidth than the ideal. These include more gradual frequency shapes that lead to more rapidly decaying time functions.

The condition of no intersymbol interference is obtained for any function whose Fourier transform satisfies

$$\sum_k X\left(\omega + \frac{2\pi k}{T}\right) = T, \qquad |\omega| \le \frac{\pi}{T}$$

$$= 0, \qquad |\omega| \ge \frac{\pi}{T}$$

We are rarely interested in spectra wider than double the ideal. We therefore only need consider two of the preceding terms, since $X(-\omega) = X^*(\omega)$. The condition is then satisfied if

$$X_r(\omega) + X_r\left(\frac{2\pi}{T} - \omega\right) = 1$$

and

$$X_i(\omega) - X_i\left(\frac{2\pi}{T} - \omega\right) = 0$$

where X_r and X_i are the real and imaginary components of X. Therefore, zero intersymbol interference is maintained if any real function that is even about $\omega = \pi/T$ and any imaginary function that is odd about $\omega = \pi/T$ are added to the ideal bandlimited specrum. Figure 1.8 illustrates a real spectrum that meets this criterion. Because of its relative smoothness, the resultant time function will decay much faster than the sinc function while maintaining its sample values at integral multiples of T.

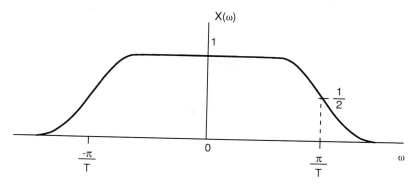

Figure 1.8   Real Nyquist spectrum.

1.4.3 Optimization of the Communication System

For a given transmitted pulse shape, channel transfer function, and noise power spectrum, the receive filter may be optimized so as to provide maximum signal-to-ratio at its output and therefore minimum probability of error in the absence of intersymbol interference. This optimum is known as the *matched filter* and is given by

$$R(\omega) = \frac{G^*(\omega)C^*(\omega)}{N(\omega)}$$

This can be multiplied by any gain factor and any delay. When the noise is white, the matched filter is the complex conjugate of its input signal spectrum, and its impulse response is therefore the time reverse of that signal.

The signal pulse shape at the output of the matched filter has the Fourier transform

$$X(\omega) = \frac{|G(\omega)C(\omega)|^2}{N(\omega)}$$

and the noise power spectrum at that point is

$$\frac{|G(\omega)C(\omega)|^2}{N(\omega)}$$

Note that the first expression is an amplitude spectrum while the second is a power spectrum, so they are not comparable even though they look nearly identical.

Let us now look at the error probability for the ideal case where the channel and the noise are both flat and there is no intersymbol interference in the output of the matched filter. That is, $C(\omega) = 1$, $N(\omega) = N_0$, and $X(\omega) = |G(\omega)|^2/N_0$ is a Nyquist shape. After some mathematical manipulation, it is found that

$$P_e = \frac{2(L-1)}{L} Q\left(\sqrt{\frac{3P_T}{(L^2-1)P_N}}\right)$$

where P_T is the transmitter power developed previously and P_N is the noise power in the Nyquist bandwidth, $|\omega| \leq \pi/T$.

With a slight modification, this error probability function is plotted in Fig. 1.9 for several values of L and with the signal-to-noise ratio, P_T/P_N, given in decibels. The probabilities shown are actually the bit error probabilities, rather than the symbol error probability given previously. Almost all errors will result from choosing levels that are adjacent to the correct one. If Grey coding is used, then such errors will result in only a single bit error. For the nonbinary curves in Fig. 1.9, the bit error probability shown is the symbol error probability divided by the number of bits per symbol, $\log_2 L$. The distinction is not very significant, since we are usually interested in order of magnitude of error probability.

The situation described, in which the channel and noise spectra are both flat, the receiver employs matched filtering, and the output of that filter is a Nyquist shape, involves joint design of the transmitter and receiver. This is accomplished simply by designing the amplitude function of both the transmit and receive filters to be the square root of the desired Nyquist shape, with complementary phase functions.

More generally, we want to minimize the receiver output noise power, subject to a fixed average transmit power, and the Nyquist constraint

$$G(\omega)C(\omega)R(\omega) = X(\omega)$$

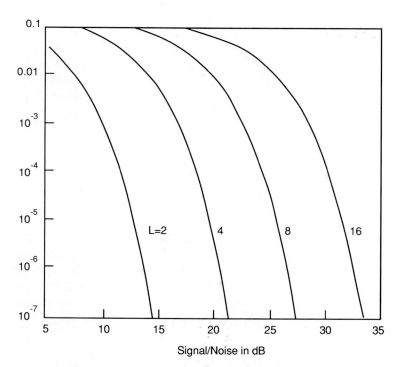

Figure 1.9 Bit error probablity for PAM.

where $X(\omega)$ is the given real Nyquist shape, and $C(\omega)$ and $N(\omega)$ are not necessarily flat.

The resultant design equations are [3]

$$|G(\omega)| = \frac{\sqrt{X(\omega)}\ \sqrt[4]{N(\omega)}}{\sqrt{|C(\omega)|}}$$

which may have any phase function; and

$$|R(\omega)| = \frac{\sqrt{X(\omega)}}{\sqrt{|C(\omega)|}\ \sqrt[4]{N(\omega)}}$$

with a phase function the negative of the combined transmitter and channel phase functions.

1.4.4 Timing Recovery

A critical function that must be performed at the receiver is sampling of the filtered signal at the correct time instants. Even a small offset from optimum timing can greatly increase intersymbol interference. Somehow a timing waveform of not only the correct frequency, but also proper phase, must be created to perform this function. In most cases the timing waveform is generated from the received signal itself. In some instances an external clock of the proper frequency may be present, but it is still necessary to adjust its phase.

Requirements of the clock include not only phase accuracy, but also stability. Any clock that is derived or adjusted by a random data sequence will be subjected to a variation of its phase, or *jitter*. A jittered clock may be thought of as a carrier subjected to a random phase modulation. The jitter is characterized by both its magnitude and rate of change or, equivalently, its frequency spectrum. In addition to degrading receiver performance, jitter can lead to serious system degradation. In a signal regenerator, the recovered clock not only controls reception but also transmission to the next regenerator. Jitter can therefore accumulate additively to a large value over a long chain of regenerators.

The first step in timing recovery is to perform a suitable nonlinear operation on the data signal so as to generate an output that contains a component centered at the symbol rate $f = 1/T$. That component will generally have substantial amplitude and phase modulation traceable to the random nature of the input to the nonlinearity. Nonlinear operations that have been employed include squaring, rectifying, and generating pulses coinciding with changes between levels, or *transitions*. The output of the nonlinearity is then filtered by a high-Q tuned circuit or a phase-locked loop in order to reduce its jitter. However, jitter components whose frequency is less than the bandwidth of this filtering operation will remain. A further phase correction may be made, controlled by some measurement of the error in the subsequent data decision operation.

The timing recovery operation requires some constraint on the transmitted signal. For example, if timing recovery is based on signal transitions, then either the symbol sequence must be assured of having a sufficient number of changes, or the basic pulse shape must be designed to provide timing information. The former approach may involve adding extraneous bits to the user's data and removing them. An alternative is to *scramble* the user's data by a suitable encoding operation and performing the inverse operation after reception. This technique assures that the data to be transmitted are truly random. With some probability, dependent on the time constants of the timing recovery operation, timing information may still be lost.

As will be seen in the next section, signal design for proper timing recovery is a very important consideration.

1.5 FURTHER TRANSMISSION TECHNIQUES

Numerous variations and enhancements to the basic PAM system can be used to accomplish purposes such as guaranteeing the ability to extract timing and fitting some particular characteristics of the channel. This section will outline some of the more common techniques.

1.5.1 Line Coding

By mapping the input information into a different sequence or by designing a particular transmit pulse shape, it is possible to achieve some of the preceding objectives. As described in the previous section, scrambling the data to assure a random sequence is an example of the former approach.

Another simple example is differential encoding of binary data to achieve polarity insensitivity. For channels such as a twisted pair of wires, it is difficult to keep track of which polarity of the signal is plus and which is minus. The differential approach obviates the need to do so. The original information is encoded so that a 1 causes the binary output of the coder to change while a 0 does not. The first bit generated after start-up is ambiguous, but this is not significant. The encoded sequence is transmitted, and after reception the original sequence is reconstructed. Since the encoding operation is one to one, there is no effect on performance.

The most common line code in existing digital transmission systems is *alternate mark inversion* (AMI), also known as *bipolar*. Binary input is converted to a ternary sequence. Zeros are transmitted as 0 signals, while ones are transmitted as either $+1$ or -1 amplitudes, with the polarity chosen such that each 1 signal is the opposite polarity of the previous 1.

It is easy to see that the AMI format provides polarity insensitivity. If the lengths of strings of zeros are constrained to be less than some number, then changes in signal level that can be used for timing extraction are guaranteed. A third desirable property of AMI is its spectral shaping. Since nonzero pulses alternate in polarity, there is no dc component in the transmitted signal. In fact, its amplitude spectrum is of the form $\sin \omega T/2$, multiplied by the spectrum of the pulse. This property is useful for channels that cannot pass zero or very low frequencies, such as channels that contain transformer coupling. A price is paid in performance to achieve these properties, since three levels are used to transmit binary information.

Instead of mapping each single bit into a ternary symbol, as in AMI, a sequence of bits can be mapped into a sequence of ternary symbols. In the 4B3T format, groups of 4 bits are encoded into sequences of three ternary symbols. This is clearly more efficient than AMI. Since there are 16 possible combinations of 4 bits, only 16 of the 27 possible combinations of three ternary digits are used. These 16 sequences are chosen such that polarity insensitivity, guaranteed transitions, and zero dc value are achieved.

Manchester coding is a particularly simple, although quite inefficient, form of line coding, which guarantees a transition in each interval so that timing information can be acquired very easily and quickly. Each information bit is transmitted as two pulses of opposite polarity. Because of its inefficient use of bandwidth, Manchester coding is only used over short distances, such as within buildings or campuses.

1.5.2 Partial Response

An interesting class of line codes involves the deliberate introduction of controlled intersymbol interference in order to achieve desirable spectral shaping. The simplest form of partial response is the *duobinary*. One way of describing this technique is the use of a transmitted pulse that produces a receiver spectrum

$$X(\omega) = 2T \cos \frac{\omega T}{2}, \qquad |\omega| \leq \frac{\pi}{T}$$

$$= 0, \qquad |\omega| > \frac{\pi}{T}$$

The pulse shape is found to be

$$x(t) = \frac{4}{\pi} \frac{\cos \pi t/T}{1 - t^2/T^2}$$

The important thing to note about the spectrum is that it occupies only the Nyquist bandwidth, but, unlike the ideal bandlimited function, it has no discontinuity. It is therefore easier to physically approximate and the time function decays faster than the sinc function. The system will also be less sensitive to timing error.

If we shift the time axis by $T/2$, then at the sampling instants

$$x\left(\frac{T}{2}\right) = 1$$

$$x\left(-\frac{T}{2}\right) = 1$$

$$x\left(\left[n + \frac{1}{2}\right]T\right) = 0, \qquad n \text{ an integer} \neq 0, -1$$

We now have intersymbol interference from one adjacent symbol.

$$y\left(\left[k + \frac{1}{2}\right]T\right) = a_k + a_{k-1} + n$$

has three possible levels (without noise) if the a_k's are binary, or $2L - 1$ levels in general. The noise performance is therefore inferior to PAM.

The signal could be decoded by assuming past decisions are correct and subtracting the previous decision from the current level. This approach, however, can lead to propagation of errors. Error propagation can be avoided by precoding the input data. Assuming a binary system, the encoding operation is to change the encoded data when the input bit is 1 and leave it unchanged for a 0, as in differential coding. The sample value at the receiver is now zero if the input bit were a 1, and either $+2A$ or $-2A$ for a 0. The input data are therefore reconstructed from single samples and error propagation is eliminated.

Another way of thinking of duobinary is the generation of a pulse plus a delayed pulse for each data symbol. The delayed pulse coincides in time with the first pulse of the next symbol. If each of these pulses is assumed to be ideal bandlimited, then

$$x(t) = \text{sinc}\left(\frac{t}{T}\right) + \text{sinc}\left(\frac{t - T}{T}\right)$$

This can be shown to be exactly equal to the expression for $x(t)$ given previously, except for a time shift $T/2$.

Another important partial response system is the modified duobinary. Here the delayed pulse is inverted and coincides with the first pulse of the symbol two steps removed.

$$x(t) = \text{sinc}\left(\frac{t}{T}\right) - \text{sinc}\left(\frac{t - 2T}{T}\right)$$

The spectrum of this signal, after shifting the time axis by T, is

$$X(\omega) = 2T \sin \omega T, \qquad |\omega| \leq \frac{\pi}{T}$$

$$= 0, \qquad\qquad |\omega| > \frac{\pi}{2}$$

This spectrum also occupies the Nyquist bandwidth without discontinuity, but in addition goes to zero at zero frequency. The previous discussion on reception and precoding, with obvious modifications, also applies to this case.

It is interesting to note that AMI can also be thought of as a partial response system. The waveform

$$x(t) = \text{sinc}\left(\frac{t}{T}\right) - \text{sinc}\left(\frac{t - T}{T}\right)$$

can be shown to be precisely that of a precoded AMI signal.

1.5.3 Modulation

For certain channels, in particular voiceband and radio channels, it is essential that the signal be confined to a particular spectral band well removed from zero frequency. Modulation is the process of using a baseband signal such as PAM to control a carrier frequency within the band of interest so as to generate an information-bearing signal of the desired spectral occupancy.

Linear modulation systems for digital signals turn out to be the most efficient in terms of spectral occupancy and immunity to noise. They are also the easiest to analyze, although not necessarily the easiest to implement. With relatively minor manipulation, linear modulation systems can be treated in terms of equivalent baseband PAM systems.

First consider simple amplitude modulation. Here the transmitter PAM signal multiplies a carrier whose frequency ω_c is in the middle of the band to be used. If the baseband signal is $s(t)$, then the modulated signal is

$$s_m(t) = s(t) \cos \omega_c t$$

Note that, unlike the familiar AM broadcasting signal, the modulation can be positive or negative. This rules out envelope detection as a receiving technique.

The spectrum of the modulated signal is

$$S_m(\omega) = \frac{1}{2} S(\omega + \omega_c) + \frac{1}{2} S(\omega - \omega_c)$$

This is the familiar double-sideband suppressed carrier spectrum, with a copy of the baseband spectrum appearing above and below the carrier frequency. Because of the doubling of the spectral occupancy, this modulation technique is rarely used for digital communications. However, it is described here because it forms the basis for the more widely used modulation systems.

After passing through the channel, the signal at the input to the receiver is

$$\frac{1}{2}[S(\omega + \omega_c) + S(\omega - \omega_c)]C(\omega)$$

The first step in reception is *coherent* or *homodyne* detection, which consists of multiplying by a local copy of the carrier, $\cos \omega_c t$, and low-pass filtering. The process of obtaining this carrier, which must have both proper frequency and proper phase, is known as *carrier recovery*. This is a problem similar to that of timing recovery. There are many different techniques for providing this function, but they will not be treated here.

Another technique, which will not be discussed in any detail, is *differential detection*. Here the problem of carrier recovery is avoided by comparing the received signal with a delayed version of that received signal. The performance of such a system is inferior to that of coherent detection due to the use of a noisy reference.

After coherent demodulation, the signal presented to the receiver filter is

$$\frac{1}{4}[S(\omega + 2\omega_c)C(\omega + \omega_c) + S(\omega)C(\omega + \omega_c)$$

$$+ S(\omega)C(\omega - \omega_c) + S(\omega - 2\omega_c)C(\omega - \omega_c)]R(\omega)$$

The first and last terms correspond to signals centered about double the carrier frequency. The receiver filter $R(\omega)$ can be expected to fully reject these frequencies. The remaining terms can be written as

$$\frac{1}{2} S(\omega)C_{eq}(\omega)R(\omega)$$

where

$$C_{eq} = \frac{1}{2}[C(\omega + \omega_c) + C(\omega - \omega_c)]$$

is the baseband equivalent of the channel. Except for the gain factor of $\frac{1}{2}$, which has no significance, it is seen that the amplitude-modulated system is fully equivalent to a baseband system. It can be shown that the noise performance is the same.

The spectral inefficiency of amplitude modulation can be eliminated by single-sideband techniques. The carrier is placed near one end of the available band, and a filter at the transmitter output rejects either the upper or the lower sideband. It can be shown that coherent demodulation will fully recover the signal with no performance degradation. If the baseband signal's spectrum includes zero frequency, the single-sideband filtering operation is very difficult. It helps if the baseband signal uses a line code with a null at dc.

Vestigial sideband transmission is an approximation of single sideband that is easier to implement. Instead of attempting to sharply filter about the carrier frequency, a more gradual but symmetric filter, with the property

$$V(\omega + \omega_c) + V(\omega - \omega_c) = 1$$

is used. No distortion results when coherent demodulation is employed.

The most common modern technique for high-performance modulated transmission of digital signals is *quadrature amplitude modulation* (QAM). This is easiest explained as the superposition of two independent double-sideband AM signals, each occupying the same band. In its simplest version, the input information is split into two streams, which amplitude-modulate carriers of the same midband frequency, but 90° apart in phase. The two modulated signals are combined for transmission. At the receiver, an identical pair of carriers is used for coherent demodulation. The two detected information streams are finally interleaved. Figure 1.10 is a block diagram of this basic QAM system.

The transmit signal is of the form

$$\sum_k a_k g(t - kT) \cos \omega_c t + \sum_k b_k g(t - kT) \sin \omega_c t$$

where a_k and b_k are each chosen from $L = 2^n$ levels and represent different sets of information bits. The possible pairs (a_k, b_k) can be represented in two-dimensional space as a square of L^2 points. This representation is referred to as the

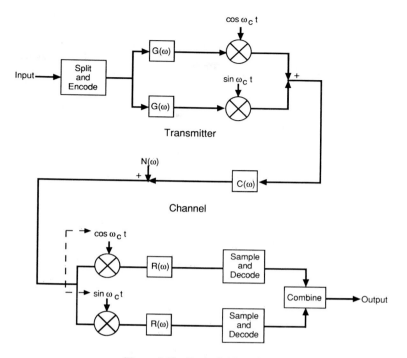

Figure 1.10   Basic QAM system.

signal constellation. Figure 1.11 shows a constellation of 16 points for which $L = 4$ and each two-dimensional symbol carries 4 bits.

Following the same analysis as for the amplitude-modulation system, when the received signal is multiplied by cos $\omega_c t$ and filtered, the result is

$$\sum_k a_k x(t - kT) + \sum_k b_k \hat{x}(t - kT)$$

where $x(t)$ is the inverse Fourier transform of

$$\frac{1}{4} G(\omega)[C(\omega + \omega_c) + C(\omega - \omega_c)]R(\omega)$$

and $\hat{x}(t)$ is the inverse Fourier transform of

$$\frac{i}{4} G(\omega)[C(\omega + \omega_c) - C(\omega - \omega_c)]R(\omega)$$

We would like to recover the values of a_k from the samples of this signal. As before, intersymbol interference from the other a_k's is avoided if $x(t)$ is a Nyquist pulse. But, in addition, interference from the b_k's must also be avoided. For this to occur,

$$\hat{x}(nT) = 0, \qquad \text{all integer } n \text{ (including 0)}$$

One obvious case in which this condition is true is where $C(\omega)$ is symmetric about

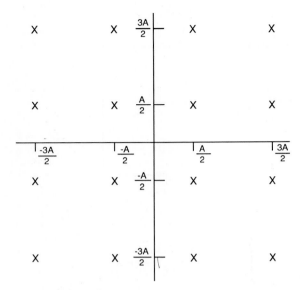

Figure 1.11 A 16-point QAM constellation.

ω_c. It should be noted that proper phasing of the receiver carriers is also essential for avoiding this cross-interference.

The conditions for recovering the b_k's after multiplying by $\sin \omega_c t$ are identical. The error probability curves of Fig. 1.9 are applicable to QAM as well as to PAM with the same value of L.

Variations of QAM include the use of constellations that are not simple squares. Here combinations of information bits determine the in-phase and quadrature components of the signal nonindependently. Some advantage in the presence of particular impairments can be achieved in this manner.

We have chosen not to discuss nonlinear modulation schemes, such as frequency and phase modulation, here. These schemes can be very easy to implement and are common in low-speed, low-cost applications. However, their inefficient use of bandwidth and their inferior tolerance to noise preclude their use where high performance is needed. It may be expected that modern technology will continue to reduce the cost of implementing QAM systems and that frequency or phase modulation will become obsolete for transmission of digital information.

1.5.4 Equalization

Until now it has been assumed that the linear channel transfer function is known and can be corrected by the transmit or receive filter. This is rarely a realistic assumption, and high-performance communication requires some form of automatic equalization to compensate for the unknown channel.

The simplest form of automatic equalization is the *automatic line buildout* (ALBO), which is widely used when the channel consists of a wire pair of known gauge but unknown length. The loss at any convenient frequency is a measure of the length and can therefore be used to correct the entire frequency response,

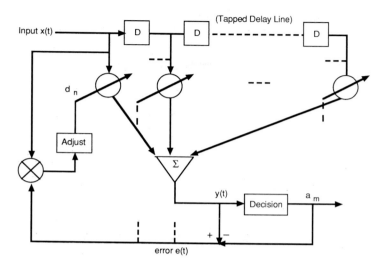

Figure 1.12   Linear LMS equalizer.

which is known *a priori* for that length of wire pair.   The ALBO is an AGC device that simultaneously varies its frequency response as it adjusts its gain.

For more general channels, automatic equalization is based on the tapped delay line or *transversal filter*.   As shown in Fig. 1.12, its output is a weighted sum of its input delayed by multiples of its tap spacing, T.   Its impulse response is therefore

$$d(t) = \sum_n d_n \, \delta(t - nT)$$

and its frequency response is

$$D(\omega) = \sum_n d_n e^{i\omega nT}$$

This is a periodic function of frequency, with period $\omega = 2\pi/T$, which can be expressed as a finite Fourier series whose coefficients are the tap weights.

There are many versions of automatic equalizer, all based on the tapped delay line.   The variations involve the tap spacing, the algorithm for adjusting the tap weights, and, in a modulated system, whether equalization is performed before or after demodulation.   However, the goal in all cases is to reduce intersymbol interference.

We will treat the simplest case here, equalization of a baseband PAM signal using a tap spacing equal to the symbol period.   We position the received signal so that the main pulse occurs near the middle of the tapped delay line, which permits correction of intersymbol interference from both leading and lagging components.

The output of the equalizer is

$$y(t) = \sum_k a_k \sum_n d_n x(t - kT - nT) + \sum_n d_n n(t - kT)$$

We wish to adjust the tap weights d_n so as to minimize the error at the sampling times. Note from the last term that the equalization process can magnify the noise.

The algorithm for adjusting the tap weights uses the principle that error is minimized when it is uncorrelated with delayed values of the input to the equalizer.

$$E \{[y(kT) - a_k]x(kT - nT)\} = 0, \qquad k \neq 0$$

The center tap, d_0, may be considered as a gain control. The other taps are adjusted according to some approximation of the preceding equation.

The *least mean square* (LMS) algorithm adjusts each tap iteratively,

$$d_n([m + 1]T) = d_n(mT) + se(mT)x(mT - nT)$$

where

$$e(mT) = y(mT) - a_m$$

The step size s is the amount of correction performed at each step of time. A small step size is necessary for insensitivity to noise and low steady-state error. However, the convergence rate of the algorithm can then be quite slow. Variations of the algorithm involve variable step size.

Typically, the equalizer operates in two modes. During initial start-up (or recovery from an outage), a known sequence is transmitted, and these known values of a_m are used in the algorithm. During normal communication, the detected symbols are used.

The LMS algorithm produces the minimum mean-square error that can be achieved for a transversal filter of a given size, including the contribution of noise to the error. The correction signal for each tap requires a true multiplication. The *zero-forcing equalizer* uses a simpler algorithm, in that only the sign of the error and the delayed signal are used in the tap adjustment algorithm. Rather than minimizing the mean-square error, it sets the intersymbol interference to zero at a number of sample points equal to the number of taps. At high signal to noise ratio, the difference between these two errors is small. The zero-forcing equalizer is guaranteed to converge only if

$$\sum_{k \neq 0} x(kT) < 1$$

The *decision-feedback equalizer* (DFE) is another form of equalization that can provide significant noise performance advantage over linear equalization when the channel's amplitude function has very wide variation. As shown in Fig. 1.13, linear equalization is still used for the leading part of the correction. However, lagging correction is performed by adding values proportional to decisions on previous symbols. Performance is quite sensitive to errors, and the conditions for convergence are not fully understood. However, DFE techniques have proved useful in practice for digital communication over channels with severe amplitude distortion.

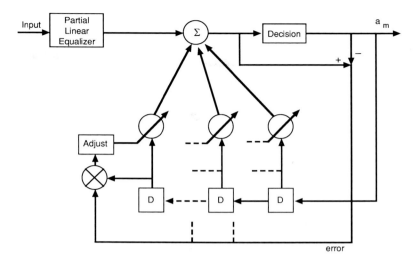

Figure 1.13   Decision feedback equalizer.

1.5.5 Full-duplex Techniques

Full-duplex communication is the capability of transmitting information in both directions simultaneously, as opposed to half-duplex, in which each end is either transmitting or receiving, but not both.   Half-duplex communication typically requires some delay in reversing direction due to required turn-around procedure.

Communication links that use separate channels in each direction are referred to as *four wire*, even if the medium is other than wire.   *Two-wire* channels are single channels that are capable of transmission in either direction.   Full-duplex communication is easily performed over four-wire channels, but for economic and other reasons it is often desirable to provide this capability over two-wire channels.

Ordinary telephony provides full-duplex conversation over two-wire circuits. However, except for very long distance connections, only a moderate separation of the signals in each direction is needed.   This is provided by a classic device known as a *hybrid*, wherever a two-wire path, such as the loop, interfaces with a four-wire path, such as the telephone transmitter and receiver or any long-haul transmission system.   A hybrid can typically be depended on to provide only about 10 dB of loss from the transmit path to the receive path.   On very long haul connections, more loss than this is required to reduce the reception of echoes. The traditional approach to this problem is the *echo suppressor*, which monitors the level in each direction and introduces loss in the quiet direction.   This prevents simultaneous two-way communication, which is generally not really desired for normal conversation.

For transmission of digital information, a hybrid is usually not adequate for keeping a transmitted signal from interfering with its colocated receiver.   An approach used for low-speed data communication over the switched telephone network is to use a different frequency band in each direction and filtering to keep the signals separate.   This technique reduces the capability of the channel by at least a factor of 2.

Another technique that was popular a few years ago for full-duplex data transmission over two-wire loops is *time compression multiplexing*, sometimes referred to as "Ping-Pong".   Source data are read into a buffer memory, and after a reasonably long block of data is accumulated, it is transmitted over the two-wire channel at a rate greater than twice the original rate.   Transmission in that direction then ceases while source data are again filling the buffer, and an identical transmission technique can take place in the reverse direction.   The channel is therefore being used in only one direction at a time, but at a much higher than normal speed. At the receiver, the high-speed data are read into a buffer in spurts and read out smoothly and continuously at the original lower speed.   Again bandwidth is used inefficiently because of the required higher-speed transmission rate.

The preferred scheme for efficient full-duplex transmission over two-wire channels is *echo cancellation*.   The motivation of this approach is to use the same full bandwidth for each direction of transmission and at each receiver to subtract out the part of the received signal that is due to the local transmitter.   Since the level of the transmitted signal is generally much higher than that of the received signal, this operation must be performed with very high precision.   Modern digital signal processing in existing systems produces over 60 dB of reduction of the interference.

Figure 1.14 is a diagram of a typical echo canceller.   A hybrid is used to partially ease its task.   The echo canceller itself is very similar to the automatic

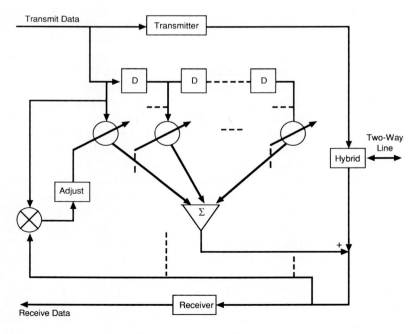

Figure 1.14   Echo cancellation.

equalizer described previously.   Note that the interference is not just a replica of the transmitted signal, but a linearly distorted version due to coupling through the local hybrid and to various echoes originating along the channel, particularly at the distant hybrid.   The signal to be subtracted is formed by a tapped delay line driven by the transmitted data.   The tap weights are adjusted as in the equalizer, using the correlation between the received signal and delayed versions of the data sequence.

1.6 CODING

Until now we have considered systems in which the information bits are more or less directly mapped into transmitted symbols.   The performance of such straight modulation schemes can be considerably enhanced by the inclusion of coding. Before discussing coding techniques, we provide motivation by outlining the very fundamental and remarkable theorem of Shannon.

1.6.1 Channel Capacity

In using any straightforward modulation system over a noisy channel, some nonzero bit error probability, p, will result.   If errors were independent, then a message of length N bits will suffer at least one error with probability $1 - (1 - p)^N$.   This approaches 1 as N grows large.   The same effect may be expected when errors are not independent.

This behavior may appear to be intuitively obvious, but Shannon's theorem shows that the error probability for a very long message can be vanishingly low. Under very general conditions, a noisy communication channel has a specific finite value of *capacity*, which may be expressed in bits per second.   As long as the rate of actual information transfer is kept below the capacity of the channel, then, in principle, long messages can be transmitted with arbitrarily low error probability. However, if one attempts to transmit at a rate higher than capacity, then it is impossible to achieve error-free performance.

To be more precise, consider a message whose true information content is m bits.   This may be thought of as a message that is chosen from a set of 2^m equally likely messages.   If that message is transmitted over a channel at a rate R bits per second, then the duration of the transmission $T = m/R$.   The transmission scheme is by no means a simple symbol-by-symbol technique as previously discussed.   Instead, a mapping is specified of each of the possible 2^m messages into a time function of duration T acceptable by the channel.   This mapping of messages into waveforms is a very generalized definition of a code.   Now, for almost any arbitrary choice of such a code, the probability that the noisy received waveform will be closer to that of a different one of the 2^m message waveforms than to the correct one will be arbitrarily small as m (and therefore T) becomes arbitrarily large.

It should be noted that the capacity theorem is an existence proof, not a constructive one.   It does not provide a recipe for transmitting below capacity at an arbirarily low error probability.   Although a random code of length $m \rightarrow \infty$

will meet the requirement with probability 1, such codes grow exponentially in complexity with length. No systematic codes, which can be implemented with linear growth of complexity, have been found that provide the performance promised by the theorem.

In spite of the lack of a constructive recipe, the capacity theorem is extremely useful in providing a bound against which practical systems can be compared and also in providing a philosophy for achieving low error probabilities. It is important to note its derivation assumes decoding of a long message as a whole, rather than in small clump of bits. This implies that high-performance communications requires large delay in arriving at a decoded output. It also implies that the waveform content corresponding to any one bit be spread over a large period of time. This means that many independent noisy samples will determine the value of each bit, therefore reducing the error probability. Conversely, each waveform sample is used in the determination of several bits.

The best known case for which the ideal capacity can easily be found is the ideal bandlimited channel with additive white Gaussian noise. The capacity for this channel is given by

$$C = W \log_2 \left(1 + \frac{P_s}{P_n} \right)$$

where W is the bandwidth in hertz, P_s is the allowed signal power, and P_n is the power of the noise in the band.

This capacity is plotted in Fig. 1.15, where the capacity is normalized to the bandwidth and the signal-to-noise ratio is given in decibels. Remember that transmission can be achieved in principle with arbitrary low error probability at any rate below this curve. We now use this curve as a yardstick against which to measure a practical system.

For the L-level PAM system, or a QAM system with L levels per dimension, the bit rate is

$$R = 2W \log_2 L$$

However, these systems do not have an arbitrarily low error probability, but an error probability that depends on the signal-to-noise ratio as shown in Fig. 1.9. For a given allowed error probability, we can find the signal-to-noise ratio required to achieve that performance for several values of L and then plot points for each L corresponding to that signal-to-noise ratio and the bit rate. Such points have been plotted on Fig. 1.15 for an error probability requirement of 10^{-6}. The signal-to-noise values are those found from Fig. 1.9.

We see from Figure 1.15 that when the signal-to-noise ratio is 32.5 dB the theoretical capacity is 10.8 bps/Hz. At the same signal-to-noise ratio, 16-level PAM (or 256-point QAM) can provide 8 bps/Hz, or 74% of capacity, provided that we are satisfied with an error probability of 10^{-6}. Alternatively, a signal-to-noise ratio of 24 dB can theoretically provide 8 bps/Hz, which is 8.5 dB better than that which permits a PAM system to achieve the same bit rate with 10^{-6} error probability. If a higher probability error could be tolerated, then rates closer to capacity can be achieved, and conversely if a lower error probability is required.

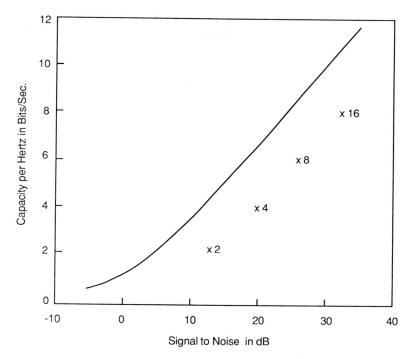

Figure 1.15 Capacity of flat-band limited channel. Also shown are achievable rates for uncoded PAM with 10^{-6} error probablity.

1.6.2 Coded Modulation

We can improve the error probability of a PAM or QAM system, or equivalently increase the bit rate for a given channel and error probability target, by introducing dependencies among the transmitted symbols and making use of these dependencies in determining the output sequences at the receiver. This approach is within the spirit of the capacity theorem and is referred to as *coded modulation.*

As an example, consider a QAM signal constellation with more points than are required for the desired bit rate. Only a subset of these points need be used at each symbol time. Which subset is used at each time depends on past values of the information sequence. The allowed sequence of subsets over several symbol intervals follows a constraint that is the coding rule. At the receiver, several past received symbol values are stored, and decisions are made so as to output the nearest, or maximum likelihood, sequence that obeys the coding rule. Note that decisions are made according to sequences of received symbols, as required by the capacity theorem, rather than individual sample values. This is the underlying philosophy of all coding schemes.

Until recently, coded modulation was considered too complex for practical implementation. However, the availability of integrated signal processors has led to the introduction of this approach in high-performance voiceband modems, and it may be expected that coded modulation will find extensive use in other communication applications. The type of coded modulation in greatest use today is *trellis coding*, with *Viterbi decoding* the preferred receiving method. These techniques are described in [3].

1.6.3 Error-correcting Codes

A more traditional approach than coded modulation is to separate the modulation and coding functions. The resultant complexity is lower, but in most cases so is the achievable performance.

In the separated approach, the modulation subsystem is surrounded by the coding subsystem. The coder accepts a bit stream from the information source and adds additional bits according to a coding rule. The encoder's output is then fed to the modulator, which in turn transmits waveforms to the receiving demodulator. The decoder then attempts to reconstruct the original information sequence from the demodulated binary output, with a lower probability of error than is present in the demodulator output.

The process of symbol-by-symbol demodulation into a bit stream is an irreversible information-destroying process, so even with the best possible coding technique, attainable rate is reduced significantly below the original channel capacity. The channel capacity theorem is broad in what can be treated as a channel, and the path from the input to the modulator to the output of the demodulator can itself be treated as a channel. The input and output are binary sequences rather than continuous waveforms, as discussed previously. In its idealized form, the *binary symmetric channel*, with rate R and error probability p, where the errors are assumed independent, has capacity

$$C = R \left[1 + p \log_2 p + (1 - p) \log_2(1 - p) \right]$$

As expected, $C < R$, but for the usual low values of p it can be quite close. If the input bit stream is of rate less than C, then in principle arbitrarily low error probability can be achieved by means of binary coding.

In practice, coding is restricted to schemes that have enough systematic structure to be implemented with far less complexity than the arbitrary codes required to achieve vanishing error probability. Practical codes do, however, greatly reduce error probability at a moderate reduction in information rate. Construction and implementation of codes is a field of intense activity, but, except for a brief outline, beyond the scope of this text. An excellent broad treatment of the subject can be found in [6].

A widely used class of codes is the linear block codes. In an (n, k) code, the message is divided into blocks of k bits, and $n - k$ check bits are formed according to a coding rule and appended to the information bits, thereby forming an n-bit block. At the decoder, the received n-bit block is converted to the k-bit block corresponding to the nearest allowed receive sequence. Nearness is determined by the *Hamming distance*, which is the number of bits that the actual received block differs from each block corresponding to a valid error-free block.

The efficiency of a code is the fraction by which the rate is reduced and is equal to k/n for an (n,k) code. The *redundancy* is $1 -$ efficiency. Clearly, a good code is one that provides a high probability of error correction at high efficiency. In addition to a good code design, a high value of k is required.

In the linear block codes, each check bit is formed by the *parity* or modulo-2 sum of some subset of the information bits. The subsets must have substantial overlap and fully cover the information bits to provide good error correction. The linearity of the codes enables the design of systematic, low-complexity decoding algorithms.

In *convolutional codes*, as opposed to block codes, encoding is performed continuously on the information stream, with check bits regularly interspersed with the information bits. Decoding is a continuous sequence estimation process. Implementation is generally somewhat less complex, since framing of blocks is not required.

1.6.4 Error-detection Codes

It is far simpler to detect the presence of errors without attempting to correct them. Particularly when errors occur in bursts rather than independently, as is common over many real communication channels, reliable correction of errors becomes extremely difficult. In error-detection systems, the receiver only detects the presence of errors and informs the transmitter via a reverse message. The transmitter then typically retransmits the block or message that was in error. In such schemes, a positive acknowledgment is sent upon successful reception. This approach is very robust in the presence of all sorts of failure modes, but this is achieved at the price of a much lower overall information throughput rate.

The same block codes that are designed for error correction can be used for error detection. However, if the received block does not agree with an allowed error-free sequence, the block is rejected rather than corrected. Hybrid schemes are possible, in which correction is performed if the received block is close to an allowed one, but rejected otherwise.

Coding for error detection can be much simpler than for error correction. A simple parity check can detect any single error (or odd number of errors). In the common ASCII code, each character consists of seven information bits plus a parity bit over them. A *longitudinal* parity check consists of adding one character to the end of a block, the first bit of which is the parity of all first bits of all characters in the block, and so on. It is easily generated on a continuous basis and provides a long span of protection.

A very common error-detection technique is the *cyclic redundancy check*, or CRC. Because of its effectiveness and ease of implementation, it has been incorporated into many data communication standards. As in the longitudinal parity check, a fixed number of check bits (usually 16) is added to the end of a variable-length block.

The CRC can be explained mathematically in terms of binary polynomials, in which coefficients of a dummy variable are either 0 or 1 and for which all arithmetic operations are modulo 2. The information sequence is treated as such a polynomial, with the highest-order coefficient denoting the first bit. This sequence is continually divided by a fixed nth-order binary generator polynomial. The resultant quotient is discarded, and only the n-bit remainder need be retained during the process. The process continues until n additional zeros are appended to the end of the information sequence (but are not transmitted), and the final n-bit remainder constitutes the check sequence that is added to the end of the block. Exactly the same process is used at the receiving end, and the resulting calculated CRC is compared against the received one. Implementation is easy, involving a short shift register and simple logic.

In spite of its simplicity, the CRC is very powerful in detecting errors. Any pattern of up to n errors will be detected. A totally garbled message will be rejected with probability $1 - 2^{-n}$.

1.7 PERFORMANCE MEASURES

The criteria for specifying and measuring the performance of a digital communication should be those that are of importance to the ultimate user. These involve overall system throughput, the delay in completing a transaction, overall reliability, and the like. These measures depend on higher-level protocols and other system components that will be discussed in subsequent chapters. Here we will only treat the performance of the single communication channel, which is a major component of the total system performance.

1.7.1 Error Probability

It is common to specify the bit error probability, which is simply the long-term average ratio of errored bits to total bits. There are at least two problems with such a criterion.

First, the error rate will usually vary slowly over the course of a day or year. Over how long a period should it be measured? It makes a very big difference to the user if the errors are widely scattered or if they occur more intensely but only during isolated intervals. In the same vein, should total outages be treated as intervals in which the bit error probability is $\frac{1}{2}$?

A second concern is the nonindependence or burstiness of the errors. Information is typically transmitted in blocks, and any number of errors in any block are equally bad. If the errors were independent, the block error probability would be $1 - (1 - p)^n$, where p is the bit error rate and n is the length of the block. However, with the usual burstiness of most channels, the block error rate will be considerably lower for the same p.

To better describe the performance as seen by the user, outages should be separated from normal operation. An outage should be defined as a time interval that is greater than some value and during which the error probability exceeds some quantity, which is close to the threshold of usability. Error probability should then be defined only in the nonoutage condition. Unless the block size is known a priori, some realistic, or typical, block size must be assumed. A common surrogate for block size is a transmission of 1-second duration. The commonly specified probability of error-free seconds, while not a perfect measure, is usually more meaningful than the bit error rate.

When error detection is employed and included as part of the channel, it is important to distinguish between detected and undetected block errors. Although the former leads to added delay due to retransmission, the latter is much more serious.

Another distinction that is frequently important is that between errors and *slips*. An error in this context is the change in the value of a bit. A slip is the addition or deletion of one or more bits so that the number of received bits differs from the number of transmitted bits. A slip can be very serious in applications that include framing, such as multiplexing or encryption. It should also be noted that error-correction codes do not cope with slips.

1.7.2 Availability

As discussed above, some reasonable definition of an outage is needed to distinguish it from short transient intervals of poor performance. Once defined, both the average number of outages over some long period of time and the fraction of time the channel is in the outage state are important. These two measures are linked by the average time duration of an outage.

1.7.3 Delay

Many factors determine the overall system response time, such as the details of the protocol that may be involved, message processing times, and transmission rate. Here we will focus on one component, the transmission channel delay, which is defined as the time required for a bit presented to the transmitter to appear at the output of the receiver.

The most obvious component of delay is the time required for the signal to travel the distance involved. If $\beta(\omega)$ is the phase transfer function of the channel per unit length, the velocity of propagation is $[d\beta/d\omega]^{-1}$, which, except for distortion, is constant over the frequency range of the signal. The propagation velocity cannot be greater than the speed of light, 300,000 km/sec. This speed is achieved over radio, while a substantial fraction of that speed is typically achieved over other transmission media.

Additional delays are introduced by analog filters in the channel, transmitter, and receiver. These delays are found from $d\phi/d\omega$, as discussed previously, and generally increase with the sharpness of the filters' frequency roll-offs. Modulation and coding also require delay, particularly the corresponding receiving functions. The more sophisticated the functions to achieve high performance, the more delay that must be introduced.

1.7.4 Jitter

Jitter is the variability of delay, which shows up as deviation of received bit times from the nominal values that would result from constant delay. It is characterized by the magnitude of the time deviation and the frequency of that deviation over time. The lower that frequency, the more difficult it is to reduce the jitter by means of synchronization regeneration techniques.

While jitter may not directly be of concern to the user, when several channels are combined in a network, jitter can lead to failure due to introduction of slips and loss of synchronization.

1.7.5 Comparison with Analog Channels

It is much easier to specify and measure the performance of a digital channel than an analog one. In the latter case it is necessary to include many more variables, such as loss, signal-to-noise ratio, and many measures of linear and nonlinear distortion.

REFERENCES

1.1. T. C. Bartee, ed., *Digital Communications*, Howard W. Sams, Indianapolis, 1986.

1.2. Bell Laboratories, *Transmission Systems for Communications*, 5th ed., 1982.

1.3. S. Benedetto, E. Biglieri, and V. Castellani, *Digital Transmission Theory*, Prentice-Hall, Englewood Cliffs, NJ, 1987.

1.4. P. Bylanski and D. G. W. Ingram, *Digital Transmission Systems*, Peter Peregrinus, Herts, England, 1976.

1.5. K. W. Cattermole, *Principles of Pulse Code Modulation*, Elsevier, New York, 1969.

1.6. D. J. Costello, Jr., and S. Lin, *Error Control Coding*, Prentice-Hall, Englewood Cliffs, NJ, 1983.

1.7. N. S. Jayant and P. Noll, *Digital Coding of Waveforms*, Prentice-Hall, Englewood Cliffs, NJ, 1986.

1.8. R. W. Lucky, J. Salz, and E. J. Weldon, Jr., *Principles of Data Communication*, McGraw-Hill, New York, 1968.

1.9. F. F. E. Owens, *PCM and Digital Transmission Systems*, McGraw-Hill, New York, 1982.

1.10. A. Papoulis, *The Fourier Integral and Its Applications*, McGraw-Hill, New York, 1962.

1.11. J. G. Proakis, *Digital Communications*, McGraw-Hill, New York, 1983.

CHAPTER 2

ISDN: A PRAGMATIC APPROACH*

PRAMODE K. VERMA

AT&T Bell Laboratories

ABSTRACT

Integrated Services Digital Network is the vision of a single integrated network that will offer a variety of services. This vision is technologically achievable on a ubiquitous basis before the end of the century. The fundamental hardware that will make ISDN realizable exists in the network today, at least partially. ISDN services have already begun in bits and pieces. The continuing challenge of ISDN will be to standardize building blocks, while allowing innovative services to be offered by competing vendors.

2.1 INTRODUCTION

In 1976, the world saw the hundreth anniversary of the telephone service.† Today it is impossible to conceive of the functioning of the society in most countries without the telephone service. Over 660 million installed telephones now serve the world, a total that continues to grow by an average of 6% [1]. Countries with the most advanced telephone systems in the world such as the United States and Sweden are approaching a telephone density of 90%. The combined gross revenues of the telephone services and the data-processing industries, technologies that are merging rapidly, amounted to $260 billion in the United States alone in 1984.

There are three major elements of a telecommunications or teleprocessing system. In general, these systems include terminal equipment, transmission systems, and switching machines.

Examples of terminal equipment are simple telephone sets used to originate or receive a call, more sophisticated integrated voice-data terminals, and data-

---

* Portions of this chapter are reprinted, with permission, from *IEEE Transactions on Communications*, Vol. COM-22, pp. 1844–1848 © 1974 IEEE, and from *Proceedings of the IEEE*, Vol. 74, pp. 1222–1230 © 1986 IEEE.

† The first telephone patent application was filed by Alexander Graham Bell in 1876.

processing machines.   Early forms of transmission facilities are pairs of wires known as lines.   Telephone communication can take place by interconnecting terminal equipment with wire pairs as shown in Fig. 2.1.   If we regard each terminal equipment as a node and each line as an edge of a linear graph, there will be $n(n - 1)/2$ lines if full interconnectability, that is, direct connection between any two telephone sets, is desired.   Even though there is no external switch in the system, switching is involved in making one telephone call another since each of the telephones must have $(n - 1)$ cross-points, one of which should be activated to connect to the desired station.   Such a system would therefore require $n(n - 1)/2$ lines and $n(n - 1)$ cross-points.   It is easy to see that, for a large number of subscribers, the cost of communication would be very high.   The positioning of a central switch will reduce both the number of lines as well as the number of cross-points.   In Fig. 2.2, a central switch is placed that requires only n lines and $n(n - 1)/2$ cross-points.   The array of cross-points shown is such that there can be up to $n/2$ simultaneous connections, which is the maximum that can be supported in an n-station configuration.   We have thus established the need for a switching machine in a telecommunications system [2].

Telephone lines that carry voice signals need a bandwidth of 3.1 kHz (4 kHz nominal) for adequate transmission.   Until the early 1960s, all telephone communications took place using the 4-kHz analog baseband.   Digital transmission was first proved in the interexchange transmission area and has subsequently proved economical for long-haul transmission as well.

The transmission system between a customer's premises and the nearest switching machine (node) is sometimes referred to as the distribution system and thus classified in a separate category.   The motivation for a separate classification arises

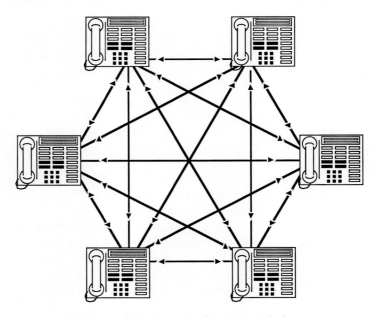

Figure 2.1   Pair-wise connection among telephones.

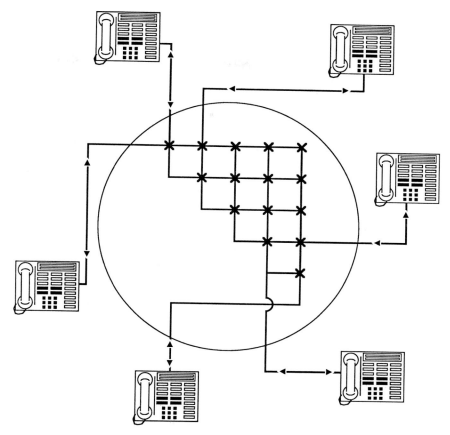

Figure 2.2   Telephone communication through a central switch.

from the fact that the trade-offs for providing economic transmission in this area are usually different from those applicable in most other situations.   For example, for residential customers of telephone services, it has generally not been economic to use multiplexing techniques on the access line to the nearest switching office, although such techniques are now being introduced.   On the other hand, the use of multiplexing techniques has been a key factor in reducing long-haul transmission costs and has resulted in the current lowered prices for domestic long-distance and global telephone services.

The present telephone network is an interconnection of switches by trans-mission systems.   It is partly analog and partly digital.   The transition between the analog and the digital domains is effected by an analog-to-digital or digital-to-analog converter, as shown in Fig. 2.3.   This transition is involuntary as far as the user is concerned.   The analog-to-digital converter provides an interface between the 4-kHz frequency spectrum on the analog side and the 64 kilobits per second (kbps) on the digital side.   (The adequacy of the 64-kbps channel capacity to handle

The Hybrid Network

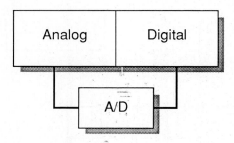

Figure 2.3 Transition between the analog and digital domains of a hybrid network.

speech signals was discussed in Chapter 1.)   The transition between the analog and digital domains can take place more than once in an end-to-end connection. These transitions do not materially affect the quality of a telephone conversation and generally the quality of voiceband data communication as well.   However, the integrity of 64-kbps digital data cannot be preserved when they transition from the digital to the analog domain through the digital-to-analog converter used in the telephone network.

The present telephone network is shown in Fig. 2.4.   Users in a particular geographic area are connected to an end office that provides for interconnection between user terminals connected to that end office and concentrates the traffic to other users served by different end offices, as shown in Fig. 2.4.   End users may be connected together directly or through a tandem office, depending on the traffic between them.   The location and interconnection of switching offices is determined by the trade-off between the transmission and switching costs.   The present telephone network functions as a highly integrated and intelligent entity. Some of its major features are discussed in the following section.

2.2 INTELLIGENT NETWORK ARCHITECTURE*

The elements of the intelligent network architecture plan are depicted in Fig. 2.5 [3].   Under this concept, the allocation of network functions and call control among network elements departs from present practice, resulting in a new distribution of these functions.   Some of this is evident in the 800 Service presently offered by AT&T.   It is also evident in some of the 800 Service plans of the local telephone companies.   In this service, the customer-dialed number is not the network address of the terminating line.   Rather, the dialed number is used as an index into a database that contains the terminating line network address, and perhaps also the identity of a long-distance service provider that the 800 Service customer has selected to carry the long-distance portion of the calls.   Also, the 800 customer will be able to specify other parameters of the service to suit his or her business plans.

* T. E. Browne, "Network of the Future," *Proc. IEEE*, Vol. 74, No. 9, Sept. 1986, pp. 1222–1230; material adapted with permission of the IEEE.

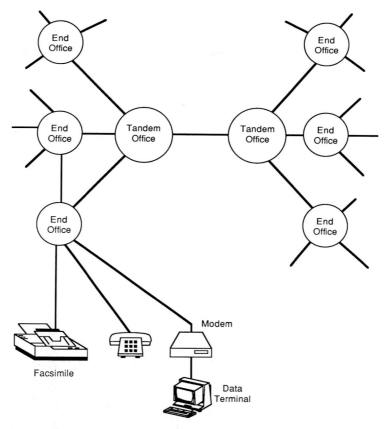

Figure 2.4 Present telephone network. © 1986 IEEE. Reprinted by permission.

For example, these parameters would allow the customer to specify a different geographic location for the call to terminate at, depending on the location of the calling customer, time of day, or day of the week.

In the present network architecture, the concentration of functionality in the software programs and hardware of the switching systems has, at times, been an impediment to the rapid introduction of new services by network providers. Also, it has complicated planning services where there has been uncertainty about whether the service falls within or outside the boundaries prescribed for the carrier by regulatory authorities.

The key elements of the intelligent network architecture are the following:

- A *service switching point* (SSP) function that controls the interconnection of transmission facilities, and receives, sends, and processes signals originating at either a user terminal or a service control point. The SSP function can be part of an end office, where it provides service for both trunk

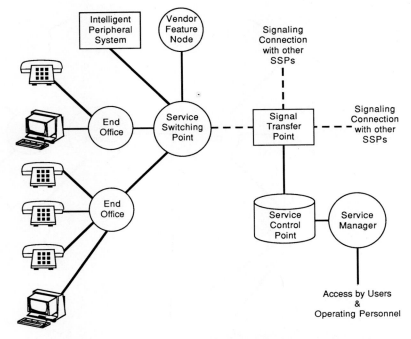

Figure 2.5 Intelligent network architecture. © 1986 IEEE. Reprinted by permission.

transmission facilities and user terminals. It can also be part of a tandem switch interconnecting only trunk transmission facilities.

- A *service control point* (SCP) function interconnected with switching systems by a common-channel signaling network.* Service logic and data at the SCP and the SSP control the actions of the other network elements in providing the service. The SCP also can collect traffic data and other measurements to support network management and administration, and it interfaces with the service management system.

- A *service manager* (SM) provides administration, coordination, and control of databases associated with the various services supported by the network. It provides the interface to operating personnel and users to specify services in terms of the linking of basic service capabilities and constructs the databases that control the real-time connection functions of the service.

- An *intelligent peripheral* (IP) system interconnected with an SSP, which provides certain telecommunications capabilities, such as announcements and DTMF (Dual tone multifrequency) digit collection, required in the course of providing a specific service. An IP has a transport and signaling links with end offices and the SSP, and it operates under control of either an SCP or an SSP.

_____

* See Section 2.2.3.

- *Vendor feature nodes* (VFN) for the distribution of some services that may not be integrated in the network, but that can be accessed by users connected to the network. This new network element is interconnected with the switch by means of a standard interface (for example, the ISDN interface) and is accessed by the user through the switch. Only minimal hardware and software changes are required in the switch to support the service. Also, the VFN can be designed to have the capacity and characteristics required for only the new service, and not all the other services that the existing switch software and hardware provide.

2.2.1 Service Control

In the intelligent network architecture plan, many of the call-processing and decision-making functions that reside in switching systems in the present network have been distributed among these new network elements.

The SSP function, for example, resembles the call-processing logic in today's network switches. It performs an analysis of the user input to determine what service capability has been requested. If the switch is equipped to fully provide the service, it does so. However, if the user request includes information specifying a service capability that the switch cannot, by itself, deliver (for example, 800 Service), the SSP requests the help of the SCP to process the service request and uses the common-channel signaling network to send the information supplied by the user to the SCP for analysis.

The SCP will interrogate information stored in databases to determine how the service request is to be satisfied. This could result in the establishment of a circuit-switched connection from the user to an interexchange carrier. Another possibility is that the SCP could effect the establishment of a connection from the user to a service vendor system providing voice message storage or perhaps a data service.

In either of these cases, the SCP might first establish a connection from the user to an intelligent peripheral system providing a voice announcement (or a data message) to the user as an indication of state of the service request.

2.2.2 Technology Implications

These simple examples illustrate the following very important aspects of the intelligent network architecture:

- Compared with present switching systems, the required switch functionality is somewhat simplified, at least conceptually. It is reduced to a set of fundamental call processing, switching, and signaling tasks common to all the services. A given service would use a subset of these fundamental tasks, and a particular subset may be used by several services, although perhaps in a different order, or with different controlling parameters specified by the SCP for the service. In this way, the software of the switch need not be upgraded to implement a new service, since the switch would already have the software for the fundamental tasks.

- The switch is directed by the SCP through the necessary fundamental tasks in completing a service request in all cases where it cannot do so on its own, whereas today's switches generally are programmed to provide certain services, and only those, and to reject all other service requests. The significance of this architectural feature is that many new services can be made available to users without having to upgrade the end offices themselves, but only the SCP.

- The use of intelligent peripherals provides for the delivery of new, user-oriented, service progress information to end users without the installation of new hardware and software in all switching systems.

- The SM provides for the distribution of new services to a large population of users, terminated on several switches, by making software changes at one place (the SM) rather than at every switch. As ISDN access lines are introduced, customers using those lines will be able to interact directly with the SM to customize network capabilities to create services satisfying their own particular requirements.

The availability of standard interfaces for connecting service nodes will provide opportunities for the implementation and economic distribution of new services using the underlying capabilities of the network. This is perhaps one of the most important aspects of the intelligent network architecture plan. Its implications in terms of technology, the economics of new services, and the achievement of some of the goals of U.S. public policy are profound.

2.2.3 Signaling Network Architecture

The architecture described here requires efficient signaling among the network elements. This is provided by a common-channel signaling network (CCS), which includes digital transmission terminals at every node interconnected with high-speed digital transmission links and signal transfer points that route the signaling messages through the network. Also, the network design will include safeguards to ensure the security of network control information and prevent a user from compromising network integrity and the quality of the service provided. This requires that the network be implemented using interfaces between network elements that are well defined and comply with the principles of an open-architecture concept.

By means of this signaling network, any element can send and receive signaling information to every other element. The information exchanged among the network elements is carried in messages that are specified according to a layered structure in which the control functions and procedures at each end of a link and at each signaling point are unambiguously defined. Signaling System No. 7 (SS7) is the internationally standardized protocol that will be used in this network. Transaction capabilities (TC) in the SS7 protocol specification provides a facility for the exchange of requests and responses between systems to remotely invoke operations in other systems. TC is the latest addition to the SS7 protocol, and it will support a variety of services that require transactions to be exchanged among the network elements in the intelligent network architecture plan. In TC, a relatively small set of nonservice-specific capabilities is provided to be used by a large variety of services.

The specifications for the messages and procedures of the SS7 protocol are given in recommendations that are being developed in national and international standards-making bodies. These specifications are being developed for application in signaling networks supporting service of both the present voice and data networks, as well as future networks in which voice and data services are integrated.

2.3 HISTORY OF DEVELOPMENTS IN DATA COMMUNICATIONS [4]

The initial needs of data communications were expeditiously and economically met by the existing telephone network (see Fig. 2.6). Network procedures and protocols were used for call setup. Once an end-to-end physical channel was set up, the use of a modem allowed digital signals to be transported over an analog medium, as described in Chapter 1.

The telephone network had the advantage of being ubiquitous. It also had a fixed bandwidth of 4 kHz nominal or 3.1 kHz actual and a level of performance designed primarily to meet the needs of voice communication. Ubiquity was a favorable factor in the use of the voice network since it provided an almost universal accessibility. The fixed bandwidth of the telephone network was a definite disadvantage, since it was uneconomic to use the entire bandwidth if the machine speed was low. This was generally the case in the early days of data communications. For example, an asynchronous (start–stop) machine operating at a line speed of 110 baud experienced a nominal information transmission efficiency of 80/4000 or 0.02 bit/sec/Hz, assuming 11 bits transmitted on line per 8-bit character. The Integrated Services Digital Network recommends an end-to-end transmission capability at 64 kbps. ISDN techniques allow this entire bandwidth to be used for data. Considering that the present analog voiceband connection can support a (switched) data speed only up to 9.6 kbps, the ISDN will provide a data capacity that is more than six times higher for every digital connection. It would appear that the need for digitizing the telephone network is due, at least in part, to the

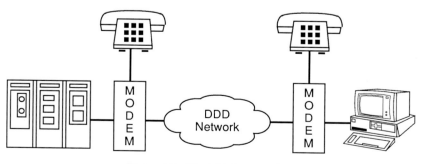

Figure 2.6 The initial approach.

fact that digitization will result in higher functionality and performance for the data user.

The telecommunication carriers' reaction in the early 1970s to the need for meeting the performance and flexibility requirements of the data communication user, in an economic way, was to provide data-transmission networks. A transmission network is a point-to-point network with fixed source–sink relationships between pairs of end points. The first such commercial network was the TransCanada Telephone System's Dataroute [5]. This was followed by AT&T's Digital Data System [6]. Both these networks resulted in enhanced performance and greater economy and flexibility to the user.

The two digital data-transmission networks mentioned above are nothing but networks of transmission facilities. These transmission facilities were first established for the transportation of voice in analog format. Subsequently, they were digitized for efficient data transmission. The cost associated with the advanced partial digitization of the existing telephone plant for digital data transmission was easily paid for by the users benefiting from lower transmission cost per bit per second and higher performance.

The major advantage of separating voice- and data-transmission environments resulted from the fact that it was possible, in the segregated environment, to regenerate data signals as frequently as desired. Selective regeneration of data signals was impossible in an integrated hybrid, that is, digital and analog, transmission environment, where facilities could be used interchangeably to transport voice in the analog format and data in the digital format. The ability to regenerate data signals was the key element in improving transmission performance. In a totally digital environment, where both voice and data are transported using digital signals, voice and data can be effectively integrated from a transmission perspective. Such an integration would provide an economy of scale while at the same time allowing transmission performance to be improved to the extent required since digital signals can be regenerated. A transmission network alone is not sufficient for effective data communication. Provisioning of transmission is just one step in meeting the total communication needs.

Teleprocessing requirements have existed since the 1950s. First they used the telephone network, as discussed earlier, for meeting all their communication needs. During the 1960s, the teleprocessing requirements gave rise to the arrangement shown in Fig. 2.7. It was a private network approach composed of leased lines and remote or local concentrators using a star topology.

A typical example of this arrangement is the IBM System/360. Essentially, all the processing was concentrated in the central host processor, befitting the technology available at the time. The front end was a transmission control unit responsible for only elementary data link control (DLC) functions. There was a lack of line sharing or terminal sharing. A given line and all terminals on it were part of the access path to only one application program. If a user wanted access to two different applications, he or she required two terminals and two lines [7].

This handicap was corrected with the release around 1974 of IBM System/370 with software and hardware releases referred to as SNA. The front end became a programmable communication controller doing DLC and a great deal more. The

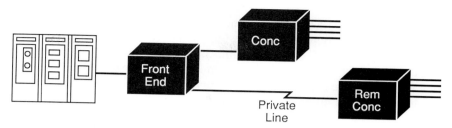

Figure 2.7 The next approach.

design allowed terminals to share a line to separate applications located in the same host.

In addition to the development of private networks typified by SNA, the concept of a public data network was also emerging simultaneously [8, 9]. It was argued that the private network approach was a fragmented approach to solving the needs of the data communications user and could be potentially expensive for the smaller customer due to lack of sufficient sharing. Lack of interconnectability among private networks, but potential demand for intercommunication among them in the future, was cited as yet another reason favoring the development of public data networks. The concept of a public data network is illustrated in Fig. 2.8.

It should be noted that a network is not merely a collection of terminals, communication lines, and computers but is an organized structure to which computers and terminals attach and through which they communicate. A network should have the ability to attach all instruments that meet a defined set of access and protocol requirements. Ordinarily, in such a network any entity will be able to communicate to any other. From a general point of view, a network is responsible for the collection, storage, processing, transmission, and distribution of information.

Along with private networks, public data networks are in existence today in several countries. Most of these operate on the principle of packet switching. Public data networks continue to grow in size, functionality, and complexity. The present trend is to have national public data networks intercommunicate with each

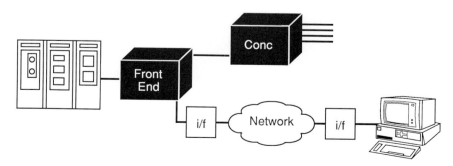

Figure 2.8 The network approach: public data network.

other through gateways.   X.75 is one example of a gateway protocol between X.25-based packet data networks.   The ISDN framework accommodates both the circuit- and packet-switching techniques in a single coherent structure.

A high-level, machine-to-machine communication between two entities or end points of a network demands much more than a simple transport connection. As an example of a higher-level communication, consider the following: When two human beings interact over a telephone, a good voiceband (4 kHz nominal) connection is a necessary requirement.   However, before they can meaningfully converse with each other, they must speak the same language, and even within the same language, where words have multiple meanings, they must have some means for resolving ambiguities should they arise.   In addition, there are usually questions related to confirmation of transmission.   Redialing the connection is used as a means to recover communication should it fail.   On a redialed connection, the communicating parties usually identify where they were cut off in order to maintain continuity with the last piece of conversation.   In any machine-to-machine communication, the functional equivalences of these operations have to take place without human intervention.   At the present time, the ISDN framework has addressed the transport issues.   Ongoing standardization activities will address issues beyond establishing a transport connection, for example, the issues involved in two application processes communicating with each other.

In 1978, the International Organization for Standardization (ISO) recognized that standards for networks of heterogeneous systems were required and initiated an activity known as Open System Interconnection (OSI).   The OSI reference model provides a layered architecture effectively breaking up the overall problem of machine-to-machine communication into manageable pieces.   The reference model is an abstract model, and adherence to the model by two different systems does not, by itself, guarantee effective communication between them.   The OSI service specifications and the OSI protocol specifications successively tighten up the abstractions, with the protocol specifications representing the lowest level of abstraction.   Two open systems with different implementations but identical protocol specifications within the OSI framework will allow them to communicate with each other.   There are seven different layers in the proposed OSI reference model. At the present time, protocol specifications for the lowest five levels (levels 1 through 5) have been agreed on by the responsible ISO committees, and work on the higher levels is in progress.   The interested reader is referred to a special issue of the proceedings of the IEEE addressing the different aspects of the OSI architecture and protocols [10].

2.4 INTEGRATION AND SEGREGATION: SOME FUNDAMENTAL CONSIDERATIONS

A major benefit of ISDN is that it provides for a common integrated infrastructure that can be used by a wide variety of communications traffic.   ISDN is thus not any specific service as such but rather an integrated means to offer a variety of services.   The underlying assumption in proposing an integrated infrastructure is that the economies of scale will allow the services to be affordable to the largest possible set of users. Another equally important reason supporting a single integrated infrastructure is that the creation of several networks, economical as they might be for specific applications, will necessarily result in the creation and management of complex interfaces whenever information has to be shared among two or more networks. Operational issues associated with the management of several networks are well known to organizations that have acquired a number of application-specific networks.

As is well known, integration of resources usually results in economies of scale. We illustrate this in the following discussion. Consider a telephone transmission system where telephone calls requesting transmission service arrive at random; that is, the probability of n arrivals during an interval of time t is given by

$$p(n \text{ arrivals in } t) = \frac{(\lambda t)^n}{n!} e^{-\lambda t} \qquad (2.1)$$

Equation (2.1) can be recognized to be the Poisson distribution. λ is a constant and can be shown to be the average rate of arrivals of calls; that is, the average number of calls arriving is an unit interval of time.

Let us assume that there are c servers in use; that is, the transmission system can handle up to c calls simultaneously. If we further assume that the holding time of calls has a negative exponential distribution and that the average holding time of a call is h, then the probability of blocking, that is, the probability that all c servers are busy handling traffic, is given by [11]

$$f(c) = \frac{(h\lambda)^c / c!}{\sum\limits_{i=0}^{c} [(h\lambda)^i / i!]} \qquad (2.2)$$

The derivation of Eq. (2.2) further requires the assumption that calls entering the system when all c servers are busy are cleared; alternatively, this discipline is also known as the lost calls cleared or the LCC discipline. Note that $h\lambda$ is a measure of the traffic intensity, since it represents the average number of servers in use.

To gain an understanding of how the efficiency of traffic handling per server increases as the magnitude or the intensity of traffic increases, one has to plot $f(c)$ as a function of $h\lambda$ or the traffic intensity, with c, or the number of servers, as a parameter. Such a curve is shown in Fig. 2.9. For example, with a total traffic such that, on the average, 12 servers are busy* ($h\lambda = 12$), and a requirement that only 1 in 100 calls attempted is lost, the number of servers required is 20. This gives an average utilization of servers as 12/20 or 0.6. If the total traffic is reduced such that only 3.8 servers are busy on the average, and if the requirement for the probability of a lost call is maintained the same as before, then the number of servers required is 9. This gives the average utilization of servers as 3.8/9 or 0.42,

---

* This measure of traffic is also known as the *Erlang*. Specifically, Erlang refers to the average number of servers occupied during the busy-hour.

Erlang "B" Load vs. Loss Curves, Infinite Sources, Lost Calls Cleared

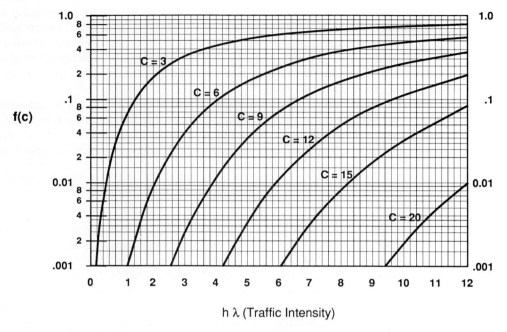

h λ (Traffic Intensity)

Figure 2.9 Traffic intensity versus probability of blocking as a function of server size.

which is significantly lower than the utilization achieved earlier. However, the advantage of the economy of scale does not continue indefinitely as the total traffic is increased. The incremental advantage progressively reduces as the traffic and the corresponding server size are increased. This can also be seen from the asymptotic nature of the curves in Fig. 2.9.

The basic reason for the economy of scale is the homogeneity of traffic. One should not be led to the conclusion that the integration of heterogeneous traffic into a common pool and its being served by a common pool of servers will always lead to higher performance from a user's standpoint. We consider it important to examine the issue of integration and segregation from a theoretical standpoint.

The general problem of integration and segregation is not specific to telecommunications traffic but arises in a variety of engineering situations. Basically, this problem is as follows: Any system generally gains from economies of scale as its size is increased, that is, as the volume of load it serves and the resources it deploys are proportionately increased. This is almost always true as long as the task the system is performing is homogeneous. In the case of the transmission system discussed earlier, this condition would amount to the incident traffic being characterized by, for example, a single distribution, the negative exponential distribution, that was assumed for the service time. However, a single system, if called on to perform a diversity of functions, may not function as well as two different systems each optimally suited to its specific task.   Modern technology, for example, can well build a machine that functions like a car on land and a boat on water.   Yet, everyone who can afford to own a car as well as a boat still has two different vehicles.   There are innumerable other situations where the segregation of identical functions, but with different characteristics when performed by two or more different systems, pays off.   For example, for minicomputers or mainframe computers, functions associated with input–output processing are almost always relegated to other microprocessors.   As yet another example, customers with fewer items in a supermarket find it more satisfying to be segregated into a different queue from those for customers buying in larger volume.   The problem of integration and segregation, therefore, is equivalent to the problem of determining when and at what point does it become desirable to segregate the functionality of a single system into two or more systems as the nonhomogeneity of functionality it provides is increased.   This determination is obviously not an easy task, since in most situations, especially in situations related to communications systems, our ability to quantify functionality (or traffic in the case of communication systems) is very limited.

In some situations, however, we can determine precisely when the segregation of communications traffic into two or more transmission systems might be better [12].   We intend to show this formally for the case of a message-switching system in the following section.

2.4.1 Message-Switching System

Consider a message-switching system with two nodes interconnected by a transmission channel of capacity C bits per second.   The average delay encountered by a message will be used as the measure of performance of the system.

Generally, an increase in the size of the message-switching system with the utilization factor ρ^* held constant, results in improved performance in the sense of obtaining a lower average message delay.   However, integrating two different message-switching systems into one, with the resultant integrated system having the combined channel capacity, need not necessarily result in improved performance.   We illustrate this in the following example.

Kendall [13] has shown that, for a single-channel system with Poisson arrivals and an arbitrary distribution of message lengths, the expected time a message spends in the system is

$$T = \frac{1}{\mu C} + \frac{\rho^2 + \lambda^2 \sigma^2}{2\lambda(1 - \rho)} \tag{2.3}$$

where $1/\mu$ = mean message length (number of characters)
  C = channel capacity (characters per second)
  σ^2 = variance of service time (sec^2)
  λ = arrival rate of messages (sec^{-1})
  ρ = utilization factor = $\lambda/\mu C$

---

* The utilization factor of a link is defined as the ratio of the average number of bits transmitted per second to the channel capacity of the link in bits per second.

Assuming an exponential distribution of message lengths, the variance of the service time can be shown to be

$$\sigma^2_{\exp} = \frac{1}{\mu^2 C^2} \tag{2.4}$$

Using (2.4) in (2.3), we obtain

$$T_{\exp} = \frac{1}{\mu C - \lambda} \tag{2.5}$$

With geometrically distributed message lengths* we obtain, after some manipulations,

$$\sigma^2_{\text{geom}} = \frac{1}{C^2} \frac{1 - \mu}{\mu^2} \tag{2.6}$$

and

$$T_{\text{geom}} = \frac{1}{2C} \frac{2C - \lambda}{\mu C - \lambda} \tag{2.7}$$

We now proceed to compare the delay performances of two segregated systems, each catering to a different class of users, against an integrated system carrying the combined traffic. The constraint in each is a fixed channel capacity C.

2.4.1.1 Average delay per message in two segregated systems each catering to a different class of users.

Let S_1 and S_2 be two segregated systems (Fig. 2.10) with specifications as shown in Table 2.1.

Before proceeding to examine whether an integrated system, S, with the given channel capacity C (which is the sum of the channel capacities of C_1 and C_2) will have an improved performance, the allocation of C between C_1 and C_2 must be optimized. The combined average message delay T_{seg} for the segregated systems S_1 and S_2 will have to be computed on this basis in order to obtain a fair comparison between the performances of segregated and integrated systems.

We have from (2.7)

$$T_1 = \frac{1}{2C_1} \frac{2C_1 - \lambda_1}{\mu_1 C_1 - \lambda_1} \tag{2.8}$$

$$T_2 = \frac{1}{2C_2} \frac{2C_2 - \lambda_2}{\mu_2 C_2 - \lambda_2} \tag{2.9}$$

Furthermore, T_{seg} is given by

$$T_{\text{seg}} = \frac{\lambda_1}{\lambda_1 + \lambda_2} T_1 + \frac{\lambda_2}{\lambda_1 + \lambda_2} T_2 \tag{2.10}$$

Substituting (2.8) and (2.9) into (2.10),

---

* In geometric distribution, the probability of a message of length 1 is given by $P(l) = \mu(1 - \mu)^{l-1}$

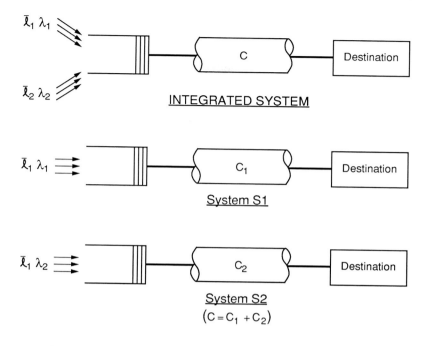

Figure 2.10 Model for integrated and segregated system. © 1974 IEEE. Reprinted by permission.

TABLE 2.1   [12]

System	Average Number of Messages per Second	Mean Message Length in Characters	Average Message Delay with an Optimum Channel Capacity Allocation
S_1	λ_1	$1/\mu_1$	T_1
S_2	λ_2	$1/\mu_2$	T_2

© 1974 TEEE.   Reprinted by permission.

$$T_{\text{seg}} = \frac{\lambda_1}{\lambda_1 + \lambda_2} \frac{1}{2C_1} \frac{2C_1 - \lambda_1}{\mu_1 C_1 - \lambda_1} + \frac{\lambda_2}{\lambda_1 + \lambda_2} \frac{1}{2C_2} \frac{2C_2 - \lambda_2}{\mu_2 C_2 - \lambda_2} \qquad (2.11)$$

If the total channel capacity C is fixed, the minimum value of T_{seg} as C_1 (or C_2) is varied can be obtained by setting

$$\frac{dT_{\text{seg}}}{dC_1} = 0 \qquad (2.12)$$

Equation (2.12) can be shown to yield the following equation:

$$\lambda_1 \frac{2\mu_1 C_1^2 - 2\lambda_1\mu_1 C_1 + \lambda_1^2}{(\mu_1 C_1^2 - C_1\lambda_1)^2}$$

$$= \lambda_2 \frac{2\mu_2(C - C_1)^2 - 2\lambda_2\mu_2(C - C_1) + \lambda_2^2}{[\mu_2(C - C_1)^2 - (C - C_1)\lambda_2]^2} \qquad (2.13)$$

Equation (13) results in a sixth-order equation in C_1, making a closed-form solution impossible. This is unlike the well-treated case [14] of exponential message length distributions where a closed-form solution is feasible.

From (2.13), we have

$$A_1 C_1^6 + A_2 C_1^5 + A_3 C_1^4 + A_4 C_1^3 + A_5 C_1^2 + A_6 C_1 + A_7 = 0 \qquad (2.14)$$

where

$$A_1 = \frac{2\mu_2}{\lambda_2} - \frac{2\mu_1}{\lambda_1}$$

$$A_2 = -\frac{8\mu_2 C}{\lambda_2} + 8 - \frac{2\mu_2\lambda_1}{\lambda_2} + \frac{4\mu_1 C}{\lambda_1} - \frac{2\mu_1\lambda_2}{\lambda_1}$$

$$A_3 = \frac{12\mu_2 C^2}{\lambda_2} - 20C + \frac{2\lambda_2}{\mu_2} + \frac{8\mu_2\lambda_1 C}{\lambda_2} - 4\lambda_1$$

$$+ \frac{\mu_2\lambda_1^2}{\mu_1\lambda_2} - \frac{2\mu_1 C^2}{\lambda_1} - \frac{2\lambda_1}{\mu_1} + \frac{2\mu_1\lambda_2 C}{\lambda_1}$$

$$+ 4\lambda_2 - \frac{\mu_1\lambda_2^2}{\mu_2\lambda_1}$$

$$A_4 = -\frac{8\mu_2 C^3}{\lambda_2} + 16C^2 - \frac{4\lambda_2 C}{\mu_2} - \frac{12\mu_2\lambda_1 C^2}{\lambda_2}$$

$$+ 12\lambda_1 C - \frac{2\lambda_1\lambda_2}{\mu_2} - \frac{4\mu_2\lambda_1^2 C}{\mu_1\lambda_2} + \frac{2\lambda_1^2}{\mu_1}$$

$$+ \frac{4\lambda_1 C}{\mu_1} - 4\lambda_2 C - \frac{2\lambda_1\lambda_2}{\mu_1} + \frac{2\lambda_2^2}{\mu_2} \qquad (2.15)$$

$$A_5 = \frac{2\mu_2 C^4}{\lambda_2} - 4C^3 + \frac{2\lambda_2 C^2}{\mu_2} + \frac{8\mu_2\lambda_1 C^3}{\lambda_2}$$

$$- 12\lambda_1 C^2 + \frac{4\lambda_1\lambda_2 C}{\mu_2} + \frac{6\mu_2\lambda_1^2 C^2}{\mu_1\lambda_2}$$

$$- \frac{6\lambda_1^2 C}{\mu_1} + \frac{\lambda_1^2\lambda_2}{\mu_1\mu_2} - \frac{2\lambda_1 C^2}{\mu_1}$$

$$+ \frac{2\lambda_1\lambda_2 C}{\mu_1} - \frac{\lambda_1\lambda_2^2}{\mu_1\mu_2}$$

$$A_6 = 4\lambda_1 C^3 - \frac{2\lambda_1\lambda_2 C^2}{\mu_2} - \frac{4\mu_2\lambda_1^2 C^3}{\mu_1\lambda_2}$$

$$+ \frac{6\lambda_1^2 C^2}{\mu_1} - \frac{2\lambda_1^2\lambda_2 C}{\mu_1\mu_2} - \frac{2\mu_2\lambda_1 C^4}{\lambda_2}$$

$$A_7 = \frac{\mu_2\lambda_1^2 C^4}{\mu_1\lambda_2} - \frac{2\lambda_1^2 C^3}{\mu_1} + \frac{\lambda_1^2\lambda_2 C^2}{\mu_1\mu_2}$$

Equation (2.14) can be solved numerically giving the optimum value of C_1 and therefore of C_2. The following argument shows that there is one and only one solution to Eq. (2.14) such that C_1 lies between 0 and C. From Eqs. (2.8) and (2.9), T_1 and T_2 monotonically decrease and increase, respectively, as C_1 is enhanced (and therefore C_2 is decreased since $C_2 = C - C_1$) over the range considered. The weighted sum of T_1 and T_2 has poles at $C_1 = 0$ and $C_2 = 0$. This results in T assuming an infinite value at both these extremes. It follows that there will be one and only one minimum value of T such that $0 < C_i < C$, $i = 1, 2$, and therefore one set of optimum values for C_1 and C_2. Using these values, T_{seg} can be computed from Eqs. (2.8) through (2.11).

A simplification of Eq. (2.13) results when $\mu_2/\lambda_2 = \mu_1/\lambda_1$, making it a fifth-order equation.

2.4.1.2 Average delay per message for an integrated system catering to two classes of users.

Let the integrated system S (see Fig. 2.10) with channel capacity C trasmit both classes of messages as given in Table 2.1. System S will have the following traffic parameters.

1. The arrival process will be a Poisson distribution with the parameter $\lambda = \lambda_1 + \lambda_2$.
2. The mean service time will be given by

$$\frac{1}{\mu C} = \frac{\lambda_1}{\lambda}\frac{1}{\mu_1 C} + \frac{\lambda_2}{\lambda}\frac{1}{\mu_2 C}$$

3. The variance of the service time can be shown to be given as

$$\sigma_{\text{int}}^2 = \frac{1}{C^2}\left[\frac{\lambda_1}{\lambda}\frac{2 - \mu_1}{\mu_1^2} + \frac{\lambda_2}{\lambda}\frac{2 - \mu_2}{\mu_2^2} - \left\{\frac{\mu_1}{\lambda\mu_1} + \frac{\lambda_2}{\lambda\mu_2}\right\}^2\right] \quad (2.16)$$

The mean delay per message for the integrated system can now be written using Eq. (2.3) as

$$T_{\text{int}} = \frac{1}{\mu C} + \frac{(\lambda/\mu C) + (\sigma_{\text{int}}^2\lambda\mu C)}{2(\mu C - \lambda)} \quad (2.17)$$

Figure 2.11 illustrates the variation of mean message delays for the segregated and integrated systems with $\lambda_1 = 25$, $1/\mu_1 = 20$, and $C = 1200$. The channel utilization is held constant at 0.92, while the ratio μ_1/μ_2 is varied to illustrate the effect of relative message lengths in determining the suitability of a segregated or

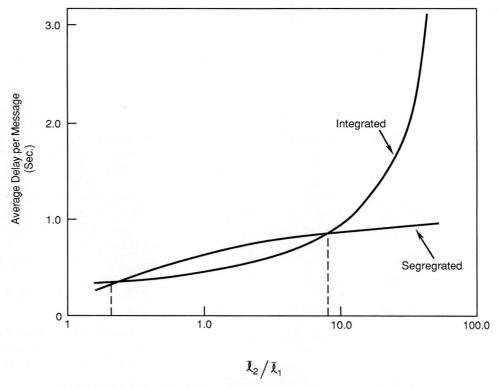

Figure 2.11 Comparison of average message delays for segregated and integrated systems as a function of ratio of message lengths. © 1974 IEEE. Reprinted by permission.

an integrated system. It can be seen from the curve that, for this particular example, the preferred region for the integrated system lies when $0.21 < l_2/l_1 < 6.6$. For all other ratios of lengths the segregated system is preferable.

2.5 A BOUND ON THE RELATIVE PERFORMANCE OF SEGREGATED AND INTEGRATED SYSTEMS

It can be remarked that, in general, as the disparity between the average message lengths increases the relative performance of the segregated system improves, and vice versa. It appears desirable to determine if a limit exists on the ratio of performance measures (in the sense defined earlier) for the segregated and integrated systems. We now increase the number of user classes to an arbitrary value N and place no restriction on the distribution of their message lengths. It is, however, assumed that the mean and variance for each class are known. We first prove the following theorem.

Theorem.   If the traffic generated by the N classes of users has the same mean and variance, then, using the same total channel capacity, the average delay per message for the segregated system is N times the average delay for the integrated system.

Proof. Let $1/\mu$, σ_l^2, and λ be the average message length, variance of message lengths, and arrival rate for each of the N classes of users, respectively.   Let C be the total channel capacity.   Then we have for the two systems the service time variances given as

$$\sigma_{\text{seg}}^2 = N^2 \sigma_l^2 / C^2$$

and
$$\sigma_{\text{int}}^2 = \frac{1}{C^2}\left[\frac{1}{N}\left(N\sigma_l^2 + \frac{N}{\mu^2}\right) - \frac{1}{\mu^2}\right] = \frac{\sigma_l^2}{C^2}$$

Furthermore, it can be easily seen that $\rho_{\text{int}} = \rho_{\text{seg}}$. Let $\rho = \rho_{\text{int}}$.   Therefore, from Eq. (2.3)

$$T_{\text{seg}} = \frac{1}{\mu(C/N)} + \frac{(\rho^2 + \lambda^2 N^2 \sigma_l^2)/C^2}{2\lambda(1 - \rho)} \tag{2.18}$$

and
$$T_{\text{int}} = \frac{1}{\mu C} + \frac{(\rho^2 + N^2\lambda^2\sigma_l^2)/C^2}{2\lambda(1 - \rho)N} \tag{2.19}$$

Comparing Eqs. (2.17) and (2.18), it is immediately obvious that

$$\frac{T_{\text{seg}}}{T_{\text{int}}} = N$$

which proves the theorem.

It can be easily shown that an integrated system with N identical user classes has lower average delay per message when compared to an integrated system with the same number of user classes but dissimilar traffic parameters under the constraint of identical channel capacity and average traffic intensity. It follows therefore, as a corollary to the preceding theorem, that the average delay per message for the segregated system can never be more than N times the average delay of the integrated system.   The converse of this corollary is not necessarily true; this can be seen by considering the case presented in Fig. 2.11 as a counterexample. It follows therefore that depending on the disparity in the average message lengths, the ratio (average message delay for integrated system/average delay per message for segregated system) could be indefinitely large.

In Sections 2.4 and 2.5 we have, rather laboriously, proved that, at least from an abstract perspective, integration of a variety of resources under a common infrastructure may not always be the most economic approach if the infrastructure is required to serve a highly diversified set of demands. While this approach may sound contrary to the ISDN approach, it really is not, since in the mathematical construct adopted to address the integrated versus segregated issue we have not really included all aspects of a large system. The issues associated with the management of large networks and our ability to quantify characteristics of the demand function, both present and future, firmly dictate an approach with a common infrastructural base for serving a variety of evolving customer requirements. ISDN is fundamentally driven from this empirical observation over the entire history of communications in all parts of the world.

2.6 MOTIVATIONS FOR ISDN

In the last few sections of this chapter and in Chapter 1, we reviewed the existing technology of the present telecommunication network. We have also seen the motivations for digitizing the network, both from transmission as well as switching perspectives. In addition, we have specifically reviewed how digitation of the end-to-end network is especially useful for the data communications user.

A digitized network is a prime requirement for integrating a variety of services that the network will support. It is appropriate to view ISDN as being evolutionary in nature and scope. The first step in the process toward realizing an ISDN is end-to-end digitization.

Digitization of the telephone network in the United States began in the early 1960s. The early digitized program largely addressed the interexchange transmission system of the metropolitan network. Use of the time division multiplexing technique, rather than the traditional frequency division multiplexing technique, resulted in an enhanced capacity of the existing telephone plant at minimal cost.

Further development in transmission systems, especially those based on fiber-optic transmission techniques, have pushed the digitization program well beyond the most optimistic projections made just a few years ago. Compared to other forms of information transport, lightware systems have proved themselves economically and will continue to be the technology of choice in the foreseeable future. From an initial transmission capability of 45 Mbps ten years ago, the capacity of lightware systems has doubled every 18 months. Presently, 1.8 Gbps systems are available, and by mid-1990, 2.2 Gbps systems will be on the commercial market [15]. End-to-end digitization is available in limited pockets in the United States today but is expected to grow sharply during the next few years. This will provide the hardware base for realizing the ISDN capability.

ISDN goes much beyond having digital switching and transmission hardware on a ubiquitous basis. The main focus of ISDN is on the support of a wide range of voice and nonvoice or integrated voice/nonvoice applications over the same network. A basic tenet of ISDN is that this service integration be achieved through a limited set of user–network interface arrangements.

Heretofore, private line and switched offerings have been made by telecommunications administrations using functionally separate networks, although they typically share transmission facilities. Circuit- and packet-switched networks, for example, are often isolated from one another, and interworking between them is usually a difficult technical issue. ISDN provides for these services within a common framework in order to benefit the end users, particularly from the point of view of assuring them, through easy interworking among different services, of the continuing usage of their applications software investment, often done at enormous expense. Without the availability of well-specified and functional user–network interface characteristics and the assurance that the network transport function can be achieved using whatever technique best meets the end user's needs, but resulting in no additional interface problems, these goals of ISDN will not be realized.

2.6.1 Basic Concepts of ISDN [16]

Recognizing the continuing growth in digitization of the telecommunications network and the advantages and additional capabilities of an end-to-end digital network, the concept of a single integrated network was born in the 1970s. Serious efforts were soon started in the CCITT, the organization that establishes international standards for public telecommunications, on a global basis. The first set of standards for ISDN were issued by the CCITT in 1984. As ISDN is established on a global basis, a variety of voice and nonvoice services can be supported over a single, homogeneous infrastructure. Analog communication will eventually disappear, resulting in enhanced quality at reduced costs.

An integrated access mechanism is a basic tenet of ISDN. The ISDN framework requires that a variety of services be accessed using common access arrangements with a limited net of access interfaces.

It is easy to recognize that there are very large fixed costs in the global telecommunications network today. Since a large discontinuity in service features and pricing will be unacceptable in the telecommunications marketplace, it is easy to see that it may be infeasible to move immediately to ISDN in many areas of the world. The full implementation of some ISDN concepts may take several years, possibly through the whole decade of the 1990s. In the meanwhile, ISDN systems and services will interoperate with the existing services. ISDN is thus an evolutionary concept from the standpoint of services to the end user.

From a networking perspective, ISDN is a new network infrastructure that will provide a single point of access to multiple networks and to different kinds of networks. ISDN exchanges will be able to interconnect with each other. In addition, ISDN exchanges will be able to connect to other existing networks, for example, X.25 packet networks. They will also interconnect with existing voice telephone networks (public and private). These interconnections will ensure that the presently available services are not disrupted while new services employing the additional capabilities of ISDN are made available to the user.

Before the advent of ISDN, the premises equipment and network services provided by the common user network were assumed to be distinct elements co-operating in only limited ways in providing an end-to-end service. The concept of ISDN specifically provides for the extension of network functions into the premises equipment, and vice versa, depending on the need of the application. This requires a rich set of signaling mechanisms between the premises equipment and the network, higher speeds of transmission that both the premises equipment and the network services must support, and an integrated set of end-to-end network management capabilities.   Within the overall concept of ISDN, all elements, whether premises based or network based, that provide a service are thus covered.   This is a revolutionary departure from the practice of communications during the last 100 years.   With the advance of technology in both hardware and software, the provisioning of complex interfaces and the realization of transmission speeds in the hundreds of megabits per second range are now achievable, making the concepts of ISDN a reality.

2.6.2 ISDN: The User's Perspective [17]

The support for any new technology must eventually be derived from the end user of the technology.   For this reason, every successful strategy for deploying new technology must view users' needs, as well as their ability to pay for the new technology, with topmost priorities.   This is especially true in a competitive environment, such as the communications environment in the United States, where telecommunications and teleprocessing services can be bought from a number of vendors and suppliers on an as needed basis.   Should the cost of a new technology prove to be overwhelming in comparison to the benefits it provides to the user in the short run, it is unlikely to go past an initial phase of excitement and will most likely be discarded by the user after a trial phase.   The PICTUREPHONE® service is a well-known example of a service that did not succeed in the marketplace.

   More than ever before the prospective user of a new service is likely to judge the value of that service through a careful analysis of its implications in the three dimensions of functionality, performance, and price. *Functionality* is the totality of functions a user demands in an application.   Functionality is thus directly related to the task the user is trying to accomplish.   Functionality is not absolute, however. It must be qualified by a set of *performance* parameters that are useful in characterizing the application under consideration and whose values are of consequence in judging the degree of effectiveness with which the application requirements are being met.   The third dimension, *price*, is the total cost to the user that could be attributed to the task being accomplished.   If the thresholds of performance levels that will satisfy the needs of the task are well known, then those alternatives that are deficient in terms of one or more parameters are discarded, making a smaller list of acceptable alternatives.   One technique frequently employed by the user is to choose the least-cost alternative from among the acceptable ones judged against the functionality and performance standpoints.

   Given these criteria, it is certain that ISDN's success in the marketplace will be based on the value it adds compared to the cost its user incurs.   Ultimately it will be up to the users to judge the effectiveness of ISDN in their respective environments.   Leading edge business organizations today view communications not only as a tool to conduct their business but, more importantly, as a strategic weapon in a competitive marketplace.

   ISDN provides an integrated infrastructure that unifies all possible telecom-

®The PICTUREPHONE is a registered service mark of AT&T.

munications and teleprocessing services. ISDN provides for 64-kbps digital channels, or its higher multiples, on an end-to-end basis. These channels can be used for transporting voice, data, or image signals. Integration of the physical media for a variety of services provides an economy of scale that would benefit all applications. The architectural framework of ISDN is driven by the users' present and evolving needs, with consideration to cost and flexibility.

2.7 IS ISDN THE ULTIMATE SOLUTION?

Despite the benefits ISDN is expected to bring to users, equipment manufacturers, and service providers, no one should anticipate that ISDN is the ultimate solution. A pragmatic view is that ISDN is the first major global step toward rationalizing a wide variety of networking systems into a coherent structure. Given the trend of the past several years, it should be clear to anyone that the need for higher speeds for nonvoice communication will continue to emerge. What is less obvious, but perhaps equally true, is that the need for lower speeds will continue to emerge as well. For example, as speech-processing techniques evolve and mature, acceptable quality of transmission might need only 32- or even 16-kbps channel capacity. The assignment of a 64-kbps, end-to-end channel capacity may thus prove to be an extravagant use of the bandwidth resource.

As far as the data communications users are concerned, some 50% of them are remote from central sites and are at the moment communicating at speeds of 4800 bps or slower [18]. A structure that supports only 64 kbps or its higher multiples for end-to-end switched communication may thus provide a very poor utilization of the bandwidth resource for such users.

Ideally, communications may be viewed as a means to transport a bit or a collection of bits at a minumum cost while meeting the user-specified characteristics of accuracy, speed, and delay. A structure that can meet this requirement is potentially the optimum structure. Unfortunately, our present state of knowledge of optimization procedures does not allow us to synthesize structures even under prespecified user demand characteristics. And it is well known that user characteristics vary with time, economic conditions, and the technological infrastructure. It is therefore impossible to determine whether the network structure imposed by the overall ISDN framework is by any means an ideal structure.

One more consideration must be taken into account in the process of determining the suitability of any new structure for networking. On a global basis, the investment in telecommunications networking is on the order of a trillion (10^{12}) dollars. If the user is to be protected from a major discontinuity in pricing or a major dislocation of existing services, the existing telecommunications base can only evolve at an acceptably small rate. ISDN does meet this requirement. It accommodates a wide variety of existing equipment and procedures, for example, those based on the North American and the CEPT* standards for digital transmission.

A major shortcoming of ISDN is that it does not, at the time of this writing,

*Conference of European Posts and Telecommunication.

provide a framework for effective local area transport capability. This is despite the fact that in the United States useful data transmission in the office environment is at 1 Mbps and higher. We fully anticipate that voids in the ISDN framework such as this will be fulfilled in due course.

The next chapter begins a detailed discussion on the physical interfaces provided by ISDN.

REFERENCES

2.1. Datapro Research Corporation, *An Overview of World Telecommunications*, Dec. 1987.

2.2. J. C. McDonald, ed., *Fundamentals of Digital Switching*, Plenum Press, New York, 1983, Chapter 1.

2.3. T. E. Browne, "Network of the Future," *Proc. IEEE*, Vol. 74, No. 9, Sept. 1986, pp. 1222–1230.

2.4. P. K. Verma, *Performance Estimation of Computer Communication Networks*, Computer Science Press, 1989.

2.5. D. J. Horton and P. G. Bowie, "An Overview of Dataroute: System and Performance," *Conf. Record. Int. Conf. Communications*, Minneapolis, June 17–19, 1974, pp. 2A1–2A5.

2.6. N. E. Snow and N. Kapp, Jr., "*Digital Data System—System Overview*," *Bell System Tech. J.*, Vol. 54, No. 5, May–June 1975, pp. 811–832.

2.7. P. E. Green, Jr., "An Introduction to Network Architectures and Protocols," *IEEE Trans. Communications*, COM-28 (12), Apr. 1980, pp. 412–424.

2.8. M. L. Ford and F. W. Davies, "International Data Networks—UK Post Office Experience and Plans," *Proceedings of the Fourth International Conference on Computer Communications*, Kyob, Sept. 26–29, 1978, pp. 4–46.

2.9. A. M. Rybczynski, D. F. Wier, and I. M. Cunningham, *Datapac Internetworking for International Services*, ibid., pp. 47–55.

2.10. *Proceedings of the IEEE*, Special Issue on Open System Interconnection, Dec. 1983.

2.11. Bruce E. Briley, *Introduction to Telephone Switching*, Chapter 5, Addison-Wesley, Reading, Mass., 1983.

2.12. P. K. Verma and A. M. Rybczynski, "The Economics of Segregated and Integrated Systems in Data Communication with Geometrically Distributed Message Lengths," *IEEE Trans. Communications*, Vol. COM-22, No. 11, Nov. 1974, pp. 1844–1848.

2.13. D. G. Kendall, "Some Problems in the Theory of Queues," *J. Roy. Statis Soc.*, Series B, Vol. 13, 1951, pp. 151–185.

2.14. L. Kleinrock, *Communication Nets—Stochastic Message Flow and Delay*, McGraw-Hill, New York, 1964, Chap. I and II.

2.15. M. Gawdon, "Future Directions in Transmission," *Telecommunications*, Dec. 1987, pp. 48–57.

2.16. R. P. Uhlig, "Technology Evolution and ISDN," *Proceedings of the Conference on Computers Communication for Developing Countries*, CCDC '87, New Delhi, Oct. 27–30, 1987, pp. 272–292.

2.17. P. K. Verma, "ISDN Technology: The User's Perspective," ibid., pp. 293–301.

2.18. John L. McElroy, quoted in *MIS Week*, Dec. 14, 1987.

CHAPTER 3

ISDN PHYSICAL INTERFACES

RYOICHI KOMIYA

Nippon Telegraph and Telephone Corporation

ABSTRACT

This chapter primarily describes physical interfaces for both basic and primary rate interfaces. These physical specifications have been best established in CCITT Recommendations I.430 ("Basic user–network interface—Layer 1 specification") and I.431 ("Primary rate user–network interface—Layer 1 specification"). This chapter also outlines the issues associated with digital subscriber line transmission systems using metallic-pair cables for ISDN basic rate access. These issues involve the technology of extending ISDN services from the central office directly to the customer using existing subscriber lines.

3.1 INTRODUCTION

The architecture of ISDN defines a small number of user–network interfaces to meet the needs of users for a variety of applications. In this chapter we discuss the ISDN basic user–network interface, as well as the primary rate user–network interface defined in CCITT Recommendations I.430 [1] and I.431 [2], respectively. The focus in this chapter is on the physical characteristics of the interfaces.

The reference configuration for the ISDN user–network interface is defined by reference points and the types of functions that can be provided between these reference points. CCITT recommendation I.411 [3] defines the reference configuration with the functional groups NT1, NT2, and TE1, as shown in Fig. 3.1.

This chapter primarily describes physical interfaces for both basic and primary rate interfaces. These physical specifications have been best established in CCITT Recommendations I.430 ("Basic user–network interface—Layer 1 specification") and I.431 ("Primary rate user–network interface—Layer 1 specification").

This chapter also outlines the issues associated with digital subscriber line transmission systems using metallic-pair cables for ISDN basic rate access. These issues involve the technology of extending ISDN services from the central office directly to the customer using existing subscriber lines.

A practical illustration of the ISDN user–network interfaces is shown in Fig. 3.2.

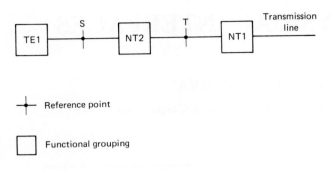

ST: ISDN user–network reference points
NT1: Network termination 1 (line transmission termination, interface
     termination, layer 1 multiplexing, layer 1 maintenance, etc.)
NT2: Network termination 2 (layers 2 and 3 protocol handling,
     switching, maintenance, etc.)
TE1: Terminal equipment 1 (ISDN standard terminal)

Figure 3.1 Reference configuration for the ISDN user–network interface.

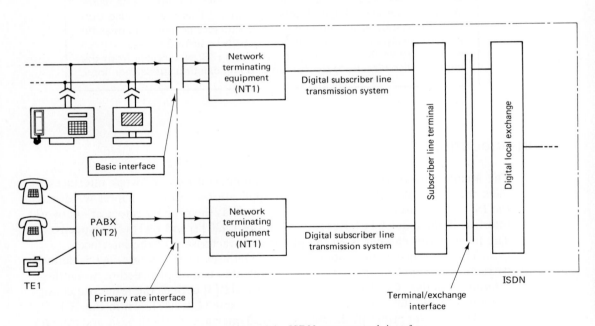

Figure 3.2   ISDN user–network interface

The ISDN basic interface provides a (2B + D) interface to the customer. It is analogous to a 4-kHz interface in the conventional analog telephone network. Four-wire metallic cable extending from the NT (network terminating equipment) is used for in-house wiring. Terminals are connected to this cable using a socket in a cable. A wide spectrum of digital services will be provided through this socket to various customer terminals. Prospective users of this basic interface range from businesses, both large and small, to residential customers.

The ISDN primary rate interface provides a (23B + D) or (30B + D) interface to the customer, directly analogous to the channelization of the primary rate interface of the existing digital hierarchy. Four-wire metallic cables are also used for in-house interface wiring. However, this interface configuration is limited to point-to-point configuration. This interface will be widely used for PBX, LAN, high-speed facsimile, and TV conferencing services.

The digital subscriber line transmission system to support the basic interface shown to the right of NT1 at the top of Fig. 3.1 is also being discussed by CCITT for standardization. A major consideration here is use of the existing two-wire subscriber cables. Time compression multiplex (TCM) and echo canceller (EC) transmission systems are the two techniques being considered for standardization.

3.2 BASIC INTERFACE LAYER 1

3.2.1 Features

Basic interface layer 1 aims at an efficient use of the existing in-house wiring, wiring flexibility, and terminal portability. The following requirements are defined to realize these objectives:

- Four-wire interface wiring
- Simultaneous communication of multiple terminals
- Interface connection by plug and jack

CCITT has adopted a multiplexed channel interface structure and a passive bus wiring configuration. This facilitates multiple terminal connections to the interface flexible wiring using existing in-house distribution cables and free installation of jacks in the cables.

The basic interface configuration is illustrated in Fig. 3.3. CCITT Recommendation I.430 specifies the physical and electrical characteristics of the basic interface to ensure digital transmission over passive bus wiring. These specifications include transmission line code, interface frame format, impedance characteristics of the cable driver/receiver, and plug and jack specifications. D-channel contention resolution is required because the channel can be accessed by multiple terminals simultaneously. Simple, layer 1, D-channel access control realizes minimum access delay and simple algorithms without any layer 1 identifiers in TE. Activation/deactivation procedures are established to save power consumption when no communication takes place. The following section describes the various layer 1 maintenance methods.

3.2.2 Electrical Interface Point

The electrical interface point depends on the interface cable length. Therefore, electrical parameter specifications vary according to the different interface points to be defined. CCITT Recommendation I.430 indicates two interface points for

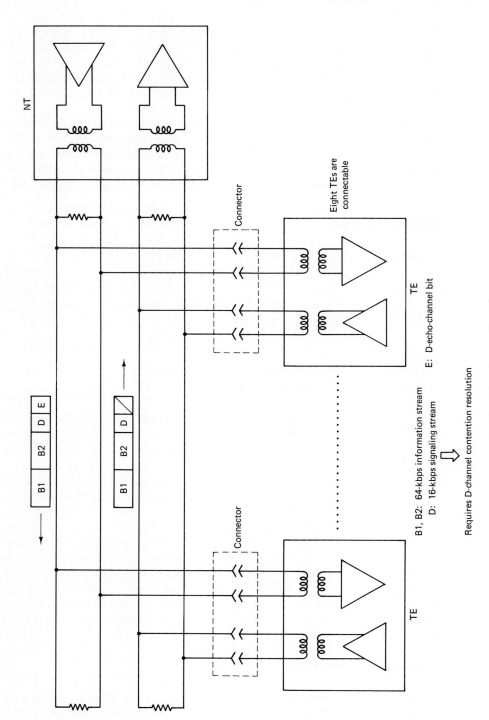

Figure 3.3 Basic interface configuration.

NT

Connector

Connector

Eight TEs are
connectable

TE

TE

| B1 | B2 | D | E |

| B1 | B2 | D |

B1, B2: 64-kbps information stream
D: 16-kbps signaling stream

Requires D-channel contention resolution

E: D-echo-channel bit

specifying electrical parameters, as illustrated in Fig. 3.4.   Interface points I_{A0}, I_{A1} ~ I_{An} are extended from terminals using less than 10 m of connecting cord.   Interface point I_B is extended from NT using less than 3 m of connecting cord.   These lengths are chosen to minimize pulse waveform distortion due to multiple terminal connections in passive bus configurations.

3.2.3 Wiring Arrangements

Wiring arrangements for the basic interface are point-to-point, short passive bus and extended passive bus, as shown in Fig. 3.5.

Point to point.   This configuration provides one transmitter/receiver at each end of the cable.   The objective for the operational distance between TE and NT is 1.0 km (d_1 in Fig. 3.5a), and the maximum objective cable loss is 6 dB at 96 kHz.

It is necessary to establish the maximum round-trip delay for any signal that must be returned from one end to the other within a specified time period limited by D-echo bits.   The round-trip delay is allocated between 10 to 42 μsec.   The lower value of 10 μsec is composed of 2-bits offset delay (see Fig. 3.8) and the negative phase deviation of -7% (see Section 3.2.5).   The upper value is composed of the following elements:

- Two bits of offset delay (10.4 μsec) (see Fig. 3.8)
- Maximum 6-bit delay permitted due to the distance between NT and TE and the required processing time (31.2 μsec)
- The fraction ($+15\%$) of a bit period due to phase deviation between TE input and output (0.8 μsec)

Short Passive Bus.   This is an essential passive bus configuration in which the TEs are connected at random points along the full length of the cable.   This means that the NT receiver must cater for pulses arriving with different delays from

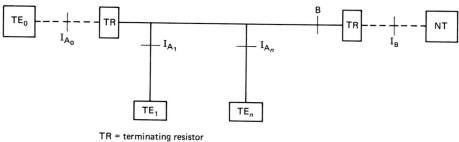

TR = terminating resistor
 I = electrical interface
 B = location of I_B when NT includes terminating resistor (TR)
TE_n = terminals

Figure 3.4   Reference configuration for wiring on customer premises.

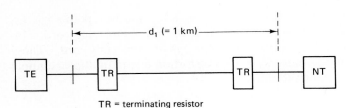

TR = terminating resistor

(a) Point to point

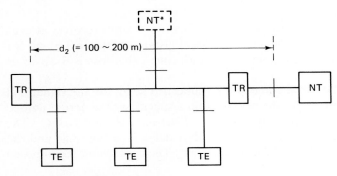

TR = terminating resistor

*In principle, the NT may be located at any point along the passive bus.

(b) Short passive bus

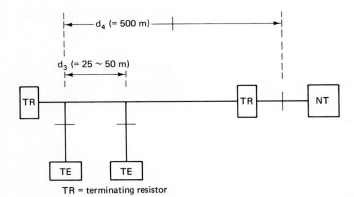

TR = terminating resistor

(c) Extended passive bus

Figure 3.5 Wiring arrangements for basic interface.

various terminals (see Fig. 3.6). Therefore, the range limit for this configuration is a function of the maximum round-trip delay and not of the loss of the interface interchange cable.

An NT receiver with fixed timing can be used if the round-trip delay is between 10 and 14 μsec. This relates to a maximum operational distance from the NT on the order of 100 to 200 m (d_2 in Fig. 3.5b). The range of 10 to 14 μsec for the

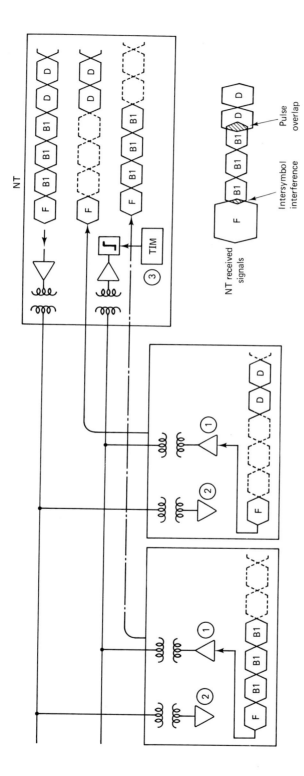

① F-bit pulse amplitude increases because terminals transmit their own F bits simultaneously on the bus, which causes increase of intersymbol interference. Amplitude-restricting driver circuit is required.
② High-impedance receiver circuit is required.
③ Retiming circuit allowing pulse overlap is required.

Figure 3.6 Technical problems in passive bus transmission.

round-trip delay is composed as follows. The lower value of 10 μsec is composed of 2 bits of offset delay (see Fig. 3.8) and the negative phase deviation of -7% (see Section 3.2.5). In this case the TE is located directly at the NT.

The higher value of 14 μsec is calculated assuming the TE is located at the far end of the passive bus. This value is composed of the offset delay between frames of 2 bits (10.4 μsec), the round-trip delay of the unloaded bus installation (2 μsec), the additional delay due to the load of the TEs (0.7 μsec), and the maximum delay of the TE transmitter ($15\% = 0.8$ μsec).

Extended Passive Bus. A configuration that may be used at an intermediate distance of 100 meters and 1000 meters is an extended passive bus. This configuration takes advantage of the fact that terminal connection points are restricted to a grouping at the far end of the cable from the NT. This places a restriction on the differential distance between TEs. The differential round-trip delay is defined as that between zero-volt crossings of signals from different TEs and is restricted to 2 μsec.

This differential round-trip delay is composed of a TE differential delay of 22% or 1.15 μsec, the round-trip delay of the unloaded bus installation of 0.5 μsec (line length 25 to 50 m), and an additional delay due to the load of 4 TEs (0.35 μsec).

d_3 (see Fig. 3.5c) depends on the characteristics of the cable to be used. The objective for this extended passive bus configuration is a total length of at least 500 m (d_4 in Fig. 3.5c) and a differential distance between TE connection points of 25 to 50 m (d_3 in Fig. 3.5c). Wiring configurations are formulated according to various in-house wiring statistics from many countries. Therefore, these configurations are applicable to almost any customer premises in the world. There will be various possible configurations other than the three types in Fig. 3.5, such as a branched configuration. Modifications of the basic three configurations are unrestricted, provided they meet electrical interface requirements.

3.2.4 Transmission Line Code and Frame Format*

Transmission Line Code. Representative line codes for digital transmission are AMI (alternate mark inversion), CMI (coded mark inversion), and 4B-3T.

All codes, including the basic interface transmission line codes, should satisfy the following requirements:

- Simple line coding
- Easy timing extraction
- DC balancing

Considering the passive bus configuration, AMI with 100% duty ratio has been selected. Since pulses received at the input side of the NT vary in phase depending on where the terminal is connected to the passive bus, pulse overlap

---

* Parts of this section are based on the texts of Sections 5.4, 6.3 and 6.3.3 of I.430.

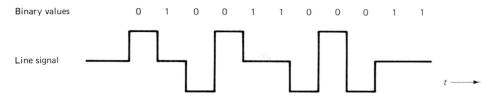

Binary values   0   1   0   0   1   1   0   0   0   1   1

Line signal

Figure 3.7   Coding rule for basic interface transmission line.

may occur at adjacent pulse edges as shown in Fig. 3.6. Received pulse phases of different channels at the input side of the NT vary depending on terminal connection points to the passive bus. Therefore, pulse overlap may occur at adjacent channel pulse edges, as shown in Fig. 3.6. A 100% duty ratio allows the maximum timing margin, even assuming pulse overlaps. The coding rule is shown in Fig. 3.7.

Frame Format.   The frame format of the basic interface has been studied from the following points:

- AMI line code with 100% duty ratio
- (2B + D) multiplexed interface structure
- Echo-bit allocation for D-channel contention resolution
- Well-organized frame alignment procedures
- Non tip-and-ring administrations of interface pair cables to facilitate maintenance and terminal installation for point-to-point application
- Symmetrical frame format for upstream and downstream frames
- Multiframing capabilities to reserve spare bits for future layer 1 maintenance control

The frame format is shown in Fig. 3.8. The F bit of the frame is detected by AMI code rule violations to facilitate frame alignment procedures. Symmetry of upstream and downstream frames is maintained for B and D channel positions. However, some differences are found for other bits within a frame. Within an upstream frame, there are dc balancing bits for each channel, which are referred to as L bits. DC balancing is required for each channel because multiple terminals transmit information on different channels. Non tip-and-ring* administration has no influence on frame alignment, which is discussed next.

Frame Alignment.   In the frame format shown in Fig. 3.8, AMI code rule violations occur twice. These are specifically (1) the first F bit and the preceding binary zero bit, and (2) the second position of the L bit succeeding the first F bit and the succeeding binary zero bit. Furthermore, the second violation occurs at the F_A bit position at latest. The distance between the first F bit and F_A bit is 13

---

* There are two copper leads in a two-wire interchange circuit pair. One lead is referred to as the tip and the other is referred to as the ring.

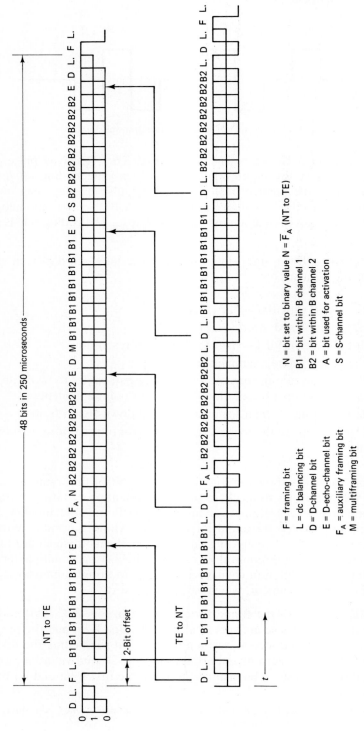

Figure 3.8 Frame format at reference points S and T.

Notes: Dots indicate those parts of the frame that are independently dc balanced.

The F_A bit in the direction TE to NT is used as a Q bit in every fifth frame if Q-channel capability is applied (see multiframe algorithm). The nominal 2-bit offset is as seen from TE (I_A in Fig. 2.2). The corresponding offset at NT may be greater due to delay in the interface cable, and varies with configuration.

F = framing bit
L = dc balancing bit
D = D-channel bit
E = D-echo-channel bit
F_A = auxiliary framing bit
M = multiframing bit

N = bit set to binary value N = $\overline{F}_A$ (NT to TE)
B1 = bit within B channel 1
B2 = bit within B channel 2
A = bit used for activation
S = S-channel bit

84

bits.   Therefore, when the first violation is detected at the F bit position, the second violation is detected within 13 bits maximum.   In other words, the frame is detected by observing two violations within a frame.   Violation detections are performed independently of violation polarity.   Therefore, there is no need to maintain wiring polarity integrity.

Multiframe Algorithm.   A multiframe structure is usually used to increase the additional bits, such as for signaling, supervising, and maintenance purposes.   The multiframe framing algorithm has been studied from the following standpoints:

- Multiframe use is optional.   Therefore, normal single-frame operation should be maintained when the NT or terminal has no multiframe function.
- The multiframe can be applied to the terminal without changing frame alignment procedures in the terminal and for the NT.   This can be achieved with minimum change to the frame alignment procedures.
- Spare bits are arranged by bit-robbing the F_A bit position of the upstream frame using multiframe format.
- When using multiframe on the passive bus configuration, a terminal with no multiframe function sends no signals on the frame's F_A bit.

Considering these requirements, a multiframe of 20 frames is adopted.   Within this multiframe, 4 F_A bits are robbed in the upstream frame for spare bits.   The F_A bit positions of every fifth frame are referred to as Q bits.   Q-bit positions in the TE-to-NT direction are identified by binary inversions of the F_A/N bit pair (F_A = binary one, N = binary zero) in the NT-to-TE direction.

The provision for identifying Q-bit positions in the NT-to-TE direction permits all TEs to synchronize transmission in Q-bit positions.   This avoids interference of F_A bits from one TE with Q bits of a second TE in a passive bus configuration. Q bits are structured into 4-bit characters (Q1 to Q4) by setting the M bit, in the NT-to-TE frame, to binary one in every twentieth frame.   This structure provides for 4-bit characters in a single channel, TE to NT.

The Q-bit position identification algorithm is shown in Table 3.1.   The TE synchronizes to received F_A bit inversions and transmits Q bits in every fifth frame, that is, in frames in which F_A bits in the NT-to-TE direction should be equal to binary ones.   Q bits are transmitted only after they are synchronized to the binary ones in the F_A bit of the NT-to-TE frame.   A TE should wrap the received Q-bit position identifier (F_A bit) into the TE-to-NT Q-bit position until multiframe synchronization is declared.

The NT requires no special Q-bit identification from the received signal.   This is because the maximum NT-to-TE round-trip delay is a small fraction of a frame. Therefore, Q-bit identification is inherent in the NT.

The algorithm for structuring the S bits into an S-channel uses a combination of F_A bit inversions and the M bit used to structure Q-bit channel.   An S-channel example is shown in Table 3.2.

TABLE 3.1 Q-BIT POSITION IDENTIFICATION AND MULTIFRAME STRUCTURE

Frame number	NT-to-TE F_A bit position	NT-to-TE M bit	TE-to-NT F_a bit position[a,b]
1	One	One	Q1
2	Zero	Zero	Zero
3	Zero	Zero	Zero
4	Zero	Zero	Zero
5	Zero	Zero	Zero
6	One	Zero	Q2
7	Zero	Zero	Zero
8	Zero	Zero	Zero
9	Zero	Zero	Zero
10	Zero	Zero	Zero
11	One	Zero	Q3
12	Zero	Zero	Zero
13	Zero	Zero	Zero
14	Zero	Zero	Zero
15	Zero	Zero	Zero
16	One	Zero	Q4
17	Zero	Zero	Zero
18	Zero	Zero	Zero
19	Zero	Zero	Zero
20	Zero	Zero	Zero
1	One	One	Q1
2	Zero	Zero	Zero
etc.			

Reproduced from Table 5/I.430.

[a] Q bits not being used by a TE shall be set to binary one.

[b] Where multiframe identification is not provided with a binary one in an appropriate M bit, but where Q-bit positions are identified, Q bits 1 through 4 are not distinguished.

3.2.5 Electrical Parameters

The electrical parameters of the basic interface are specified very carefully to achieve multiple terminal operations on the passive bus configuration. The crucial parameters are the interface driver/receiver impedance characteristics, the jitter and bit-phase relationship between TE input and output, and NT jitter characteristics.

Transformer-coupled interface interchange circuits are used to achieve good longitudinal balance. A phantom circuit configuration is applied to power feeding through the interface line. Thus, all electrical parameters are specified at the transformer input/output. The principal electrical parameters are summarized next.

TABLE 3.2   S-CHANNEL STRUCTURE

Frame number	NT-to-TE F_A bit position	NT-to-TE M bit	NT-to-TE S bit
1	One	One	SC11
2	Zero	Zero	SC21
3	Zero	Zero	SC31
4	Zero	Zero	SC41
5	Zero	Zero	SC51
6	One	Zero	SC12
7	Zero	Zero	SC22
8	Zero	Zero	SC32
9	Zero	Zero	SC42
10	Zero	Zero	SC52
11	One	Zero	SC13
12	Zero	Zero	SC23
13	Zero	Zero	SC33
14	Zero	Zero	SC43
15	Zero	Zero	SC53
16	One	Zero	SC14
17	Zero	Zero	SC24
18	Zero	Zero	SC34
19	Zero	Zero	SC44
20	Zero	Zero	SC54
1	One	One	SC11
2	Zero	Zero	SC21
etc.			

Output Jitter.   The output jitter is specified as $\pm 5\%$ peak to peak for NT and $\pm 7\%$ peak to peak for TE to facilitate respective receiver timing circuit design.

NT Receiver Input Delay Characteristics.   Received pulse overlaps are specified at the NT input to facilitate timing circuit design.   Round-trip delay is specified between the zero-volt crossings of the framing pulse and its associated balance bit pulse at the transmit and receive sides of the NT by considering the following:

- Two-bit offset delay between transmit/receive frames at the TE input/output
- Transmission delay on the passive bus
- Output jitter and delay between input and output of a terminal.

The round-trip delay including TEs is specified from 10 to 14 μsec for a short passive bus.

The PLO or PPLO generates the retiming clock at the NT receiver [4]

Waveform for Test Configurations.   Several waveforms are specified to define receiver sensitivity and retiming circuit parameters in TE and NT for three different interface wiring configurations.

Input–Output Impedance of Line Driver/Receiver.   The input–output impedance of the line driver/receiver should be maintained sufficiently high to reduce
waveform distortion due to passive bus transmission.   The NT input–output impedance template is defined in Fig. 3.9.   A 600-pF capacitance is considered for the
high-frequency band because the NT connection cord is shorter (3 m) than that of
TE.

   The terminal input–output impedance template is also defined in Fig. 3.10
by considering circuit feasibility.   This impedance template assumes over 2.5-kΩ
resistance for the mid-frequency band, over 20-mH inductance for the low-frequency band, and less than 800-pF capacitance (including a maximum 10-m cord)
for the high-frequency band.

Transmitter Output Pulse Amplitude and Waveform.   The following specifications are set for output pulse amplitude and waveform according to NT or TE
output port termination conditions.

   1. NT or TE transmitter output pulse: Both ends of the passive bus
      are terminated by 100 Ω.   Nominal pulse amplitude is then defined
      across the equivalent of 50-Ω terminating resistance with 750 mV
      o-p (millivolts zero to peak) nominal figure.   The transmitter pulse
      template is shown in Fig. 3.11.

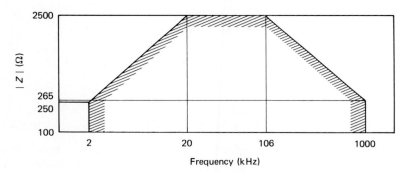

Figure 3.9   NT impedance template.

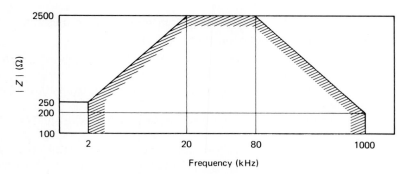

Figure 3.10   TE impedance template.

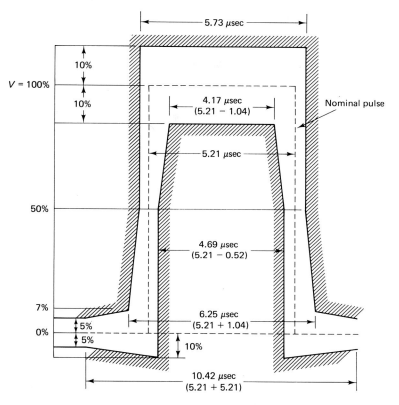

Figure 3.11   Transmitter output pulse template.

2. Transmitter output pulse where multiple TEs transmit pulses simultaneously onto a passive bus: Output pulse amplitude is defined within 90% to 160% of the nominal value for 400-Ω termination (equivalent resistance when eight terminals transmit binary zero simultaneously). This specification is required for the F and F_A bit positions. This is because these bits from eight terminals can overlap and increase the amplitude, causing intersymbol interference to adjacent bits in a frame. The pulse template is illustrated in Fig. 3.12.

3. Other: To guarantee over 50-Ω internal impedance when transmitting binary zero, the TE output pulse is defined at less than 20% of the nominal value across a 5.6-Ω terminating resistance.

3.2.6 Power Feeding from the Interface*

Power feed from the interface varies according to the decisions of individual countries' operating companies regarding the necessity of telephone service continuity even during power failure. Therefore Recommendation I.430 specifies three op-

* Parts of this section are based on the texts of Sections 9.2 and 9.3 of I.430.

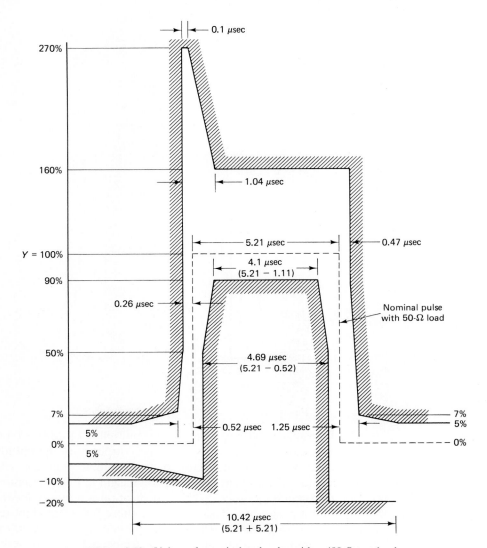

Figure 3.12 Voltage for an isolated pulse with a 400-Ω test load.

tions for power feeding from the user–network interface reference point: (1) normal and (2) restricted power feeding from power source 1 and (3) power feeding from power source 2. Each administration may select the power feeding method most appropriate to its network from within these options.

The reference configuration for power feeding is shown in Fig. 3.13.

Two power feeding methods will be discussed here.

Power Source 1.   Power source 1 derives its power from the network or local batteries or both. The source may be either an integral part of NT or physically separate and connected at any point in the interface wiring. Power source 1 is

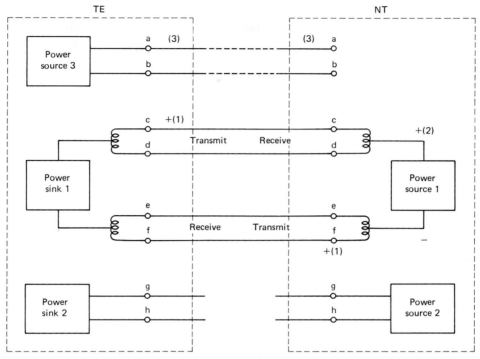

(1) Indicates framing pulse polarity.
(2) Indicates power polarity during normal power condition.
(3) The access lead assignments indicated in this figure are intended to
    provide for direct interface cable wiring. That is, each interface pair
    conductor may be connected to access leads having the same number
    at TEs and NTs.

Figure 3.13   Reference configuration for signal transmission and power feeding
in normal operating mode.

connected to the sink by phantom circuits used for bidirectional transmission of
the digital signal.

The following two conditions are specified for power source 1:

- *Normal power conditions:* voltage at a TE interface shall be a maximum
  of 40 V + 5% and a minimum of 40 V − 40% (24 V) when drawing up
  to a maximum permitted power consumption of 1 W.
- *Restricted power conditions:* nominal value of the voltage at TE inputs shall
  be 40 V when drawing up to a maximum permitted power consumption of
  400 mW (380 mW for a designated TE and 20 mW for other TEs).

When power source 1 can only supply restricted power due to ac main failure,
it should indicate this condition by reversing its wiring polarity. In this case only
the restricted power functions of TEs are allowed to consume power from source
1.

If power source 1 can supply power in both normal and restricted power conditions, power source 1 may change from normal to restricted power condition when power source 1 cannot supply the normal level of power due to ac main failure.

Power Source 2.   Power source 2 derives its power from local commercial power or batteries or both.

Power source 2 may be located either in the NT, as indicated in Fig. 3.13, or separately.   Access lead pair (g-h) is used for power transfer.

The following conditions are also specified for power source 2:

- Normal power conditions; voltage at a TE interface shall be a maximum of 40 V + 5% and a minimum of 40 V − 20% when the TE is drawing up to a minimum available power of 7 W.
- Restricted power conditions: when power source 2 cannot provide 7 W, it may go to a restricted power condition where it provides a minimum power of 2 W.
- The nominal voltage values at TE inputs shall be 40 V + 5% maximum and −20% minimum.

Power Source 3.   Power source 3 may be located either within a terminal or separately, assuming applications to TE-to-TE connections.   However, this power source is beyond the scope of CCITT Recommendations.

Power feeding specifications are summarized in Table 3.3.

3.2.7 D-channel Contention Resolution*

The basic interface has a frame structure based on (B + B + D) for upstream and downstream.   The D-channel is used by all terminals connected to the bus interface.   There is no contention state downstream from the NT when it broadcasts 2B + D information to all terminals because every terminal can access any channel when required.   However, there is contention state upstream because multiple terminals simultaneously originate communications to a limited number of channels.   In this case, respective terminals can access B channels using D-channel signaling.   Thus no B-channel contention occurs.   By contrast, multiple terminals use the D-channel to send signaling or packetized data.   Thus contention states occur easily.

In Recommendation I.430, the contention resolution is performed by layer 1 as follows.

D-Channel Access Procedure.   The following procedure allows several TEs connected in a multipoint configuration to access the D-channel in an orderly fashion.   The procedure always ensures that, even when two or more TEs attempt to accesss the D-channel simultaneously, only one TE will successfully transmit its

---

* Parts of this section are based on the text of Section 6.1 of I.430.

TABLE 3.3 POWER FEEDING SPECIFICATIONS

		Power source 1		Power source 2	
		Normal power condition	Restricted power condition	Normal power condition	Restricted power condition
Power feeding direction		NT → TE		NT → TE	
Power feeding method		Four-wire phantom feeding		Two-wire feeding	
Power source location		Network or ac mains (or battery)		ac mains (or battery)	
Power source location		Inside or outside NT	Inside or outside NT	Inside or outside NT	
Available power	NT output	Note 1	Max. 420 mW	Note 1	
	TE input	Active state or local action state: Max. 1 W (Max. 1.5 W, note 2) Deactivated state: Max. 100 mW	Designated terminal Active state or local action state: Max. 380 mW Deactivated state: Max. 25 mW (Max. 100 mW, note 2) Other terminals Max. 3 mW/TE Max. 20 mW/ all TEs	Over 7 W	Over 2 W
Supply voltage	NT output	40 V $^{+5\%}_{-15\%}$	40 V $^{+5\%}_{-15\%}$	40 V $^{+5\%}_{-(\text{note 1})\%}$	40 V $^{+5\%}_{-(\text{note 1})\%}$
	TE input	40 V $^{+5\%}_{-40\%}$	40 V $^{+5\%}_{-20\%}$	40 V $^{+5\%}_{-20\%}$	40 V $^{+5\%}_{-20\%}$
Power condition indication		Normal	Reverse	Not specified	

Notes: 1. This is beyond the scope of CCITT.
       2. Provisional value until the end of 1988.

information.   This procedure relies on the use of layer 2 frames delimited by flags consisting of the binary pattern 01111110.   Zero-bit insertion is used to prevent flag imitation.   The procedure also permits point-to-point TE operation.

Interframe (Layer 2) Time Fill.   When a TE has no layer 2 frames to transmit, it shall send binary ones on the D-channel; that is, the interframe time fill in the TE-to-NT direction shall all be binary ones.

When an NT has no layer 2 frames to transmit, it shall send binary ones or HDLC flags; that is, the interframe time fill in the NT-to-TE direction shall be either all binary ones or repetitions of the octet 01111110. The flag that defines the end of a frame may also define the start of the next frame.

D-Echo Channel (See Fig. 3.14). When the NT receives a D-channel bit frame from the TEs, it shall reflect the binary value in the next available D-echo channel bit position toward the TE(s).

D-Echo-Channel Monitoring (See Fig. 3.14). A TE shall monitor the D-echo channel, counting consecutive binary one bits. When a zero bit is detected, the TE shall restart the count of consecutive one bits, because it indicates that the D-channel has already been used by another terminal. The current value of the count is called C.

Priority Mechanism. Layer 2 frames are transmitted such that signaling information receives priority (priority class 1) over all other types of information (priority class 2). Furthermore, to ensure that all competing TEs receive fair access to the D-channel within each priority class, a TE is given a lower priority level within its class after successfully transmitting a layer 2 frame. The TE is returned to its normal level within a priority class when all TEs have had an opportunity to transmit information at the normal level within that priority class.

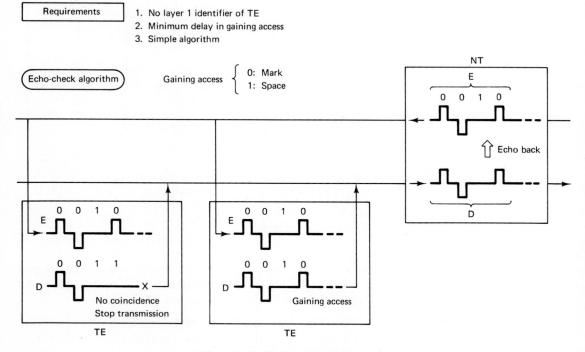

Figure 3.14 D-channel access control.

The priority mechanism is based on the requirement that a TE may start layer 2 frame transmission only when C, the current value of the count, is equal to or exceeds the value X_1 for priority class 1 or is equal to or exceeds the value X_2 for priority class 2. For the signaling access to the D-channel from a terminal, the value of X_1 is eight for the normal priority level and nine for the lower level.

For packetized data access to the D-channel from a terminal, the value of X_2 is 10 for the normal priority level and 11 for the lower level.

In a priority class the value of X_1 or X_2 changes from the normal priority level to the value of the lower priority level (that is, higher value) when a TE has successfully transmitted a layer 2 frame of that priority class. The value of X_1 or X_2 changes from the lower priority level back to the value of the normal priority level when C equals the value of the lower priority level (that is, higher value).

Note that C need not be incremented after the value 11 has been reached to avoid the overflow of the counter.

Collision Detection. While transmitting information in the D-channel, the TE shall monitor the received D-echo channel and compare the last transmitted bit with the next available D-echo bit. If the transmitted bit is the same as the received echo, the TE shall continue its transmission. If, however, the received echo is different from the transmitted bit, the TE shall cease transmission immediately and return to the D-echo-channel state.

Priority System. An example of how the priority system may be implemented is shown in Fig. 3.15.

3.2.8 Activation/Deactivation Procedures

Layer 1 activation/deactivation procedures are specified to save power consumption in a terminal when no communication takes place.

Principal sequences for both call origination and call arrival are described to make these procedures readily understandable (Figs. 3.16 and 3.17). Definitions of INFO signals used in these figures are summarized in Table 3.4.

Activation for Call Origination. A terminal connected to the bus interface transmits an INFO 1 signal to NT. This signal is the specific digital sequence with asynchrous clocks to the network clock. The NT then sends an INFO 2 signal to all terminals connected to the bus interface. Upon receiving the INFO 2 signal, all terminals transmit an INFO 3 signal, synchronized to the INFO 2 signal, to NT.

At this point NT acknowledges the frame alignment establishment between NT and TEs. This information is then sent to layer 2, while NT simultaneously sends an INFO 4 signal to all TEs. Terminals receiving the INFO 4 signal carry out the frame alignment establishment and report activation accomplishment to layer 2.

Activation for Call Arrival. When a call arrives, the NT sends an INFO 2 signal to all terminals connected to the bus interface according to network layer 2 instructions. Each terminal connected to the bus interface then sends an INFO 3

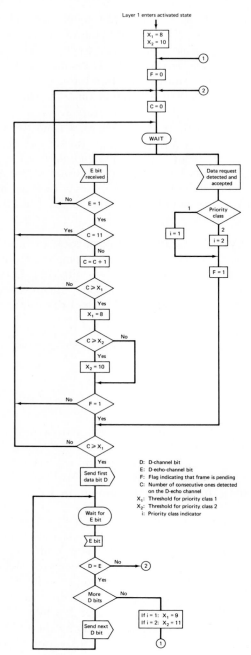

Figure 3.15 Possible implementation of D-channel access.

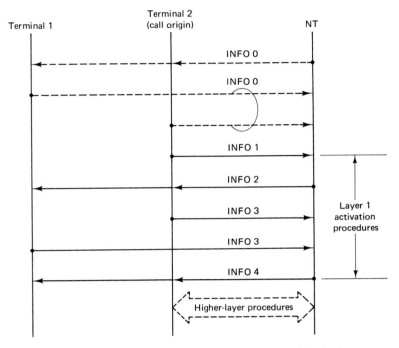

Figure 3.16 Layer 1 activation procedures (call origination).

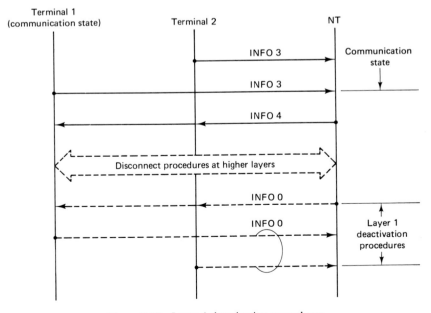

Figure 3.17 Layer 1 deactivation procedures.

TABLE 3.4 DEFINITION OF INFO SIGNALS

Signals from NT to TE	Signals from TE to NT
INFO 0 No signal	INFO 0 No signal
INFO 2 Frame with all bits of B, D, and D-echo channels set to binary ZERO. Bit A set to binary ZERO. N and L bits set according to the normal coding rules.	INFO 1 A continuous signal with the following pattern: Positive zero, negative zero, six ones.
	Nominal bit tate = 192 kbit/s
INFO 4 Frames with operational data on B, D, and D-echo channels. Bit A set to binary ONE.	INFO 3 Synchronized frames with operational data on B and D channels.

Reproduced from Table 2/I.430

signal synchronized to the INFO 2 signal.   This procedure is followed by procedures identical to call origination.   Layer 1 activation is then established for both terminals and network.

Deactivation.   NT stops sending an INFO 4 signal to terminals according to disconnection instructions from network higher layers, and simultaneously reports layer 1 deactivation to higher layers.   Every terminal-connected bus interface detects the loss of NT signals, stops sending any signals, and reports layer 1 deactivation to the terminal higher layers.

3.2.9 Maintenance

Possible locations of test loopbacks for maintenance of the ISDN basic user–network interface are shown in Fig. 3.18.   Tables 3.5 and 3.6 summarize the characteristics applicable to each recommended, desirable, and optional loopback.

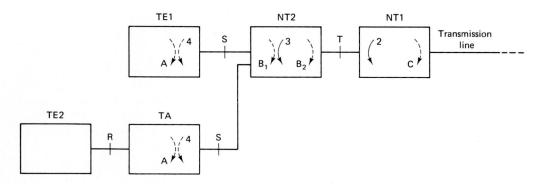

Figure 3.18   Location of test loopbacks.

TABLE 3.5 CHARACTERISTICS OF RECOMMENDED LOOPBACKS

Loopback	Location	Channel (S) looped	Loopback type	Control point	Control mechanism	Implementation
2	In NT1, as near T reference point as possible, toward ET[a]	2B + D channels	Complete, transparent or nontransparent	Under control of local exchange	Layer 1 signals in transmission system	Recommended
3	In NT2, as near S reference point as possible, toward ET	2B + D channels	Complete, transparent or nontransparent	NT2	Local maintenance	Desirable[c]
				NT2	Layer 3 messages in D-channel or in-band signaling in B channel[b]	

Reproduced from Table 1-1/I.430.

[a] For a combined NT1 and NT2 (that is, an NT12), loopback 2 is located at the position within the NT12 equivalent to the T reference point.

[b] Activation/deactivation of loopback 3 may be initiated by request from a remote maintenance server by layer 3 messages in the D-channel or by other signaling in the B channel. However, the NT2 generates the test pattern over the loopback.

[c] From a technical standpoint, it is desirable, although not mandatory, that loopback 3 can always be implemented. Therefore, protocol design for loopback control should include loopback 3 operation.

TABLE 3.6 CHARACTERISTICS OF OPTIONAL LOOPBACKS

Loopback	Location	Channel (S) looped	Loopback type	Control point	Control mechanism	Implementation
C	In NT1	B1, B2[a]	Partial, transparent or nontransparent	TE, NT2	Layer 1[b]	Optional
				Under control of local exchange	[c]	
B$_1$	In NT1, at subscriber side[d]	B1, B2[a]	Partial, transparent or nontransparent	TE, NT2	Layer 1 or layer 3	Optional
B$_2$	In NT2, at network side	These loopbacks are optional in the TE/NT2. When used, for example, as part of an internal test, no information should be sent toward the network interface. That is, INFO 0 should be transmitted to the interface.				
A	In TE					
4	In TA or TE	B1, B2[a]	Partial, transparent or nontransparent	NT2, local exchange, remote maintenance server or remote user	Layer 3	Optional

Reproduced from Table 1-2/I.430.

[a] B$_1$ and B$_2$ channel loopbacks are controlled by separate control signals. Howevver, both loopbacks may be applied simultaneously.

[b] Layer 3 service messages may be exchanged between TE (or NT2) and the digital local exchange prior to the use of the layer 1 control mechanism. However, the TE (or NT2) may not receive a reply in the following situations: (1) the message cannot be transmitted when the interface has failed; (2) a network that does not support the layer 3 signaling option need not respond.

[c] The control mechanism in this case is the same as in footnote a except that the network controls the loopback using spare capacity in the transmission system.

[d] Loopback B$_1$ is applicable to each B channel at reference point S.

Specifically, the control point, control mechanism, loopback type, and loopback location are identified.   The loopback type indicates whether a complete, echoing, or logical loopback is required and whether the loopback should be transparent or nontransparent.   The choice of loopback mechanism is dictated by the protocol layers available at the looping point and the addressing requirements.   Thus, for instance, loopback 3 is controlled via layer 2 since selection of a particular S interface may be required.

3.2.10 Connectors

It is just as important to specify the mechanical characteristics of interface features, such as connectors, as the electrical characteristics.   CCITT has given much attention to connector requirements.   The principal requirements are as follows:

- Small, lightweight, and cost effective
- Easy plug in/unplug mechanism
- No tools required to plug in or unplug
- Should include latch mechanism to prevent disconnection

ISO has selected a minimodular connector to meet these requirements.   A photograph of the plug and jack is shown in Fig.3.19.

3.3 PRIMARY RATE INTERFACE LAYER 1

3.3.1 Features

Frame formats and bit rates of the primary rate interface have been determined based on the primary digital hierarchy of existing trunk transmission systems.

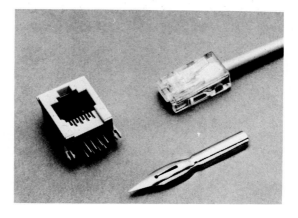

Figure 3.19 Plug and jack.

Therefore, CCITT Recommendation I.431 recommends two primary rate interfaces operating at 1544- and 2048-kbps bit rates.

Recommendation G.703 specifies the electrical characteristics for the primary rate digital hierarchy interfaces [5]. Therefore, Recommendation I.431 refers to G.703 regarding the electrical characteristics of primary rate interfaces. In-house interface wiring uses four-wire metallic cables. However, this interface configuration is limited to point-to-point application. This interface will be widely used for PBX, LAN, high-speed facsimile, and TV conferencing services.

The interface structures for primary rate interfaces are summarized in Table 3.7.

The primary rate interfaces can provide any of the following: 64-kbps B and D channels; 384-kbps H0 channel; a mixed mode of B and H0 channels, or 1536- and 1920-kbps H1 channels [6].

3.3.2 Electrical Interface Point

The electrical characteristics for 1544- and 2048-kbps interfaces are defined on the input of the receiver and the output of the transmitter at the interface exchange circuits. The only wiring configuration applicable to the primary rate interface is point to point.

TABLE 3.7   INTERFACE STRUCTURES FOR PRIMARY RATE INTERFACES

Interface Bit Rates	Interface Structures		Remarks
	Designations	Structures	
1544 or 2048 kbps	B channel interface	23 B + D (1544 kbps) 30 B + D (2048 kbps)	D = 64 kbps
	H0 channel interface	4 H0 or 3 H0 + D (1544 kbps) 5 H0 + D (2048 kbps)	D = 64 kbps For 4 H0, the D channel of another interface provides H0 channel signaling
	H1 channel interface	H11 (1544 kbps) H12 + D (2048 kbps)	D = 64 kbps The D channel of another interface provides H11 signaling
	Combined B and H0 channels interface	nB + mH0 + D	D = 64 kbps

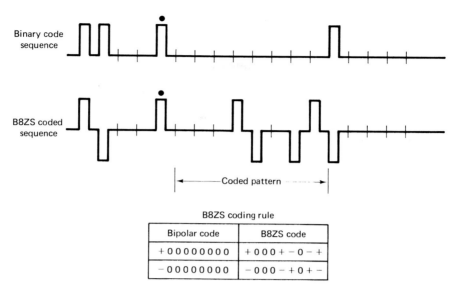

Figure 3.20   B8ZS line code.

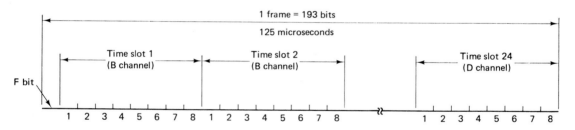

Figure 3.21   Frame format of 1544-kbps interface.

3.3.3 Transmission Line Code and Frame Format

3.3.3.1 1544-kbps interface*

1. Line Code: B8ZS (bipolar with eight-zero substitution) (Fig. 3.20).   This code is selected to facilitate timing extraction at both sides of the interface.

2. Frame format: Frame format is shown in Fig. 3.21.   Each frame consists of 193 bits, including an F-bit followed by 24 consecutive time slots numbered 1 to 24.   Multiframe format is shown in Table 3.8 [7].   Each multiframe is 24 frames long.   It is defined by the multiframe alignment signal (FAS) formed by every fourth F bit.   Bits e1 to e6 are used for error checking.   The m bits are used for operation and maintenance.

* Parts of this section are based on the texts of Sections 2.1.1 and 2.1.2.2. of G.706.

3. Frame alignment procedure [8]

a. Loss of frame alignment: The frame alignment signal is monitored to determine whether frame alignment has been lost. Frame alignment loss is detected within 12 msec. It is confirmed over several frames to avoid unnecessarily initiating frame alignment recovery procedures due to transmission bit errors. The frame realignment procedure commences immediately once loss of frame alignment is confirmed.

b. Frame realignment procedure: The frame is realigned by detecting a valid frame alignment signal. When the CRC-6 code is used to monitor error performance at the receiving end, CRC-6 information may be coupled with the framing algorithm to ensure that a valid frame alignment signal contained within the 24 F bits is the only pattern onto which the reframe circuits can permanently lock. This procedure is illustrated in Fig. 3.22.

TABLE 3.8 MULTIFRAME FORMAT

Multiframe frame number	Multiframe bit number	F Bits		
		Assignments		
		FAS	m bits[a]	CRC bits
1	1	—	m	—
2	194	—	—	e1
3	387	—	m	—
4	580	0	—	—
5	773	—	m	—
6	966	—	—	e2
7	1159	—	m	—
8	1352	0	—	—
9	1545	—	m	—
10	1738	—	—	e3
11	1931	—	m	—
12	2124	1	—	—
13	2317	—	m	—
14	2510	—	—	e4
15	2703	—	m	—
16	2896	0	—	—
17	3089	—	m	—
18	3282	—	—	e5
19	3475	—	m	—
20	3668	1	—	—
21	3861	—	m	—
22	4054	—	—	e6
23	4247	—	m	—
24	4440	1	—	—

Reproduced from Table 1/G.704.

FAS: Frame alignment signal (. . . 001011 . . .).

[a] The m bits will be used for operational and maintenance information.

3.3.3.2 2048-kbps interface

1. Line code: HDB3 (high density bipolar of order 3) (Fig. 3.23).

2. Frame format: The frame format is shown in Fig. 3.24. Each frame consists of 256 bits, including 32 consecutive time slots numbered 0 to 31.

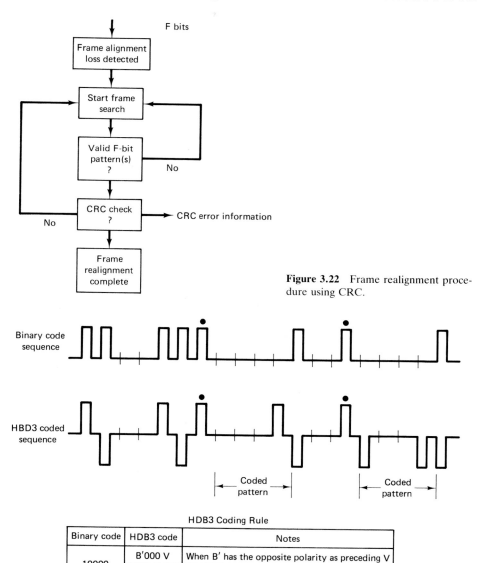

Figure 3.22 Frame realignment procedure using CRC.

HDB3 Coding Rule

Binary code	HDB3 code	Notes
10000	B'000 V	When B' has the opposite polarity as preceding V
	B'B00 V	When B' has the same polarity as preceding V

B: bipolar pulse; V: pulse violating bipolar rule

Figure 3.23 HDB3 line code.

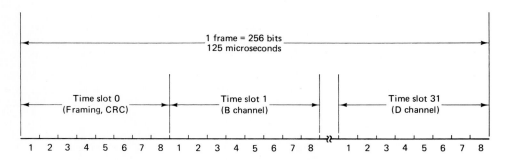

Figure 3.24 Frame format of 2048-kbps interface.

The bits of time slot 0 are used for framing, CRC, and remote alarm indication. The multiframe is established to use a cyclic redundancy check 4 (CRC-4) procedure, as shown in Table 3.9 [7]. The CRC-4 multiframe alignment signal has the form 001011.

3. Frame alignment procedure [8]

  a. Frame alignment loss: Frame alignment is assumed to have been lost when three consecutive incorrect frame alignment signals are received. To limit the effect of false frame alignment signals, the following procedure may also be used: Frame alignment is assumed to have been

TABLE 3.9 CRC-4 MULTIFRAME STRUCTURE

	Sub-multiframe (SMF)	Frame number	Bits 1 to 8 of time slot 0							
			1	2	3	4	5	6	7	8
Multiframe	I	0	C1	0	0	1	1	0	1	1
		1	0	1	A	Sa	Sa	Sa	Sa	Sa
		2	C2	0	0	1	1	0	1	1
		3	0	1	A	Sa	Sa	Sa	Sa	Sa
		4	C3	0	0	1	1	0	1	1
		5	1	1	A	Sa	Sa	Sa	Sa	Sa
		6	C4	0	0	1	1	0	1	1
		7	0	1	A	Sa	Sa	Sa	Sa	Sa
	II	8	C1	0	0	1	1	0	1	1
		9	1	1	A	Sa	Sa	Sa	Sa	Sa
		10	C2	0	0	1	1	0	1	1
		11	1	1	A	Sa	Sa	Sa	Sa	Sa
		12	C3	0	0	1	1	0	1	1
		13	Si	1	A	Sa	Sa	Sa	Sa	Sa
		14	C4	0	0	1	1	0	1	1
		15	Si	1	A	Sa	Sa	Sa	Sa	Sa

Reproduced from Table 4b/G.704.

Key: Si, spare bits specified for international use.

  Sa, additional spare bits.

  C1, C2, C3, C4, cyclic redundancy check 4 (CRC-4) bits.

  A, remote alarm indication.

lost when bit 2 in time slot 0 in frames not containing the frame alignment signal has been received with an error on three consecutive occasions.

Frame alignment can also be lost by an inability to achieve CRC multiframe alignment or by exceeding a specified count of CRC error-message blocks.

b. Frame realignment procedure: Frame alignment is assumed to have been recovered when the following sequence is detected:

- The first occurrence of the correct frame alignment signal
- The absence of the frame alignment signal in the following frame, detected by verifying that bit 2 of the basic frame is a 1
- The second occurrence of the correct frame alignment signal in the next frame

To avoid states in which no frame can be achieved due to false frame alignment signals, the following procedure may be used: When a valid frame alignment signal is detected in frame n, a check should be made to ensure that a frame alignment signal does not exist in frame $n + 1$ and also that a frame alignment signal exists in frame $n + 2$. Failure to meet one or both of these requirements should cause a new search to be initiated in frame $n + 2$.

3.3.4 Electrical Parameters

3.3.4.1 1544-kbps interface. Primary electrical parameters for 1544-kbps interface are summarized in Table 3.10.

3.3.4.2 2048-kbps interface. Primary electrical parameters for 2048-kbps interface are summarized in Table 3.11.

3.3.5 Connector

Detailed requirements for primary interface connectors are almost the same as for basic interface connectors, except for working voltage and nonintermatability of

TABLE 3.10 ELECTRICAL PARAMETERS FOR 1544-KBPS INTERFACE

Parameters	Specifications
Line bit rate	1544 kbps $\pm$ 50 ppm
Test load impedance	100-Ω resistance
Code	B8ZS
Pair in each direction of transmission	One symmetrical pair
Nominal pulse width	324 ns
Nominal peak voltage of a mark pulse	3 V

Reproduced from Table 4/G.703.

TABLE 3.11   ELECTRICAL PARAMETERS FOR 2048-KBPS
INTERFACE

Parameters	Specifications
Line bit rate	2048 kbps $\pm$ 50 ppm
Test load impedance	120-Ω resistance
Code	HBD3
Pair in each direction of transmission	One symmetrical pair
Nominal pulse width	244 ns
Nominal peak voltage of a mark pulse	3 V

Reproduced from Table 6/G.703.

primary rate and basic access connectors.   These issues are now under discussion
in Subcommittee 6, Working Group 3, of the International Standards Organization
(ISO).

3.3.6 Maintenance

Possible locations of test loopbacks and their characteristics regarding the maintenance of the ISDN primary rate user–network interface are identical to those
of the basic interface discussed in Section 3.2.9.

3.4 SUBSCRIBER LINE TRANSMISSION SYSTEMS USING
METALLIC PAIR CABLES TO SUPPORT BASIC INTERFACE

3.4.1 Features

Developing an economic digital subscriber transmission system is one of the most
important steps in providing ISDN services.   Telephone subscribers are connected
to the local exchange via metallic-pair cables.   It has required much time and
money to construct subscriber loop plants.   Therefore, the development of a two-
wire digital subscriber transmission system is the key to providing digital services
to more customers without further investment in subscriber loop plants.
     Several approaches have been attempted in many countries.   To date, two
transmission systems have been tested and evaluated by several telephone companies around the world.   These two transmission systems are (1) Echo canceler
with hybrid and (2) time compression multiplex (Ping-Pong) [9].   They are discussed in Section 3.4.2.   In the United States, the echo canceler transmission system
supports the basic interface with line code 2B1Q [10].
     In the transmitter successive pairs of bits in the binary data stream are as-
sociated with a quaternary symbol as follows [10].

First bit	Second bit	Quaternary symbol
1	0	+3
1	1	+1
0	1	−1
0	0	−3

It has been adopted as the national standard to meet the electrical and physical requirements of existing metallic subscriber loops.

Digital subscriber line transmission systems utilizing two-wire metallic pair cables do not fall within the scope of ISDN physical interfaces. However, CCITT has been discussing possible recommendations for digital subscriber line transmission systems since 1985.

Transmission technology is the key to developing the (2B + D) interface to customers extensively and economically. Therefore, this chapter includes a description of digital subscriber line transmission systems.

3.4.2 Two-wire Digital Transmission Systems

In local areas, a significant number of subscribers still have only a two-wire facility. Thus, rather than running extra cable pairs to existing subscribers, it is more appropriate to utilize two-wire lines for bidirectional digital transmission. The major problem then is how to achieve bidirectional transmission of digital signals over a pair of wires. Several approaches to this problem have been exlored in the past. There are two basic alternatives for achieving two-wire transmission of digital signals, as shown in Fig. 3.25.

3.4.2.1 Time compression multiplex. Digital signals from the transmitting end of a subscriber's set or an office terminal are compressed into bursts. These bursts are periodically transmitted over the two-wire subscriber line with pause intervals in between. At the receiving end, bursts are expanded to reconstruct the original continuous bit stream. The bit rate for transmitting the bursts then must be selected to cater for objective maximum cable propagation delay avoiding transmit/receive burst collision on the cable. Central office equipment controls synchronization and timing for upstream/downstream separation equally in all systems within the cable. Therefore, bursts are simultaneously transmitted in the same direction in all pairs. This avoids near-end crosstalk, which limits transmission length or reduces the number of systems that can use the same cable. Only far-end crosstalk is of major concern.

3.4.2.2 Echo canceller with hybrid. The two signal directions are separated using a hybrid circuit. Adaptive echo, cancellation is also used to improve separation to achieve signal separation between input and output. The advantage of the hybrid balancing technique over TCM is its narrower transmission bandwidth. However, the inherent near-end crosstalk between hybrid systems themselves cannot be eliminated.

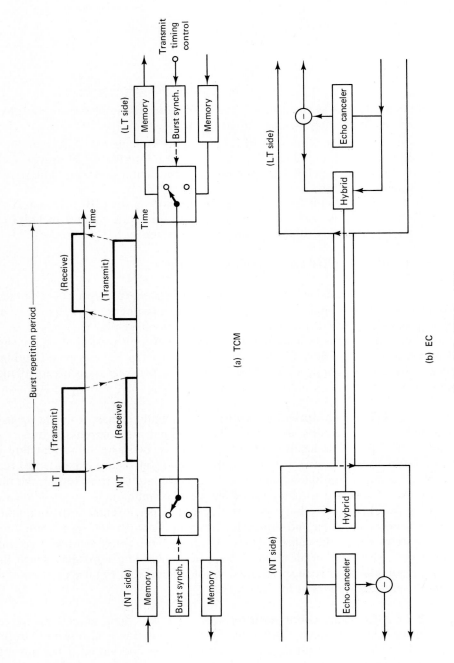

Figure 3.25 TCM and EC.

(a) TCM

(b) EC

3.4.3 Typical Transmission Impairments Anticipated on Existing Metallic-pair Cables

Transmission impairment factors that can be observed on existing metallic-pair cables are illustrated in Fig. 3.26.   The digital transmission capability of the present loop plant will be determined by evaluating these range-limiting factors.

These factors are summarized in Table 3.12.   A bridged-tap equalization technique is required to avoid pulse distortion due to bridged taps.   Crosstalk from other systems and various impulse noises restrict the transmissible length and the attainable line bit rate.   During the digitalization process in an analog environment, impulse noises coming through analog subscriber loops degrade digital transmission performance.   Short interruptions caused by oxidization in cable splices affect the design of signal frame synchronization circuits.   Feeding direct current into sub-scriber loops effectively reduces the bit error rate due to short interruptions.

3.4.4 Transmission System Selection Guidelines [11] [12]

3.4.4.1 Range-limiting factors.   The EC and TCM techniques each have inherent transmission range-limiting factors.   Primary range-limiting factors for EC and TCM are shown according to ISDN penetration stage in Table 3.13.   Burst-synchronized TCM avoids near-end crosstalk (NEXT) by synchronizing transmission bursts.   The range limitation due to far-end crosstalk (FEXT) is insignificant for both EC and TCM.   More significant are the limitations imposed by impulse noise induced from conventional analog telephone lines and NEXT induced from similar digital subscriber line transmission systems operating within the same cable unit.   Thus the primary range-limiting factors are impulse noise and NEXT for EC and impulse noise for TCM.   Transmission technique selection depends on these noise characteristics in existing loop plants.

3.4.4.2 System range comparison.   EC and TCM transmission perform-ances are compared on the basis of their expected system range.   EC and TCM system ranges derived from their range-limiting factors (Table 3.13) are shown in Fig. 3.27.   EC and TCM system parameters are shown in Tables 3.14 and 3.15.   NEXT loss of power sum for $X\%$ confidence level computed using Nassel's model [13] is shown on the horizontal axis in Fig. 3.27.   (Actual values of X are determined by individual telephone companies.)   EC and TCM loop losses at Nyquist frequency are shown on the vertical axis.   Loop loss limitation caused by NEXT is inde-pendent of transmission pulse level.   It is computed assuming that the NEXT loss spectrum decreases at 4.5 dB/octave and that the equalized signal spectrum is a raised cosine 100% roll-off).   Loop loss limitations caused by impulse noise, which depend on transmission pulse level and bit rate, are shown for the conditions listed in Appendix A, Table 3.A1, and impulse noise limitations for other transmission pulse levels and bit rates are shown in Figs. 3.A2 and 3.A3.

3.4.4.3 Transmission system selection guidelines.   Transmission system selection guidelines for 160-kbps EC and 320-kbps TCM are shown in Fig. 3.27.

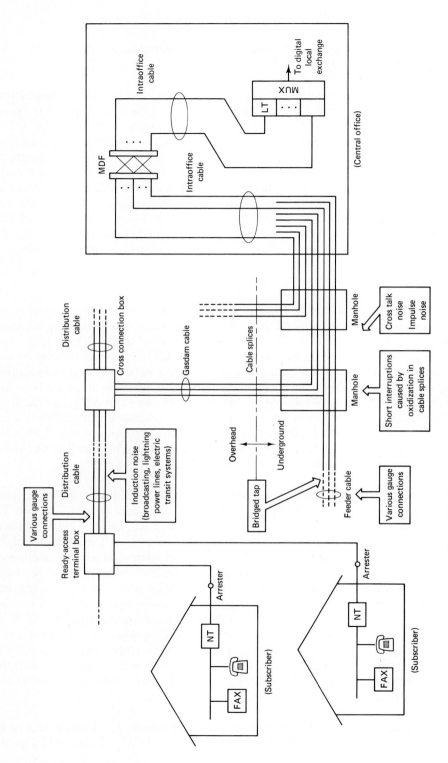

Figure 3.26 Transmission impairments of existing subscriber loop plants.

112

TABLE 3.12 TRANSMISSION RANGE-LIMITING FACTORS IN EXISTING
SUBSCRIBER LOOPS AND THEIR INFLUENCE ON DIGITAL SUBSCRIBER LINE
TRANSMISSION SYSTEM DESIGN

Factors	Present Situation	Influence on digital subscriber line transmission system design
Bridged tap[a]	Cumulative bridged-tap number distribution 56%: zero tap 31%: one tap 9%: two taps 3%: three taps 1%: over four taps	Bridged-tap equalizer
Noises	Induction noise (broadcasting, lightning, power lines, electric transit system) Crosstalk noise Impulse noise	Longitudinal balance for the system Pair segregation within cables System range
Cable splices	Short interruptions caused by oxidization in cable splices	Power-feeding system from central office to wet pair-splicing points Guard time optimization for frame synchronizer

[a] NTT's statistics.

TABLE 3.13 PRIMARY RANGE-LIMITING FACTORS

ISDN penetration Systems	Early stage	Advanced stage
EC	Impulse noise[a]	Intrasystem NEXT[b]
Burst-synchronized TCM	Impulse noise[a]	Intrasystem FEXT[b]

[a] Induced from conventional analog telephone lines.

[b] Induced from similar DSLs.

It is clear from the figure that the system selection point is the 52-dB (80 kHz) NEXT loss of power sum. That is, when the NEXT loss of power sum is greater than 52 dB, 160-kbps EC is recommended. When the NEXT loss of power sum is lower than 52 dB, 320-kbps TCM is recommended. This is summarized in Table 3.16.

3.4.5 Transmission Systems under Study in Several Countries

Since the electrical and physical parameters of existing subscriber cables vary from country to country, many different transmission systems have been proposed and tested. The intended application range of these transmission systems is summarized in Table 3.17 [10], [14–19].

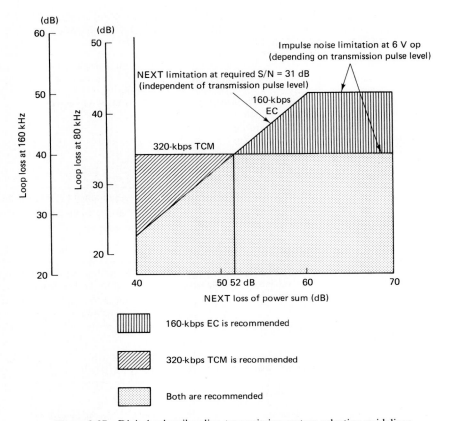

Figure 3.27 Digital subscriber line transmission system selection guidelines.

TABLE 3.14 EC SYSTEM PARAMETERS

Factors	Parameters
Bit rate	160 kbps
Line code	Scrambled 50% AMI, 6 V op
Transmission capacity	144 kbps + 8 kbps + 8 kbps (2B + D) (C^a ch) (frame)

^{a} Control channel (e.g., activation/deactivation, maintenance, etc.).

TABLE 3.15 BURST-SYNCHRONIZED TCM SYSTEM PARAMETERS

Factors	Parameters
Burst repetition period	2.5 ms
Bit rate	320 kbps
Line code	Scrambled 50% AMI, 6 V op
Transmission capacity	144 kbps + 3.2 kbps + 3.2 kbps (2B + D) (Cᵃ ch) (frame)

ᵃ Control channel (e.g., activation/deactivation, maintenance, etc.).

TABLE 3.16 DIGITAL SUBSCRIBER LINE TRANSMISSION SYSTEM SELECTION GUIDELINES

NEXT loss of power sum for $X\%^a$ confidence level (80 kHz)	Recommended system
Greater than 52 dB	160 kbps EC
Less than 52 dB	320 kbps burst-synchronized TCM

ᵃ Value determined by individual telephone companies.

TABLE 3.17 DIGITAL SUBSCRIBER LINE TRANSMISSION SYSTEMS UNDER CONSIDERATION

Countries	Transmission system	Line code	Baud rate (kbaud)	Intended application range
United States	EC	2B1Q	80	100% coverage for nonloaded cables
Canada	EC	2B1Q	80	100% coverage for nonloaded cables
Federal Republic of Germany	EC	4B3T	120	5 km for 0.4-mm pair cable
Netherlands	EC	4B3T	120	5 km for 0.4-mm pair cable
United Kingdom: STC	EC	3B2T	108	45-dB loss coverage at 100 kHz
GEC	EC	Biphase	160	4.3 km for 0.4-mm pair cable (45-dB loss coverage at 100 kHz)
France	Fourwire		160	4 km for 0.4-mm pair cable
	TCM	AMI	384	2.2 km for 0.4-mm pair cable
	EC		160	4 km for 0.4-mm pair cable
Sweden	EC	Biphase	320	40-dB loss coverage at 120 kHz
Italy	EC	AMI	160	4 km for 0.4-mm pair cable
Japan	TCM	AMI	320	99% coverage for existing cables

TABLE 3.A1 LOOP LOSS LIMITATIONS (IN DECIBILS) AT NYQUIST FREQUENCY

Bit rate	Kilobits per second			
transmission pulse level (V op)	120[a]	160	200	320
2	35.1	33.8	32.7	30.8
3	42.6	37.3	36.3	38.3
6	44.6	43.3[b]	42.3	40.3[b]

[a] When using 4B3T code, the value of loop loss limitations may decrease by 1.5 to 2.5 dB, because one symbol error corresponds to 1.5 to 1.8 average bit error.

[b] These values are impulse noise limitations shown in Figs. 3A1 and 3A3.

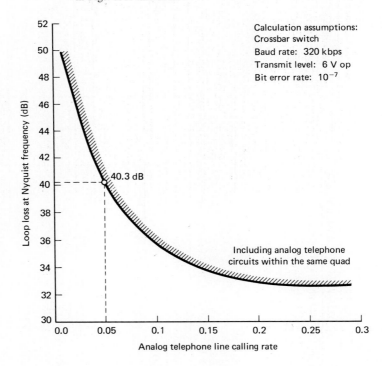

Calculation assumptions:
Crossbar switch
Baud rate: 320 kbps
Transmit level: 6 V op
Bit error rate: 10^{-7}

Including analog telephone circuits within the same quad

Figure 3.A1 System range limited by impulse noise.

Appendix A: Impulse Noise Characterization

Loop loss limitations by impulse noise, measured in typical NTT loop plants, are shown for 320-kbps TCM with a transmission pulse level of 6 V op in Fig. 3.A1. The limitations depend on both transmission pulse level and bit rate, as shown in Figs. 3.A2 and 3.A3.   Table 3.A1 summarizes loop loss limitations for various bit rates, calculated from Figs. 3.A1, 3.A2, and 3.A3.

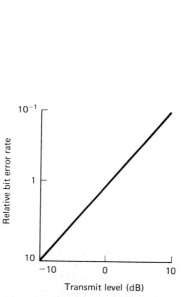

Figure 3.A2 Dependence on transmission pulse level.

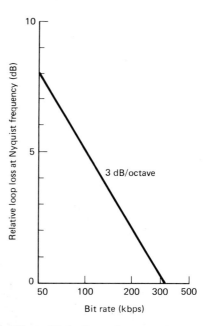

Figure 3A.3   Dependence on bit rate.

REFERENCES

3.1. *CCITT, "Recommendation I.430: Basic User Network Interface—Layer 1 Specification," COM VXIII-R21 (C), 1986, pp. 2–71.

3.2. CCITT, "Recommendation I.431: Primary Rate User Network Interface—Layer 1 Specification," *Red Book*, Volume III, Fascicle III.5, 1984, pp. 178–184.

3.3. CCITT, "Recommendation I.411: ISDN User–Network Interfaces—Reference Configurations," *Red Book*, Volume III Fascicle, III.5, 1984, pp. 125–132.

3.4. Y. Okumura and others, "Circuit Design and Transmission Performance for ISDN Basic Interface," *Proceedings of ICC-86*, 1986, pp. 1651–1654.

*These Recommendations, reproduced respectively from CCITT COM XVIII—Report 25 (C)-E and CCITT COM XVIII—Report 21 (C)-E have, in conformity with CCITT Resolution No. 2, been provisionally approved, but not yet adopted definitively by the CCITT Plenary Assembly.

3.5. CCITT, "Recommendation G.703: Physical/Electrical Characteristics of Hierarchical Digital Interfaces," *Red Book*, Volume III, Fascicle III.3, 1984, pp. 44–69.

3.6. CCITT, "Recommendation I.412: ISDN User Network Interfaces—Interface Structures and Access Capabilities," *Red Book*, Volume III, Fascicle III.5, 1984, pp. 132–137.

3.7. *CCITT, "Draft Recommendation G.704: Synchronous Frame Structures Used at Primary and Secondary Hierarchical Levels," COM XVIII-R25 (C), 1986, pp. 34–54.

3.8. *CCITT, "Draft Recommendation G.70X: Frame Alignment and CRC Procedures Relating to Basic Frame Structures Defined in Recommendation G.704," COM XVIII-R25 (C), 1986, pp. 2–10.

3.9. S. Yamano and others, "Design Philosophy and Performance for ISDN Basic Access Digital Subscriber Loops," *Proceedings of ICC-87*, 1987, pp. 591–595.

3.10. CCITT, "Information for Draft of ISDN Basic Access System Recommendation," Contribution (U.S.A.) No.D.1104/XVIII, 1987, pp. 1–65.

3.11. R. Komiya and others, "The Loop Comparison between TCM and Echo Cancellar under Various Noise Considerations," *IEEE Trans. Communications*, Vol. COM-34, No. 11, Nov. 1986, pp. 1058–1067.

3.12. CCITT, "Network Requirements for Basic Access Digital Subscriber Loop Transmission Systems," Contribution (NTT, Japan) No.D.1050/XVIII, 1987, pp. 1–8.

3.13. I. Nassel, "Some Properties of Power Sums of Truncated Gaussian Variables," *Bell System Tech. J.*, 1976, pp. 2091–2110.

3.14. Eckart Elor, "Fundamental Performance, Network Requirements and Economical Aspects of the U-interface in the Deutsche Bundespost Network," *Proceedings of ISSLS '86*, 1986, pp. 239–243.

3.15. CCITT, "Standards at the Network Side of NT," Contribution (STC, U.K.). No.D.1363/XVIII, 1987, pp. 1–6.

3.16. CCITT, "A Suitable Digital Line System for ISDN Basic Access Based on Binary Bi-phase Line Coding," Contribution (GEC, U.K.) No.D.1102/XVIII, 1987, pp. 1–2.

3.17. P. Deffin and others, "GOELAND: An Universal On-line Engineering Tool for Digital Transmission in the local Network," *Proceedings of ISSLS '86*, 1986, pp. 315–320.

3.18. B. Carlqvist and others, "A VLSI Implementation of an ISDN Echo Canceller," ibid., pp. 244–249.

3.19. CCITT, "Digital Transmission System on Metallic Pair Cable for the ISDN Basic Access," Contribution (Italy) No.D.1395/XVIII, 1987, pp. 1–8.

CHAPTER 4

ISDN Signaling Protocols

SADAHIKO KANO

Nippon Telegraph and Telephone Corporation

ABSTRACT

This chapter discusses the ISDN user–network interface signaling protocols. Reference is made to the interexchange signaling protocol, Signaling System No. 7, and its interworking with the user–network interface protocols. The user–network interface protocols responsible for providing packet-switched services are addressed as well.

4.1 INTRODUCTION

Signaling in this chapter means the method of transfer of control information to set up, maintain, and clear down a connection between two nodes of a telecommunication network. The nodes could be user terminal equipment, a local exchange, a transit exchange, a network operations center or a new service center, as shown in Fig. 4.1. Signaling protocols in ISDN can be classified into the following three categories:

1. User–network interface signaling protocols, applied to the ISDN user–network basic rate interface (2B + D) and to the primary rate interface (23B + D or 30B + D). The same set of protocols (CCITT Q.920–Q.931) is applied to both the basic rate interface and the primary rate interface. It is also applicable to PBX-to-extension terminal equipment interfaces and to direct PBX-to-PBX interfaces via leased-line circuits.

2. Interexchange signaling protocols, applied to the interface between local and transmit exchanges and between an exchange and a network operations/new service center. In this case, CCITT Signaling System No. 7 (SS No. 7) protocol is applied, and the signaling information is carried by a common channel interoffice signaling (CCIS) network, composed of signal transfer points (STPs).

3. Interexchange packet signaling protocols, applied to the interface between packet transit exchanges. In this case, the protocol to be used is not

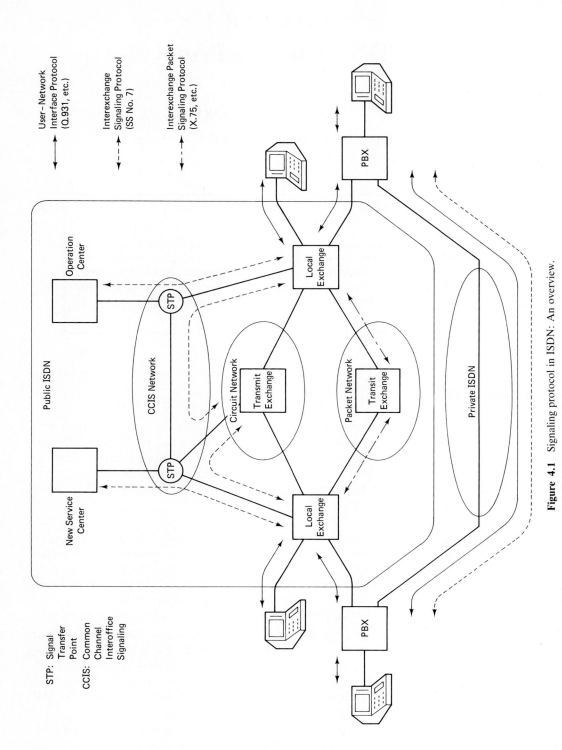

Figure 4.1 Signaling protocol in ISDN: An overview.

STP: Signal Transfer Point

CCIS: Common Channel Interoffice Signaling

User–Network Interface Protocol (Q.931, etc.)

Interexchange Signaling Protocol (SS No. 7)

Interexchange Packet Signaling Protocol (X.75, etc.)

Public ISDN

Operation Center

New Service Center

CCIS Network

STP

STP

Circuit Network

Transmit Exchange

Packet Network

Transit Exchange

Local Exchange

Local Exchange

Private ISDN

PBX

PBX

standardized internationally, but it could be CCITT X.75, which is defined as the internetworking protocol between two packet networks.

All these protocols are studied and standardized by CCITT on the basis of the layered concept of the Open Systems Interconnection (OSI) reference model studied jointly by CCITT and ISO. National and regional standards organizations such as T1 in the United States, CEPT in the European countries, and TTC in Japan set up national or regional standards based on CCITT Recommendations.*

This chapter discusses mainly the user–network interface signaling protocols. Reference is made to the interexchange signaling protocol SS No. 7 in relation to its interworking with the user–network interface protocols. Interexchange packet-signaling protocols are not dealt with as there is no standardized protocol as described above. However, ISDN packet-switched services and the user–network interface protocols as seen by the user are fully discussed.

4.2 USER–NETWORK INTERFACE SIGNALING PROTOCOLS

4.2.1 Introduction

ISDN user–network interface signaling protocols refer to data link layer (layer 2) and network layer (layer 3) protocols specified in CCITT Recommendations Q.920–921 (layer 2) [1] and Q.930–Q931 (layer 3) [2]. They will be applied, together with the physical layer (layer 1) Recommendations I.430 (for 2B + D) and I.431 (for 23B + D or 30B + D), to the S reference point (for example, an interface between a PBX and its extension terminal equipment) and the T reference point (for example, an interface between a local exchange and terminal equipment or between a local exchange and a PBX). Although different standards are provided at the physical layer, I.430 for the basic rate interface (2B + D) and I.431 for the primary rate interface (23B + D or 30B + D), the same layer 2 and 3 protocols, Q.921 for layer 2 and Q.931 for layer 3, apply to both basic and primary rate interfaces. Also, layer 2 and 3 protocols were designed in a symmetrical way so that they could be applied to direct PBX-to-PBX signaling applications in a private network.

One of the most important concepts of ISDN is a clear definition of the user–network interfaces and protocols to be applied there. This will enable terminal portability and independent evolution of user side equipment and the network. The study on ISDN user–network interface signaling protocols was started by CCITT in 1981 along with other studies on ISDN. The first results of these studies were published in the 1984 (*Red Book*) CCITT Recommendations. Studies are still going on at CCITT and other national and regional standards bodies to enhance

---

* CCITT: International Telephone and Telegraph Consultative Committee
  ISO: International Standards Organization
  CEPT: European Conference of Posts and Telecommunications
  TTC: Telecommunications Technology Committee

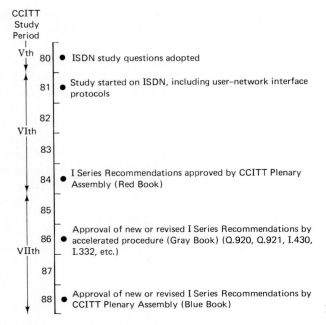

Figure 4.2   ISDN study at CCITT.

the protocols for basic services, as well as to define them for supplementary services and for operation, administration, and maintenance (OAM) applications. Figure 4.2 shows the history of ISDN studies at CCITT.

4.2.2 Requirements

4.2.2.1 New features. In comparison with existing user–network interface protocols, such as X.21 for circuit-switched data networks and X.25 for packet-switched data networks, the ISDN user–network interface signaling protocols have the following new features to satisfy the basic requirements of ISDN:

1. Support of both circuit- and packet-switched services by the same interface.
2. Support of a variety of customer premises configurations such as a point-to-multipoint (passive bus) configuration in addition to a point-to-point configuration.
3. Support of multiple calls in progress across a single interface by means of out-of-band signaling using the D channel.
4. Support of compatibility checking between the calling and the called terminals to check if they are compatible and thus can communicate with each other.

4.2.2.2 Easy use by ordinary customers. Another important requirement is that it be easy to use by ordinary customers such as "my mother" or "your grandfather," as the original ISDN designers at CCITT used to say. That is, the protocols have to allow an ordinary customer to buy a terminal at a nearby supermarket, bring it home, plug it into the interface socket, and start using it, without preregistration to the network provider or presetting of terminal parameters, for example, by rotary switches. In other words, terminal equipment must be handled with the same ease as today's electrical appliances, such as radios, TVs, and refrigerators.

Figure 4.3 illustrates some of the requirements described in 4.2.2.1.

4.3 DATA LINK LAYER (LAPD)

4.3.1 Basic Features Common to the HDLC Family of Protocols

The function of the data link layer (layer 2) is to reliably transfer a block of data, usually called a *frame*, from one node to an adjacent node using the physical layer (layer 1) that interconnects the two nodes. The data link layer protocol of the ISDN user–network interface signaling protocols is called the LAPD, for link-access procedure on the D channel. It belongs to the family of data link layer protocols based on the high-level data link control (HDLC) procedures defined by ISO. The X.25 LAPB is another member of the family. This section explains the basic data link layer technologies commonly adopted in this family of protocols.

The best way to understand data link layer technologies is to look at the data link layer frame format. Figure 4.4 shows the format of an HDLC frame and that part of a frame format that is specific to the LAPD. In the following subsections, explanation is given on the function and use of the fields that appear in the format.

4.3.1.1 Delimitation of a frame by the flag. A frame is delimited by a bit pattern of 01111110, called the *flag*. That is, when the sending side sends a frame, it first sends an opening flag, followed by a data stream to be transmitted, and then it attaches a closing flag at the end. To distinguish the flag from a data stream having the same bit pattern, the 0-insertion/deletion operation is performed on the data stream. According to this operation, the sending side inserts a 0 after every five contiguous 1s in the data stream, as illustrated in Fig. 4.5. The receiving side first looks for the flag pattern and, if it is not detected, the bit stream is checked by the *0 deleter*, which deletes every 0 after five contiguous 1s in the data stream. Thus, the original bit pattern is restored in the receive-data buffer. When the closing flag is detected, the bit stream in the receive-data buffer constitutes the frame received.

4.3.1.2 Error detection by the frame check sequence (FCS) bits. To detect a transmission error, the sending side generates a 16-bit error-detection code, called the *frame check sequence* (FCS) and attaches it at the end of data to be transmitted. The receiving side checks the FCS, and only when the received data pass the check are they made available for further processing. If the data

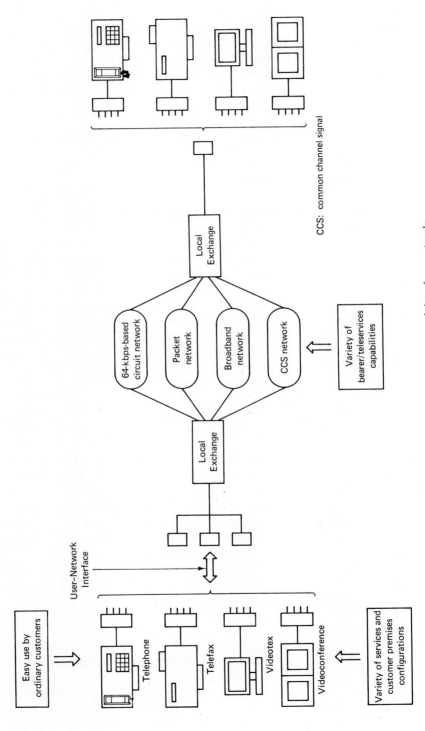

Figure 4.3 ISDN requirements on user–network interface protocols.

CCS: common channel signal

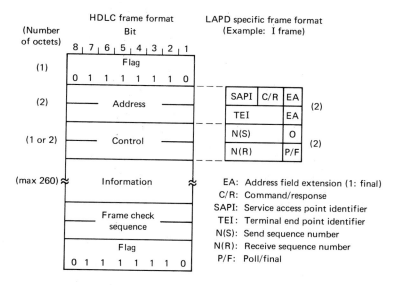

Figure 4.4 Data link layer frame format (HDLC and LAPD).

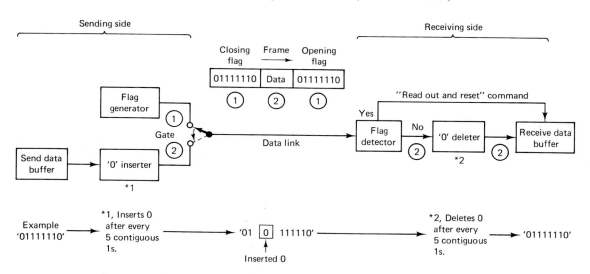

Figure 4.5 Delimitation by a flag pattern: principle of 0 insertion/deletion operation.

fail the check, they are discarded. The generation and checking algorithm of the error-detection code is beyond the scope of this book, and interested readers are referred to other books, such as reference [3].

4.3.1.3 Sequence numbering of frames.

For the purpose of error correction by the retransmission of a corrupted frame, the sending side sequentially numbers the frames that it is transmitting to the receiver. The number is sent to the receiver in the "send sequence number" or N(S) field. The receiver first checks the FCS for a possible transmission error, and if the check fails, the frame is discarded. If the frame passes the check, then the receiver checks whether the send sequence number is in sequence to that of the last frame correctly received. If it is, the receiver acknowledges the receipt of the frame by sending back the next expected frame number in the "receive sequence number" or N(R) field. If the receiver detects that the number is not in sequence, it asks the sending side to retransmit all the frames that have been transmitted but have not been acknowledged by the receiver.

Since the N(S) and N(R) fields are 7 bits long, the range of sequence numbers in the LAPD is from 0 to 127. Thus, it is called modulo 128 sequence numbering. In the HDLC and the LAPB, the length of the N(S) and N(R) fields are optional and could be either 3 or 7 bits long. Modulo 128 numbering of LAPD allows it to be applied to both satellite and surface circuits.

4.3.1.4 Procedure. Figure 4.6 illustrates a typical example of a data link operation procedure. After the physical layer connection is established (see Chapter 3), the normal way to operate a data link is to first initialize it by setting N(S),

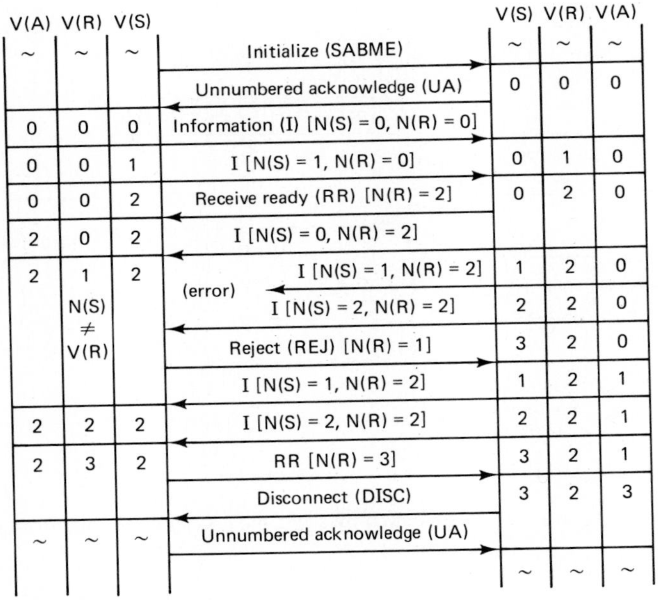

V(A)	V(R)	V(S)		V(S)	V(R)	V(A)
~	~	~	Initialize (SABME)	~	~	~
			Unnumbered acknowledge (UA)	0	0	0
0	0	0	Information (I) [N(S) = 0, N(R) = 0]			
0	0	1	I [N(S) = 1, N(R) = 0]	0	1	0
0	0	2	Receive ready (RR) [N(R) = 2]	0	2	0
2	0	2	I [N(S) = 0, N(R) = 2]			
2	1 (N(S) ≠ V(R))	2	(error) I [N(S) = 1, N(R) = 2]	1	2	0
			I [N(S) = 2, N(R) = 2]	2	2	0
			Reject (REJ) [N(R) = 1]	3	2	0
			I [N(S) = 1, N(R) = 2]	1	2	1
2	2	2	I [N(S) = 2, N(R) = 2]	2	2	1
2	3	2	RR [N(R) = 3]	3	2	1
			Disconnect (DISC)	3	2	3
~	~	~	Unnumbered acknowledge (UA)			
				~	~	~

V(S): Send state variable
V(R): Receive state variable
V(A): Acknowledge state variable
N(S): Send sequence number
N(R): Receive sequence number
~ denotes "don't care" state

Figure 4.6 Typical example of a data link layer procedure.

$N(R)$, and other control parameter values to zero on both sides of a data link connection. This initialization is activated by either side by sending a command frame called set asynchronous balanced mode (SABM) or SABM Extended (SABME). SABM is used to initialize a data link connection having modulo 8 numbering and SABME for modulo 128 numbering. In the LAPD, only SABME is used because it has only modulo 128 numbering. However, in the HDLC and the LAPB, either SABM or SABME is used depending on whether modulo 8 or modulo 128 numbering is opted. The side receiving the SABM or SABME command initializes its control parameter values and acknowledges the receipt of the SABM or SABME command by sending an unnumbered acknowledgement (UA) response frame. On reception of the UA response frame, the side that has sent the SABM or SABME command sets its control parameter values to zero, thus completing the initialization procedure.

When initialization is completed, either side can start sending information frames (I frames) with appropriate $N(S)$ and $N(R)$ values. These values are determined on both the sending and receiving sides with the help of the following variables:

Send state variable or $V(S)$ denotes the sequence number of the next I frame to be transmitted. The value of $V(S)$ is incremented by 1 with each successive I frame transmission.

Receive state variable or $V(R)$ denotes the sequence number of the next in-sequence I frame expected to be received. The value of $V(R)$ is incremented by 1 with the receipt of an error-free, in-sequence I frame having an $N(S)$ equal to $V(R)$.

Acknowledge state variable or $V(A)$ identifies the last frame that has been acknowledged by the other side. Actually, $V(A) - 1$ equals the $N(S)$ of the last acknowledged I frame.

Furthermore, in Fig. 4.6, the receive ready (RR) command appears, which is sent to acknowledge previously received I frames when there are no I frames to be sent from this side to carry the $N(R)$ value. The RR command can be used for other purposes as well.

Figure 4.6 also includes the reject (REJ) command, which is sent to request the retransmission of I frames starting with the frame indicated by the sequence number in $N(R)$.

When a data link connection is no longer needed, either side can disconnect the connection by sending a disconnect (DISC) command, which should be acknowledged by a UA response from the other side.

4.3.2 Features Specific to LAPD

4.3.2.1 Multiple data link connections. The LAPD, HDLC, and LAPB provide the address field to identify a data link connection. Before explaining what a data link connection is, some examples are given in Fig. 4.7 to facilitate the reader's understanding. In the LAPB, only one data link connection can be established over one physical layer connection, as illustrated in Fig. 4.7a. However, in the LAPD, multiple data link connections need to be established to satisfy

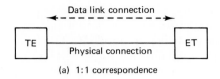

(a) 1:1 correspondence

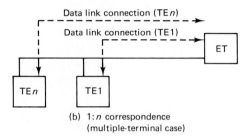

(b) 1:n correspondence
(multiple-terminal case)

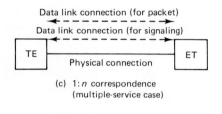

(c) 1:n correspondence
(multiple-service case)

ET: exchange terminal
TE: terminal equipment   **Figure 4.7**   Data link connection.

the point-to-multipoint customer premises configuration as illustrated in Fig. 4.7b. Another example of multiple data link connections in the LAPD is the need to distinguish between the data link connection for transferring signaling information for circuit-switched calls and that for transferring user packet data, as shown in Fig. 4.7c.

As such, a data link connection can be defined as a connection established between two data link layer entities that are exchanging frames. The numbering of frames takes place on a per data link connection basis. Also, control mechanisms such as flow control and other control parameters are applied on a per data link connection basis. In the case of a point-to-multipoint configuration, as in Figure 4.7b, it is easier to understand the need for different data link connections because they are associated with different terminals. However, even in the case of the point-to-point configuration, as in Figure 4.7c, there is a need to provide two data link connections, because the data link connection for the transfer of signaling information for circuit-switched calls requires different flow control and other control parameter values than that for the transfer of user packet data.

To distinguish a data link connection in the LAPD, the address field is divided into two subfields, the service access point identifier (SAPI) subfield and the terminal end point identifier (TEI) subfield, as shown in Figure 4.4.

The SAPI identifies a point at which data link layer services are provided by a data link layer entity to a layer 3 or management entity. Consequently, the SAPI specifies a data link layer entity that should process a data link layer frame and also the layer 3 or management entity that is to send or receive information carried by the data link layer frame. In the current Q.921, the SAPI values are allocated as shown in Table 4.1.

The TEI normally identifies a terminal equipment on a passive bus. However, a terminal equipment may contain one or more TEIs. Therefore, more accurately, the TEI is said to be used to identify a specific data link connection end point within a given service access point. TEI values are assigned on a per digital subscriber line basis, that is, on a per D-channel basis. The range of TEI values is allocated as shown in Table 4.2.

Nonautomatic TEI values are selected by the user, and their allocation is the responsibility of the user. Automatic TEI values are selected by the network, and their allocation is the responsibility of the network.

The TEI value of 127 (all 1s) is defined as the group TEI and identifies a broadcast data link connection. The broadcast data link connection is used in the direction from the network to the user to broadcast a message to all the terminal equipments in a point-to-multipoint configuration. A typical example of the use of the broadcast data link connection is to broadcast the incoming call setup message to all the terminal equipment in a multipoint configuration so that each can receive the message and check to determine if the incoming call is compatible. If so, any compatible terminal equipment may start alerting the user.

A data link connection is thus identified by the SAPI and the TEI; therefore, the data link connection identifier (DLCI) consists of the SAPI and the TEI. An overview diagram of the relationship between SAPI, TEI, and DLCI is shown in Fig. 4.8.

TABLE 4.1   SAPI VALUES IN Q.921

SAPI value	Related layer 3 or management entity
0	Call control procedures
1	Reserved for packet-mode communications using Q.931 call control procedures
16	Packet communication conforming to X.25 level 3 procedures
63	Layer 2 management procedures
All others	Reserved for future standardization

TABLE 4.2   RANGE OF TEI VALUE ALLOCATION

TEI value	User type
0–63	Nonautomatic TEI assignment-type user equipment
64–126	Automatic TEI assignment-type user equipment
127	Group TEI

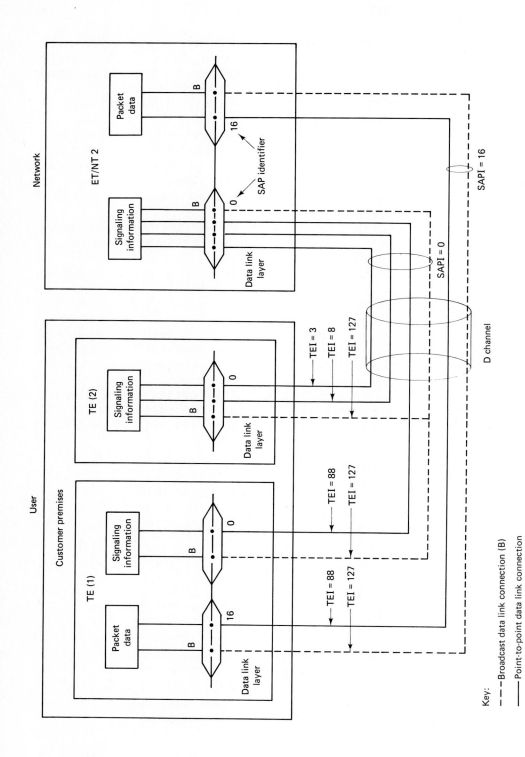

Figure 4.8 Overview description of the relationship between SAPI, TEI, and DLCI.

Key:

– – – Broadcast data link connection (B)

——— Point-to-point data link connection

DLCI = SAPI + TEI

130

4.3.2.2 Terminal portability and TEI management procedures. Terminal portability is a feature that allows a user to move a terminal equipment that is not in an active call-handling state from one interface socket to another, even on a different digital subscriber line, without preregistration or presetting of the pararmeters associated with that equipment. To achieve terminal portability, the TEI management procedures are provided in the LAPD.

The TEI management procedures consist of the following:

1. TEI assignment procedures that allow automatic TEI equipment to request the network to assign a TEI value that the data link layer entities within the requesting user equipment will use in their subsequent communications.
2. TEI check procedures that allow a network to check whether or not a TEI value is in use or whether multiple TEI assignment has occurred.
3. TEI removal procedures that allow a network to remove a previously assigned TEI value from specific or all user equipment.
4. TEI identify verification procedures that allow user equipment to request the network to invoke TEI check procedures as an option.

Figure 4.9 illustrates a typical example of how these procedures work in moving a terminal from one interface socket to another. A terminal equipment, when it is plugged into an interface socket, requests the network to assign a TEI value. The network looks at the TEI assignment table that keeps track of the TEI values already assigned out of the possible values of 64 to 126. The table is provided on a per digital subscriber line basis and assigns an available value to the requesting terminal equipment and marks the value as used. When the network finds out that the number of available values has become small, it updates the table by invoking the TEI check procedure, in which the network sends an ID check request message to all the terminals, using the broadcast data link. All the terminals receiving the ID check request message must respond to it by the ID check response message and report their respective TEI values. Thus, multiple assignment of a TEI value to more than one terminal should not happen among automatic TEI assignment terminals or between an automatic TEI assignment terminal and a nonautomatic TEI assignment terminal.

However, among nonautomatic TEI assignment terminals, there is a possibility that more than one of them with the same TEI value will be connected to the same digital subscriber line. Furthermore, there is always a chance that multiple assignment of a TEI value may happen because of some kind of design error or program bug. Figure 4.10 illustrates a typical example of such a multiple assignment of a TEI value. When a new terminal equipment with the same TEI value used by another on the same digital subscriber line is plugged in and tries to initialize the data link connection by sending the SABME command with its TEI value, the network sends a UA response with the same TEI value to acknowledge the initialization. Then the other terminal equipment with the same TEI value also receives this UA response, although it has not solicited link initialization or link disconnect. Therefore, a terminal equipment that receives an unsolicited

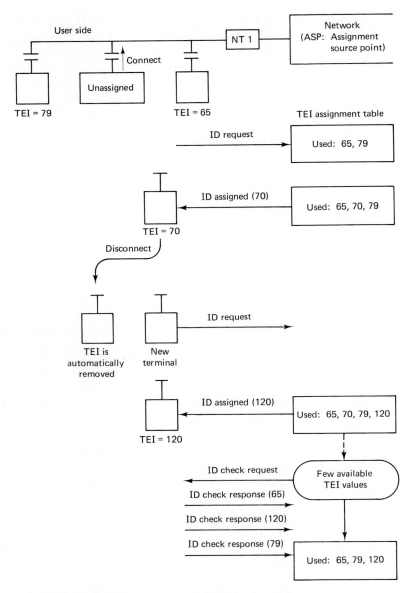

Figure 4.9 TEI assignment and check procedures.

UA response should ask the network to activate the TEI check procedures. Upon completion of the TEI check procedure, if the network finds that there is indeed a multiple assignment case, it asks the terminal equipment with the same TEI value to remove it by the TEI removal procedure. Then automatic TEI assignment terminals will start the TEI assignment procedures to obtain a new TEI value, while nonautomatic terminals should notify the user of the need for corrective action.

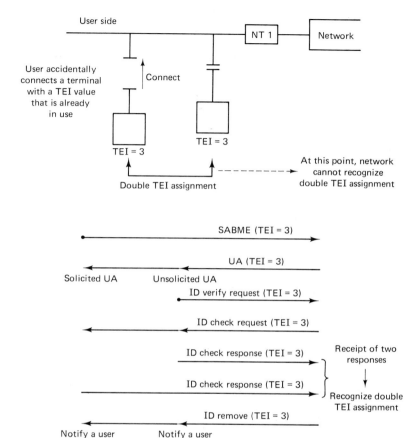

Figure 4.10   Double TEI assignment and verify procedure.

4.3.3 Status of LAPD Standardization

The basic framework of the LAPD was laid out by 1984 (*Red Book*) Recommendations Q.920 (general aspects) and Q.921 (specifications). Study at CCITT was then directed toward completing the specification on further study items and reducing the options as much as possible for simplification and for enhancing terminal portability. Thanks to the hard work and spirit of cooperation among the world's leading experts participating in the study, the work proceeded very rapidly and resulted in the production of a revised version. The revised version has no further study items and has deleted four options that existed in the 1984 version. This revised version was unanimously approved by the responsible study group at CCITT (Study Group XI) in November 1986 and was approved by accelerated procedure in June 1987. Thus, the standards work on the LAPD is completed, and many

LSI manufacturers are either in the process of implementing it on an LSI chip or are planning to do so.

4.4 NETWORK LAYER: LAYER 3

4.4.1 Introduction

The network layer (layer 3) of the ISDN user–network interface signaling protocols is specified by CCITT Recommendations Q.930 (general aspects) and Q.931 (specifications). They define the protocols for establishing, maintaining, and clearing such network connections as the following:

- Circuit-switched connections using the B channel
- Packet-switched connections using either the D or B channel
- User-to-user signaling connections using the D channel

The main features of the protocols can be summarized as follows:

1. Out-of-band signaling: the signaling information to control network connections is transferred by a separate channel or data link connection from that used for the transfer of user information. The arrangement gives the capability of exchanging control information at any time regardless of the state of a call.

2. Support of circuit-switched, packet-switched and user-to-user signaling connections through the same interface: to select an appropriate service on a call-by-call basis, the user informs the network at the time of the call setup of the bearer capability he is requesting from the network.

3. Application of the same protocol to both the basic rate (2B + D) interface and the primary rate (23B + D or 30B + D) interface, as well as to both point-to-point and point-to-multipoint configurations: to handle the point-to-multipoint configuration, an incoming call setup message is broadcast to all the terminal equipment connected to a called digital subscriber line, using the layer 2 broadcast data link connection.

4. Definition and transfer of information for compatiblity checking between the calling and the called terminal equipment: a called terminal checks the contents of the compatibility information element, and it will respond to the call only if it finds that the calling terminal is compatible.

5. Symmetrical protocol for outgoing and incoming calls to enable the control of direct user-to-user connection, for example, direct PBX-to-PBX connection over leased-line circuits. This includes symmetrical call clearing, by which clearing of a connection can be initiated either by the calling party or by the called party.

6. Modular message structure: the Q.931 message format consists of two main

parts, the common part, which is common to all the messages, and the message-specific part.   The message-specific part is composed of a number of *information elements* that are either mandatory or optional for a particular message.   The information elements follow the common coding rules and serve as the building blocks of Q.931 messages.

7. Alignment with the Signaling System No. 7 ISDN User Part (ISUP): specification is provided for the interworking of Q.931 and Signaling System No. 7 ISUP on a network level.   To facilitate the interworking, alignment is achieved, for example, by way of allocating the same code point values for the "Cause" information element in Q.931 and the "Cause" parameter in the ISUP.

4.4.2 Circuit-switched Call Control

4.4.2.1 Overall procedure.   A typical message flow for a circuit-switched call at an ISDN user–network interface is shown in Fig. 4.11.   The calling terminal initiates a call by sending a Setup message to the network.   The Setup message contains, among other information elements, the called party number and the bearer capability information elements to indicate the destination of the call and

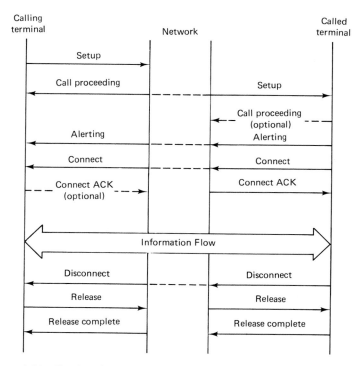

Figure 4.11   Circuit-switched call control message flow (normal sequence typical example).

the characteristics of the requested bearer service, respectively. If the requested call is acceptable and the information contained in the Setup message is sufficient, the network returns the Call Proceeding message to the calling terminal and starts to process the call across the network.

When the destination local exchange receives a call, it sends the Setup message to the called terminal. The called terminal may send back the Call Proceeding message. This is an option added to make the Setup–Call Proceeding message sequence a completely symmetrical procedure across both the calling and the called user–network interfaces. If the called terminal needs to alert its user of the arrival of a call, for example by ringing a bell, as is the case with conventional telephone sets, the terminal starts alerting the user and sends back the Alerting message to the network. The Alerting message is transferred to the calling terminal to inform the calling user that the called terminal has started alerting. When the called terminal answers the call, the Connect message is sent to the network, requesting to establish a connection to the calling terminal. The Connect Acknowledge message is sent from the network to the called terminal to inform that the call has been awarded to it.

As illustrated in Fig. 4.12, in a point-to-multipoint configuration, more than one terminal may respond to the call by sending a Connect message. In this kind of collision case, the terminal that sent the Connect message first gets the call on a first-come, first-served basis. The other terminals, which could not get the call,

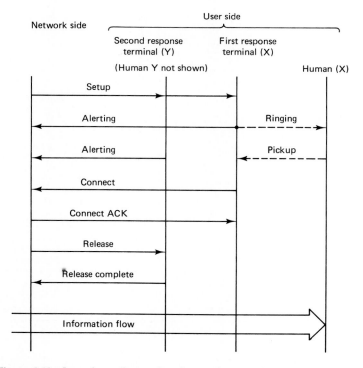

Figure 4.12 Incoming call procedure for a point-to-multipoint configuration.

receive the Release message instead of the Connect Acknowledge message. Normally, to a basic rate (2B + D) interface, the network sends the Setup message on a broadcast data link and is prepared to receive more than one Alerting and/ or Connect message, assuming a point-to-multipoint configuration at the customer's premises. However, on a primary rate (23B + D or 30B + D) interface, only a point-to-point configuration is allowed, and the network sends the Setup message on a point-to-point data link connection.

The Connect message from the called terminal will be conveyed across the network to the calling terminal. The calling terminal may respond to the Connect message by sending the Connect Acknowledge message. This is again an optional message to make the procedure completely symmetrical. This completes the end-to-end connection, and user information can now be conveyed over the B-channel.

When the communication is over, either side can start clearing the connection by sending the Disconnect message and disconnecting the B channel. Then the Disconnect message is conveyed across the network to the terminal on the other side of the connection. The clearing sequence is completed by an exchange of the Release and the Release Acknowledge message sequence on a link by link basis. This releases the Call Reference number and the B channel for use by the next call.

4.4.2.2 Message format. The Q.931 message format consists of the common part and the message-specific part as shown in Fig. 4.13.

The Common Part. The common part appears at the head of all Q.931 messages. It consists of protocol discriminator, call reference value, and message-type information subfields and normally occupies four octets for the basic rate interfaces and five octets for the primary rate interfaces.

The protocol discriminator identifies the protocol with which the message is associated, as shown in Table 4.3. All the Q.931 messages have the value 8, that is, Q.931 user–network call control messages. The purpose of this discriminator is to allow the use of the D channel for the transfer of other protocol messages, such as X.25 packet-level control messages.

The call referernce identifies the call with which a message is associated. By virtue of the call referernce, one D channel is capable of carrying the call control messages of multiple calls in progress across the basic rate (2B + D) or the primary rate (23B + D or 30B + D) interface. The call reference has only a local significance at the local user–network interface and does not have an end-to-end significance across ISDN. The call reference may be of variable length, and its length is indicated by the "length of call reference value" subfield. The normal value for basic rate interfaces is one octet and for primary rate interfaces, two octets.

Message type identifies the message being sent, such as Setup, Call Proceeding, Alerting, Connect, Disconnect, Release, and Release Complete messages.

4.4.2.3 Information elements.

Coding Rules. There are two categories of information elements in Q.931, as shown in Fig. 4.13: variable-length information elements and single-octet in-

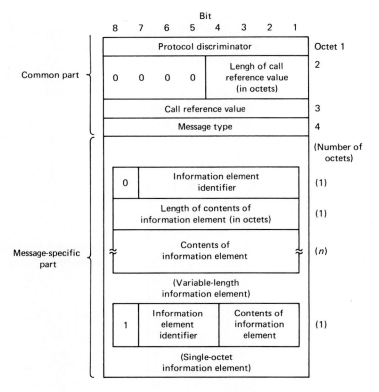

Figure 4.13   Q.931 message format.

TABLE 4.3   PROTOCOL DISCRIMINATOR CODING

Value	Protocol
0	User-specific protocol (used only in user–user information element)
1	OSI high-layer protocols (used only in user–user information element)
8	Q.931 user–network call control messages
16–63	Reserved for other network layer or layer 3 protocols, including X.25 (used to discriminate from the first octet of an X.25 packet including the general format identifier)
64–71	Reserved for national use
80–254	Reserved for other network layer or layer 3 protocols, including X.25 (used to discriminate from the first octet of an X.25 packet including the general format identifier)

formation elements.   Variable-length information elements in a particular message appear in the ascending numerical order of the code values of the information element identifier subfield.   This allows the receiving equipment to detect the presence or absence of a particular information element without scanning through an entire message.   Single-octet information elements may appear at any point in the message.

Typical Information Elements.   A bearer capability information element indicates a requested bearer capability defined in I.211 to be provided by the network. It is coded as shown in Fig. 4.14.   The "information transfer capability" subfield identifies the network capability to be provided.   For example, the value "speech" indicaes a network capability that can transfer voice information but not voiceband coded modem data information, while the value "3.1 kHz audio" indicates a network capability that can transfer both voice and voiceband coded modem data information.   The value "unrestricted digital information" indicates a network capability to transfer user's digital information transparently across an ISDN.   The "transfer mode" subfield identifies whether the requested network capability is circuit mode or packet mode.   The "information transfer rate" subfield indicates the bit rate of a circuit-switched connection, while for a packet-switched connection, it is intended to indicate the throughput rate.   Since the definition of throughput rate has not been established yet, the value of this field for a packet-mode connection is to be coded as all 0s for the time being.

The high-layer compatibility information element provides a means for a remote user to perform compatibility checking on the layers 4 to 7 characteristics. It is coded as shown in Fig. 4.15.   The high-layer compatibility information element is transported transparently by an ISDN from a calling user to the addressed entity by the called party number (for example, called user or high-layer function network node).

High-layer compatibility information can take a variety of forms, but the one currently standardized is by means of the "protocol profile" concept.   A protocol profile identifies a specific service for which a particular combination of protocols in layers 4 to 7 is applied.   Such specific services currently defined in Q.931 by the protocol profile concept are Telephony, Facsimile Group 2/3 and 4, Teletex, Videotex, Mixed Mode, Message Handling Systems services, and OSI application services.   For OSI application services, it is assumed that further compatibility checking is performed according to the OSI protocol using the B channel.

Similarly, the low-layer compatibility information element provides a means for a remote user to perform compatibility checking on the layers 1 to 3 characteristics.   The format and coding are the same as for the bearer capability information element.

4.4.2.4 Compatibility checking.

ISDN will accommodate a variety of terminal equipment that may not necessarily be able to communicate with each other, for example, a telephone set and a telefacsimile terminal.   Furthermore, such terminal equipment may possibly be connected to the same digital subscriber line in a point-to-multipoint customer premises configuration.   Therefore, it is essential before establishing an ISDN connection to check that the terminal equipment on both sides of the connection are compatible, that is, that they can talk to each other.   This checking is called *compatibility checking* and can be performed as follows.

As shown in Fig. 4.16, when the calling terminal originates a call, it includes in the Setup message the bearer capability information element (mandatory) and, optionally, the high-layer and/or low-layer compatibility information elements.

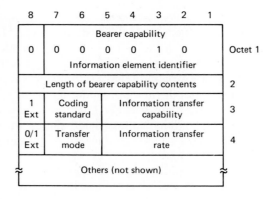

Information transfer capability (octet 3)

Bits

5 4 3 2 1

0 0 0 0 0	Speech
0 1 0 0 0	Unrestricted digital information
0 1 0 0 1	Restricted digital information
1 0 0 0 0	3.1-kHz audio
1 0 0 0 1	7-kHz audio
1 1 0 0 0	Video

All other values are reserved.

Transfer mode (octet 4)

Bits

7 6

| 0 0 | Circuit mode |
| 1 0 | Packet mode |

All other values are reserved.

Information transfer rate (octet 4)

Bits

5 4 3 2 1	Circuit mode (kbps)	Packet mode
0 0 0 0 0	—	(Note)
1 0 0 0 0	64	—
1 0 0 0 1	2 × 64	—
1 0 0 1 1	384	—
1 0 1 0 1	1536	—
1 0 1 1 1	1920	—

All other values are reserved.

Note: The definition of throughput rates for packet-mode bearer capabilities is for further study; 00000 shall be used for packet-mode calls.

Figure 4.14 Bearer capability information element.

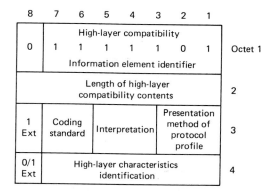

High-layer characteristics identification (octet 4):

Note: The coding below applies in the case of "coding standard" = "CCITT standard" and "presentation method of protocol profile" = "high-layer protocol profile."

Bits
7 6 5 4 3 2 1
Bits	Description
0 0 0 0 0 0 1	Telephony (Recommendation G.711)
0 0 0 0 1 0 0	Facsimile group 2/3
0 1 0 0 0 0 1	Facsimile group 4
0 1 0 0 1 0 0	Mixed mode (Recommendations T.61, T.62, T.70, T.73)
0 1 1 0 0 0 1	Teletex (Recommendations T.62, T.70, T.101)
0 1 1 0 0 1 0	Videotex
0 1 1 0 1 0 1	Telex
0 1 1 1 0 0 0	Message Handling Systems (MHS) (Recommendation X.400 series)
1 0 0 0 0 0 1	OSI application (Recommendation X.200 series)
1 1 1 1 1 1 1	Reserved

All other values are reserved.

Figure 4.15 High-layer compatibility information element.

The network establishes the connection based on the bearer capability information element down to the local exchange to which the called customer is accommodated, while transparently passing the high-layer and/or low-layer information elements. The destination local exchange then sends to the called customer the Setup message on a broadcast data link connection, including the bearer capability, and high-layer and/or low-layer compatibility information elements, if they exist. Then it is the responsibility of each receiving terminal to check its compatibility based on the contents of the bearer capability, high-layer compatibility, and low-layer compatibility information elements and to respond with either the Connect or the Alerting message if compatible, or to ignore the Setup message if incompatible. In the example given in Fig. 4.16, because the high-layer compatibility information element says that the calling terminal is a telefacsimile terminal, only the telefax terminal on the called digital subscriber line responds to the call, while the telephone set ignores it.

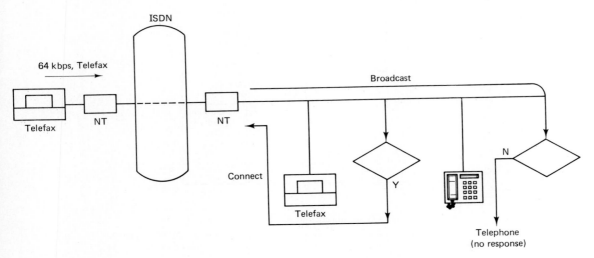

Figure 4.16 Compatibility checking.

4.4.3 Packet-switched Call Control

4.4.3.1 Packet-switched services in an ISDN. The approach taken by the current (1984/1988) version of ISDN packet Recommendation X.31 [4] to offering packet-switched services in an ISDN is to make the best use of the existing packet protocol developed for packet data networks, that is, X.25 [5], and existing packet data networks based on X.25.   In this approach, a connection is first established from an ISDN packet-mode terminal to an X.25 packet-handling function according to normal ISDN procedures, and then packet communication between the two will take place over the established connection according to normal X.25 procedures.
There are two main cases of packet-switched services in an ISDN as illustrated in Fig. 4.17:

> Case A: Packet-switched services using a circuit-mode connection to packet-switched public data networks (PSPDNs)
>
> Case B: Packet-switched services within an ISDN

In case A, an ISDN provides a switched or nonswitched (semipermanent) 64-kbps circuit-mode connection to the access port of a PSPDN, called the access unit (AU).   In the switched connection case, a circuit-switched connection is first established from the calling terminal to the AU according to the normal Q.931 setup procedure.   The AU is identified by the ISDN number in a Q.931 SETUP message.   Then, using the circuit-switched connection, the calling terminal proceeds with the normal X.25 procedures, starting with an X.25 Call Request packet containing the PSPDN address of the called terminal.   In this case, only the B channel can be used at the user–network interface.
In case B, ISDN has full packet-switched service offering capability.   A packet

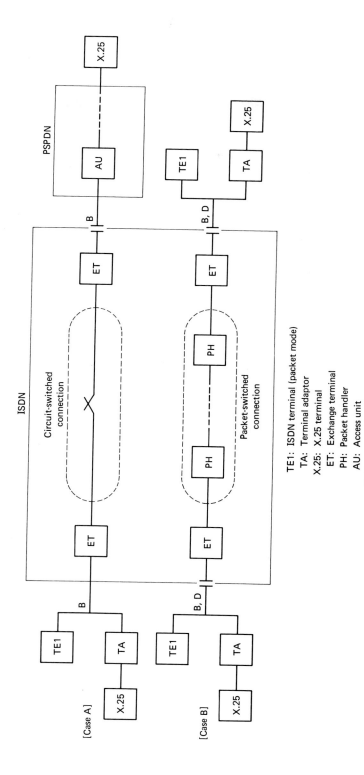

Figure 4.17 Two cases of packet-switched services in an ISDN.

TE1: ISDN terminal (packet mode)
TA: Terminal adaptor
X.25: X.25 terminal
ET: Exchange terminal
PH: Packet handler
AU: Access unit
PSPDN: Packet-switched public data network

call may be placed on either the B or D channel, and it is routed to the packet handler (PH) in an ISDN, where the complete processing of an X.25 call can be carried out. The PH may be placed anywhere within an ISDN, for example, at a local exchange, at a remote exchange, or at a packet-switching module. The routing of packet calls to the PH is done on the basis of the requested bearer capability (transfer mode = packet mode) and, therefore, the user does not provide the called party number in his Q.931 Setup message. The address of the called terminal is contained in the X.25 Call Request packet. In case B, it is important to note that the terminating side can choose to use either the B or D channel completely independently of the channel used at the originating side.

As for the packet-mode terminals in an ISDN, they could be either newly developed terminals conforming to the ISDN user–network interface standards (TE1s) or existing X.25 terminals connected to an ISDN via terminal adaptors (TAs). From the viewpoint of an ISDN, an X.25 terminal and its TA are equivalent to a packet-mode TE1. Also, they could be connected to a point-to-point configuration and to a point-to-multipoint configuration with other packet- and circuit-mode terminals.

4.4.3.2 Procedural examples. There are a variety of packet-switched connection types resulting from the combination of the choices in cases A and B, on the use of the B or D channel, or on the use of switched or nonswitched circuit connections as described in the previous section. Therefore, there are a number of procedures to control various packet-switched connection types. However, their basic principle is the same; that is, a connection is established first according to normal ISDN procedures between the packet-mode terminal (TE1 or X.25 terminal + TA) and the entity that performs the X.25 protocol control, the PSPDN (case A) or the packet handler (case B). Then packet communication takes place over the connection established between the two according to normal X.25 procedures.

In this section, the following two procedures are explained as typical examples:

1. Packet call setup procedure for a call using the B channel
2. Incoming packet call offering procedure for a call using the D channel

Packet Call Setup Procedure for a Call Using the B Channel. Figure 4.18 illustrates the packet call setup procedure for a call in which packet communication takes place over a B-channel connection. In the figure, a packet call is originated by an X.25 terminal connected to an ISDN via a terminal adaptor (TA). The terminal sends an information (I) frame containing an X.25 Call Request packet, expressed as I[X.25 CR], to the TA. The TA then initializes the LAPD data link connection to the originating local exchange by sending a SABME command with SAPI = signaling, which is to be acknowledged by a UA response from the originating exchange. (For abbreviations such as SABME, SAPI, and UA, see Section 4.3.)

Then the TA sends a Q.931 SETUP message requesting the establishment of an X.25 packet call and the use of the B channel indicated by the bearer capability

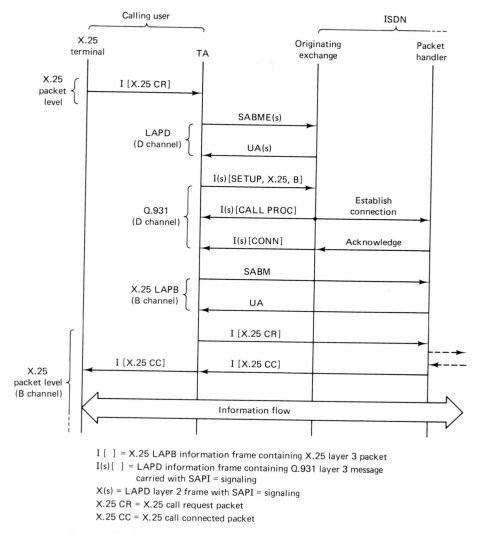

I [ ] = X.25 LAPB information frame containing X.25 layer 3 packet
I(s)[ ] = LAPD information frame containing Q.931 layer 3 message
        carried with SAPI = signaling
X(s) = LAPD layer 2 frame with SAPI = signaling
X.25 CR = X.25 call request packet
X.25 CC = X.25 call connected packet

Figure 4.18 Packet call setup procedure (an example using the B channel).

and the channel indication information elements, respectively. This Q.931 SETUP
message is expressed as I(s)[SETUP, X.25, B], in which (s) means the use of the
LAPD data link connection of SAPI = signaling. The originating exchange then
establishes a connection to a packet handler in the ISDN, while acknowledging the
receipt of the SETUP message by sending back a CALL PROCeeding message to
the TA. The connection to the packet handler could be either packet mode (virtual
circuit connection) or circuit mode. When the packet handler acknowledges the
establishment of the connection, the originating exchange sends a Q.931 CONNect
message to the TA.

The TA then initializes an X.25 LAPB data link connection to the packet handler by sending a Set Asynchronous Balanced Mode (SABM) command, which is to be acknowledged by an Unnumbered Acknowledgment (UA) response. Both the SABM command and the UA response in this case will be coded according to the X.25 LAPB frame format. Then, using the initialized X.25 LAPB data link connection, normal X.25 packet-level procedures will take place, starting with the sending of an X.25 Call Request packet containing a called user address. This packet will be transferred to the called user, and when the called user accepts the call, the X.25 Call Connected packet will be returned to the TA, which relays it to the originating X.25 terminal. Thus an X.25 packet-level connection is established over which packet information is to be exchanged according to the normal X.25 procedures.

Incoming Packet Call Offering Procedure for a Call Using the D Channel. This example differs from the previous one in two aspects. First, instead of the call setup procedure at the originating side, the incoming call procedure at the terminating exchange is explained. Second, instead of the B channel, the D channel is used for packet communication. After having studied these two examples, the readers are invited, as an exercise, to work out the other two combinations:

1. The packet call setup procedure for a call using the D channel
2. The incoming packet call offering procedure for a call using the B channel

Figure 4.19 illustrates the incoming packet call offering procedure for a call using the D channel. When a packet handler at the terminating side receives an X.25 Call Request packet, it sends to the terminating exchange a SETUP message indicating that the call is an X.25 packet call and the channel to be used. The channel to be used is negotiable between the packet handler and the called user, and it can be decided on completely independently of the channel used at the originating user–network interface. In this particular example, the packet handler indicates that any channel is acceptable to it.

The terminating exchange then sends a Q.931 SETUP message indicating that the call is an X.25 packet call and that any channel is acceptable to it in this particular example. As for the choice of the channel, the terminating exchange makes its own decision on the basis of the channel indication given to it from the packet handler and of the current availability of B channels and the D channel. The channel indication in the Q.931 SETUP message is given by the channel identification information element and can be any one of the following:

- Any Bi* channel or the D channel
- Any Bi channel, but no D channel
- Bi channel preferred, but other B channels or the D channel acceptable
- Bi channel preferred, other B channels acceptable, but no D channel

---

* Bi stands for either B1 or B2 in a basic rate interface and one of B1 through B23 or B30 in a primary rate interface.

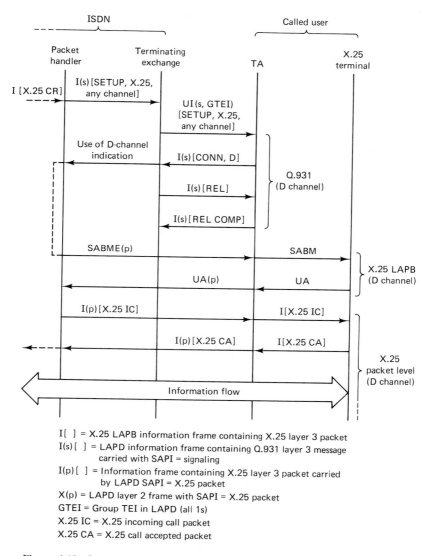

I[ ] = X.25 LAPB information frame containing X.25 layer 3 packet
I(s)[ ] = LAPD information frame containing Q.931 layer 3 message
       carried with SAPI = signaling
I(p)[ ] = Information frame containing X.25 layer 3 packet carried
       by LAPD SAPI = X.25 packet
X(p) = LAPD layer 2 frame with SAPI = X.25 packet
GTEI = Group TEI in LAPD (all 1s)
X.25 IC = X.25 incoming call packet
X.25 CA = X.25 call accepted packet

Figure 4.19 Incoming packet call offering procedure (an example using the D channel).

- Bi channel exclusively or D channel exclusively
- Bi channel exclusively, no D channel
- D channel exclusively

In the figure, the Q.931 SETUP message sent to the called user is expressed as UI(s, GTEI) [SETUP, X.25, any channel], indicating that the message is sent by an unnumbered information (UI) frame with the SAPI = signaling over the broadcast data link, which is indicated by the use of the group TEI (GTEI). As such, the message is of the same form as that for an incoming circuit-switched call except for the indication in the bearer capability information element that the call is an X.25 packet call.   In this way, the signaling procedures for a circuit-switched call and a packet-switched call are integrated.

Upon the reception of the Q.931 SETUP message, all the terminals including the terminal adaptors (TAs) connected to the called user–network interface perform compatibility checking.   Those packet-mode terminals including TAs that have found the call to be compatible with them answer the call by sending a Q.931 CONNect message, indicating the channel to be used by the channel identification information element.   In this particular example, the use of the D channel is indicated, expressed as I(s)[CONN,D].   This information is then sent to the packet handler.

At the same time, the terminating exchange sends a RELease message to the selected terminal with the indication that "the call is delivered over an established channel." This RELease message to the selected terminal is sent only when the selected channel is the D channel or an already established B channel, in order to release the call reference value reserved by the selected terminal.   When a new B channel is selected, the call reference value needs to be retained and, therefore, the RELease message is not sent.   In any case, the terminating exchange sends a RELease message to those terminals that have answered the call by returning a CONNect message but have not been selected with an indication that the call was not awarded to them.   In all these cases, the RELease message is to be acknowledged by a RELease COMPlete message from the called terminal or TA.

When the packet handler receives an indication to use the D channel, it establishes the SAPI = X.25 packet data link connection within the D channel by sending a SABME command to the called TA, expressed in Fig.4.19 as SABME(p). The TA then initializes the X.25 LAPB data link connection to the X.25 terminal by sending an X.25 LAPB SABM command, expressed simply as SABM in the figure.   The command is to be acknowledged by a UA response from the terminal, which will be converted by the TA into a UA response to the network over the X.25 packet data link connection, expressed as UA(p).   This completes the establishment and initialization of the data link connection.

Then the packet handler sends an X.25 incoming call packet to the TA over the X.25 packet data link connection, expressed as I(p)[X.25 IC], which will be relayed to the called X.25 terminal on an X.25 packet data link connection, expressed as I[X.25 IC].   The X.25 terminal answers the call by sending an X.25 call accepted packet to the TA, which will be relayed to the network over the X.25 packet data link connection.   The packet handler sends the X.25 call accepted packet across the network to the other packet handler at the calling side, which will convert the packet into the X.25 call connected packet and send it to the calling terminal (see Fig. 4.18).   This completes the packet-level network connection between the calling terminal and the called terminal, and packet information can now be exchanged according to the normal X.25 procedures.

4.4.3.3 Evolution of packet-mode services in ISDN.   The packet-mode services according to the procedures described are to be considered as the first step

in the evolution of packet-mode services in ISDN. The following evolutionary steps are recognized at CCITT:

Step 1: Services according to the current X.31 procedures as described in the previous section. They are characterized by a two-stage connection, the first stage being the establishment of an ISDN connection (either circuit-mode connection over the B channel or packet-mode connection within the D channel) between the terminal and the packet handler, and the second stage being packet communication according to the X.25 layers 2 and 3 procedures over the established ISDN connection.

Step 2: Extensions of step 1 services based on layer 2 multiplexing in the B channel. In step 1, only a single X.25 packet data link connection can be established over the B-channel connection between the terminal and the packet handler. In step 2, the LAPD is to be applied also to the B-channel connection, which allows multiple data link connections to be established between the terminal and the packet handler over a single B-channel, circuit-mode connection. Each data link connection can then be processed separately at the packet handler, for example, by extending a data link connection to an adjacent packet handler in the network. This means routing of a LAPD frame on the basis of the layer 2 address, that is, the data link connection identifier (DLCI) currently consisting of the SAPI and the TEI. Therefore, it is often called *frame relaying*. When the frame reaches an entity within the network that processes layer 3, layer 3 packet-level communication takes place over the established data link connection according to the X.25 packet-level procedures.

Step 3: New packet-mode services based on (1) layer 2 multiplexing as in step 2 and (2) out-of-band call control signaling at layers 2 and 3. Item (1) is already explained in relation to step 2. As for item (2), it should be noted first that the packet call control signaling in steps 1 and 2 is performed according to the X.25 procedures, that is, at layer 2 using the same data link connection that transfers the user information, and at layer 3 according to the X.25 packet-level protocol, which is different from the Q.931 ISDN circuit-switched call control protocol in both procedures and messages.

In the proposed step 3 approach, out of multiple data link connections established over a B-channel connection or within a D channel between a packet-mode terminal and the packet handler in the ISDN, one data link connection is dedicated as the signaling data link for packet-mode calls. Currently, a SAPI value of 1 is reserved for it, as shown in Table 4.1. As a result, all the control signals for packet-mode calls on multiple data link connections will be carried by this signaling data link connection. Since call control signals are transferred over a different data link connection from that used for the transfer of user packet information, this arrangement is called *out-of-band signaling*.

Consequently, at layer 3, since the out-of-band signaling arrangement is the same as for circuit- and packet-mode calls, the same Q.931 procedures and messages are to be applied for the control of calls in the two modes. Integration is thus achieved even at layer 3, which is expected to simplify the concept, specification, and implementation significantly for the support of both circuit- and packet-mode services. Out-of-band call control enhances flexibility since (1) signals can be sent at any time regardless of the state of a call, and (2) information not associated with a call can also be sent.

Step 4: New packet-mode services applicable to both broadband and narrowband ISDN services and able to support voice, video, and high-speed data in addition to medium- to low-speed data.   Since this step provides the highest degree in integration in terms of both services (narrowband and broadband) and technology (circuit and packet), it is a challenging goal, attracting the attention of the world's telecommunications research and development community.   The technology to be applied is referred to by various names, for example, fast packet, broadband packet, asynchronous transfer mode, and even fast circuit.   As such, the concept as well as the technology is still in the embryonic stage and thus beyond the scope of this book.

It should be noted that these four steps are identified only as conceptually possible evolutionary steps.   In reality, many networks may skip one or more steps or provide one or more steps simultaneously depending on such factors as market demands and progress in technology.

4.5 INTERWORKING BETWEEN Q.931 AND SIGNALING SYSTEM NO. 7

Interexchange signaling in an ISDN is performed according to the Signaling System (SS) No. 7 protocol.   The protocol consists of the common message transfer part (MTP) and the application-specific user parts, such as the ISDN user part (ISUP), telephone user part, data user part, signaling connection control part, and transaction capability application part.   Since the description of SS No. 7 in its entirety would require a large number of additional pages, here in this chapter only the interworking aspects of the ISDN user part (ISUP) with Q.931 are described.   SS No. 7 ISUP and its interworking with Q.931 are documented in the CCITT Recommendations. [6, 7]

Figure 4.20 illustrates the interworking between Q.931 applied at the user–network interface and SS No. 7 ISUP applied at the interexchange interface for a circuit-switched connection in a full ISDN.   The Q.931 SETUP message is translated into the SS No. 7 initial address message (IAM) at the originating local exchange and is sent to the succeeding exchange in the ISDN.   The circle mark with a slanted cross ($\otimes$) indicates the state of through-connection at an exchange. In the case of a circuit-switched connection with a bearer capability of 64-kbps unrestricted digital information, only a backward channel, that is, in the direction from the called to the calling user, is interconnected at the time of the call setup. This is to prevent fraudulent use of the connection before charging will start.   The SS No. 7 IAM is translated into the SETUP message at the terminating exchange and sent to the called user.

When a called terminal decides that the call is compatible, it starts alerting the called user and sends an ALERT message.   The ALERT message is translated at the terminating local exchange into the SS No. 7 address complete message

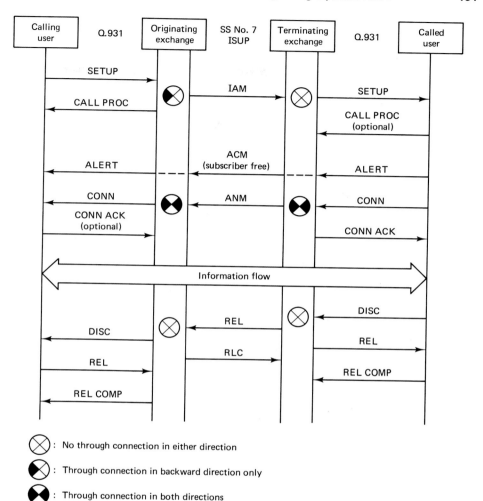

Figure 4.20   Q.931–SS No. 7 ISUP interworking in an ISDN (unrestricted 64-kbps circuit-switched connection example.

(ACM) with an indicator notifying the subscriber-free condition. Then the ACM message will be translated back into the ALERT message at the originating local exchange and sent to the calling user. When the called user answers the call by sending the CONNect message, the terminating local exchange completes the connection of both forward and backward channels, and the CONNect message is translated into the SS No. 7 answer message (ANM). At the reception of the ANM message, the originating exchange through-connects the forward channel also and sends the CONNect message to the calling user, which completes the call establishment.

The asymmetric through-connection at the originating local exchange before the call is answered is done to prevent a fraudulent use of the established connection after the reception of the CONNect message at the terminating exchange and before the ANM message travels across the network and reaches the originating exchange, which triggers the duration-based charging.   This asymmetric through-connection is applied to calls requesting a bearer capability of the 64-kbps unrestricted digital information.   For calls requesting a bearer capability of the 3.1-kHz audio or speech, symmetric through-connection is normally applied to prevent speech clipping when the called user answers the call.

To release an established connection, either side can send the Q.931 DISConnect message, which will be translated into the SS No. 7 RELease message. The RELease message will be acknowledged by the release complete (RLC) message when the connection at the exchange is released, and the interexchange circuit becomes available for another call.

It is rather unfortunate that Q.931 messages and SS No. 7 messages have to be translated back and forth at originating and terminating exchanges as described. This is the result of past history in CCITT in that Q.931 and SS No. 7 were standardized by different groups without a sufficient amount of coordination during the 1981–1984 study period.   In 1985, recognizing the need for coordination, the two groups established a joint group to let the two protocols interwork correctly and harmonize message names and detailed codings as much as possible to facilitate the interworking.   Unfortunately, some of the message names have been left as they were, since they are so well known already among the experts and the implementers who are working on each of the two protocols.   In any case, an interworking Recommendation is being drafted by the group to be recommended by CCITT in 1988.

4.6 INTERWORKING BETWEEN ISDN AND PSTN

ISDNs will evolve from today's public switched telephone networks (PSTNs) by introducing digital switching and transmission equipment into them over a period of one or more decades.   During this migration period, ISDNs have to interwork with other existing networks, notably the PSTNs, which are by far the largest and most numerous among the existing networks.   For example, a digital telephone set connected to an ISDN basic rate (2B + D) interface certainly needs to be able to talk with a conventional telephone set connected to the conventional PSTN.

Figure 4.21 illustrates a typical interworking example between an ISDN and a PSTN for the bearer capability of speech or 3.1-kHz audio.   In the interworking with the existing networks, it is assumed that no change will be required by the existing networks and that protocol conversion will be provided at the ISDN interworking exchanges.   Therefore, when the interworking exchange receives an initial address message (IAM) of SS No. 7 ISUP from a preceding exchange in an ISDN, it first checks to determine if the call can leave the ISDN and enter into the PSTN by looking at the bearer capability requested by the calling user. If the calling user is requesting either speech or 3.1-kHz audio bearer capability, the interworking exchange assumes that the call may enter into the PSTN and sends

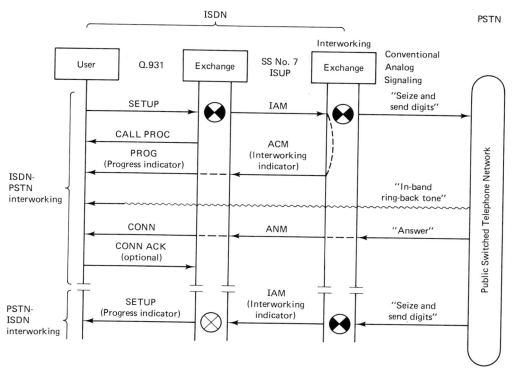

Figure 4.21 ISDN-PSTN interworking (speech or 3.1-kHz audio bearer capability example).

an appropriate seizure signal, followed by signals conveying the digits of the called party number to the PSTN by the conventional analog signaling system used in the PSTN.

At the same time, the interworking exchange returns an address complete message (ACM) with an interworking indicator indicating that the call is leaving ISDN and that further call progress information may be available in-band. The ACM is translated into a Q.931 PROGress message at the originating local exchange, with the progress indicator indicating the same situation. This will enable the calling terminal to take an appropriate action, for example, to switch on the in-band tone receiver to be activated or to hang up the call if interworking is not desired. In the example, the call proceeds within the PSTN, and when the called user is alerted, an in-band ring-back tone is sent from the terminating local exchange in the PSTN toward the calling user. This in-band tone in analog form within the PSTN is converted into PCM-coded digital form at the interworking exchange and sent to the calling user in the B channel. The tone receiver at the calling terminal will convert the tone into an appropriate audible tone for the human user. When the called user answers within a PSTN, the answer signal will be converted at the interworking exchange into the answer message (ANM) of SS 7 ISUP and then into the Q.931 CONNect message of at the originating exchange.

As shown at the bottom of Figure 4.21, in the PSTN to ISDN direction, interworking takes place when a call arrives at an ISDN interworking exchange from a PSTN by appropriate means to signal the seizure of a trunk circuit and to send the digits of the called ISDN subscriber according to the conventional analog signaling system adopted in the PSTN. The interworking exchange then sends an initial address message (IAM), with an interworking indicator indicating that the call has come from a PSTN. The IAM will be converted by the originating local exchange into a Q.931 SETUP message, with the progress indicator indicating the same situation. The SETUP message is broadcast to all the terminals connected to the addressed called subscriber line, and the receiving terminals perform compatibility checking on the basis of the contents of the progress indicator information element in addition to the bearer capability information element.

As explained previously, the assumption is that there will be no change in the existing networks to enable interworking with an ISDN. Therefore, because of the limited signaling capability of the existing networks, the services provided to an ISDN user are limited in some aspects in the interworking case as compared with those provided within a full ISDN. For example, neither high-layer compatibility information nor user-to-user information is available for a call between an ISDN and a PSTN. Therefore, the current arrangement does not allow, for example, a PSTN telefax terminal to make a call to an ISDN telefax terminal connected to a multipoint 2B + D interface with other terminals because another terminal may answer first and get the call. However, if an ISDN telefax terminal connected to a multipoint 2B + D interface is assigned an ISDN number, the calling user can dial that number and establish a connection to that telefax terminal. The assignment of ISDN numbers to specific terminals in a multipoint configuration is under study at CCITT.

4.7 STATUS OF NETWORK LAYER STANDARDIZATION AT CCITT

As of July 1987, most of the protocols for the basic services, that is, setting up, maintaining, and clearing down a connection, were completed for both Q.931 and SS No. 7 ISUP. The specification for the interworking between the two, including the interworking cases between an ISDN and a PSTN, is also completed. The major remaining task concerning the network layer is completion of the specification on the services and protocols for the supplementary services, such as conference calls, call waiting, credit card calling, and completion of a call to a busy subscriber. Service negotiation between a user and a network is also another important item under study.

For services and operation of an ISDN, higher-layer protocols need to be standardized also, and this work is going on at CCITT and at other national and international standards organizations.

REFERENCES

4.1. CCITT Recommendations Q.920 (I.440) and Q.921 (I.441), "ISDN user–netork interface layer 2—General aspects (Q.920) and specification (Q.921)," 1st version (1984), revised version (accelerated approval 1987, 1988 planned).

4.2. CCITT Recommendations Q.930 (I.450) and Q.931 (I.451), "ISDN user–network interface layer 3—General aspects (Q.930) and specification (Q.931)," 1st version (1984), revised version (1988 planned).

4.3. W. Peterson and others, *Error-Correcting Codes*, 2nd ed.   MIT Press, Cambridge, Mass., 1972.

4.4. CCITT Recommendation X.31, "Support of packet mode terminal equipment by an ISDN," 1st version (1984), revised version (1988 planned).

4.5. CCITT Recommendation X.25, "Interface between data terminal equipment (DTE) and data circuit terminating equipment (DCE) for terminals operating in the packet mode and connected to public data networks by dedicated circuit," 1st version (1976), revised versions (1980, 1984, 1988 planned).

4.6. CCITT Recommendations Q.761–766, "Integrated Services Digital Network User Part of Signalling System No. 7," 1st version (1984), revised version (1988 planned).

4.7. CCITT Recommendation Q.xxx (not numbered yet), "Specification of interworking between Q.931 and Signalling System No. 7 ISDN User Part," 1st version (1988 planned).

4.8. S. Kano, "Layers 2 and 3 ISDN Recommendations," International Communications Conference 1985, Chicago, June 1985.

4.9. S. Kano, "ISDN user–network interface layers 2 and 3 protocols: new developments after 1984," International Communications Conference 1986, Toronto, June 1986.

CHAPTER 5

The ISDN Standardization Process

ANTHONY M. RUTKOWSKI*

ABSTRACT

This chapter provides an overview of the ISDN Standardization Process. It discusses the standards-making bodies and the forums and legislative procedures employed by these bodies. A description of important developments occurring in the principal global ISDN forum at the time of writing this book is also presented

5.1 INTRODUCTION

The ISDN standardization process occurs within a complex maze of global, regional, and domestic organizations and committees that provides for the interaction of thousands of telecommunication professionals representing nearly every segment of the industry. It is an immense collective endeavor, annually disseminating tens of thousands of documents, consuming millions of hours of corporate and institutional resources, and producing the standards, specifications, operating procedures, and regulations necessary to implement telecommunication networks, present and future.

It is a process that has been exponentially increasing during the 1980s in every dimension: scope, complexity, number of organizations and meetings, level of detail, and throughput. In some meetings, more than half the time is now spent in hearing liaison summaries of related work in other forums.

It is also a process without precise boundaries. The subject matter of some groups is clearly and explicitly focused on ISDN. In other cases, only a segment of the activity concerns ISDN. In still other instances, the subject matter may only peripherally be related, such as with the Open Systems Interconnection (OSI) model.

This chapter provides an overview of the forums and legislative procedures employed by these bodies. It concludes with a description of important devel-

---

* Research Associate, Massachusetts Institute of Technology. Mr. Rutkowski is presently an official with the International Telecommunication Union, Geneva, Switzerland, which has not approved in any manner the contents of the chapter.

opments occurring in the principal global ISDN forum at the time of this book's publication.

5.2 STANDARDS-MAKING FORUMS, METHODS, AND PRODUCT

The importance of the complex of organizations and their activities to the development and implementation of digital communication networks and equipment cannot be emphasized enough.   Although many leading-edge companies are frequently reluctant to reveal proprietary new approaches through their active participation in these forums, today's emerging world of integrated information and telecommunication systems militates against "going it alone." Some minimal, stable, well-defined standards and procedures must exist at the interfaces among networks and terminal equipment.   However, the very nature of integrated services digital networks fosters common models for both facilities and services.

In the United States, regulatory agencies have almost entirely abandoned this domain to the private sector, a seemingly preferable condition vis-à-vis an all-encompassing governmental involvement.   There are now hundreds of private corporations participating in these forums, although the most significant involvement is that of the largest network operators and manufacturers.

However, most other countries and regions exercise at least a minimal government role to facilitate the work and minimize the immense and frequently redundant resources required by manufacturers, service providers, and users to participate.   And for the many nations in which the network is owned and operated by a governmental agency, generally a Ministry of Posts and Telegraph and Telephone (PTT), the government involvement is inextricably a part of their national or regional planning process.

This wide range of participants with differing scopes of interest and motivation, as much as historical, operational, and market reasons, results in the complex of forums and procedures that constitute the ISDN standardization process. The forums discussed next are the *principal* ones dealing with ISDN.

5.2.1 Global Forums

At the global level, the two most active organizations devising digital communication standards are the International Telecommunication Union (ITU) and the International Organization for Standardization (ISO).*   The former has traditionally been a focal point for telecommunication system coordination, while the latter has focused on information systems.   As these systems have begun to merge, each organization has shifted its focus to encompass integrated systems.

5.2.1.1 International Telecommunication Union (ITU).   The ITU, which traces its origins to the founding of the International Telegraph Union in 1865, is

---

* In the early 1980s the organization officially changed its name to the International Organization for Standardization from the International Standards Organization, but the acronym was left as ISO.

the world's specialized international organization of nations and network operators for telecommunication matters. The purpose of the ITU is to promote cooperation and development in the field of telecommunication, especially in the provision of worldwide service capabilities.

Only administrations, that is, national governments, may be ITU members. In early 1989, nearly every nation in the world, 166 in all, was a formal member. However, recognized private operating agencies (RPOAs) (for example, AT&T), scientific and industrial organizations (SIOs) (for example, IBM), and international organizations of all kinds may also participate in most facets of ITU work. Indeed, the ISDN work is largely pursued in ITU forums by private sector representatives rather than those from governments, although the participants at the larger meetings may nominally be on a delegation of the government.

Structurally, the ITU consists of both temporary and permanent bodies. The temporary ones are legislative/managerial in nature: the Plenipotentiary Conference, Administrative Council, Administrative Conferences, the International Telegraph and Telephone Consultative Committee (CCITT), the International Radio Consultative Committee (CCIR). The permanent ones provide a variety of important functions and include the General-Secretariat (headed by a secretary general and a deputy), the CCITT Secretariat (headed by a director), a CCIR Secretariat (headed by a director), and the International Frequency Registration Board (headed by five board members). The permanent staff is located at a single headquarters in Geneva, Switzerland. The structure and functions are set out in the current International Telecommunication Convention (Nairobi, 1982), which is a treaty signed by nearly all countries.

Most of the activity on ISDN matters is confined to the International Telegraph and Telephone Consultative Committee (CCITT), although some issues relating to radio are considered within the International Radio Consultative Committee (CCIR). This work is largely carried out through scores of technical bodies within the CCITT, involving many thousands of participants. The results are published as international standards termed *Recommendations* of the consultative committees, although some provisions, largely relating to radio, are adopted as treaty agreements referred to as *Regulations*. However, the World Administrative Telegraph and Telephone Conference (WATTC) which convened in December 1988 in Melbourne adopted new International Telecommunication Regulations of a treaty nature that indirectly affect digital network operations. Currently, some 20,000 pages of CCITT Recommendations have been adopted.

The process of adopting Recommendations normally proceeds in the context of discrete *questions*, although those relating to radio are done in the context of *projects*. The Recommendations normally proceed from initial drafts to adoption in the context of specific four-year activity periods that both begin and end with major formal convocations called Plenary Assemblies. At the end of each period, the work on a question is either adopted and/or continued into the next four-year period. Adoption nearly always occurs by consensus. However, this process was significantly altered in late 1988, and "Accelerated Procedures" can now be used.

The process of adopting Regulations nominally proceeds in the context of a single Administrative Conference at which adoption normally occurs by consensus.

For virtually all matters except those relating to radio, most of the substantive work actually occurs within the Consultative Committees.

International Telegraph and Telephone Consultative Committee (CCITT). Although the terms "telegraph and telephone" constitute the CCITT's name, the formal jurisdiction is defined in the International Telecommunication Convention in terms of all telecommunication matters, except those specifically relating to radio. In fact, relatively little of the CCITT's current work relates explicitly to telegraph and telephone systems.

The CCITT consists of a Plenary Assembly that meets every four years and numerous Study Groups established by the Plenary. The last Plenary (the ninth since the formerly separate Telegraph and Telephone Consultative Committees were merged in late 1956) was convened in Melbourne November 14–25, 1988. As discussed at the end of this chapter, many important ISDN-related standards were adopted at that meeting.

Each Study Group in turn has its own plenary meetings and divides its work up among numerous working parties, working teams, and rapporteurs. The rapporteurs are individuals appointed to perform some specific drafting or liaison activity. This activity is assisted by the CCITT Secretariat staff located at ITU headquarters. The principal staff are the CCITT director, elected by the ITU Plenipotentiary Conference (as of 1989), assisted by a small permanent staff of counselors and administrative assistants. The counselors are technically knowledgeable consultants who are generally assigned to a particular study group to facilitate the work of that group.

The groups shown in Table 5.1 consider matters directly or indirectly involving ISDN. This organized focus on ISDN is at least partially due to the leadership at

TABLE 5.1 CCITT STUDY GROUPS

Group	1989–1992
I	Services
II	Network Operation
III	Tariff and Accounting Principles
IV	Maintenance
V	Protection against Electromagnetic Effects
VI	Outside Plant
VII	Data Communication Networks
VIII	Terminals for Telematic Services
IX	Telegraph Networks and Telegraph Terminal Equipment
X	Languages for Telecommunication Applications
XI	Switching and Signaling
XII	Transmission Performance of Telephone Networks and Terminals
XV	Transmission Systems and Equipment
XVII	Data Transmission over the Telephone Network
XVIII	ISDN

the study group level provided for nearly two decades by the present CCITT director, Theodor Irmer of Germany, elected to that position in 1984 and reelected in 1989.   The work involves the consideration and production of four kinds of documents.   The normal submissions to any meeting are referred to as *regular contributions* or *white documents*.   These are furnished to the CCITT Secretariat 2 to 3 months prior to the meeting, allowing their translation and dissemination to all the participants well in advance of their arrival at the meeting.

The CCITT ISDN activity has been occurring so rapidly, however, that such formal contributions are no longer the norm.   Rather, the documents are simply brought to the meetings by the hundreds and distributed there.   These are known as *delayed documents*.   During the course of a meeting, a number of documents are typically submitted by rapporteurs or officers, prepared by drafting groups, and adopted by the meeting.   These are known as *temporary documents*.   Several months later, the temporary documents comprising the report of the meeting are translated into all three working languages of the ITU (English, French, and Spanish), typed, and distributed as *reports*.   Each type of document has its own numbering scheme and color of paper.

The standardization process generally consists of the introduction of a contribution at a study group meeting, usually early in the four-year cycle.   The contribution sets forth the rationale for a new or amended standard, a draft text, and ties the standard to a one or more study questions.   The matter will then be referred to a working party, which in turn will refer it to a drafting group or rapporteur.   Rapporteurs are variously dedicated to particular questions or used in an ad-hoc fashion to undertake a drafting or study effort spanning periods of time beyond one meeting.   These practices are different among the study groups and adapted to fit the circumstances.   If there is substantial support for the standard, a text is produced that is introduced back up through the infrastructure.   At some point it must be assigned a permanent identifier and approved by the Study Group Plenary, and then the CCITT Plenary Assembly.   This process is specified in CCITT's A series of Recommendations.

The ultimate product of the CCITT is Recommendations.   The entire field of telecommunication (except radio) has been codified by the CCITT, with each major subdivision represented by a prefix letter.   For example, the fairly universal packet-switching standard X.25 is one of the X series of Recommendations on Data Communication Networks.   These Recommendations are formally adopted at each Plenary Assembly and known by the color of the outer covers of the published set of volumes and fasicles.   The former CCITT Recommendations adopted by the Eighth Plenary Assembly in 1984 are referred to as the *Red Book*, and those adopted at the Ninth in November 1988 are contained in *Blue Books*. It is likely in the near future, however, that the material will be disseminated in various electronic or optical formats.

Perhaps the most prominent of the CCITT Study Groups is XVIII, which has been the global focal point for most ISDN activities.   The others, as can been seen from their titles in Table 5.1, address nearly every aspect of communication network and terminal design and operation and have become highly active, global focal points for all these subjects. (The CCITT designates its study groups using

Roman numerals to differentiate them from those of the CCIR, which uses Arabic numerals.)

The dynamic nature of CCITT's work has resulted in constant reorganization during the last decade or two. The current Study Groups are shown in Table 5.2. After 1992, several of these groups are scheduled for merger or elimination.

The VIIIth CCITT Plenary Assembly in October 1984 attempted to secure a more functional infrastructure to accommodate the ISDN environment. During the 1981–1984 activity period, Study Group XVIII had nearly exclusive jurisdiction over ISDN matters and coordinated ISDN-related work of other groups. That approach was changed somewhat in the organization after 1984, which in effect orients most of the CCITT Study Groups around ISDN and diffuses more of the responsibilities. This trend is continued at the 1988 Plenary Assembly.

In addition to the groups shown in Table 5-1, a joint CCITT/CCIR Study Group on television transmission networks, Special Autonomous Groups (referred to by their French acronym as the GAS groups), and Joint Plan Committees occasionally address ISDN matters.

TABLE 5.2 OUTLINE OF CCITT RECOMMENDATIONS

Series	Title
A	Organization of the work of the CCITT
B	Means of expression (definitions, symbols, classification)
C	General telecommunications statistics
D	General tariff principles
E	International telephone operation, network management, and traffic engineering
F	Telegraph, telematic, message handling, and directory services: operations, quality of service, and definition of service
G	Transmission systems and media, digital systems and networks
H	Line transmission of nontelephone signals
I	Integrated Services Digital Networks (ISDN)
J	Transmission of sound programs and television signals
K	Protection against interference
L	Construction installation, and protection of cable and other elements of outside plant
M	Maintenance: international transmission systems, telephone circuits, telegraphy, facsimile, and leased circuits
N	Maintenance: international sound programs and television transmission circuits
O	Specifications of measuring equipment
P	Telephone transmission quality, telephone installations, and local line networks
Q	Telephone switching and signalling
R	Telegraph transmission
S	Telegraph services terminal equipment
T	Terminal equipment and protocols for telematic services
U	Telegraph switching
V	Data communication over the telephone network
X	Data communication networks
Z	Programming languages

The process of standards adoption within the CCITT at the time of this book's publication in 1990 continues to undergo significant review. A much faster process for adopting new and amending old Recommendations has been established, and changing the titles of these provisions from recommendations to standards, and other alterations are being considered. The term recommendations is a holdover from a controversy that emerged in the early 1920s regarding the role of the newly instituted international consultative committees and a fear that they would infringe on the perogatives of government plenipotentiaries to the treaty-making conferences. It was that same fear, coupled with the relatively leisurely pace of telecommunication developments 40 years ago, that resulted in the four-year plenary periods.

If there is widespread consensus that the matter is important enough, the existing process can proceed with surprising rapidity, considering the frequent complexity of the subject matter, the important trade-offs embedded in the standards, and the number of parties involved from around the world. The most notable recent success story was the adoption of the new Broadband-ISDN/Asynchronous Transfer Mode Recommendation described near the end of this chapter. This effort proceeded from the introduction of a totally new concept to a detailed standard in less than 24 months.*

Study Group XVIII. At the international level, important ISDN-related work is done in many of the study groups, particularly VII, XI, and XVIII. The most important of all these groups, however, has been and remains Study Group XVIII. It is the global driver for standardization, R&D, and policy on ISDN. This group evolved out of former Special Study Group A in 1976 and was led by Theodor Irmer of Germany until October 1984, when Irmer was rewarded for his pioneering effort by election to the post of CCITT director. During the 1989–1992 study period, Hans K. Phyffer of Switzerland serves as the chairman.

During the 1985–1988 plenary period, the number of contributions in SG XVIII forums increased to new records for the CCITT, nearly 4000. This reflected a remarkable evolution in the direction of what is commonly referred to as broadband ISDN, which occurred within this same time period and is described at the end of this chapter and in Chapter 9. What is encompassed under the term broadband, however, is an entire new complex of technologies and services that can provide narrowband, as well as high capacity (that is, 150 Mbps and up), capabilties. And during 1986–1987, it so captured the ISDN planning community that it became clear a revolution was in the making.†

Study Group XVIII is best described in terms of the structure and identities of its work. The infrastructure of working groups during the 1989–1992 study period is depicted in Table 5.3.

---

* See Report of Working Party 2 (Methods of Work), Final Report of Special Study Group S, Geneva, 7–16 December 1987.

    † See, for example, Minzer, "Towards a Universal Broadband Standard," *Telecommunications,* Vol. 21, No. 10, Oct. 1987; "The View from Copper Mountain: T1D1's Summit on Advanced Digital Networks," *Telecommunications at 75,* Vol. 21, No. 7, July 1987; "Telecommunication's New Terminology," *Telecommunications at 91,* Vol. 21, No. 7, July 1987.

TABLE 5.3 CCITT STUDY GROUP XVIII, WORKING GROUPS, 1989–1992 STUDY PERIOD

Working Party XVIII/1:	General aspects and coordination
Working Party XVIII/2:	Interworking APBMS and field trials
Working Party XVIII/3:	Interfaces layer 1 characteristics
Working Party XVIII/4:	Architecture and models
Working Party XVIII/5:	Network capabilities
Working Party XVIII/6:	Performance
Working Party XVIII/7:	Digital hierarchies
Working Party XVIII/8:	General B-ISDN aspects

At the IXth Plenary Assembly, 23 questions concerning ISDN were assigned to Study Group XVIII, as listed in Table 5.4. All contributions to the working parties must generally address one or more of these questions and be indicated on the cover page of the contribution.

During the 1980–1984 study period, an initial structure for ISDN recommendations with a new I series was adopted, and an initial set of recommendations was adopted. The new outline of Recommendations adopted at the IXth Plenary in November 1988 is set forth in Table 5.5.

International Radio Consultative Committee (CCIR). The CCIR is an ITU body similar to the CCITT. However, its methods of work and Recommendations are significantly different due to the nature of the subject matter and the divisions that have historically existed between the two groups.

The CCIR work has been largely confined to radio propagation and facilities. However, as radio transmission systems and networks have increasingly employed digital techniques and are envisioned as an extension of ISDN capabilities, the CCIR study groups devoted to specific radio services have adopted relevant study programs and Recommendations. There has been markedly increased liaison with the relevant CCIR and CCITT groups on matters, particularly those involving mobile radio services and digital television signals. Some work has been involved satellite systems in ISDN circuits.

CCIR Recommendations may be found in a set of "green books" (they have always been green) that are published by the ITU.

5.2.1.2 International Organization for Standardization (ISO).

The ISO is the specialized international agency for standardization, at present comprising the national standards bodies of 91 countries. A *member body* of ISO is the national body "most representative of standardization in its country." Member bodies are entitled to participate and exercise full voting rights on any technical committee of ISO, are eligible for Council membership, and have seats in the General Assembly. By January 1989, the number of member bodies was 73. The American National Standards Institute (ANSI) represents the United States.

A *correspondent member* is normally an organization in a developing country that does not yet have its own national standards body. Correspondent members

TABLE 5.4 QUESTIONS ASSIGNED TO CCITT STUDY GROUP XVIII

Question	Short title
1/XVIII	General aspects of ISDN
2/XVIII	Asynchronous Transfer Mode (ATM)
3/XVIII	Network aspects of digital hierarchies
4/XVIII	Network application of Synchronous Digital Hierarchy with reference to the Network Node Interface (NNI)
5/XVIII	General aspects of Quality of Service and network performance in digital networks including ISDNs
6/XVIII	Network performance objectives for ISDN circuit mode information transfer
7/XVIII	Performance objectives for timing and controlled slips (synchronization), filter, wander, and propagation delay
8/XVIII	Network performance objectives for ISDN connection, processing, and packet mode information transfer
9/XVIII	Performance objectives for ISDN availability
10/XVIII	Impact of signal processing on ISDN
11/XVIII	Interworking of ISDNs with other networks, including compatibility checking and terminal selection
12/XVIII	Interworking between networks using different digital hierarchies—Layer 1 functionality
13/XVIII	Network capabilities for the support of broadband services in ISDNs
14/XVIII	ISDN network capabilities for the support of additional and/or new services
15/XVIII	ISDN packet mode bearer services—services and user-network interface aspects
16/XVIII	ISDN architecture and functional principles, characterization methods, and reference configurations (including user-network interfaces)
17/XVIII	ISDN Protocol Reference Model
18/XVIII	ISDN Connection Types
19/XVIII	Network capabilities for the integration of mobile network services into the ISDN
20/XVIII	Layer 1 characteristics of ISDN interfaces and ISDN access
21/XVIII	Vocabulary for ISDNs
22/XVIII	Broadband ISDN influence on principles for video encoding
23/XVIII	Guidelines for implementing ISDN field trials in developing countries

do not take an active part in the technical work, but are entitled to be kept fully informed about the work of interest to them.

The purpose of the ISO is to promote the development of standardization and related activities in the world with a view to facilitating international exchanges of goods and services and to developing cooperation in the sphere of intellectual, scientific, technological, and economic activity. The results of ISO technical work are published as *International Standards*.

The scope of the ISO covers standardization in all fields except electrical and electronic engineering standards, which for equipment are the responsibility of the International Electrotechnical Commission (IEC). For several decades, the ISO has been the major forum for devising international information systems standards, principally through its Technical Committee 97. Telecommunication standards

TABLE 5.5 GENERAL STRUCTURE OF THE I SERIES RECOMMENDATIONS

PART I: GENERAL STRUCTURE—THE I.100-SERIES

Section 1: Frame of I Series Recommendations; Terminology
I.110   Preamble and general structure of the I Series Recommendations
I.111   Relationship with other Recommendations relevant to ISDNs
I.112   Vocabulary of terms for ISDN
I.113   Vocabulary of terms for broadband aspects of ISDNs

Section 2: Description of ISDNs
I.120   Integrated Services Digital Networks (ISDNs)
I.121   Broadband aspects of ISDNs
I.122   Framework for providing additional packet made services

Section 3: General Modeling Methods
I.130   The method for the characterization of telecommunication services supported by
                 an ISDN and network capabilities of an ISDN

Section 4: Telecommunication Network and Science Attributes
I.140   Attributes for the characterization of telecommunication services supported by
                 an ISDN and network capabilities of an ISDN
I.141   ISDN charging capability attributes

PART II: SERVICE CAPABILITIES—THE I.200 SERIES
I.200   Guidance to the I.200 Series

Section 1: General Aspects of Services in ISDN
I.210   Principles of telecommunication services supported by an ISDN and network
                 capabilities of an ISDN
I.211   Bearer services supported by an ISDN
I.212   Teleservices supported by an ISDN

Section 2: Common Aspects of Services in ISDN
I.220   Common dynamic description of basic telecommunication services
I.221   Common specific characteristics of services

Section 3: Bearer Services Supported by an ISDN
I.230   Definition of bearer services
I.231   Circuit mode bearer services categories
I.232   Packet mode bearer services categories

Section 4: Teleservices Supported by an ISDN
I.240   Definition of teleservices
I.241   Teleservices supported by an ISDN

Section 5: Supplementary Services in ISDN
I.250   Definition of supplementary services
I.251   Number identification services
I.252   Call offering services
I.253   Call completion services
I.254   Multiparty services
I.255   "Community of Interest" services
I.256   Charging services
I.257   Additional information transfer services

PART III: OVERALL NETWORK ASPECTS AND FUNCTIONS—THE I.300 SERIES

Section 1: Network Functional Principles
I.310   ISDN—network functional principles

TABLE 5.5 (continued)

Section 2: Reference Models

I.320	ISDN Protocol reference model
I.324	ISDN network architecture
I.325	Reference configurations for ISDN connection types
I.326	Reference configurations for relative network resource requirements
I.32x	ISDN hypothetical reference connections

Section 3: Numbering, Addressing, and Routing

I.330	ISDN numbering and addressing principles
I.331(E.164)	Numbering plan for the ISDN era
I.332	Numbering principles for interwork between ISDNs and dedicated networks with different numbering plans
I.333	Terminal selection in ISDN
I.334	Principles relating ISDN numbers/subaddress to the OSI reference model network layer addresses
I.335	ISDN routing principles

Section 4: Connection Types

I.340	ISDN connection types

Section 5: Performance Objectives

I.350	General aspects of Quality of Service and network performance in digital networks, including ISDNs
I.351	Recommendations in other Series including network performance objectives that apply at T reference points of an ISDN
I.352	Network performance objectives for call processing delays

PART IV: ISDN USER–NETWORK INTERFACES—THE I.400-SERIES

Section 1: ISDN User–Network Interfaces

I.410	General aspects and principles relating to Recommendations on ISDN user–network interfaces
I.411	ISDN user–network interfaces—Reference configurations
I.412	ISDN user–network interfaces—Interface structures and access capabilities

Section 2: Application of I Series Recommendations to ISDN User–Network Interfaces

I.420	Basic user–network interface
I.421	Primary rate user–network interface

Section 3: ISDN User–Network Interfaces: Layer 1 Recommendations

I.430	Basic user–network interface—Layer 1 specification
I.431	Primary rate user–network interface—Layer 1 specification
I.43x	Higher rate user–network interfaces

Section 4: ISDN User–Network Interfaces: Layer 2 Recommendations

I.440(Q.920)	ISDN user–network interface data link layer—general aspects
I.441(Q.921)	ISDN user–network interface data link layer specification

Section 5: ISDN User–Network Interfaces: Layer 3 Recommendations

I.450(Q.930)	ISDN user–network interface layer 3—general aspects
I.451(Q.931)	ISDN user–network interface layer 3 specification for basic call control
I.452(Q.932)	ISDN user–network interface layer 3 specification—generic procedures for the control of ISDN supplementary services

Section 6: Multiplexing Rate Adaptation and Support of Existing Interfaces

I.460	Multiplexing, rate adaptation, and support of existing interfaces

TABLE 5.5 (continued)

I.451(X.30)	Support of X.21 and X.21bis and X.20bis based Data Terminal Equipments (DTEs) by an Integrated Services Digital Network (ISDN)
I.462(X.31)	Support of packet mode terminal equipment by an ISDN
I.463(V.110)	Support of Data Terminal Equipments (DTEs) with V Series type interfaces by an Integrated Services Digital Network (ISDN)
I.464	Multiplexing, rate adaptation, and support of existing interfaces for restricted 64 kbit/s transfer capability
I.465	Support by an ISDN of data terminal equipment with V Series type interfaces with provision for statistical multiplexing

Section 7: Aspects of ISDN Affecting Terminal Requirements

I.470	Relationship of terminal functions to ISDN

PART V: INTERNETWORK INTERFACES—THE I.500 SERIES

I.500	General structure of ISDN interworking Recommendations
I.510	Definitions and general principles for ISDN interworking
I.511	ISDN-to-ISDN Layer 1 internetwork interface
I.515	Parameter exchange for ISDN interworking
I.520	General arrangements for network interworking between ISDNs
I.530	Network interworking between an ISDN and a public switched telephone network (PSTN)
I.540(X.321)	General arrangements for interworking between Circuit-Switched Public Data Networks (CSPDNS) and Integrated Services Digital Networks (ISDNs) for the provision of data transmission services
I.550(X.325)	General arrangements for interworking between Packet Switched Public Data Networks (PSPDNs) and Integrated Services Digital Networks (ISDNs) for the provision of data services
I.560(V.202)	Requirements to be met in providing the telex service within the ISDN

PART VI: MAINTENANCE PRINCIPLES—THE I.600 SERIES

I.601	General maintenance principles of ISDN subscriber access and subscriber installation
I.602	Application of maintenance principles to ISDN subscriber installation
I.603	Application of maintenance principles to ISDN basic accesses
I.604	Application of maintenance principles to ISDN primary rate accesses
I.605	Application of maintenance principles to static multiplexed ISDN basic accesses

have generally been left to the International Telecommunication Union. However, with the integration of these systems, the activity of the ISO increasingly overlaps with that of the ITU.

The ISO brings together the interests of producers, users (including consumers), governments, and the scientific community in the preparation of International Standards. ISO work is carried out through some 2200 technical bodies. More than 20,000 experts from all parts of the world participate each year in the ISO technical work, which to date has resulted in the publication of 4917 ISO standards.

Structurally, the ISO consists of a General Assembly that meets once every three years, a Council that meets at least once a year, a president, a vice-president, a treasurer, a secretary general, a Central Secretariat, technical committees and, if necessary, technical divisions.*

* See Arts. 5-7, ISO Constitution (1982).

The ISO process of adopting a standard normally proceeds in the context of a *project formal description* (FD) that has four phases: WD (working draft), DP (draft proposal), DIS (draft international standard), and IS (international standard). A ballot procedure is used to advance the standard to the next higher stage. The process typically takes 2 to 3 years.

All the ISDN-related activity in the ISO is confined to one major technical committee, JTC1. Extensive formal liaison activity occurs between all levels of the JTC1 and CCITT infrastructures.

Joint Technical Committee 1. Information Technology. JTC1 is responsible for one of the most dynamic areas in international standardization, information technologies. The secretariat for JTC1 is not the ISO headquarters staff at Geneva, but rather the American National Standards Institute at New York City. Its work takes place in an environment that is constantly changing and expanding in scope and importance. The organization of its work has been recently altered in order to keep up with these dynamics, including redesignation from TC97 to JTC1.

Within JTC1, an important division is Subcommittee 6—Telecommunications and Information Exchange between Systems. SC6 is responsible for more than 50 projects to develop standards for telecommunications and information transfer. This work is reflected in the subdivision of labor among four working groups that focus on the first four layers of the OSI model. The Committee acts as a liaison on multilayer issues. This includes such subjects as naming and addressing; connectionless data transmission; multi end-point data transmission; service conventions; conformance; management; developing the concepts necessary to model the use of multiple subchannels and relevant aspects of common channel signaling systems; understanding the relationship of particular facilities provided by ISDN to OSI; and harmonization in conjunction with CCITT of the architectures of OSI and ISDN.

Another important division, SubCommittee 21, focuses on open systems support services, including the Open Systems Interconnection (OSI) Reference Model, the OSI Management Framework, and their continuing development. This is the seven-layer model serving as a nearly all-encompassing master standard for the integrated telecommunication–information systems environment. Even the CCITT now follows this model.

SC21 therefore stands at the center of all the work going on in the field and has numerous liaisons with dozens of other groups inside and outside the ISO structure. Its closest relationship is with SC6 as the work affects layers 1 to 4.

5.2.1.3 Other global organizations. In addition to the ITU and ISO, other global international organizations have been or may be serving as forums for dealing with digital communication network matters.

Increasingly, user and business groups have begun to shape the standards process. The most prominent of these are the International Telecommunications Users Group (INTUG). INTUG is private international association of associations. It is concerned with the representation of the user community, mainly the business user in international matters. The members consists of users groups from ten nations and one other international organization, plus a number of transnational corporations. INTUG not only participates in the work of the CCITT as an organization, but also hosts occasional meetings on ISDN and exchanges information among its members.*

The International Telecommunications Satellite Organization (INTELSAT) also has a consultative committee and has international organization status to participate in CCITT activities. INTELSAT's ISDN-related activity has principally consisted of participation in CCITT and CCIR meetings relating to the use of satellite networks within ISDNs.

To a varying extent, other public and private international organizations such as the International Electrotechnical Commission (IEC) (recently integrated with ISO), the International Maritime Satellite Organization (Inmarsat), and the Society for Worldwide Interbank Financial Telecommunications (SWIFT) have similarly participated in CCITT ISDN forums and exchanged ISDN-related information within their own organizations and among their membership.

5.2.2 Regional Organizations

At the regional level, the European Conference of Postal and Telecommunication Administrations (CEPT) has been very active and influential in the digital network standardization process although in 1988 it transferred all of this activity to the new European Telecommunication Standards Institute. In addition, the European Computer Manufacturers Association (ECMA) promulgates important information systems standards for regional application. The Commission of European Communities (EC) began in 1986–1987 to become actively involved in many issues related to ISDN developments. This resulted in the mid-1987 adoption of a Green Paper on the development of a common market for telecommunication services and equipment that will likely significantly shape the processes and institutions within Europe regarding ISDN.† Indeed, coordinating the deployment of ISDN, including broadband ISDN, and the RACE (Research on Advanced Communications in Europe) program broadband research is one of the specific principal objectives of the EC effort.

5.2.2.1 European Telecommunication Standards Institute (ETSI). The European Telecommunication Standards Institute, located at Sophia Antipolis, France, is a mechanism for coordinating the positions of the European telecommunication community (especially for CCITT) and for promulgating European-wide standards. This activity was largely created from the former CEPT standards making infrastructure, known as the CCH.

The influence of this activity is illustrated by the work of the former Har-

---

* See *The International Telecommunication Users Group, Workshop on ISDN* (Cologne, 19 October 1984), ArTech House, 1985.

† See "Towards a Dynamic European Economy, Green Paper on the Development of the Common Market for Telecommunications Services and Equipment," Commission of the European Communities, Doc. COM(87) final, Brussels, 30 June 1987.

monization Coordination Committee (CCH) which created a Special Group on ISDN. The group became a means of coordinating plans and strategies on ISDN by developing common contributions for submission and support within CCITT Study Groups, especially XVIII. In the context of this activity, one of the most cohesive and influential documents on ISDN, entitled *ISDN in Europe*, was published in 1982.*

CEPT committees also have become increasingly active and influential in some of the most important ISDN developments. These principally include broadband ISDN, mobile digital systems, and integrated network management systems, where the Commercial Action Committee (CAC) work has been strongly influential in instituting new work in Study Group XVIII. The studies and reports of all these committees are models for the timely, comprehensive management of research, policy, and institutional activity and significantly shape the ISDN standardization process.

5.2.2.2 European Computer Manufacturers Association (ECMA).

The aim of the European Computer Manufacturers Association (ECMA) is to study and develop, in cooperation with other national and international organizations, standardized methods and procedures for use in conjunction with data-processing systems. It presently consists of 48 members and has a permanent secretariat in Geneva.

The focal point on the digital communications standards is Technical Committee 32 on OSI. ECMA seeks to develop standards and procedures that complement existing recommendations of CCITT and CEPT. This is illustrated by its recent release of a technical report on the maintenance at the interface between data processing equipment and private switching network in a European ISDN environment.

It is a project undertaken in the 1987–1988 time frame, however, that is having the greatest impact on ISDN developments: alternative models and architectures for interoperation of public and private digital networks. In late 1987, its issuance of a draft report on this subject has not only substantively contributed to global ISDN work, but spurred considerable interest in pursuing this work on a much larger scale. At the close of this chapter, it will be noted that the subject is now slated as a major area of activity for CCITT Study Group XVIII.

The development of a new universal framework that obeys certain rules by preserving compatibility with the OSI Reference Model was seen by ECMA as the best solution for promoting the convergence of various implementations of operations modes and the convergence of protocols for use with these modes. In the definition of the three models, attempts were made to maintain consistency with the CCITT Protocol Reference Model and the IEEE 802.1 Reference Model for local area networks. Although ECMA's fourth Draft Technical Report issued in late 1987 was restricted to data applications, development work on the architectural framework continues on the architectural modeling of signaling and nondata ap-

---

* See "ISDN in Europe," Special Group ISDN (GSI) 1982 Report on Integrated Services Digital Network Studies, CEPT Doc. T/CCH (82)30, Doc. T/GSI (82)71, Stockholm, November 1982.

plications that pertain to integrated services and integrated voice and data applications. This Technical Report is the product of ECMA committees, TC32 and TG7.

5.2.3 United States Organizations

A wide variety of organizational forums in the United States actively deals with digital communication standards. These forums can be grouped into four categories, although the boundaries frequently overlap: government policy making, international preparatory, domestic standards making, and professional colloquia. People, papers, and ideas regularly course their way through many of these forums in a continuing complex process of refinement and persuasion.

There are two dominant characteristics of these forums in the United States: most are nongovernmental and participation in all of them is overwhelmingly by the private sector. The activity typically brings together hundreds of experienced personnel from major telecommunications companies of the United States who use these forums to share their views and achieve a consensus on issues ranging from the minute details of a connector to the broad policies of network interconnection and interoperation. Of these people, the staff of the American Telephone and Telegraph Company (predivestiture) and ATT Communications, ATT Information Systems, and Bell Communications Research (postdivestiture) have clearly played a leading role.

5.2.3.1 Exchange Carriers Standards Association (ECSA). Prior to the AT&T divestiture, the massive Bell System Technical Standards provided the technical and operational specifications to allow the national telephone network to function in an integrated fashion. The only standards promulgated by the FCC were those for interconnecting simple telephone-type instruments to the network. AT&T de facto handled every other aspect of network operations.

It was realized that with the divestiture of the Bell Operating Company local exchange facilities, as well as with the increasing number of alternative interexchange carriers, some kind of organization was necessary to carry out the national network integration functions formerly assumed by AT&T. Out of this need, the Exchange Carriers Standards Association was born.

The ECSA consists of several different forums and committees and a small permanent staff with headquarters in Bethesda, Maryland.

Committee T1.   The focal point in ESCA for network standards is the "Standards Committee T1—Communications," usually simply referred to as T1. (It should not be confused, however, with digital primary rate service, also commonly referred to as T1.)

From the outset, Committee T1 has served as much more than a standards-writing body. The Committee is clearly a major focal point for many of the technical concerns of the industry and, for ISDN purposes, the national equivalent of the CCITT. Some of its meetings are even attended by representatives from other governments and standards bodies around the world. In some respects the draft standards and technical reports that are now emerging from the Working Groups and Technical Subcommittees are only the "tip of the iceberg." A major accomplishment of these groups is their success in bringing issues into focus, analyzing alternatives, and developing consensus.

Committee T1 operates in accordance with bylaws that define the scope and responsibilities, membership requirements, infrastructure, meeting requirements, and due process procedures for adoption and appeal of its actions. This process is complemented with similar procedures required as part of T1's association with the American National Standards Institute.*

Supporting the mission of Committee T1 are the resources of 89 member organizations representing exchange carriers, interexchange carriers and resellers, manufacturers, and vendors, as well as users and general interest participants. Elected officers of the T1 Committee consist of a chair, vice-chair, and 12 interest group representatives, and technical subcommittee chairs and vice-chairs.

Projects flow into T1, where they are addressed within a structure of Technical Subcommittees. Projects intended to yield candidate American National Standards are submitted to ANSI.

T1's work program also includes liaison projects related to continuing work in international forums, such as the International Telegraph and Telephone Consultative Committee (CCITT). In this case, industry positions are formulated and submitted to the U.S. Department of State's USCCITT public advisory committee. T1 is the principal source of U.S. submissions to CCITT on ISDN and Common Channel Signaling System No. 7. A third activity is the development of technical reports. These reports represent the consensus view of the committee and may precede the development of an industry standard or may present data or procedures that would not necessarily result in a standard. During 1988, T1 was engaged in approximately 70 standards development and study projects.

Committee T1 consists of a main committee, an elected Advisory Group and six Technical Subcommittees. Each subcommittee establishes Working Groups, as needed, to address specific projects.

All elements of T1 are subordinate to the main committee. This committee establishes the organizational structure, elects officers, approves standards and study projects, and approves draft standards for submission to ANSI. Technical subcommittees and authorized to communicate directly with external groups to assure appropriate liaison.

Advisory Group. The T1 Advisory Group (T1AG) provides advisory and managerial functions for the T1 membership. The voting members of the T1AG are the T1 chair, T1 vice-chair, and elected representatives or their alternates. Nonvoting members include the Technical Subcommittee chairs and the T1 secretary.

During the past year T1 assisted the Office of the U.S. Trade Representative by presenting its standards-making procedures to representatives from Japan and

---

* See Bylaws of Standards Committee T1, *Telecommunications*, August 21, 1987; *Procedures for the Development and Coordination of American National Standards*, American National Standards Institute, 1983.

the Commission of European Communities.   A T1-like committee, the Telecommunications Technology Council (TTC), was formed in Japan in 1985, and functions like Committee T1, but also integrates radio technologies.   It is expected that ongoing liaison with the Japanese TTC will be developed over time.

T1 subcommittees and their work are described next. To some extent, however, the organization of this work changed in 1987 with the creation of a new T1 Subcommittee T1S1 for Services Architecture and Signaling, into which former T1D1 ISDN-related activities were merged.

Technical Subcommittee T1E1: Network Interfaces. This subcommittee recommends standards and develops technical reports related to the interfaces between customer premises equipment (including private networks) and the networks of exchange, interexchange, and other carriers.   Work includes the physical and electromagnetic characteristics of the interfaces, as well as the transmission, signaling, and protocol definitional aspects of these interfaces.

Technical Subcommittee T1S1: Integrated Services Digital Networks. This subcommittee recommends standards and develops technical reports related to all aspects of Integrated Services Digital Networks. The work includes ISDN services, user-to-network and network-to-network interfaces (including signaling), gateways and protocols, protocol architecture; ISDN layer specifications; numbering plans and administration; and other necessary matters.

The T1S1 Working Groups are:

T1S1.1–ISDN Architecture and Services
T1S1.2–ISDN Switching and Signaling Protocols
T1S1.3–Common Channel Signaling
T1S1.4–Individual Channel Signaling Interfaces

In addition to these three groups, a fourth, the T1D1.1 Subworking Group on Broadband ISDN (BB), has grown very rapidly in size and activity during late 1986–1987 as the U.S. counterpart to the CCITT Study Group XVIII Broadband Task Group (BBTG).

Current T1S1 projects include the entire panoply of ISDN standardization matters before the CCITT, as well as some that are unique to the U.S. environment. These include:

- All matters related to broadband ISDN
- Principles of user–network access interfaces
- Definition of ISDN service aspects
- Network aspects of ISDN
- Maintenance and operations principles
- ISDN architecture functional model
- ISDN protocol reference model
- Numbering and addressing principles

- Definition of internetwork interfaces
- Interworking of ISDN services with services on existing networks: ISDN routing principles
- ISDN basic access interface for application at reference points S and T—Layer 1 specification
- ISDN primary rate interface for application at S and T reference points—Layer 1 specification
- Standard for ISDN basic access interface for application at the network side of NT1—Layer 1 specification
- Standards for rate adaptation
- Multiplexing and support of existing interfaces
- Standard for ISDN data link layer protocol (LAPD)
- Standard for call control protocol involving ISDNs and for related user equipment
- User-to-user signaling
- Minimal ISDN user–network signaling specification
- ISDN call control interworking standards

Many American National Standards have recently been adopted. Some deal with the minimal user–network signaling specifications for basic access and primary access interfaces. Others address the development of a basic access layer 1 interface standard for application on the network side of NT1 or U interface. Development of specifications for basic and primary access interfaces at the S and T reference points (layer 1 and layer 2) has reached maturity as well as exchange–interexchange signaling protocols.

In addition to work directed toward developing American National Standards, T1S1 has been the principal source of contributions to the U.S. CCITT ISDN Joint Working Party, mainly for CCITT Study Groups XVIII and XI.

Technical Subcommittee T1M1: Internetwork Operations, Maintenance, Administration and Provisioning. This subcommittee recommends standards and develops technical reports related to internetwork planning and engineering, internetwork operations, testing and operations support, and equipment and administrative support. The work includes traffic routing plans; measurements and forecasts; trunk group planning; circuit and facility ordering; network tones and announcements; network management; circuit and facility installation, lineup, restoration, routine maintenance, fault location, and repair; contact points for internetwork operations; network access; operator interfaces; methods for charging; and accounting and billing data.

With a new interest within international ISDN forums on intelligent networks and network management capabilities, the work of T1M1 achieved a more prominent level of interest, particularly in the area of protocols for OS/NE interfaces.

In addition to work directed toward American National Standards, T1M1 also made contributions to the USCCITT Study Group C on the subject of man–machine languages (CCITT Study Group X) and to SG IV on OS/NE interfaces.

Technical Subcommittee T1Q1: Performance. This subcommittee recommends standards and develops technical reports related to performance within the U.S. telecommunications network at and between the carrier-to-carrier and carrier-to-customer interfaces. The work includes the development of network performance objectives from the customer interface-to-customer interface, focusing on the performance for voice, voiceband data, audio program, television, digital, and wideband analog telecommunications.

In addition to work directed toward developing American National Standards, T1Q1 has submitted contributions to USCCITT Study Groups C and D and the ISDN Joint Working Party for performance questions in CCITT Study Groups VII and XVIII.

Technical Subcommittee T1X1: Digital Hierarchy and Synchronization. This subcommittee recommends standards and develops technical reports related to the interconnection and interoperability of telecommunications networks. The work focuses on interfaces between carriers. Included are the physical, electromagnetic, and protocol aspects of these transmission and switching interfaces.

The T1X1 Working Groups are:

T1X1.3—Synchronization Interfaces
T1X1.4—Metallic Hierarchial Interfaces
T1X1.5—Optical Hierarchical Interfaces
T1X1.6—Tributary Analysis Interfaces

The T1X1.5 working group is particularly important with respect to broadband ISDN because of the pioneering work done in developing the Synchronous Optical Network Standard (SONET), which appears to be the preferred near-term transport technique. In addition to work directed toward developing American National Standards, T1X1 has been the principal source of U.S. contributions to the CCITT on common channel signaling questions, but in 1988 the work was transferred to T1S1.

Technical Subcommittee T1Y1: Specialized Subjects. This subcommittee recommends standards and develops technical reports related to specialized telecommunications projects not addressed by other T1 subcommittees. The work includes the development of standardized processing of voice, audio, video, and data signals and the development of environmental standards for exchange and interexchange carrier networks.

5.2.3.2 Federal Communications Commission (FCC).

The Federal Communications Commission (FCC) is the government agency in the United States generally responsible for the regulation of telecommunications. It is known as an independent regulatory agency because it is a creature of the United States Congress and is not part of the Executive Branch, which has its own agencies that regulate government use of telecommunications. The FCC's regulatory scope is broadly subdivided into two major categories under its statutory charter, the Communications Act of 1934: common carrier telecommunication services and the use of radio stations. In addition, the commission has a kind of general jurisdiction over all telecommunication services, common carrier and otherwise, which has been interpreted to include ancillary information systems.

The FCC exercises its power in a variety of ways. It *authorizes* companies or individuals to provide common carrier services or use radio facilities or undersea cable facilities. It *prescribes* certain technical and operational criteria for telecommunication systems and equipment and the rates that market dominant providers of common carrier services may charge. It *certifies* that equipment complies with certain technical standards. The FCC also, in cooperation with the Departments of State and Commerce, *determines* U.S. positions with respect to activities of international organizations and negotiations with foreign governments.

The commission must exercise this authority through fairly formal processes that are almost entirely public and subject to judicial review. Most of its general policies and its specific rules are published in tentative form and public comment received prior to adoption. The important documents adopting rules and policies are published as part of the commission's permanent legal record, the FCC Reports, as well as in the *Federal Register*. The commission's rules are contained in Title 47 of the Code of Federal Regulations. All the materials associated with any particular proceeding are contained in a *docket* file at Commission headquarters.

The FCC's authorization processes vary in formality from the simple filing of a form to formal mechanisms similar to rule and policy making. This is particularly true when the authorization process invokes a request for a waiver of some general rule or policy.

Although the FCC's explicit standards on ISDN are nonexistent, it is the commission's policies emanating from rule and policy making proceedings and the authorization of particular services under tariff that can have far-reaching effects on digital network standards. The *Computer III Decision* mentioned above has a profound effect. Other examples include such areas as ISDN, centrex, and protocol processing.

The commission clearly has a significant basis for involvement in ISDN matters. It is, however, a rather complex involvement because most of the ISDN work has been occurring entirely within the research and development efforts of private companies, or within private-sector organizations, or within the context of U.S. participation in international organizations. The commission has a broad regulatory purview over the first two of these activities and shares the third with Executive Branch agencies, especially the Department of State and the Department of Commerce.*

In 1983 the Commission took the rather rare step of instituting a policy-

---

* The Department of Commerce has established a specialized division, the National Telecommunication and Information Administration (NTIA), for dealing with telecommunication and related matters. See, generally, Executive Order 12046 (regarding the respective roles of the FCC, Department of State and Department of Commerce on international telecommunication policy). In addition, the National Communications System (NCS) plays a significant role in coordinating national-security-related policies.

making proceeding largely looking prospectively at ISDN issues, but has done nothing further on ISDN, except for a brief section in its *Computer III* ruling.

5.2.3.3 Department of State (DOS). The Department of State is indirectly involved in communication standards largely because of the CCITT, a body of the ITU that was created by a treaty instrument among governments and has historically served as a meeting ground for government representatives. The State Department has chosen to discharge its representational responsibility in two ways. The first is through two public advisory committees, the United States Organization for the International Telegraph and Telephone Consultative Committee (CCITT) and a similar organization for the CCIR that recommend U.S. policies and contributions. These committees are often referred to as the USCCITT and USCCIR, and the State Department maintains approved charters defining the responsibilities and structures of both organizations.

The second means by which the department effects the representation of the United States in these forums is through the formation, accreditation, and conduct of delegations to many of the CCIR and CCITT meetings, or otherwise bestowing the title of "recognized private operating agency (RPOA)" or "scientific and industrial organization (SIO)" on U.S. companies. These designations allow companies and organizations, upon payment of a contribution to the ITU, to participate in their own name (as opposed in the name of the United States) in CCITT or CCIR activities.

On substantive policy matters, an Executive Order on international telecommunications policy directs the Department of State to look to both the FCC and NTIA for advice in most telecommunications matters.* In the case of the CCITT, however, the Department of State had historically relied on the companies actually involved in the provision of telegraph and telephone service, Western Union, AT&T, RCA and a few other international carriers, to perform most required policy-making and representational functions. During the last two decades, the number of companies involved in these activities has significantly increased, along with the scope and importance of the work. Nonetheless, this activity has remained largely a private sector function. Consonant with this, organizations such as ECSA have been used increasingly as a preclearance mechanism for documents.

In the case of the ISO, however, the Department of State has deferred entirely to the American National Standards Institute (ANSI), a private organization, to represent the United States in all its activities.

The charter for the USCCITT specifies the following purposes for the advisory committee(s):

(a) promote the best interests of the United States in CCITT activities;

(b) provide advice on matters of policy and positions in preparation for CCITT Plenary Assemblies and meetings of the international CCITT Study Groups;

(c) provide advice on the disposition of proposed contributions (documents) to the international CCITT;

---

* See Executive Order 12046.

(d) assist in the resolution of administrative/procedural problems pertaining to United States CCITT activities.

The USCCITT infrastructure specified in its charter consists of a National Committee, which is a steering body having purview over the agendas and work of four study groups and a joint working party:

A. U.S. Government Regulatory Policies
B. Telegraph Operations
C. Worldwide Telephone Network
D. Data Transmission ISDN Joint Working Party

In practice, however, the National Committee has largely concerned itself with the CCITT Plenary Assembly occurring every four years, and the study groups and working party have operated fairly autonomously. They determine de facto the disposition of proposed contributions to the CCITT.

Of these USCCITT groups, the ISDN Joint Working Party assumed a leading role in approving U.S. contributions to CCITT study groups and working parties when it was first created in the early 1980s.

Notice of the meetings must be published at least 15 days in advance in the *Federal Register*. The role of the Joint Working Party in practice is, however, rather limited. The documents it considers are almost invariably made available only at the meetings. Typically hundreds of pages of complex and detailed material are disposed of in only a few hours, with little discussion of underlying policies or rationale. However, the use of preparatory committees of the Exchange Carriers Standards Association (ECSA) beginning at mid-1984 has improved this situation. The ECSA Committee T1S1 on ISDN currently serves as a preclearance mechanism for most documents destined for CCITT major study group meetings.

The work of the CCIR in ISDN matters has been minimal. The USCCIR operates in a similar fashion to the USCCITT, except it generally has a domestic infrastructure that directly parallels that of the international groups. For example, there is a USCCIR Study Group 1 to prepare for the work of the international CCIR Study Group 1. The focus of USCCIR groups on ISDN remains almost nonexistent.

5.2.3.4 American National Standards Committee (ANSC) Subcommittee on Information Processing Systems.

The American National Standards Institute (ANSI) was founded in 1918 as nonprofit organization that coordinates voluntary standards activities in the United States. Its membership consists of approximately 220 nonprofit organizational members and almost 1000 company members representing virtually every facet of commerce, trade, and industry. It is governed by a board of directors and most of its work is carried out under the direction of various councils. An extremely wide range of standards is developed and adopted on a consensus basis within the elaborate infrastructures of accredited committees. ANSI also represents the United States in two international telecommunication and information-related organizations, the International Organization for Standardization (ISO) and the International Electrotechnical Commission (IEC).

Two accredited standards committees operate under the procedures of ANSI that are directly related to digital communication standards: X3, Information Processing Systems; and T1, Telecommunications. Committee T1 is a creature of the ECSA, discussed previously. Committee X3 is a large and complex organization dealing with a wide range of information-processing systems matters, with secretarial support provided by the Computer and Business Equipment Manufacturers Association (CBEMA). The focal point for digital communication activities in X3 is the subgroup on communications, Technical Committee X3S3.

Committee X3 and its various task groups serve as clearinghouses for information brought to the meetings by liaisons from virtually all the other relevant international and domestic groups, as well as a mechanism for directly effecting U.S. participation in ISO JTC1 and indirectly in the CCITT. Committee X3 performs this latter function through the preparation of contributions and position papers adopted by consensus, with extensive use of balloting by mail.

5.2.3.5 Institute of Electrical and Electronic Engineers (IEEE).

The most prominent and active professional organization in the United States focusing on digital communication standards is the Institute of Electrical and Electronic Engineers (IEEE). The IEEE and its various subdivisions largely disseminate information through their publications and meetings. They also engage in some important standards development activity.

The IEEE was founded as the Institute of Radio Engineers at the turn of the century and merged in January 1963 with the American Institute of Electrical Engineers to form the IEEE. It is headquartered in New York City. Its major specialty subdivisions are known as societies and operate somewhat autonomously.

With the Computer Society, the 802 Committee on Local Network Standards has been working since February 1980 on local area networks. It began its effort by studying the subject of LANs generally, and wound up developing four specific, important standards: a carrier sense multiple access standard (CMSA/CD) for the workstation environment, a token bus standard particularly useful to manufacturers, a token ring standard used by IBM for its PCs, and a link layer protocol common to all networks. The committee's meetings are now experiencing extensive participation, and 802 is the focal point for a broad range of work on local networks, including metropolitan area and broadband fiber-optic networks.

The IEEE Communications Society is very active in providing many forums for disseminating information concerning digital communication networks, but sponsors no standards groups. Nevertheless, the *IEEE Transactions on Communications*, biannual symposia on ISDN, annual Globecoms, International Conferences on Communication, and International Switching Symposia all provide extensive opportunities for individuals throughout the industry to collectively discuss important issues and developments.

The IEEE's 802 Committee on Local Network Standards has been working for several years on a local area network standard. The standard may be used in conjunction with ISDNs in the provision of local services.

The IEEE Instrumentation Society sponsors committee work devoted to digital communication for measurement applications and has developed the 488 bus standard for that purpose.

5.2.3.6 Federal Telecommunications Standards Committee (FTSC).

Within the U.S. government, there exists a Federal Telecommunication Standards Committee (FTSC) under the aegis of the National Communications System (NCS). The NCS is the government agency charged with providing integrated telecommunications among the separate facilities of the other U.S. government agencies. Some ISDN issues have been considered within the NCS/FTSC, information disseminated, and issues analyzed in its technical bulletins. Within the U.S. government, NCS has remained substantively involved in the ISDN standards-making process and coordinates ISDN standards making within the government community.

5.2.3.7 Corporation for Open Systems (COS).

On January 9, 1986, more than 30 of the largest telecommunications and information companies in the United States came together to charter and fund the nonprofit Corporation for Open Systems (COS). Its purpose is "to provide an international vehicle for accelerating the introduction of interoperable multi-vendor products and services operating under agreed-to open systems interconnection, integrated services digital network, and related international standards to assure acceptance of an open network architecture in world markets."

Like similar efforts now getting underway in Europe and Japan (SPAG and POSI, respectively), COS is not a public forum for devising ISDN standards. Nonetheless, its role in promoting such standards and embellishing them through conformance testing specifications and programs merits its inclusion here.

COS is presently headquartered in the Washington, D.C., suburb of Vienna, Virginia. Most of the standards-related activity is now centered in the Architecture Committee under the guidance of the Strategy Forum Committee.

5.3 NEW DEVELOPMENTS

In 1988–1989, several highly significant developments have occurred in Study Group XVIII that are worthy of note.

At the last general meeting during the 1985–1988 period of the ISDN Experts Group (Seoul, January 25 to February 5, 1988) agreement was reached on a new recommendation on broadband aspects of ISDN, designated I.121. As the foreword to the text notes, "this recommendation is the first one on broadband aspects of ISDN, a new subject of standardization." It will likely be the major reference document for all the standards and networking planning work subsequently unfolding on the new high-speed switching and transmission technologies described in Chapter 9.

The Recommendation sets forth planning targets, service descriptions, architecture models, asynchronous transfer mode (ATM) characteristics, broadband channel rates, user–network interface (UNI) specifications, network characteristics, and adaptation between ATM and non-ATM parts of ISDN. The section on "evolution" states:

Target network. Asynchronous transfer mode (ATM) is the target solution for implementing a B-ISDN. It will influence the standardization of digital hierarchies and multiplexing structures, switching, and interfaces for broadband signals.

ATM is used in this recommendation as addressing a specific packet oriented transfer mode using asynchronous time division multiplexing technique, i.e., the multiplexed information flow is organised in fixed size blocks, called cells. A cell consists of a user information field and header, where the primary role of the header is to identify cells belonging to the same virtual channel on an asynchronous time division multiplex. Cells are assigned on demand, depending on the source activity and the available resources. Cell sequence integrity on a virtual channel is guaranteed by the ATM network.

ATM is a connection-oriented technique, where header values are assigned to each section of a connection at call set-up and released at the end of the call. Signalling and user information are carried on separate virtual channels.

ATM is designed to offer a flexible transfer capability common to all services.

Evolution steps. B-ISDNs will be based on the concepts developed for ISDNs and may evolve by progressively incorporating additional functions and services (e.g., multimedia applications).

The deployment of B-ISDN may require a period of time extending over one or more decades. Thus arrangements must be developed for the interworking of services on B-ISDNs and services on other networks.

In the evolution towards a B-ISDN, digital end-to-end connectivity will be obtained in part via plant and equipment used in existing and planned networks, such as digital transmission and switching. Relevant Recommendations for these constituent elements of a B-ISDN are contained in the appropriate series of Recommendations of CCITT and of CCIR.

In the early stages of the evolution of B-ISDN, some interim user–network arrangements (e.g., combinations such as Synchronous Transfer Mode and ATM techniques) may need to be adopted in certain countries to facilitate early penetration of digital service capabilities.

The achievement of global agreement on this recommendation within a period of 24 months attests to the importance accorded to these developments.

In addition to adopting I.121, the Seoul meeting developed the basic plan of work for Study Group XVIII for the 1989–1992 period. The subject matrix is reproduced in Table 5.6, and the subject list is reproduced in Table 5.7. As can be noted, the work is heavily oriented around ATM and other broadband developments, as well as intelligent network and network management concepts. In

TABLE 5.6 CCITT STUDY GROUP XVIII MATRIX OF ITEMS FOR NEW STUDY
GROUP XVIII QUESTIONS 1989–1992 STUDY PERIOD

	Reference Configurations; Architecture and Modeling	Network Aspects of Services	General Principles of User–Network Interfaces	Layer 1 User–Network Interfaces	Network Aspects of ISDN	Network Interworking	Vocabulary
Broadband ISDN	R, S	B, L	N	P	C, D–H	K	A, T
64-kbps ISDN	S	I, J, M	N	Q	D–H, I, J	K	A, T
Intelligent network capabilities	S	M				K	A, T
Network management control	S	M					A, T
Private networks	S				D–H	K	A, T
Mobile networks	O, S	M	M	Q	D–H	K	A, T

TABLE 5.7 CCITT STUDY GROUP XVIII DRAFT OUTLINE OF AREAS OF STUDY 1989–1992
STUDY PERIOD

A. General question on ISDN

B. Asynchronous transfer mode (ATM)
    For which applications
    Definition of basic characteristics
    General principles for introducing ATM into existing environments
    Impact on network functions and capabilities (signaling, switching, transmission, support of services, etc.)
    Relation between user–network interface (UNI) and network node interface (NN1)

C. New digital hierarchy
    Synchronous hierarchy
    NN1
    Impact on ATM

D–H. Performance aspects
    Continuation of questions 13–17 modified as necessary and enlarged to include B-ISDN, mobile, private network issues as well as hypothetical configurations for multipoint and broadcast services

I. Impact of new types of signal processing/encoding on network capabilities of the 64-kbps ISDN (such as signaling, routing, interworking); for example:
    Audiovisual services
    Speech packetization
    32- and 64-kbps encoding

J. New and/or additional requirements/functions to be implemented in an ISDN arising from, for example:
    Capabilities for effecting charging

TABLE 5.7 (continued)

	Numbering/routing
	Terminal selection
	Support of other Study Groups
K.	Interworking of ISDN with:
	PSTN
	PSPDN
	CSPDN
	ISDN
	Telex
	Private networks
	B-ISDN
	Intelligent networks
	Mobile services (including satellite-based mobile services networks)
L.	Impact of broadband services on network capabilities including:
	Service rates required
	Multipoint and broadcast connections
	Stage 2 description of services
	Signaling and control functions
	Numbering
M.	Use of network capabilities of the 64-kbps ISDN for the support of new services, including stage 2 of the service descriptions, and specification of any additional network capabilities needed to support new or improved services; for example:
	Audiovisual services
	Teleaction services on the D channel
	Additional packet-mode bearer service
	Intelligent network services/VANS
	Mobile network services
	Maintenance and management services
	Universal personal telecommunication services
N.	General principles of user–network interfaces, including:
	Updating, as necessary, reference configurations for 64-kbps ISDN
	Reference configurations for user–network interfaces of mobile services
	Reference configurations for B-ISDN user–network interfaces
O.	Integration of mobile network services into ISDN, including reference configurations
P.	Layer 1 characteristics of B-ISDN
Q.	Layer 1 aspects of 64-kbps ISDN, including:
	Updating/completing Recs. I.430, I.431
	Extensions, if any, for mobile services in ISDN
R.	Architectures, models, and connection types and reference configurations for B-ISDN including broadcast and multipoint
S.	Additions to modeling, architectures, and methodologies to incorporate the needs of:
	Further capabilities of the 64-kbps ISDN
	Network management and control functions
	Private networks
	Mobile networks/services
	Intelligent network services
T.	Vocabulary and definition of terms
U.	Impact of B-ISDN capabilities on coding techniques

addition, there is significant interest in establishing reference models and inter-operation approaches for private and mobile networks.

This focus is sure to be mirrored in the entire panoply of global, regional, and national forums constituting the ISDN standardization process. This appears to be the predominant future of ISDN.

In addition, the following international developments related to the ISDN standardization process are also worthy of note.

- The European Commission has emulated the U.S. ONA concept in the form of Open Network Provisioning (ONP), which is being broadly specified by the EC and specified within the new European Telecommunication Standards Institute (ETSI).

- Numerous technologies and techniques that are collectively dealt with under the concept of broadband ISDN have had substantial impacts on the standards-making forums worldwide. Also of significant importance are ISDN matters that proceed under the concept of intelligent network. This involves, for example, Operations Systems work, which proceeds in the international arena under the name Telecommunications Management Network (TMN), Signaling System No. 7, and others.

- Considerable ISDN work is now carried on in CCITT Study Groups I, II, III, XI, and XV, as a result of decisions taken at the Melbourne IXth Plenary.

- Digital mobile radio delivery of ISDN capabilities is receiving substantial attention in standards groups with considerable liaison between nonradio and radio activities.

- The U.S. National Bureau of Standards, re-formed as the National Institute for Science and Technology (NIST), is playing a significant role in establishing ISDN standards and assuring conformance with OSI models.

CHAPTER 6

Components for ISDN: Partitioning, Definition, and Realization

GUSTAV LAUB

Intel Corporation

ABSTRACT

This chapter discusses the requirements for application-specific components for ISDN. The architectures of the functional groups most numerous in the system, TE and NT, are presented. A large number of functional blocks that are used in these systems are discussed. It is found that these blocks can be partitioned into a small number of components useful in many applications of interest, if some local component interface standards are followed to allow "mix and match." This is compared with the approaches of several commercial component manufacturers, taking into account the market segment each has targeted. It is concluded that further integration will continue in current directions, concentrating most heavily on the TE, which is both the most numerous and the most cost-sensitive system node.

6.1 OVERVIEW

Two classes of applications within ISDN have been identified as good candidates for semicustom VLSI components. These are terminal equipment (TE) and network terminations (NT), each of which encompasses a large range of complexities. Network termination equipment is the equipment that lies around the periphery of the ISDN network, just inside the terminals; it can be specified to a large extent with the CCITT I-series protocols. Terminal equipment interfaces either to non-ISDN equipment or directly to the user, and is thus dependent on both ISDN and non-ISDN protocols.

Collectively, these applications represent a very large percentage of the total number of nodes within any given system. They are where the communications channels are least multiplexed. To minimize the number of components per line, where line usually refers to the basic user rate of 2B + D, fixed functions have been integrated into VLSI components, which can be produced in large quantities at low incremental cost. Standards were agreed on when it became clear that the market would be maximized not by isolated islands of proprietary protocols and hardware, but by a global network using a uniform set of standards.

The I-series recommendations for ISDN systems [1] presently define protocols to be used on layers 1, 2, and 3 at TE and NT nodes. They do not, however, define how or where the protocols are to be implemented. Some applications require only that layer 1 functions be present, as in the NT1, which is a physical-layer relay station; some require that all layers be present, as in an ISDN phone, which, although outwardly simplistic, must realize protocols for all seven levels of the OSI model. The system designer retains some freedom to determine an attractive solution given a particular set of constraints, architectural, commercial, legal, financial, and practical. The standard diagram of two seven-layer protocol stacks connected by a physical medium does not present the situation in its entirety. The complexities of the protocols require significant amounts of hardware and/or software at each level. In some cases the distinction between levels is blurred by the combined implementation of related functions. The final partitioning between blocks and between hardware and software is an exercise in capturing a moving target. These constraints have as much to do with the final form of an implementation as any of the formalized protocols. Architectures must always be chosen to be flexible, to allow future expansion, adaption, and integration.

The ISDN physical, link, and network layers provide low layer services to both ISDN and non-ISDN systems. Protocols of the D channel must always be followed since it is used for all supervisory functions. The B channels do not require the use of ISDN protocols because they provide a physical-layer service on which other protocols may be superimposed, although for broadest compatibility they should be used. The requirements of each level necessary to perform the functions outlined by the 1984 CCITT Redbook I-series recommendations are summarized in Table 6.1. The height of the protocol stack at any node determines

TABLE 6.1 FUNCTIONS DIVIDED BY CHANNEL AND LAYER

Layer	Common	D Channel	B Channels
L1	Interface to medium Activation Transmission Error detect Channel identification Power provisions Interface to L2	Priority resolution	Transmit enable I.515 protocol identification
L2	Interface to L1 Interface to L3	Packetization Elements of procedure	Packetization Elements of procedure Rate adaption
L3	Interface to L2 Interface to L4	Connection management Network services	Link management User services

the exact protocols needed.   The TE must implement all OSI levels, while the simplest NT can be strictly a level 1 device.

Although different protocols are used on the B and D channels, it is evident that the types of tasks to be done at each level are similar, whether for B or D. However, because of the very different nature of the information conveyed and the multiplexing of the channels in time, they are generally routed to physically separate processors.   The majority of initial ISDN standards work has been done for the D channel.   The B channels have been assumed to be largely transparent, to be host to existing protocols such as V.24 [2] and X.25 [3].   More recent developments have produced B-channel specific protocols such as V.110 (to adapt the synchronous X.21 R interface using block codes) and V.120 (to adapt asynchronous protocols using HDLC packets).

Because the D channel carries the signaling packets, it must be processed in the network as well as the terminal; the B channels need not be.   This creates a difference between NT and TE hardware.   A terminal must perform several layers of processing for the information in both B and D channels.   Where the NT implements only layer one, higher layer processing is done at the terminal and deeper within the network.   The large amount of processing and signaling bandwidth necessary to implement D-channel processing centrally for an entire switch often leads to the decision to implement some D-channel preprocessing at the network periphery.   This provides a mechanism to separate signaling packets from user data packets for routing through different network hardware.

D-channel services fall into three categories: supervisory services, where the network arbitrates the allocation of B-channel bandwidth between a pair of subscribers; end services, in which the network itself is the endpoint of the message exchange with a subscriber; and packet services, as one node in a large packet network.   The last two may be grouped together as connectivity functions, where the network passes packets between upper layers of applications but does nothing to the data itself.   Supervisory messages must always be interpreted within the switching network.   When the connectivity involves other network switches, it is necessary to generate messages in a common connectivity protocol, such as CCITT Signaling System No. 7, a standard used between networks over trunks.   In these cases, the local switching system serves as a layer 3 node within the global network.

6.2 PARTITIONING OF FUNCTIONS

The recommendations are very careful not to limit the ways in which one may realize a conforming system.   The three lowest layers most important to the development of ISDN hardware can be built in many ways, from strictly serial processing (three strictly separated blocks) to fully merged (one comprehensive block), as shown in Fig. 6.1.

The realities of equipment design tell us that the more "boxes" we define, the more interfaces there are.   These in turn require more coordination and specification.   It is easier to specify the external behavior of a group of functions than it is to specify that plus several internal interfaces.   Some efficiency of realization

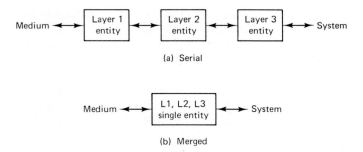

(a) Serial

(b) Merged

Figure 6.1 Serial and merged architectures.

may also be gained by having broader and more efficient access to information passed between levels, combining the functions of several levels in one software or hardware block. We will see when discussing specific commercial products that several significantly different approaches have turned up.

For discussion, we will assume initially that processing for each level is realized in a physically separate processing unit, or block. Later we will return and discuss the possibilities of combining functions. Since the OSI model is most cleanly applied to packet communications we will use the example of D-channel signaling packets. The packets are assumed to have been separated from the combined 2B + D flow in the layer 1 block. The CCITT recommendations include descriptions of *primitives* to be exchanged between layers (control/status bits and messages), but not of means to transfer either the data or the primitives. Thus, where each layer is realized as a separate entity, it is left to the implementer to establish the details of the interface between layers. Figure 6.2 shows the complete set of interface primitives necessary for implementation of D-channel layers 1, 2, and 3 in three separate blocks.

The system designer must minimize the complexity of the overall system. If he has chosen to implement layer 2, for example, as a separate entity, he needs to specify how all the primitives and the data (packets) are transferred between layers 1 and 2, between layers 2 and 3, and between layer 2 and the management entity. In each case, the frequency of transfer, data rate, physical distance of

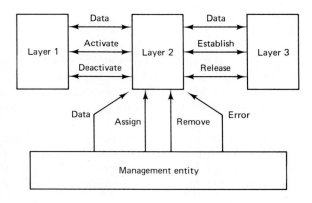

Figure 6.2 Primitive interfaces for D channel.

transfer, and importance (for example, response time) of the entity to be transferred play a part in determining the type of realization. The connection types most often used are shown in Table 6.2. Standards have been established by manufacturers for most of these connection types. Many of them predate ISDN, but because ISDN has been designed around some constraints of the preexisting voice network and interfaces to preestablished communications protocols, many non-ISDN-specific components can be used within the overall system. Where real-time connectivity is maintained to level 2, serial connections are most often used; once data, especially packets, leave the synchronous world for processing, they are transformed to a parallel representation for use in microcomputer systems.

Partitioning of functions must be considered across two axes, level and channel, because of the widely varying requirements for processing B and D channels at different network nodes. As the basic user interface on the physical-level multiplexes a minimum of four channels (B1, B2, D, and layer 1 signaling), there are quite a number of possible partitionings. Proposals must be evaluated on flexibility, extensibility, completeness, and simplicity so that many applications may be covered with small variations on a single architectural theme.

6.3 SOFTWARE PROTOCOL PROCESSING

Software and hardware both can be effectively used to process layers 2 and 3 of LAP-D or LAP-B. Several microcoded firmware components are available that take the hardware approach for layer 2, the more concisely defined of the two layers. Software solutions have the cost advantage of being able to use higher-volume general-purpose components and retain the flexibility of easy upgrades, but they have the disadvantage that the initial software development investment is quite high. With the availability of complete hardware/software bundles, the software development cost is overcome, and the implementation is as straightforward with the general-purpose components as with the ISDN-specific ones. Only

TABLE 6.2 CONNECTION TYPES

Type	Example
Parallel dedicated lines	Printer interface
Parallel shared lines	Microprocessor bus
	Some backplanes
	IEEE-488
Serial dedicated lines	V.24
	X.21
	RS-232C
	SLD
	ST-bus
Serial shared lines	Ethernet
	PCM
	Token ring
	FDDI

at very high data throughput (many D channels in a common processor) does a hardware solution become advantageous: instruction fetch times and the interpretation inefficiencies inherent in the instruction sets of general-purpose processors limit the maximum traffic the software engine can support.

Several blocks are common between hardware and software implementations of the same protocol. DMA is used to move packets into and out of the processor. Timers are needed at various points in the protocols. The central processing engine steps through the protocols, but whether it is implemented as a processor running a program or as a complex hard-wired state machine is not a large issue. The processor's program requires separate memory, but the dedicated state machine needs some type of supervisory processor to pick up those portions of the protocol that invariably appear late in the design cycle or are special cases for a particular application. Here one advantage of the purely software implementation is clear; it is much easier to update and maintain software in a ROM or EPROM than to revise the firmware in a dedicated device's control store.

The data rates in basic-rate ISDN are low enough that common microprocessors do not have trouble executing code for levels 2 and 3 of both B and D channels at a terminal, or for several D channels on a linecard. When packet traffic exceeds the capacity of a reasonable microprocessor system, as when D-channel processing is centralized for a large group of lines in a switch, it is more attractive to use dedicated hardware. However, the flexibility of software implementations makes them quite attractive for systems such as ISDN that are likely to have a dynamic set of services. Thus, a trade-off must be made between flexibility and capacity at any given cost.

6.4 FUNCTIONAL GROUPS

The CCITT I-series recommendations (I.411) refer to the equipment at a network node by their function, not by name, and collectively they are called *functional groups* TE and NT. The members of each category vary from very simple, usually single-function low-end equipment to complex, programmable, expandable high-end equipment. This section will describe the functions necessary within each group at a high level. Following will be sections to present in more detail the blocks used to implement the functional groups.

6.4.1 Terminal Equipment: TE

Because it represents the periphery of the ISDN network, terminal equipment and associated hardware must implement all seven OSI protocol layers. Those TE's that are required to provide a wide variety of high-feature end user functions will necessarily be quite complex, but we will discuss several types that implement extremely simple high-level protocols and are themselves simple.

Four major functions are served by terminal equipment: terminal adapters (TA) allow non-ISDN equipment (TE2) to communicate over the network; voice-only ISDN phones fill the role of the traditional telephone; data-only low-bit-rate terminals allow automatic remote operation of alarms, telemetry, and message exchange; full-feature ISDN terminals combine all these services with the ability to be programmed for additional protocols. The equipment types that are service endpoints in themselves are TE1. There is some overlap between categories, but the basic distinctions are similar to those among modems, telephones, telemetry devices, and networked personal computers, respectively. Figure 6.3 illustrates the uses of the four types of terminal equipment.

The terminal adapter is used in an environment where ISDN transmission is used to network equipment using older protocols, including voice equipment. It is usually designed to have only the features necessary for basic adaptation using a fixed set of protocols. An office environment would take advantage of this configuration where each desk is equipped with low-feature voice and data sets: telephones and keyboard/display terminals. This keeps computing centralized but takes advantage of the flexibility and simplicity of ISDN architecture. The functions necessary in such terminal adapters are listed in Table 6.3.

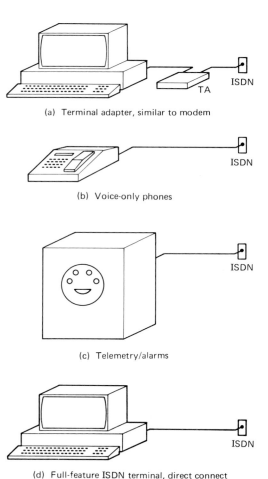

(a) Terminal adapter, similar to modem

(b) Voice-only phones

(c) Telemetry/alarms

(d) Full-feature ISDN terminal, direct connect

Figure 6.3 TE types.

TABLE 6.3   FUNCTIONS NECESSARY IN A TA

Layer 1 interface
Layer 2 LAP-D
Layer 3 D channel
V.120 B-channel packetization
V.110 bit-rate adaption
Codec/filter
Tone generation
User-interface protocols
Higher-level applications
Maintenance
Test

The terminal adapter, which generally supports only a minimum of upper-layer functions, can be a featureless black box with jacks for the ISDN level 1 media interface, the voice terminal, and the data terminal. A simple user-interface protocol can be set up so that no local keyboard or display is necessary. The industry standard AT command set originated by Hayes [16] for voiceband modems is an example of such a protocol. One popular type of terminal adapter is a board that plugs into a personal computer. While the board external to the PC box is a terminal adapter, when it is plugged in, the PC becomes a full-feature ISDN terminal. This is in line with the CCITT reasoning that, taken together, a TA and a TE2 may be considered a TE1.

An ISDN phone (voice terminal) needs a set of functions similar to that of the terminal adapter. B-channel packetization or rate adaptation is not necessary. Some of the software or firmware relating to B-channel services may be dropped, allowing the use of smaller memories. A requirement on ISDN voice-only sets is that they be able to function on only a few hundred milliwatts in an emergency-power condition. In addition, if they are not locally powered, they should consume very little current in the on-hook mode yet still be able to alert for an incoming call.

Low-bit-rate terminals for telemetry are a step further backward from the voice systems. They do not need the codec/filter function for voice and may delete software necessary for B-channel call setup. They do need a hardware interface to the equipment they are intended to monitor, but that is normally very minimal. Telemetry systems that operate only in a polled mode can also do away with call-origination software.

Full-feature ISDN terminals incorporate additional software and hardware for extended data services over both B and D channels. It is here that many upper-layer protocols are supported. This TE is distinguished from the TA/TE2 set by the fact that the hardware and software are developed together and complement each other. This provides for a broad feature set and allows coordinated plans for extension of both hardware and software, as in open-architecture personal computers.

6.4.2 Network Termination Equipment: NT

As its name suggests, the NT is a network layer node (L3) and thus generally implements protocols from layers 1, 2, and 3. The need for processing B or D channels in NTs generally depends on whether any multiplexing is done, and whether the upstream and downstream ports have the same capacity. Complex NTs may use timeslot multiplexing to compress a high downstream B-channel capacity (many subscriber lines) into a limited upstream bandwidth (a trunk) and statistical multiplexing to combine many sparsely-used downstream D channels into a single upstream D channel.

Some NT equipment does not process D-channel data, passing it on instead to a further node, which may be designed to process many channels in parallel. B channels generally pass through the equipment unaltered, even if they are switched or multiplexed. Thus, for the B channels, the NT functions are strictly level 1. For the D channel(s), the protocols often include levels 2 and 3.

The CCITT I.411 definitions of NT equipment are extremely broad, covering everything from an S-T relay device to a full private branch exchange, including its switching function. We will confine discussion to the more peripheral functions, corresponding to those network nodes where the largest amount of ISDN-specific VLSI is used. These include the NT1 as defined by the CCITT, which is a level 1 protocol translator and which we will refer to as the simple NT; the remote multiplexer or remote switch, which may have switching capability and pair gain, which we will refer to as an intelligent NT; and the linecard (LT), where the ISDN S or U [11] lines first enter a major switching node. These types of NTs are illustrated in Fig. 6.4.

6.4.3 Simple NT

The simple NT performs no functions above layer 1 and thus can be very simple (thus its name). It may include multiplexing functions, but consists of little more than several transceivers. Since the D channel on the S/T interface contains a contention-resolution mechanism, it is possible to multiplex several S/T lines into one T or U line at the simple NT. The channels from multiple S/T lines may be ANDed together to continue the D-channel contention resolution through the NT1. B channels are allocated by higher-level protocols to terminals with unqiue identifying addresses, so they need no layer 1 contention-resolution mechanism. Most simple NTs are 1:1, however, one line in, one line out. Layer 1 maintenance issues are difficult to manage if there is more than one loop downstream of the NT1 (on the subscriber side) because of the ambiguity of the information.

If we assume an NT1 is a 1:1 layer 1 protocol converter, what is needed there is an upstream-protocol transceiver, a downstream-protocol transceiver, a format converter, some maintenance circuitry, and optionally some provision for power feeding. Data are passed transparently for B and D channels. Maintenance channels must be interpreted and controlled either in firmware or by a simple microcontroller.

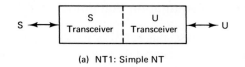

(a) NT1: Simple NT

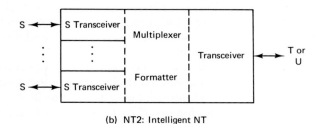

(b) NT2: Intelligent NT

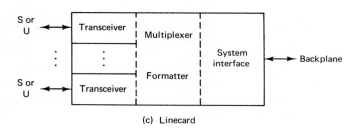

(c) Linecard

Figure 6.4   NT types.

6.4.4 Intelligent NT: NT2 and NT12

To differentiate an NT from a linecard, we will specify that the NT is an autonomous piece of equipment, whereas the linecard is a peripheral part of a larger piece of equipment. The downstream interfaces may be identical, but the upstream interfaces are to transmission media in the NT versus internal communications buses (backplanes) in the linecard. The NT upstream interface may be one or more basic rate interfaces or may be a primary rate interface. To be able to serve several terminals simultaneously, when the upstream interface is basic rate, it is necessary to include some basic switching functions in the NT; when it is primary rate, this is not necessary.

D channel packets need to be multiplexed in the upstream direction and demultiplexed in the downstream direction. This requires level 2 capability for flow control upstream and destination identification downstream. Higher levels may be implemented at the NT but are again not necessary if switching and supervisory functions are implemented further upstream.

The intelligent NT must include a subsystem to execute protocols from layers 2 and above; this will normally be centered around a general-purpose microprocessor with dedicated hardware for lower levels. Level 2 is often split between hardware and software.   Levels 3 and above are well suited to software implementation and will likely remain so for flexibility.   The intelligence contained in an NT is used to concentrate D channels at level 2 and to execute protocols for supervision, management layer 1 maintenance, B-channel control and switching if applicable, activation, and so on.   Most of the secondary protocol tasks occupy a very small portion of any real time scenario.   The system thus is not loaded by them but must provide suitable additional software.

6.4.5 Linecard

The ISDN linecard is the entry point of several S, T, or U loops into a switching system.   In some systems, their function is confined to layer 1, and the D-channel processing task is passed on to a central processor for the higher levels.   In others this is extended with level 2 and 3 processing on the linecard to offload the central processor.   The great majority of ISDN linecards have a microprocessor for some minimal amount of supervision and management.   The choice of extending this system to LAP-D processing for distribution of processing power versus concentration of all processing in one node favors distributed processing.   Economies of scale that are realized in producing a large number of linecards are not seen if all the function is concentrated at one point.   Layers 2 and 3 are processed on the linecard, and higher layers are processed deeper within the switch.   Protocols may be split on the D channel to route supervisory messages to a different network than user data and telemetry.

The functions necessary on the linecard are thus the appropriate layer 1 transceiver, processing for layers 2 and 3 of the D channel, layer 1 maintenance, and the normal supervision and management.   Normally, there are eight basic rate interfaces or one primary rate interface per linecard.   Some type of timeslot assignment must be done to map the external interface B and D channel information into the appropriate internal format.   Power feed toward the NT and terminals is required to provide basic emergency service in the public network.

6.5 TE, NT, LT TIMING ISSUES

The hierarchy of clocks in a wide-area ISDN system must be very well controlled to maintain a good degree of data integrity.   Without it provision must be made for continual phase adjustment by dropping or repeating data, causing a high number of transmission errors.   To avoid this problem, a master clock is established within a geographic region, and all switching systems within it are very closely synchronized to it by means of bit stuffing.   Each switch passes its timing out from the linecards to NTs and TEs.   Synchronous terminals (TE2s) adapted by TAs must run off the clocks derived from the loop.   This strict specification of global timing assures minimal loss of data on circuit-switched connections.

Where network-wide synchronization is not guaranteed, it is necessary to provide mechanisms to guard against and recover from errors, which may be either missing or added bits.   While 64-Kbps voice is generally not sensitive to such errors, data exchange requires error detection and provision for correction or retransmission in the protocol used. Some networks may attempt to reduce these errors by confining them to periods between packets if it is known that packet data are being exchanged, but it is best to build the error tolerance into the terminal equipment data protocols. For this reason, packet-based protocols have been used exclusively for signaling, and nearly exclusively for data. These include a frame-check sequence for error detection and packet acknowledgment to request retransmission if necessary. Forward error correction algorithms have not yet found widespread use, and are not specified within ISDN. With packet sizes tailored to expected bit error rates in the system, the throughput obtained using only error detection is acceptable. Forward error correction is more useful where channels are expected to have fairly high error rates.

6.6 REQUIREMENTS OF ISDN FUNCTIONAL BLOCKS

This section will review the blocks most often found in ISDN basic-rate components. The blocks are useful at the TE, NT, and LT nodes. Partitioning and implementation will be discussed in the next section. Some functions can be covered in software, as is discussed where appropriate. Eventually, it is expected that many functions will be integrated together with a programmable core to obtain both maximum integration and a high degree of flexibility. This is a discussion only of the peripheral functions necessary for ISDN and will not include evaluation of microprocessors and microcontrollers that are used for software-based protocol implementation.

6.6.1 Microprocessor Interface

A microprocessor interface allows a host processor access to control, status, and data in these components. It must operate at the highest speed possible to allow compatibility with high-bandwidth parallel buses. All serial subchannels and all control/status should be accessible from this interface, as it serves as the main test, control, and maintenance access to the device. It is not absolutely necessary to have such a port on a device if slower access to internal information does not reduce system performance. Alternate control interfaces may be implemented serially or with dedicated input and output pins. This will be especially desirable when sensitive analog circuitry is included on the same device with a large amount of digital circuitry, especially a microprocessor port. If the device is at all complex, however, testing becomes much more of a problem without a microprocessor port.

A byte-wide interface will suffice for most ISDN systems because of the octet organization of much of the transferred information. An increase to 16-bit-wide access is not necessary because basic user data rates are low enough compared to microcomputer bus transfer rates that they do not interfere significantly with other bus activities. Package pin count and current spikes during read cycles (especially if analog circuitry is incorporated within the same device) lead one to prefer a narrower bus. Fully digital devices on a heavily utilized bus may choose the 16-bit width if their internal architecture supports it.

Access to internal data may be direct or indirect. Direct access requires data transfer across the internal bus essentially simultaneously with the external bus transfer. Indirect access separates the internal and external transfers by making use of temporary storage registers for data and address (see Fig. 6.5). Many chips adopt a compromise approach in which the most frequently accessed information is available through direct access and less important information is indirectly accessed. Direct access requires additional hardware to interface synchronous and asynchronous sections of a system. This generally requires that each accessible register bit be a master/slave pair of latches. The slave must have time to resolve to a full level before or during access, lengthening access time somewhat. Indirect

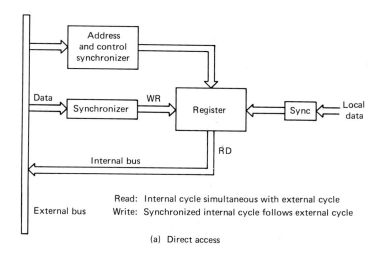

(a) Direct access

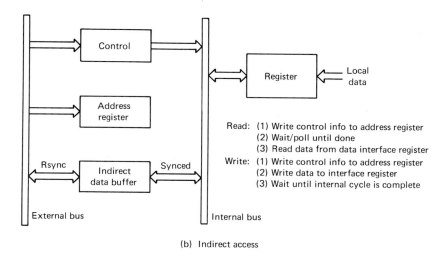

(b) Indirect access

Figure 6.5 Microprocessor access schemes.

access requires considerable software overhead, however, so direct access at least to often-used registers is well worth the additional complexity.

6.6.2 Internal Bus Structures

It is very useful to separate the data stream from the control stream. Simpler internal transfer timing results, without contention between synchronous and asynchronous events. In layer 1 devices, this generally means having separate data and control buses. In higher-level devices, where the data become less "real time" due to packetization and interlayer buffering, this becomes less necessary. Because of the serial nature of many of the external connections used in communications, it is useful to consider not only parallel but also serial bus structures.

Parallel bus structures are well suited to interface any control or data structure to a microprocessor system. Serial bus structures are useful when an external serial bus is connected to multiple internal blocks, especially when channels are significantly interleaved as in I.430. Most serial connections defined within the ISDN system are synchronous or isochronous (containing embedded time information), derived from the 8-KHz synchronous sampling in voice systems. The frame structures of these define timeslots or subframes that may carry a variety of different types of information. A serial connection may be shared in a multipoint manner either on a chip level or on a system level if timing conventions are followed to avoid contention.

A synchronous bus, whether parallel or serial, generally transfers frames of information on a regular basis (at the frame rate). The frames are divided into groups of bits referred to as subframes or timeslots. The most common use of such connections in telecommunications has been on PBX or central office switch backplanes, where both parallel and serial connections are used, and on trunk lines between switches, which are exclusively serial. Such a bus consists at a minimum of data, clock, and framing signals. The clock may be contained within the data stream, and framing can be indicated with unique codes. An extreme example could be the isochronous S/T interface, which multiplexes all framing, timing and data information into a single signal.

Synchronous systems need to have a strictly defined timing hierarchy. Each bus must have its timing derived from a master clock located at one node. Other nodes on the bus derive their clocks from the signals received from the timing master. Often the same node that is the timing master is also the master in other control hierarchies. The maintenance of this synchronization over large geographical areas such as an entire country or continent requires very tight specifications on the phase error allowed at each stage of clock regeneration. Central clocks use extremely stable timebases to minimize the maximum jitter expected at the most remote slaved node.

Jitter propagation and accumulation become a problem when synchronous connections are to be made between two systems that are either quite distant in a single timing hierarchy tree or are not in connection trees whatsoever. Buffering is necessary to absorb the maximum allowed phase or timing offset, and a graceful means of recovery from buffer overflow must be defined for the case where there is a long-term frequency offset, causing the accumulated phase difference to exceed buffer capacity.

6.6.3 Central Timing Unit

A central timing unit is often very useful to control data transfers on synchronous buses. It is slaved directly or by means of a phase-locked loop to one set of external timing signals. A digital PLL may be used in less important nodes but where regenerated timing is passed further down the tree it will be necessary to use an analog PLL to minimize jitter generation and avoid the use of extremely high frequency DPLLs. Where serial data must be converted to parallel data and/or to a different serial format, the timing unit can control a fixed sequence of events to move data between shift registers, buffers, and interface registers regularly each frame. The core of the timing unit is a state machine, but additional complexity can vary quite significantly. The simplest devices will require only a fixed repetitive function such as indicating transfers for B1, B2, and D data. The most complex provide programmable internal timeslot control and support multiple interface formats.

6.6.4 Reformatter: Subchannel Extraction

The data reformatting section is the crossroads where all data paths meet. Since it is necessary to have a controlling state machine for this section, which is similar to the central timing unit, the two may be merged, but where interconnect becomes a problem, it may be easier to realize them separately. The task of this unit is to adapt the synchronous data between data ports that have different formats, but that transfer similar data (for example B1 + B2 + D or B1 + B2 out of the basic access frame). The most straightforward way of doing this is to convert each serial channel to a parallel format for transfer to temporary storage, then a further transfer to the output destination. The need for parallel data buffers also means a parallel local exchange bus is necessary. This can be extended outside the reformatter to any unit that would like to access the data in a parallel manner, such as the microprocessor interface. Because of possible contention between synchronous access (internal origin) and asynchronous access (external origin) on this bus, it is not desirable to merge this bus with the control/status bus that talks to the microprocessor interface. Figure 6.6 illustrates the structure of an S-PCM reformatter.

This unit is also a good place to implement loopbacks, which are required for maintenance purposes such as fault location and bit error rate monitoring. Normal buffer register transfers are modified so data are reflected back to the same interface from which they arrive, instead of being passed through to the other interface.

6.6.5 Serial Data Interfaces

Except for the initial generation and final resolution of a transfer of data, the OSI model consistently shows transfer of data through a block with additional connection to a management entity. The block may cover one or multiple OSI layers.

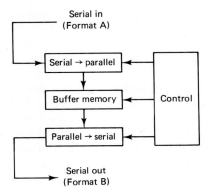

Figure 6.6 Reformatter.

This leads to a basic block structure consisting of two ports for data (for example, 2B + D) and a third for control (often a microprocessor interface). To reduce pin counts, the data ports are often serial. At a node where it is necessary to separate data, multiple serial ports may be used on one side. This can be used to separate B1, B2, and D data or may be used to separately process packets from different logical links (DLCIs).

One popular way to separate B1, B2, and D data that requires no analysis of the data and no extra pins is external separation on the serial bus itself. The multiplexing is done by the external devices dedicated to individual subchannels of the serial interface. To allow multiplexing of more bandwidth than is available on the serial link or to allow flexible subframe assignment when a large number of channels are being time-multiplexed, the multiplexing may be made programmable, as is the case with timeslot assignment for PCM backplane connections.

Many basic rate interlayer "standard" serial interfaces are quite similar, based on a four-byte structure. The B1 and B2 octets occupy two bytes; the remaining two bytes contain D-channel information and some type of control/status structure that requires protocol execution units on each end of the link. One may take advantage of this similarity to make each serial data interface programmable in several modes, without expending a great amount of hardware. These interfaces may be easily piped into common synchronous HDLC devices for processing of layer 2.

6.6.6 Timeslot Assignment

Timeslot assignment is used to allocate bandwidth on a high-capacity serial bus to multiple data channels. It was originally used to multiplex 64-Kbps digitized voice channels onto primary-rate (usually 1.544 or 2.048 Mbps) serial channels for routing between linecards and switching nodes or between physical switches on trunk lines. Where nonblocking architectures are used, the timeslot assignment can be fixed, but in the public network blocking is tolerated and timeslot assignments must be programmable. In ISDN, timeslots are used on interdevice interfaces and on the multipoint S interface. In both cases, programmable multiplexing is necessary.

PCM backplane timeslot assignment can get quite complex when maximum flexibility is required, but a large number of simplifications can be made so the amount of control logic required does not get out of hand. Common features of PCM interfaces include (1) an ability to interface to multiple PCM highways, (2) programmable delay after sync pulse to start of frame, (3) operation at several clock frequencies, and (4) independent timeslot programmability for each data channel.

A fully programmable PCM interface is only an absolute necessity where the PCM links are used throughout the system, including for switching, and the system is allowed to be blocking, meaning not all users may simultaneously be active in all channels. Many applications do not require full timeslot programmability and can accept fixed assignment of timeslot blocks for each subscriber line. This is especially true at a terminal, where a very simple timeslot structure may suffice because the multiplexed loop signal is interfaced only to a microprocessor system for data and a codec/filter for voice.

6.6.7 Timeslot Interchange (Switch Matrix)

A timeslot interchange, although not a per line component, is useful in components such as NT2 or NT12 that are hubs for multiple loops. It can serve as the heart of a remote switch in a small private system. It is another function that can be done with software on a small scale but is most efficiently done with dedicated hardware. It consists of two RAM banks, one for timeslot assignments and one for data (see Fig. 6.7). Two data ports interface to the system's internal data paths. A control interface allows timeslot map programming.

Data received on the input side in timeslot T are written into data memory location T. Data to be transmitted are read from the location pointed to by location T in the timeslot assignment map memory. Features can include broadcasting, timeslot phase programmability, and asynchronous operation, but the core of the device is quite straightforward. This is the same serial/parallel/serial structure used on a smaller scale in the reformatter, but here the timing of data transfers is quite simple.

6.6.8 Command Execution Units

When a component needs to operate in an application without an attached microprocessor, control and status information must be exchanged over the serial interfaces. Bits in addition to the basic 2B + D must be reserved for this purpose, and an interchange structure must be defined. The resulting protocol may be simple, if little is to be exchanged, or complex, if the serial interface is replacing a parallel microprocessor interface to a complex device. Examples of simple protocols include the ANSI S interface S and Q channels, and the ANSI U interface M and EOC channels.

All ISDN physical layer interfaces include a maintenance channel that is used for monitoring and testing performance of the loop, and thus the quality of the physical medium. These are not very complicated but generally are defined in a bit-mapped fashion that cannot be handled efficiently by a microprocessor without

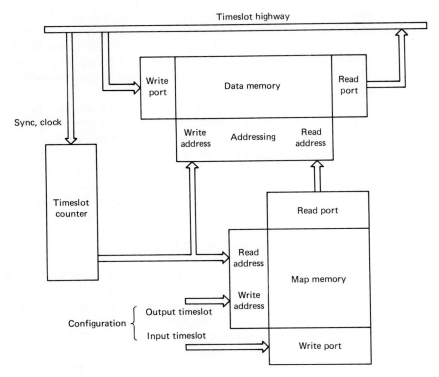

Figure 6.7 Timeslot interchange.

a special peripheral processing unit. The bit rate is low (800 bps in the TE-to-NT direction for I.430), but the fact that the data are interspersed through a superframe makes transmission and accumulation of messages very overhead intensive. A dedicated unit for this must buffer messages, supervise superframe synchronization, and be able to interrupt the processor when a new or different message is received.

Some messages transferred across the maintenance channel are commands to perform loopbacks or self-tests. At some physical-layer nodes, such as NT1, a microprocessor may not be desirable; in these cases it is necessary to implement a small state machine to interpret and execute these commands. This may be incorporated as a part of any other channel processor included in the device.

If the component has no parallel interface whatsoever, maintenance and test requirements normally dictate that the serial control interface have complete access to all internal registers and state variables. In this case, it is necessary to define read and write cycles akin to microprocessor bus cycles. A command processor can access internal registers on request over the serial interface. Unless the interface bit rate is quite high, the serial communication leads to long test times. A completely internal self-test may be defined to circumvent this problem; but if it does not test absolutely everything, the access problem still exists. Where normal application modes restrict access speeds, test complexity can be reduced with test modes that reconfigure pins for parallel access.

6.6.9 Bit-level Functions

It is well accepted that bit-level operations such as those done for HDLC [17] packetization and depacketization are best done in dedicated hardware. Microprocessor instruction sets are not tailored toward the bit-serial operations required for these functions, especially when they must be done continuously at high speed. Their relatively simple nature makes them a good fit for a peripheral unit. Functions that fit into this category and are usually done in dedicated hardware include HDLC bit processing, serial scramblers and descramblers, encryption and decryption, error-correction coding and decoding, and bit rate adaption.

The HDLC serial channel protocol is well-established and widespread. It allows detection of transmission errors, unambiguous demarkation of packet beginning and end, and receipt acknowledgment. All these functions are done on a serial stream; the protocol does not assume byte alignment of data and does not produce byte-aligned code on the line. This protocol has been extended for use on the D channel of ISDN and one of the protocols for B channel data transmission (V.120).

A scrambler is implemented with very similar hardware to that which generates the HDLC frame check sequence. In this case, however, the data normally sent are passed through the logic on a continuous basis, and there is no frame check sequence. This is used to suppress correlation between the transmitted signal and any other signal of interest, such as a constant level (to increase the amount of timing information) or the received signal (very important in echo canceling systems). One problem inherent in a scrambler is error propagation. A 1-bit transmission error can cause a series of errors as long as the scrambling polynomial in the descrambled data. Encryption may use this scrambling as part of an algorithm that provides security for sensitive data sent through a public network.

V.110 synchronous rate adapters use block codes to map low-speed V-series links into B channels or subchannels [2]. These simple bit-level maps include user data, rate information, signaling fields, and framing indication. A state machine to implement this protocol should be programmable for the various V-series bit rates so it can cover the variations of block mapping to the 64-bit B-channel frames. V.110 also includes provision for multiplexing several R interfaces onto one ISDN B channel.

6.6.10 Data Channel Buffering

When a data channel is routed to a microprocessor, it is usual to provide some buffering between the serial link and the registers accessible to the microprocessor. The buffer depth required is determined by the maximum acceptable interrupt latency or poll interval and the minimum acceptable number of bytes transferred. Although data transfer rates over ISDN are not fast in comparison with disk drive or LAN bit rates, transfers done without DMA may overburden the processor if the amount of task-switching necessary is not reduced by increasing the size of each task. For the transfer of data from the buffer to more permanent memory, a larger number of bytes per block move means a more efficient overall system. Often a very simple microprocessor system is responsible for these transfers, further transfers to another system, all tasks necessary for levels 1, 2, and 3, and additional supervisory tasks. When this expands to include several channels, as at an NT2 or NT12 node, significant buffering becomes an absolute necessity. When a processor is responsible for both transfers and packet processing, it must be allowed enough time for both in the highest-traffic conditions expected. DMA may steal some time on the bus from the microprocessor, but it doubles or triples the time available to process packets by doing the block transfers more efficiently.

When several blocks serially process a given packet of data, much can be gained by minimizing the number of times that packet must be moved from one memory to another, between processors, and so on. By leaving the packet in one place, the headers from several levels can be processed independently and only pointers need be passed to the next level of processing. This favors multiple-port memory and/or consolidation of software from several levels into a single package run on one processor.

6.6.11 Direct Memory Access

DMA is often used to remove the task of block transfers of packet data from a microprocessor that is intended to process the packets. The most effective DMA is tightly coupled with the packet transmitter or receiver and interrupts the processor only when a complete packet is available for further action. Coupling with level 2 is also useful so that the processor is not involved in retransmissions and rejections. Two types of DMA transfers are common: (1) single-cycle "fly-by" transfers that address the requesting device with a dedicated acknowledge signal, and (2) two-cycle memory/buffer/memory transfers.

Each DMA channel requires a considerable amount of hardware: address registers, transfer counters, and control registers. The unit as a whole must also include a bus master and arbitration unit (see Fig. 6.8). Since the DMA controller represents such a large hardware investment, its benefits are worthwhile only when many transfers must be coordinated, as in an NT2 or on a linecard where multiple basic user interfaces are managed.

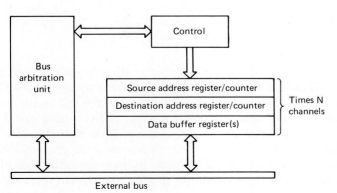

Figure 6.8 DMA master.

If a DMA controller is available elsewhere in the system, DMA request circuitry may be included. This gets the data into memory, but not in a location known to the requesting unit, so it cannot do anything further with those data. If an intelligent peripheral is to be responsible for packet processing, it must have a means of cataloging packets by datalink and frame sequence number. Separate requests for several channels cannot effectively be used because of the number that is needed in a general-purpose device. DMA is thus a key item when full support of level 2 is desired in a dedicated device.

6.6.12 Level 2 and 3 Machines

Since information packets drag around a large information field with the headers used by level 2 or level 3 processors, moving the entire packets from a level 1 entity to a level 2 entity to a level 3 entity and so on is not efficient. The system designer would like to minimize the number of transfers the host must supervise and eventually the total number of transfers to avoid tying up the bus. Ideally, the level 2 controller operates on a packet autonomously, and the host processor is not bothered until the level 2 (or higher) functions are complete and the packet has been transformed into the proper format for the level of protocol delegated to it.

A dedicated controller for level 2 is the core for several fairly complex devices already on the market [7, 14]. Approximately 20 basic states exist for each end of each datalink. These are managed by a state machine, which is supported by several additional hardware blocks. To be able to manage a large number of datalinks, records are stored in external memory containing the state of each datalink, window and address information, and data. A record manager must be defined to load and unload these records. The device should be a bus master so it can access all packet data itself. Level 2 of all packetized ISDN protocols is based on HDLC and includes the usual bit-level functions, error detection, sequencing, and flow control. ISDN protocols support multiple simultaneous logical links, sharing the bandwidth of one physical channel between several data and/or signaling "conversations." Each of these must be separately supervised, necessitating the storage of a number of sets of state variables and datalink descriptors. Address recognition logic differentiates between datalinks and can reduce processing time by ignoring packets not addressed to the local node.

A common architecture for ISDN devices is a flow-through architecture, with two ports designed to talk to hardware of adjacent OSI levels. Dedicated level 2 devices have been implemented with one serial port, toward level 1, and one parallel port, toward level 3. Standards recommendations do not restrict implementations, however, and an equally valid memory-based architecture would be based on a single parallel microprocessor port. This architecture encourages software protocol implementations, with the single parallel port being actually the bus interface of a microprocessor or microcontroller. It also allows complete packet processing without ever moving the packet in memory.

The flexibility of a software implementation is an advantage when the network protocols or application features are expected to change over time. Software may also be downloaded to allow upgrades. However, low-cost general-purpose processors have performance limitations that make them unsuitable at high-throughput nodes where many channels are processed. Here the dedicated hardware controller can relieve the processor of much work.

Level 3 is most often implemented in software because of its managerial function. Whereas level 2 is responsible for the fairly well defined task of transferring packets between layer 3 entities, layer 3 manages the allocation of B-channel bandwidth and D-channel datalinks. It is much more a system function than a hardware function. Because of the wide range of possible system architectures, the easy customization of software makes it more attractive than hardware for the level 3 function. Again, however, when traffic at a node becomes very high and the protocols become well established, dedicated hardware will become popular. The blocks necessary to assist a core controller in layer 3 hardware would be similar to those in a layer 2 machine.

6.6.13 Timers

Many of the ISDN protocols require timers that escape from an abnormal sequence of events to indicate an error condition. A counter and comparator may provide a time-out signal to the local microprocessor for this purpose. When many timers are simultaneously needed, for example, when multiple D-channel datalinks are active within the control of a single microprocessor, separate hardware for each is excessive. It is preferable to use the counter as a clock and to implement the timers in software. A periodic interrupt source may be useful to begin a status check of all active software timers. In some cases, once-per-frame or once-per-superframe interrupts may be available from physical-layer devices; these can be used as a coarse timebase.

Another very useful function in stand-alone microprocessor systems is the *watchdog timer*. This timer performs a system reset if a unique set of events is not performed within a given period of time that resets its counter. It protects against software bugs and noise that might cause the processor to begin execution out of an undefined area of memory.

6.6.14 Phase-Locked Loops

Phase-locked loops are necessary in many synchronous systems to regenerate the timing information embedded in a data signal. A local oscillator is slaved to a remote reference by extracting phase information from the incoming signal, comparing that with the phase of the local oscillator, integrating, and feeding back the result to control the frequency (rate of phase change) of the local oscillator. Jitter describes the variations in phase offset between the local and remote clocks; it is often called wander when periodic with low frequency. PLLs can follow wander of the reference to a certain extent, but generate both wander and jitter as phase tracking error.

Digital PLLs, which rely on division of a high-frequency local clock by a variable divisor, are straightforward to implent, but result in a large amount of jitter that can be tolerated in many systems.   If an extremely high frequency clock is used, the jitter may be held low, but the expense and complications of the high-frequency clock are usually greater than those from an analog PLL.   The usual DPLL does not use a loop filter, but simply switches the "oscillator" between two frequencies by changing the divisor.   Intelligent algorithms may be added to a DPLL to reduce the overall jitter by averaging the phase detector output over a period of time before an actual correction is made.   This is a type of loop filter; it reduces the effects of noise on jitter, but only to the granularity afforded by the divisor.

Analog phase-locked loops can provide much more precise control than their digital counterparts.   Instead of step changes in phase, analog phaselocked loops track by making stepped or ramped changes in frequency.   Where the global architecture of a synchronous system such as ISDN allows only a very small jitter budget per node, they are the rule.   It is usually only the interface beween synchronous and asynchronous systems, that allows the use of digital PLLs.   Analog PLLs, however, are more difficult both to design and to manufacture due to their analog circuitry, loop stability analysis, and the process control or trimming necessary to center a monolithic oscillator's free-running frequency.

An attractive compromise to some of the difficulties with analog PLLs is the use of a voltage-controlled crystal oscillator (VCXO).   When a system is known to be slaved to a very well controlled frequency, the small range of a VCXO may suffice.   The frequency of a crystal oscillator may be moved about $+/-$ 100 ppm by placing additional capacitance in parallel with it.   At some maximum capacitance, the crystal ceases to oscillate.   Very close attention must be paid to oscillator parasitics to achieve a wide enough control range.

6.6.15 Compatibility of Analog with Digital

ISDN transmission line interfaces are generally implemented with analog functional blocks to be able to meet specifications over a sufficiently wide range of power supplies, temperature, and loop characteristics.   These analog blocks require a somewhat controlled environment to perform as well as possible, requiring low-noise power supplies and some amount of substrate isolation.   Noise from clocked circuitry, large buffers such as clock generators and output buffers, especially those for parallel buses, must be kept isolated from the analog circuitry.   Where clock feedthrough into analog circuitry such as switched-capacitor filters is a problem, it is necessary to add a buffer stage that uses the quiet power supplies.

Analog circuit performance is degraded by the use of low power supply voltages, which are the rule for digital compatibility.   Internal signal-to-noise ratios suffer on both ends.   Maximum signal swing is decreased by the absolute reduction in power supply voltage (not linearly).   Noise tends to increase with smaller processes because the same trap density has a larger effect with smaller geometries. Designs can compensate for this to some extent, but the struggle to get enough headroom for voice components at 5 V has been translated to lower-voltage, higher-frequency circuitry for ISDN.   High-performance circuitry can take advantage of digital signal-processing techniques when a high signal-to-noise ratio is very difficult to maintain through many stages of analog circuitry, keeping only a front-end A/D or D/A analog.

Careful separation of power supply traces and substrate connections can isolate a group of analog functions from noisy digital circuitry. However, when the signal-to-noise ratio in the analog section must be above about 40 dB, the restrictions on the digital section so that it does not interfere become too great, and separate power supply connections must be provided. In addition, a quiet supply must be connected to the substrate. When these steps are taken, the digital section is free to be as noisy as it wants, as long as it does not overload the substrate connection. This allows interface to very fast parallel buses, something which is difficult when common power supplies are used.

6.6.16 Common Analog Blocks

The analog circuitry of an ISDN transceiver is built of general-purpose functional blocks that are usually designed and characerized separately before being assembled into a larger unit. The recent migration from 10 V supplies to 5 V supplies follows a similar trend in digital devices and has caused analog designers problems similar to those previously encountered by their digital counterparts. More complex analog circuits have been developed that perform as well as previous techniques that do not translate well to low supply voltages.

Opamps, comparators, and buffers to drive resistive loads are closely related circuits. Often several types of each are used within a single circuit. Each usually consists of a differential input stage, a second gain stage, and in the case of buffers a current gain stage. Opamps are internally compensated so that stability is assured when they are used with external feedback. They may be used open loop with or without compensation as comparators. A compensation capacitor may also double as an offset-storage device when we wish to make a zero-offset comparator.

Many simple CMOS opamps have very high output impedance and are best used only for driving capacitive loads [12, 13]. When it is necessary to drive any significant current into a resistive load, especially off-chip, a buffer must be added to the circuit. The output stages of an opamp usually operate class A and can deliver a maximum current only equal to the bias current. A buffer output stage operates in class AB (push/pull) and is capable of delivering currents an order of magnitude or more higher.

Resistors are often made in a polysilicon gate layer because of its good linearity and reproducibility. When large-value linear resistors are necessary, thin-film layers may be deposited at the end of processing. Low-concentration implanted layers such as wells can be used where their nonlinearity can be tolerated or if thin-film costs are too great. Capacitors are usually realized with a thin oxide as the dielectric between two layers of polysilicon. If this structure is not available, it is possible to use a deep-depletion MOS device, but this again results in a small nonlinearity that must be considered in design.

Temperature- and supply-stable voltage references may be included using one of several methods. The structure most often used adds the positive-tempco voltage across a resistor to the negative-tempco V_{BE} of a bipolar device (available in most CMOS processes), passing a current proportional to temperature. Supply voltage independence is assured by adequate cascoding, and with proper design the temperature coefficients cancel to give a very stable reference. Another reference design directly uses the threshold difference between two MOS transistors of the same type that have different channel implants.

6.6.17 Transmitters

An ISDN transmitter is a fairly straightforward subsystem, but is dependent on the existence of one or more reference voltages or currents. The transmitter must be able to source large amounts of current at accurately controlled voltages and must switch rapidly between several states; to get accurate output levels, the driver must be an analog circuit. The bandwidth of the circuit should be controlled to reduce current transients when switching output states. An important system design issue is the amount of power expended in transmission. Most systems couple power to the loop through a transformer; the higher the transformer ratio, the lower the device output current and the more efficient the transmitter. In transmission formats using echo cancellation, the linearity of the transmitter influences the complexity of the receiver.

Some logic is usually associated with the transmitter. It must translate binary signals internal to the device to the line code used for transmission and adapt timing appropriately to the line symbol rate. Some buffering may be included to ensure correct timing on the output. Activation signals, often different than the data in normal frames, may also be generated within the transmitter block.

6.6.18 Receivers

A digital communications receiver must perform a number of basic functions to recover the data from its input signal: equalization, symbol timing extraction, detection, and frame alignment. Echo-canceling transceivers must in addition implement some type of hybrid to remove the transmitted portion from the composite signal before it enters the equalizer.

Basic equalization serves to flatten out the frequency response of the transmission system between the remote transmitter and the local equalizer, resulting in the reproduction of the original transmitted waveform. In addition, filtering may be added to remove noise or other expected signal corruption. Equalization becomes rapidly more complex as the length of the loop increases beyond about 2 Km, or the point where significant response to a pulse one symbol wide occupies several symbol intervals. This situation is known as intersymbol interference and causes the received signal to be a function not only of the data represented in the present symbol but also of the data in previous symbols. An important issue is that of bridged taps, unterminated lines connected to the main loop, that can cause the pulse response to have several lobes. These are present in much of the public loop plant, but are generally not used in private systems (PBXs) and have not been used in Europe. These can usually be corrected by an adaptive equalizer, but extreme cases may arise where the major lobe is not the first one. Since we wish to use the largest signal possible for detection, these precursors must be removed with a special equalizer. Since very few existing loops exhibit this type of response, they can generally be ignored.

Three classes of equalizers have been used in ISDN receivers. Low pass or bandpass filters may be used simply to remove high-frequency noise in a simple system such as the I.430 S interface. A modified AGC section that boosts mainly the frequencies around the major spectral peak can be used in simple systems that are not used in the presence of bridged taps, but that have extended pulse responses. The high-frequency emphasis restores edges that are dulled during transmission.

The most general but also most complex system is the feedback equalizer, generally realized digitally (DFE). When the loop pulse response extends over several symbols, the DFE is used as an FIR filter, feeding back the expected tails from the last several received symbols. It thus removes intersymbol interference from the received signal. These have been used in both echo-canceling and TCM (Ping-Pong) systems. A DFE may be constructed for use in either a linear or nonlinear system. A linear DFE may be used when the entire transmission system is sufficiently linear that the superposition of received and transmitted signals does not distort either one significantly when they are separated with the hybrid or echo canceler. A nonlinear DFE should be used if transformer, transmitter, or front-end saturation is expected. The nonlinear DFE requires much more coefficient memory, especially when a large number of taps is used, and is avoided when possible.

An echo-canceling receiver must use a second filter similar to a DFE as an adaptive hybrid to remove the transmitted signal and any vestigal replicas of it that may be echoed back into the receiver from splices, bridged taps, or even the other end of the loop. The two may be combined into a single functional block for ease of implementation.

The DFE and echo canceler may be implemented as analog circuits with digital control or, with an A/D at the front end, in a purely digital fashion. The analog implementation is more straightforward and area efficient but cannot attain the performance of the digital structure. In the digital implementation, the sensitive circuitry rests solely in the A/D converter, which is a well-investigated subject and can meet any reasonable design goal. One elusive target, however, is the capability of manufacturing precision analog blocks such as A/Ds without the need for trimming. The recent development of self-calibrating structures begins to open the door to such possibilities.

Symbol timing extraction is done in the time domain by making an assumption about the shape of the received signal and searching for that characteristic. From an initial random starting phase, the receiver is synchronized by making periodic phase corrections in response to an error signal generated by a phase detector. The unit is essentially a phase-locked loop with a specialized phase detector. The complexity of the phase detector is dependent on the type of line code used. The AMI line code used on the S interface and the biphase code used in several early echo-canceling systems contain enough timing information that zero crossings may be used to accurately extract timing. Some filtering may be used to reduce high-frequency jitter. Codes with higher low-frequency content and no built-in balance, such as the 2B1Q used on the ANSI U interface, contain significantly less timing information. Here we must filter the extracted information over many symbols before using it to make phase corrections.

Digital and analog phase-locked loops may be used, depending on system jitter requirements. Analog PLLs, often utilizing VCXOs (voltage-controlled crystal oscillators) can be designed to keep jitter extremely low, but are avoided when digital PLLs can be used because of design and manufacturing complexity. Digital PLLs require a clock at a much higher frequency than the symbol rate if they are to maintain tight phase lock. Such a clock is usually available in basic rate (2B + D) systems, allowing the use of DPLLs. One complication arising from the use of DPLLs in conjunction with echo cancelers is the fact that a sudden shift in receiver phase with respect to the transmitter causes the estimated echo to be generated for the wrong instant within the symbol. This necessitates the generation of a second set of canceler coefficients before the switch is made, and thus doubles the required canceler memory size. Analog PLLs that change their frequency and thus slowly ramp the phase offset allow the echo canceler to track more easily.

Once the received signal is equalized and isolated, it is passed through a detector to translate it into the binary environment. The baseband signals used in ISDN transmission require fairly straightforward level detection. An AGC stage or adaptive thresholds may be used for best performance in the presence of noise where multiple-level line codes are used. Framing is established from the detected data by recognizing unique codes that appear periodically.

6.6.19 Line Interfacing

Interfacing to the actual subscriber loop requires several components necessary for functions similar to the BORSHT functions necessary in a voice system (battery, overvoltage, ringing, signaling, hybrid, test). Battery feed is done with a high-voltage supply from the network that is to be efficiently converted to the voltages required at the NT or TE. Overvoltage protection from induced mains voltages and lightning strikes is an important reliability issue. Signaling emergency power conditions is done by reversing the polarity of the battery feed. Most test functions again are performed over the physical layer, but testing the transmission medium requires hardware associated with the battery feed circuitry. The hybrid is necessary only in echo-canceling systems and is usually done within the transceiver. Ringing is not done with high-level signals in ISDN.

Since the manufacturing processes used for transceivers cannot support the high voltages (up to 70 V) necessary for battery feed over subscriber lines and cannot provide the needed fault protection, external components are necessary. Transformer isolation of the transceiver device from the line provides ground fault protection to the user and allows the network to supply power to the NT and terminal for emergency use when local power is not available, as is the case in the present public voice network. An efficient switching power supply is used to convert the high-voltage feed to the power needed at the NT or TE. The power supply continues to be a significant part of the cost of the node, because few of its functions can be reduced in size or integrated.

6.6.20 Testability and Self-Test

Much attention must be paid to the testability of each unit within a device to be able to assure proper functionality within a reasonable test time. Some VLSI devices have embedded state machines, counters, and so on, that live in a very slow environment, and if not provided with special modes, they can be tested only at great expense (long test time). Several design techniques have been developed to assure complete testability that are very general methodologies intended to ensure access to every internal state variable. The most popular, *scan path design*, provides a serial path through state machine state variables that are normally difficult to access. To assure both complete testability and reasonable test time, testability should be discussed in the specification of the block: whenever a function or parameter is described, the appropriate method of test and time to do so should be included. This results in the very quick development of a test known to be extremely thorough.

ISDN components are a breed apart because of their serial multichannel nature. They often require fairly fast clocks, although the data streams they manipulate are not fast. This requires a very large number of cycles to execute a test. Loopback modes, mainly for maintenance and test once installed in a system, can be used effectively to reduce test time. The clocks used in a block that extracts a subchannel and processes it can be sped up, often by a factor of 5 to 10, once it is isolated in an internal-loopback mode. If a data-processing block has an independent control structure, it can be given test modes that extract it from the normal data paths, substitute data accessible from the device pins, and give faster-than-normal operation. If each block can be tested in this manner, only the interfaces between blocks needs to be tested in a fully operational mode. The overall test time is thus considerably reduced while at the same time good test coverage is assured.

Analog blocks need special attention during test. Even when there are no explicit external specifications, each block has its functions, which need to be verified. If an internal block does not meet its design goal, it may be extremely time consuming to find this out by testing the device in its normal operating mode. Therefore, it is necessary to include test modes for analog blocks as well as digital and to specify the performance expected from the blocks when isolated.

6.7 COMPONENTS TO SUPPORT BASIC RATE SERVICE

After reviewing the content and purpose of functional blocks in the ISDN environment, we can now begin assembling them into a system and, where necessary and logical, partitioning them into components. We will discuss the functions necessary at the most numerous nodes within the network:

1. NT1: S/U physical layer adapter
2. NT2 subscriber linecard (S or U interface)
3. TE/TA: full function voice-data terminal adapter

Flexibility and expandability must be considered. The physical layer transmission format will not be considered in detail; the transceiver simply acts as a converter between a serial digital format and a layer 1 protocol. Minimal consideration will be given to interfaces between blocks until partitioning limits currents and wire counts. Only merged processing of layers 2 and 3 will be considered.

The simplest system, the NT1, is discussed first because of the applicability of some of its blocks to functions at the other nodes. To complete the set of ISDN-specific functional blocks, the NT2 is discussed before the TE, that includes blocks which interface to the non-ISDN world. Where sets of blocks are used at several node types, "least supersets" can be identified during partitioning, resulting in more generally useful components and reducing the number of different components necessary in the entire system.

6.7.1 NT1: Physical Layer Adapter

The functions of an NT1 are confined to layer 1, and as such it can be a relatively simple device. It is basically two transceivers, but in addition it is necessary to establish protocols for transfers of level 1 activation and maintenance information. This requires processing blocks associated with each transceiver and bandwidth between them to transfer the information. Maintenance protocols also require self-test capability, and manufacturing tests require access to internal registers and buses for thorough testing. This requires another small processing unit, with its own set of commands. Common functions that are useful at other nodes are collected together, keeping blocks usually associated with each transceiver tightly coupled.

Figure 6.9 shows the NT1 block diagram. The two halves are nearly identical because the types of transceivers used are not specified. In a U/S NT1, the transceivers are different, but U or S repeaters may use two of the same type. The control/maintenance blocks are masters of the asynchronous control/status bus. They generate and interpret command and status information transferred in the layer 1 maintenance channel. Each is responsible for the protocol on the type of layer 1 connection used by the associated transceiver. A common protocol is used between the two control blocks that covers activation and maintenance. The NT1 is transparent to both B and D channels. They need only frame format adaptation.

Timing is extracted by the upstream transceiver and passed to the downstream subsystem. System jitter requirements determine the accuracy of the local time-base and what type of phase-locked loops should be used. A digital PLL will usually suffice, but in some cases the tighter tracking of an analog PLL will be desired to reduce the complexity of the transceiver.

Power is usually not an issue in private (PBX) systems, where each piece of equipment can be mains powered, but must be considered in equipment designed to be placed in the public network. There the NT1 must draw power from the upstream line and provide it to the terminals further downstream. This requires a very efficient switching power supply. The most critical case is in the loss of local power, where the NT must supply a minimum amount of power (approxi-

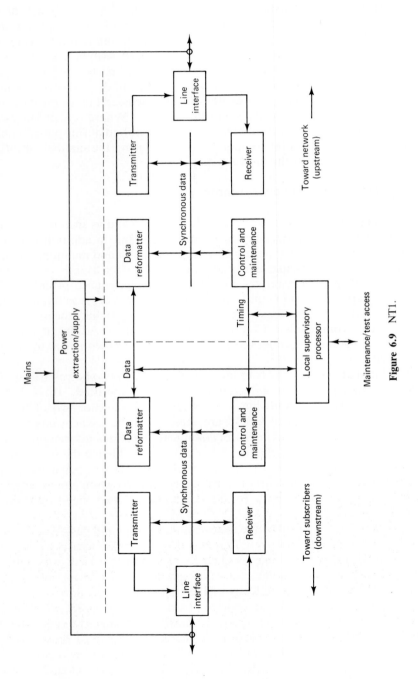

Figure 6.9 NT1.

Mains

Power extraction/supply

Toward network (upstream)

Toward subscribers (downstream)

Line interface

Transmitter

Receiver

Synchronous data

Data reformatter

Control and maintenance

Timing

Data

Local supervisory processor

Maintenance/test access

mately 400 mW) downstream to the terminal(s) for emergency service. In non-emergency cases the NT may be locally powered and may not need to provide the terminals with power.

The control and supervision blocks must be able to execute an internal self-test so that systems maintenance can locate problems in the network. To be complete, this should test all data paths, memories, state machines, and so on that are not fully exercised by loopback modes. This can be a difficult requirement to meet without introducing a large amount of unwanted complexity. To eliminate this, it may be desirable to include a test mode designed to be controlled by an external device, such as a microcontroller. Some system design guidelines do not accommodate microcontrollers at the NT1 node because of the resulting need for them to test themselves, although this is possible to a certain extent. A trade-off must be made between self-test coverage, test logic complexity, and the goals of the self-test.

External equipment is employed during manufacturing tests, and a simple protocol can be used to access registers, memories, and the like, internal to the transceivers. Special test modes and access ports can be provided to reduce test time and equipment complexity. This is a different environment than the self-test because the equipment can be almost arbitrarily complex and can test the device from the outside in a real operating mode instead of in somewhat artificial test modes. While minimal test coverage is not sufficient for manufacture, it may be sufficient for in-service maintenance, as long as it checks all basic functions.

6.7.2 NT2 Subscriber Linecard

The NT2 consists of a number of subscriber line interfaces, a core processor, which may have some switching capability, and one or more upstream links to further switching nodes. The linecard handles upstream subscriber line interfacing and peripheral protocol processing for a number of lines. The upstream links are similar to those of the NT1, so we will concentrate here on local protocol handling and the downstream links. If the NT2 is only present for layer 1 functions, higher-level D-channel functions are pushed off to the exchange group processor, where the task becomes very cumbersome because of the interleaving of the many channels. Thus we will concentrate on the NT2, which includes D-channel level 2 and 3 processing, with a higher-level (virtual) connection to the exchange group processor.

Figure 6.10 illustrates the architecture of a multiple-subscriber NT2. The network-side interface may use T, U, or V (trunk) protocols as stand-alone equipment and may be primary rate. The diagram has been extended to illustrate a remote multiplexer, remote switch, and full PBX. The multiple-interface downstream side remains unchanged for all these network functions, while upstream control and data connections vary. The remote multiplexer will generally have primary rate upstream data connections, so it is nonblocking (all upstream channels can simultaneously be active without bandwidth restrictions). The multiplexer has no switching functions and can utilize a fixed timeslot map from the upstream to downstream channels. The remote switch is most common in larger public network

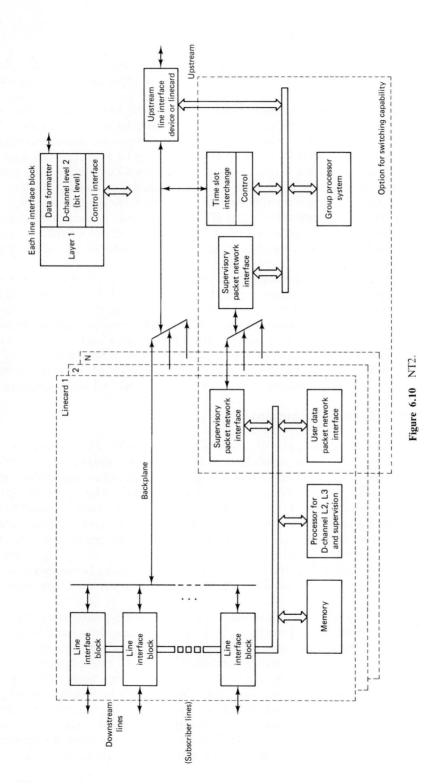

Figure 6.10 NT2.

systems and often does not provide enough upstream bandwidth to be nonblocking. It therefore cannot use fixed timeslot mappings and must contain programmable timeslot interchange logic. A remote switch is slaved to the central switching node, but with the addition of higher-level protocols and services, the same architecture becomes a PBX. The linecard is the downstream interface module in any one of these systems.

Each subscriber line on the linecard, of which there are traditionally eight, requires a transceiver and several associated formatting and processing blocks. The transceiver and layer 1 maintenance channels are very similar to those found in the NT1. The B channels (circuit-switched connections) pass transparently and require only a reformatting block. To allow processing of the D channels, the synchronous circuit-switched connections must be terminated and interfaced to the layer 2 LAP-D processor. This in turn can exchange packets in memory with the local microprocessor for layer 3 processing.

The several methods of distributing the D-channel packet processing differ mainly in the placement of the three main D-channel processing blocks: (1) packet assembly and disassembly, (2) the layer 2 elements of procedure, and (3) layer 3. Generally, all are covered on the linecard, but (2) is variously mapped into hardware or software.

Not only must the subscriber line D channels be processed, but also the corresponding channels on the upstream side of the NT2. Some systems separate signaling traffic from user data and telemetry traffic to eliminate the need for doing so at nodes deeper within the system where the traffic is more concentrated. If the NT2 is a remote concentrator or a remote switch with only a single D channel toward the network, this separation cannot be done. Thus a total of nine or ten bidirectional packetized channels must be processed. The bit-level functions cannot very effectively share hardware, so most implementations utilize one PAD (packet assembler/disassembler) per channel. The rest of level 2 and 3 processing may be done in a common processor once the packets are restored to bytes and placed in memory.

In the nonlinecard applications, a timeslot interchange and a local master processor may be necessary. The timeslot interchange may be used for B-channels, signaling channels, and packet data channels. All can be routed serially and switched using timeslots. The local master group processor system supervises the signaling protocol for the group of lines under its control. A second processor may be used as the entry point to a packet network for user data and telemetry packets which are separated from the D-channel stream at the linecard.

6.7.3 Terminal/Terminal Adapter

The general architecture for ISDN terminals and terminal adapters consists of several core blocks common to all varieties and a multitude of application-oriented blocks that interface layer 1 either with higher levels of ISDN protocol or to non-ISDN protocols. The basic core contains the transceiver, as discussed above, a D-channel processor for levels 1 to 3, and a vestigial formatting section to provide access to B and maintenance channels in more complex equipment. Most basic-rate terminals implement protocols above layer 1 in software, except bit-oriented functions such as packetization.

The most minimal implementations are those for telemetry. These have very simple interfaces to transducers and use only the D channel. The simplest implementations can get by with a transceiver, an HDLC controller for the D channel, and a microcontroller with 8K to 16K bytes of program memory. These blocks provide only the most basic packet exchange capability. This is all that is necessary, however, for automatic utility meter monitoring, for example. The same core transceiver can be used for all NT and TE applications. The HDLC block is the same as used for many other purposes, with a buffer size customized to the D-channel application. The controller software for basic D-channel communication is common to all TEs. Application-specific software modules fill out the main terminal hardware, and a power extraction block completes the design of a fully autonomous telemetry device.

This basic core can be extended for B-channel and more complete D-channel capabilities with the addition of appropriate hardware or software modules. Figure 6.11 illustrates the expansion possible from the telemetry core to a full capability ISDN terminal or terminal adapter. The layer 1 maintenance channel should be fully supported at a data terminal by a block dedicated to data buffering. Automatic execution of layer 1 maintenance directives (loopbacks, self-tests) is not necessary, as it can be covered by the local processor. A DMA master is of great value for reducing the overhead of D-channel block moves that bog down a processor. When the DMA master is more closely associated with the processor that handles the layer 2 protocols, a multiplexed interrupt source is sufficient to inform the processor that it needs to set up the transfers. B-channel serial reformatter blocks may be used to adapt data protocols such as V.24, X.21, and X.31 to ISDN. Voice service can be provided by connecting codec/filter components to a similar reformatting block which adapts to one of several popular serial telecom interfaces. Finally, the ISDN interface device is a peripheral to a microprocessor and should have a parallel bus interface.

The human or data storage that is the actual end point of the ISDN data exchange is reached through higher levels of protocol and other interface components. These are no longer ISDN specific and as such are TE2 components that interface to the ISDN TA via the R-interface (microprocessor bus or serial connection). Serial data connections are made to voice codecs and dumb terminals. The local host microprocessor system includes the keyboard, display, and memory devices that make up the remainder of the terminal.

The voice-only ISDN terminal deserves some special mention. The most important feature of this terminal is its ability to function in an emergency power situation when local power is not available, drawing a minimum of power from the loop. When not in use, it must draw an extremely low current, yet still be able to recognize and wake up to service an activation request, either local or from the loop. The power specifications do not preclude the primary emergency terminal from providing other services when local power is available, but data and power isolation would be necessary between the normal and emergency sections to allow a personal computer card TA (for example) to double as an emergency ISDN

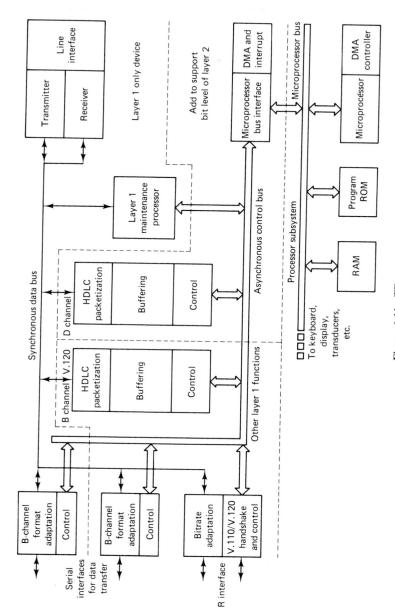

Figure 6.11 TE.

phone. (This additional complexity is generally not desirable on the PC card.) Thus the "ISDN telephone" becomes a line-powered device similar to the telemetry TE, with the addition of a B-channel extraction block, a codec/filter device, and D-channel protocol software for voice call setup.

6.8 PARTITIONING AND INTERFACES

The building blocks presented must be partitioned into larger groups for the final design and realization of components for actual systems. Since this may be done in many ways, some figures of merit should be set up to evaluate different overall partitionings. These should be based on cost, complexity, user friendliness, and reliability. Where the market segment to be addressed is limited so that only a portion of the possible network functions is planned, the figures of merit should be modified. The discussion here will be general, to address the entire range of terminal, NT, and linecard functions.

If we inspect Figures 6.9, 6.10, and 6.11, several blocks can be identified that are useful in a number of applications. Generality of application guarantees a larger market for a device. If generality can be built in without too much added complexity, economies of scale lead to even further advantage. We can thus discuss similar blocks found in multiple applications and find the "least superset"—the simplest extension that covers all architectural variations.

6.8.1 Transceiver Block

Each line-connected component requires a transceiver to implement layer 1 protocols. The S and U transceivers are very different, but the functions of the downstream and upstream transceivers for one format are quite similar. The transceiver block should include all functions closely associated with the physical layer: timing recovery, data buffering, maintenance channel extraction, and multipoint functions. It must also interface to higher-layer functions and to the local management entity. This usually results in a block with several generic serial interfaces and one parallel (microprocessor) control interface.

Timing must be recovered from the upstream side and used to drive the rest of the transceiver and other downstream components. This requires a phase-locked loop in each transceiver. If a transceiver is timing slaved to an internal interface, as on the subscriber side of an NT, recovered receive timing is only used to assure good receiver performance and is not distributed to other parts of the system. In this case the node synchronization is determined by the upstream-side transceiver, which passes timing information to the node's timing block for distribution.

The transceivers must interface their data to the rest of the local system in a predictable manner. Buffering is necessary to adjust the timings of the internal data streams to fit external system requirements. For example, at the upstream transceiver, the buffering must take into account different loop propagation delays and adapt the received data stream to internal timings. Format conversion is usually needed to interface to the external serial buses, requiring buffering for the serial/parallel/serial conversions.

Standardized level 1 protocols include a low-bit-rate maintenance channel to control loopback and self-test of devices such as an NT1, which are not accessible over other channels. Similar logic can be used at each end of the loop to transmit and receive the maintenance codes, but a special machine would be necessary to execute and generate them. This would be used only at an NT1 if no microprocessor was desired. A trade-off must thus be made there between hardware and software costs, including development.

The I.430 basic rate S interface defines a D-channel contention resolution scheme for multipoint topologies that is implemented as a part of the level 1 device. This requires different logic at the TE and NT, but the extent of each is small. Another TE function necessary for I.430 multipoint operation is the transmit enable for B channels at the TE.

6.8.2 D-Channel Processing Block

The most widely used block for D-channel processing is the HDLC packet processor and buffer, which converts between asynchronous byte-wide data and the synchronous bit stream that is exchanged on layer 1 entities. Except for the contention-resolution support necessary at the S terminal, the same block can be used at all D-channel link layer nodes. Address and control-byte recognition may be added to eliminate unnecessary processing at terminals and to separate packet types at the linecard. Many layer 2 implementations are software-based past this point, using the linecard or terminal adapter microprocessor as the host. The advantage of this method is that the same processor can also be used for level 3 processing. Where a large amount of packet traffic is concentrated on a single node for protocol execution, as in a group controller, dedicated hardware processors are better able to handle the task than general-purpose processors. Existing products can support only a limited number of links, however, without external preprocessing, so we will assume that layer 2 elements of procedure and layer 3 are software based. Thus the D-channel hardware block should consist of HDLC packetization, address recognition, contention-resolution support, and data buffering. Software-based processing requires an extension of the "management entity" system but no special functional blocks.

As further integration demands dedicated processors for higher layers of the protocols, the software that had been based in the management microprocessor can be offloaded to embedded peripheral processors. To take advantage of the existing software, a compatible processor can be integrated as a core with the PAD function to complete the layer 2 functions. Where the investment is justifiable, some silicon area reduction may be found if a custom processor is built for this protocol alone. However, question of flexibility versus speed will continue to plague the custom approach.

6.8.3 B-Channel Processing Block

B-channel processing blocks must implement only layer 1 functions, but may also include layers 2 and 3. Because B channels are (virtual) circuit-switched connections, these blocks are used only at the terminal. Bit rate adaptation such as V.110 are straightforward layer 1 functions, but require special functional blocks because of the incompatibility of the required bit-oriented functions with microprocessor instruction sets. Packet protocols such as V.120, X.25, and X.31 can be implemented with blocks very similar to the D-channel packet processor. Since B-channel communication is generally point to point, the address recognition and contention resolution are not necessary. A larger data buffer is required for the B channel than for the D channel because of the higher data rate. Byte-oriented protocols are easily implemented with a microprocessor, but require buffering to reduce overhead. This can be realized by bypassing the bit-level front end of the HDLC block.

6.8.4 Interfaces Between Blocks

Since all ISDN functions are not going to be integrated in a single device anytime soon, it is necessary to define interfaces between devices that each implement a number of functional blocks. Several interfaces that have been developed by component manufacturers intent on establishing de facto standards. However, not being supported by CCITT and ANSI, they are not as complete or general as might be expected. Their general format is a serial bidirectional link at some multiple of 256K bps. These are physical-level interfaces, and thus carry 2B + D plus maintenance and primitive control channels. They are intended for use between layer 1 components, as at an NT1, or between layer 1 and layer 2 components at a terminal or NT2. Higher levels are generally transferred over a standard parallel processor bus. Master and slave control relationships are established, propagating outward from the microprocessor in control of the group of components (the NT1 is thus slaved to the linecard microprocessor). The interfaces consist of data, clock, and framing lines. Timing is propagated downstream by means of the clock and framing lines. Local multipoint connections are allowed, which enable distribution of D and B channels to appropriate processing units (in terminals) or for multiplexing several lines at the primary rate (at the NT2).

Some layer 1 components must be remotely controlled over these interfaces because they do not interface to a microprocessor bus. Only layer 1 primitives and data need to be exchanged: B, D, and maintenance channel data, and the primitives for activation, deactivation, D-channel priority, loopback specification, and so on. The more complete protocols allow communication with internal registers at the remote nodes by means of device-specific control protocols. This allows maintenance tricks such as locating a line fault by reading back the coefficients of an echo-canceling filter.

When a distributed series of layer 1 devices is connected by such a protocol, activation proceeds in a serial fashion, beginning at the requesting processor, through both standard and nonstandard physical interfaces, until all links are activated. If activation is thought of as the transfer of primitive signals for activate request, activate command, and acknowledgment between connected devices in a serial chain, each primitive signal is transferred along a layer 1 chain between nodes with higher-layer processing capability that initiate the process. Similarly, maintenance messages are propagated from the L1 management entities, which are usually associated with the L2/L3 nodes, to the appropriate device in the chain. The addressed device may automatically respond to acknowledge the message with a reply or acknowledgment or may be polled.

When a device is to be operated without direct connection to a microprocessor, but is slaved by means of such an interface to a remote control entity, a command processor must be included to execute commands and generate requests. Its functions must at the minimum include all primitives used at that layer for activation, data transfer, and maintenance. So that the device is testable within a reasonable amount of time, additional maintenance and test features must be included. For network maintenance, duplicate access to such features should be provided over the interdevice interface.

Several devices can be locally paralleled on such an interface by means of time division multiplexing (TDM). This is the basis of the widely accepted serial TDM or PCM (pulse code modulation) codec interface, defined for standardization of the digitized linecard interfaces to voice switches. A point-to-multipoint topology with one master node (or conceptually so) distributes the bandwidth outgoing from the master node among several slaves. In the other direction, the data are multiplexed from the slaves back into the master. A common use of this in ISDN terminals is the separation of B1, B2, and D information at the transceiver interface for connection to their respective voice, data, and signaling processors.

6.9 POWER FUNCTIONS

Devices for power extraction and power feeding remain in a different category from the VLSI used for the bulk of ISDN functions. Because of the high voltages and relatively high currents involved, these are normally manufactured on high-voltage bipolar processes, incompatible with the low-voltage CMOS used for most other components. Among themselves, however, there is a limited range of functions that need be done. Therefore a small number of devices can provide all the functions necessary throughout a network. The two basic functions are simply power feeding and power extraction. Variations on these for optimum efficiency in different power ranges or for polarity indication to detect emergency power conditions can be included in the basic device for broader applicability.

6.10 COMMERCIAL ARCHITECTURES AND PRODUCTS

Two architectures have become popular among manufacturers of data-path components for ISDN. The serial architecture emphasizes the separation of levels and explicitly defines new interface structures for use among them. The merged architecture is an expansion of that of digital voice switches to ISDN without overly complicating the data path. Components have been placed on the open market from both captive manufacturers, associated with switch makers, and from independents, which support each partitioning. There is some crossover as well, as manufacturers realize the longer-term advantages that both architectures offer. With higher levels of integration, the natural tendency will be toward the merged architecture, but neither partitioning is so advantageous that is can be predicated to dominate until full integration obviates the serial architecture.

The main distinguishing features are the partitioning of processing elements for layers 2 and above of both B and D channels. Above layer 2 the protocols are well suited to software implementations and the differences disappear. At layers 1 and 2, much of the architectural difference is due to different market segments targeted by each manufacturer. The total number of components and the complexity of each should be minimized by each manufacturer to most efficiently approach the market. Where only a small number of applications are considered, for example, only the TA and TE1, a small number of very complex components can be an appropriate solution. If it is necessary to cover the entire range of TA, TE, NT, and linecard possibilities, a more modular line of less complex components allows the most flexibility for mix-and-match solutions.

The traditional markets of each manufacturer are a good gauge of the focus of their ISDN architectures. Thus, semiconductor merchant manufacturers prefer the higher-integration merged approach because their customers are oriented more toward the terminal market, while captive producers within switch manufacturers need to provide capabilities for the entire range of ISDN nodes and thus take the modular route.

The serial architecture, placing processing for each level in one component or group of components, is best exemplified by the Siemens ISDN product line [4]. Being closely associated with a switch manufacturer, the component developments paralleled that of the CCITT I-series recommendations. Since the recommendations needed to fit well with one another to form the larger whole, it was a good strategy to identify one component development with each recommendation. The close association with both systems people and standards people gave the overall project solid structure and good direction.

A good example of the merged architecture is provided by the components from Advanced Micro Devices. This independent semiconductor manufacturer is known for producing high-complexity, high-performance devices, integrating many functions into a single device; that same strategy has been followed for their ISDN components. The independent manufacturers strive to minimize the number of components developed and maximize the volume of each, giving good functionality at reasonable cost.

6.10.1 Serial Architecture

The Siemens architecture is organized such that each protocol level of each channel (D, B) is handled by one device. A multipoint local interface (IOM) is used between the single layer 1 component and several layer 2 components. This separates the channels to individual processing blocks at the TE and allows circuit switching the B channels while doing local processing of the D channel at an NT2 or linecard. The components that belong to this family include several transceivers, a D-channel-oriented HDLC processor, a B-channel-oriented dual-channel HDLC processor, and a timeslot-assignment/HDLC "linecard controller" that interfaces to serial backplanes. Layers 3 and above are handled in software by one or more processors attached to the bus ports of the layer 2 components.

The modular design of the serial system is the key to its flexibility. Subsystems of hardware and appropriate software can be developed around each module and assembled for different applications. Where separate hardware is necessary for incompatible B channel functions, independent subsystems can be developed and multiplexed in a bus fashion on the serial interface between the layer 1 transceiver and the layer 2 components. Figure 6.12 shows how the Siemens components map into the functions for NT1, NT2 and TE, nodes.

Although they remain the primary example of a well-planned serial system, one limitation restricts the use of the Siemens layer 2 components: the level 2 controllers do not support multiple logical links without a significant amount of help from a microprocessor, which must effectively take over protocol execution. Where this restricts system performance unacceptably, more complex bus-master layer 2 components may be used. These include devices from Motorola, the MC68606 LAPD Controller and the MC68605 X.25 Contoller [7], and from Western Digital, the WD2511 X.25 Packet Network Interface [14]. These are advanced components that handle level 2 for multiple logical links and large window sizes and include DMA bus masters to completely unload the processor from level 2 activities. Similar to the less complex layer 2 devices, however, they require further support from a microprocessor to execute higher-level protocols. Their complexity and cost make them somewhat less desirable in application to the low data rates of a basic-rate interface. Primary-rate and multiple-channel applications are a better fit, where the high data rates may exceed the capacity of software-based processing.

6.10.2 Semi-Propietary Interfaces between Components

Several serial interfaces have been developed by Siemens, alone and in conjunction with other manufacturers, to connect these components together. It is interesting to look at their history as an example of the development of ISDN-related proprietary protocols. Three schemes are pictured in Fig. 6.13.

The SLD (subscriber line data) interface, supported by a number of manufacturers [4, 6], uses a ping-pong data lead and thus is difficult to use as anything but a point-to-point interface. It was originally used as an interface in advanced voice network and has carried over for use in ISDN. Four bytes are transferred in the upstream and downstream directions at an 8-KHz rate, two of which are used for the B channels. The other two channels carry component-dependent control and status information. The linecard controller supports using the third byte for packetized control and status, while the fourth is intended for slow-speed bit-mapped signaling.

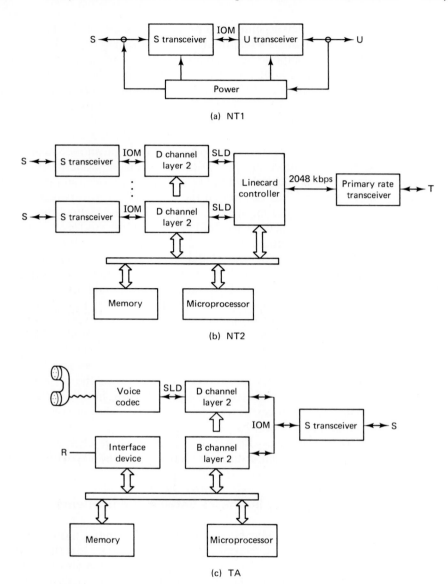

Figure 6.12   Functional group realization using serial architecture components.

The IOM (ISDN-oriented modular) interface is an outgrowth of SLD that uses one data lead in each direction and standardizes some commands and responses [4].   The data lead separation allows multipoint connections and simple interfaces to other unrelated interconnect schemes.   For example, a gating signal that identifies a B-channel octet can enable the clock when data are transferred into an HDLC device and can enable a driver for the data when multiplexed onto the data

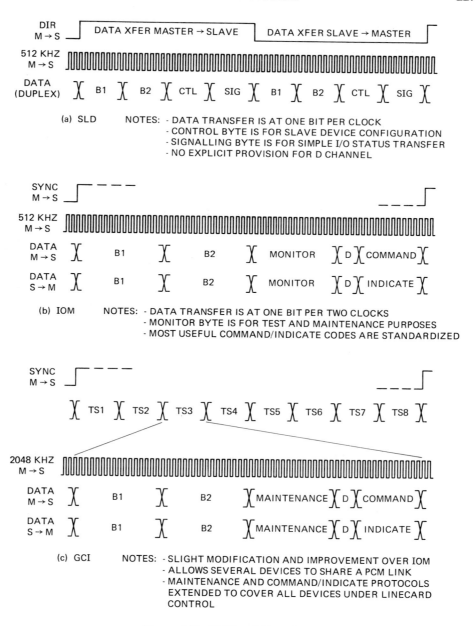

Figure 6.13 ISDN serial interfaces.

line in the other direction. This enables generic synchronous communications devices to be used without customization or complicated interfaces in the ISDN environment. Standardization of L1–L2 primitive commands and responses allows interchangeability of L1 components without any need to change the layer 2 software.

The GCI (general circuit interface) has been developed by the European consortium of Alcatel, Italtel, Plessey, and Siemens as a further refinement in this series of protocols [18]. It extends IOM in two important areas. It allows the use of a high-speed interface clock at the same speed as that used on PCM backplanes, but minimizing timeslot assignment complications by simply multiplexing the data of eight basic-rate subscriber lines onto the higher speed link. It also extends the control/status transfer capability past the local system. This allows the linecard to control and maintain all nodes in the line out toward the subscriber, e.g. a U-interface repeater and an NT1. With GCI, a flexible and well-thought-out system of interconnect is put in place.

The Siemens set of components is best suited to the hardware and software architecture of its own switching systems. Other switch manufacturers have incompatible systems, requiring custom components at the hardware interface and protocol translators at the software interface if they are to be able to use these same components. Mitel has developed a similar family of components around their ST-bus, a 2.048-MHz interface similar to the 32-timeslot backplane standard [8]. The ST-bus definition has adapted the existing digitized-voice PCM for use as an ISDN intercomponent link by defining control protocols. Similar to the protocols mentioned above, four bytes are used to transfer the basic rate 2B + D bandwidth plus signaling and control information.

6.10.3 Merged Architecture

Although serial architecture provides inherent flexibility, easier development because of the simplicity of each module, and the ability to better customize the final system design to the application, there are similar arguments in favor of merged architecture. Here the user needs to deal with only one component and one set of software routines to cover an entire spectrum of applications. Component complexity is higher, but manufacturing experience shows that a reduction in package count often leads to a reduction in system cost. This drives the normal course of component evolution toward higher integration and lower cost per function.

Advanced Micro Devices provides the best example of a high-integration ISDN part in their AM79C30 Digital Subscriber Controller (DSC) [9]. This integrates a DSP-based codec/filter voice block, an S tranceiver, an HDLC bit-level processor for the D channel, a serial port, and a microprocessor port. A complete terminal adapter can be constructed with this device, a dedicated LAP-D processor subsystem, and components to support the desired external B-channel data interface. This normally will be the population of a personal computer plug-in board.

This AM79C30 represents the integration of most of the functions of three of the components of the Siemens serial product line: the transceiver, the codec/filter, and the front-end bit-level functions of the HDLC LAP-D machine. It is by no means, however, a stand-alone TE. The complexity of a number of the blocks is reduced when compared with less highly integrated devices so that the codec/filter can be accommodated: the transceiver has been pared down to only those functions necessary at the TE; the D-channel processing block has been restricted to a small buffer and only minimal status/control logic; and minimal support has been given to the maintenance channel. However, these simplifications do not seriously limit the applicability of the device; all reduced functions can be taken over by the supervisory microprocessor. Figure 6.14 shows the partitioning of Fig. 6.11 as realized in a 79C30-based TE.

6.10.4 Other Partitionings

A large number of semiconductor manufacturers have offered devices for the ISDN network. Mitel is the most notable switch manufacturer with a broad product line based around their ST bus. They offer several components for proprietary U-type interfaces, and the MT8930, an S-interface device that is similar to the AMD 79C30 without the codec/filter. The transceiver can function in both NT and TE modes, and the D-channel HDLC processor is somewhat more versatile than that on the AMD device, allowing the local processor more time for other functions. Existing codec/filters are used for voice service, interfaced via the ST bus. Similar devices (with different interfaces) are available from Siemens (the PEB 2085), AMD (the 79C31), Intel (the 29C53) [6], and ATT (the T7250A) [5].

A very logical partitioning of functions has been proposed by National Semiconductor for their ISDN product line [15]. Since the analog functions in transceivers make them difficult to integrate with a very large amount of digital circuitry, they have separated the transceiver from the layer 2/3 functions. A single device (HPC16400) handles layers 2 and 3 for both D and B channels, using dedicated machines for the bit-oriented front-end functions of each channel and executing the bulk of the protocols with software. The processor for the software is built into the layer 2/3 device with the front-end processors. Its instruction set has been tailored for packet processing.

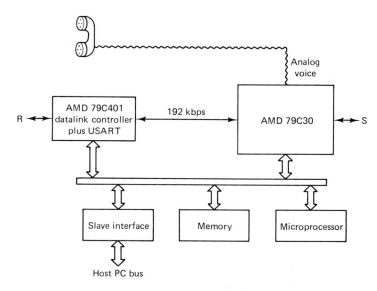

Figure 6.14 Merged-architecture components.

Because of the late development of U interface specifications and the expectation that terminals at least in the public network will be based on the S-interface, little work has been done on integrating U transceivers with other functions. Since U-interface transceivers are much more complex than those for the S-interface, this partitioning will continue to dominate for quite some time.

Late appearing in product portfolios are B-channel protocol translation blocks, as described in section 6.6. Presently, a certain amount of "glue" hardware is necessary to interface older hardware (X.25, V.24) with ISDN layer 1 components. The need for this glue will eventually disappear. Bit-rate adaptation blocks for V.110 and similar protocols also will be forthcoming, likely integrated with layer 1 blocks.

6.11 SOFTWARE

One of the largest hurdles in implementation of ISDN has been the software in switching systems. While the general form of switch software has been able to support ISDN-like services since the advent of digital switching systems, widespread installation of thoroughly tested software that implements the stadardized protocols has taken many years. Because of the importance of the switch as a part of the entire network, extremely thorough testing of all software has been necessary. This has been done with field trials conducted on ISDN islands, where all aspects of both hardware and software are debugged. Switch software reliabilty and robustness are as important as the services offered. Terminal equipment uses a smaller set of software, having a smaller set of functions. Terminal equipment must be certified for compatibility with the network and conformance to the necessary standards. It is the switch, however, that is the reference point. Thus the ultimate responsibility for the introduction of ISDN on a large scale lies with the successful implementation, verification, and deployment of software in PABX and public switching systems. The terminals, which enable subscribers to access network services, have no capabilities without the network; the hardware, similarly, sits idle without the higher layers.

Many tasks in ISDN are easily handled by the software of a small microcomputer system or a microcontroller. Most sections of the link access protocols are well suited to implementation in software. Those that are not are those for which most processors do not provide appropriate instructions, resulting in inefficient code. Processors usually concentrate on parallel byte and word operands. When the data are serialized and must be processed in a serial fashion, as is done in HDLC or bit-rate adaptation protocols, dedicated hardware is better suited to the task than general purpose. These functions, although operating on fairly slow bit streams, use large numbers of state variables and require large amounts of task-switching overhead if executed as one of a number of tasks by a general-purpose processor. Similar difficulties are found if one attempts to implement B-channel rate adaption protocols such as V.110 with a standard processor.

Protocol handling is generally divided between hardware and software such that serial bit-stream processing is done in hardware and parallel byte or word-oriented processing is done in software. The capacity of simple microcomputer systems is exceeded when the packet throughput exceeds that required by 2B + D on levels 2 and 3. Several component manufacturers offer hardware controllers that cover all of level 2, to unload some tasks from the processor when significantly more throughput is needed. In many cases, however, a more economical and equally valid solution is to use a more powerful processor in a faster system.

Much software is necessary to support level 2 and 3 protocols of the D channel alone. Some B-channel packet protocols such as X.31 are quite similar in concept to LAP-D, but there is not significant overlap. Several independent parties have developed software for layers 2 and 3 of LAP-D, for several different processors, usually arriving at a code size of between 64K and 128K bytes. If two such protocols (LAP-D and LAP-B) are executed by one processor, for example at a TE, this would require a code space of approximately 256K bytes. Additional packet buffer memory is needed for the data. The size of this code suggests that the processor needs to support a large address space, but this is not necessarily so. The code size is relatively independent of the type of processor, and speed is not a significant limitation for basic-rate applications, so even a modest 8-bit microcontroller has the capacity to support 2B + D if program memory paging is implemented.

The amount of code necessary to support ISDN is very large, and it represents as significant an investment as the hardware. Just as the hardware is being standardized by these protocols, so will the software become standardized. A small number of user interface communications software packages (representing the upper layers of protocols) will become dominant, as are several such packages for existing lower-speed serial protocols, such as the V series. Testing and validation during the development of large software packages is at least as important as that for hardware. Operating under the auspices of CEPT and ANSI, certification bodies have appeared with the charter to approve equipment for use on the ISDN network. The enormous amount of effort needed to both develop and certify such a large amount of code will encourage software standardization.

6.12 TRENDS AND DIRECTIONS

When we compare the hardware composition of TAs or full-feature TEs that employ devices from the serial and merged architectural extremes, we see that these significantly different design philosophies result in only a minor difference in the overall result: the three Siemens ISDN devices are covered by the one from AMD. Little of significance in terms of cost or design complexity is seen unless we look at simpler functional groups, such as ISDN phone or the NT1. As volumes and competition grow, the costs of each of the applications will be reduced by the employment of higher and higher levels of integration. The most cost-sensitive nodes will be tackled first (NT1 and ISDN phone), followed by the more complex functions. ISDN hardware will follow the same learning curves as all high-volume semiconductor applications.

The high volume is a key. Those applications generating the most volume will create the most competition, resulting in the most efficient and highest-integration implementations. The NT2 application, whether for use as a linecard, a remote switch, or a remote multiplexor, will lag behind because of the lack of consumer orientation. These functions usually fall under the design and manufacturing jurisdiction of the switch manufacturer. The terminal market will be much more open than the switch, with very well defined interfaces, protocols, and services. Upgrades to the switch side will most often be to the software in order to provide additional services.

The most likely course of integration is for all TE digital functions to be integrated before the analog functions are added. This allows some time for further evolution of transmission standards and standardization of applications. Architectures similar to that of the National Semiconductor 16400 (processor with dedicated peripherals) will be emulated by numerous vendors, especially those with popular microprocessor architectures. Eventually, program and data memory will be included within the device to complete the digital functional complement. Finally, the transceiver and codec/filter blocks will be added. When the ISDN network appears in the home, the demand for the single-chip ISDN phone will assure the completion of this evolution.

ACKNOWLEDGMENT

For helpful discussion and suggestions, the author is grateful to colleagues George Hayek, Gary Thomas, and Pat Weston.

REFERENCES

6.1. The International Telegraph and Telephone Consultative Committee, Blue Book, Volume III, Fascicle III.8, *Recommendations of the Series I*, International Telecommunications Union, Geneva, 1989.

6.2. The International Telegraph and Telephone Consultative Committee, Blue Book, Volume VIII, Fascicle VIII.1, *Recommendations of the Series V*, International Telecommunications Union, Geneva, 1989.

6.3. The International Telegraph and Telephone Consultative Committee, Blue Book, Volume VIII, Fascicle VIII.2, *Recommendations of the Series X*, International Telecommunications Union, Geneva, 1989.

6.4. Siemens Components USA, "Telecommunications Data Book," Santa Clara, Calif., 1987.

6.5. AT&T Technologies, "Communication Devices Data Book," Allentown, Pa., 1987.

6.6. Intel Corporation, "Microcommunications Handbook," Santa Clara, Calif., 1988.

6.7. Motorola Semiconductor Products, Inc., "Telecommunications Products," Austin, Tex., 1987.

6.8. Mitel Semiconductor, "Microelectronics Data Book," Kanata, Ontario, 1988.

6.9. Advanced Micro Devices, "Semiconductors for Telecommunications Applications, Condensed Catalog," Sunnyvale, Calif., 1987.

6.10. Exchange Carriers Standards Association, American National Standards Institute, Inc., "ISDN Basic Access Interface for S and T Reference Points, Layer 1 Specification," Bethesda Md., 1988.

6.11. Exchange Carriers Standards Association, American National Standards Institute, Inc., "ISDN Basic Access Interface for Use on Metallic Loops for Application on the Network Side of the NT, Layer 1 Specification", Bethesda Md., 1988.

6.12. Gray, Paul R., and Robert G. Meyer, *Analysis and Design of Analog Integrated Circuits, 2nd Ed.*, Wiley, New York, 1984.

6.13. Tsividis, Y., and Antognetti, P., eds., *Design of MOS VSLI Circuits for Telecommunications*, Prentice-Hall, Englewood Cliffs, N.J., 1985.

6.14. Western Digital Corp., "Communications Products Handbook," Irvine, Calif., 1984.

6.15. National Semiconductor Corp., "Telecommunications Databook," Santa Clara, Calif., 1987.

6.16. Hayes Microcomputer Products, Inc., "Smartmodem 2400 TM User's Guide," Norcross, Ga., 1985.

6.17. International Organization for Standardization, "Data communication—High-level data link control procedures—Frame structure," ISO 3309, Geneva, 1979.

6.18. Group-of-Four Companies (Alcatel-Italtel-Plessey-Siemens), "General Circuit Interface (GCI)," 1988.

CHAPTER 7

ISDN Applications

EDWARD K. BOWER

Edward K. Bower, Inc.

ABSTRACT

As the ISDN spreads to larger numbers of users, with greater geographical extension and higher bit rates, the bulk of today's telecommunications tasks will be supported. Voice and data services for business applications will lead the advance of ISDN, with residential and high-bit-rate applications to follow. Many of the early applications depend on a single ISDN feature, the ability of the called party to learn the calling party's number. In the future, ISDN's flexible, multipurpose interfaces will be employed for a multitude of applications that have not yet been conceived. The cost of basic voice telephone service can approach today's rates, while many novel applications involving voice, data, and their combination will motivate the conversion of present-day networks to ISDN compatibility. The benefits of an open, multivendor telecommunications environment outweigh the cost of upgrading present equipment and services. The ultimate goal of ISDN is to provide a worldwide information utility.

7.1 INTRODUCTION

Previous chapters have described the origin, objectives, specifications, and implementation of ISDN. The purpose of this chapter is to present the principal applications of ISDN, as seen by its end users. A distinction is made between the *services* provided by an ISDN and the *applications* that may be supported by these services. An example of a service is a 64-kbps clear channel synchronous data path with out-of-band signaling; a voice telephone call is one of the applications, or uses, that may be made of this service.

The CCITT specification of ISDN details the interfaces and services that the network provides, but the applications of ISDN are not formally specified. This was done to avoid limiting ISDN to those uses that could be identified at the time the specifications were established. The study groups that contributed to the ISDN specification had many specific applications in mind, and tailored the definition of the services to support these uses, while not restricting the future addition of novel applications.

The ultimate goal of the ISDN is to provide a worldwide information utility. A model for this service is the electric utility, which provides electric power capable of driving an enormous range of appliances via a standardized wall outlet. An information utility would provide access to communications, database information retrieval, computation, and similar services through a standard interface. To this end, ISDN defines a small number of interfaces, each capable of supporting multiple applications. The groups that formulated the specifications of these interfaces performed delicate trade-offs in order to select the most useful and economical set of interface types. If a single interface were to support all the functions of the information utility, it would require a very high bit rate and would need to provide all the capabilities of the most sophisticated user. On the other hand, specifying the most cost-effective interface for each application on an individual basis would lead to a very large number of incompatible interfaces. A compromise between these two extremes resulted in the ISDN interface family, a small number of multipurpose standards.

Since ISDN is intended to support nearly all the present telecommunications activities, its applications include many familiar uses. The emphasis of this chapter is on the new applications that ISDN enables and those that are simplified by the unique features it provides.

7.1.1 Basic Telephone Service

The bulk of the use of the telephone network is for voice communication. This will continue to be the case for the foreseeable future. Therefore, ISDN must strive to provide basic voice telephone services on an economical basis. This goal is to be accomplished by realizing economies from digital switching and transmission, as compared with an analog telephone plant. With the use of VLSI circuitry, the basic digital telephone handset should not be more costly to manufacture than the analog telephone.

7.1.2 Enhanced Features

In addition to providing basic voice calls, ISDN supplies a variety of enhanced features to its users. Both voice and data users will enjoy new capabilities, while a number of applications that integrate voice and data will emerge.

Many of the new features depend on one ISDN capability: the transfer of the caller's number to the called party via the D channel. Equipment designers have selected this particular new capability as the building block upon which to implement a surprisingly large array of applications.

7.1.3 First Business, Then Residential Use

The conversion of the world's present telephone system into an integrated digital network will require several decades to accomplish. An enormous global investment has been made in the present equipment, which cannot be discarded overnight. The only economically feasible approach is to gradually replace the telephone network, upgrading components and facilities as they wear out or as new capacity is added.

ISDN will first penetrate the business, or office, market and then later the residential sector. Business users have greater economic incentives to upgrade their applications to make use of the new services than do residential voice subscribers. Businesses have come to view their communications resources as an important tool to enhance productivity. They demand that their facilities be at least as capable and efficient as those of their competitors.

A single large corporation may contribute a significant fraction of a local carrier's revenue and therefore have much more leverage than an individual residence in obtaining desired services. If ISDN services are not provided locally, the corporation has the alternative of constructing transmission paths to the nearest offices of an interexchange carrier that can support the corporation's needs. This competitive environment will compel many local and regional operating companies to upgrade their offerings to include ISDN functionality. Since bypassing the local carrier is not feasible for the residential subscriber, business applications will receive attention first. Once the ISDN backbone network is in place, carriers will be positioned to provide its benefits to individual homes on an economical basis.

7.1.4 Importance of Applications

Integrated services digital networks expect to realize savings in the areas of digital transmission and switching, as compared to the analog telephone plant. It is widely recognized that these savings will be difficult to obtain during the deployment phase of ISDN. Initially, small quantities of ISDN units are built, so the eventual economies of manufacturing scale are not realized.

A basic tenet of ISDN is that the end user must be able to send any arbitrary sequence of bits in the B channel, fully utilizing all 64 kbps for its purposes; this is known as *clear channel* capability. In pre-ISDN T1 links, the user is prohibited from sending long strings of 0 bits, which lack the transitions necessary for timing to be recovered from the received waveform. The bipolar eight zero substitution (B8ZS) technique solves this problem by encoding groups of eight 0 bits into a unique pattern containing transitions. However, most of the presently installed intermediate multiplexers will not pass this unique pattern transparently, so a significant number of devices must be upgraded to allow the T1 network to support clear channel capability.

Thus, it is initially more expensive to provide ISDN services than traditional telephone service. If some part of these extra costs are to be paid by the subscriber, then ISDN services are more expensive than traditional services, at least on initial deployment. Subscribers cannot be expected to subsidize ISDN with higher fees to gain its eventual advantages. Governments may compel some subsidization in the form of user fees or access charges, but corporate users have considerable flexibility to construct bypass arrangements or non-ISDN private networks to avoid these charges.

These considerations lead to the conclusion that the success of ISDN, as measured by the rate of its deployment, depends strongly on the willingness of its users to pay a premium for the extra services they receive. Their desire for ISDN services depends, in turn, on the applications that those services support. Thus, the value of the various applications, as perceived by their end users, is the key to the success of ISDN.

As we will see in the rest of this chapter, a wide range of applications and features are made possible by ISDN. In addition, numerous capabilities of the pre-ISDN network are enhanced and simplified by the availability of ISDN services. Many corporations around the world are investing substantial sums to develop and implement various aspects of ISDN, with the expectation that the value of the new applications will outweigh their cost.

7.2 BUSINESS APPLICATIONS

7.2.1 Simultaneous Voice and Data Calls

The basic rate interface (BRI) has been described in detail in earlier chapters. It consists of two simultaneous, full-duplex, clear-channel, 64-kbps paths with associated signaling, denoted the 2B + D configuration. Why should the *basic* interface be defined as *two* paths? Wouldn't it be more natural to specify a single connection as the basic building block (a B + D configuration) and then define the 2B + D arrangement in terms of this more fundamental unit? After all, ISDN is built upon the existing telephone plant, whose basis is the voice call, a single bidirectional path. To develop insight into the motivation for defining BRI in terms of dual paths, we must consider a commonplace office application involving telecommunication service.

Suppose an incoming voice caller is requesting information about a product, a service, a price, or a schedule. The call is received by an attendant or PBX and routed to an appropriate agent. The caller asks questions of the agent, who performs a database inquiry to find the answer and then relays the information to the caller. In a very small company, a single agent can maintain the database on a local personal computer. In larger organizations, a number of different agents could have answered the call at their individual offices. Since they need to share a single database, some communication between multiple offices and the database is required.

In this scenario, the voice call must be maintained while the database inquiry takes place, since the caller desires an immediate response. Thus, the agent's duties involve two simultaneous conversations: one voice call from a human and one data call to a computer. In the pre-ISDN environment, a telephone and a separate data terminal occupy the agent's desk, shown in Fig. 7.1. The telephone is connected by twisted-pair wiring to the PBX, while the data terminal is typically connected to a host computer by a separate 25-conductor cable or local area network bus.

A 2B + D configuration allows an integrated voice/data terminal to perform both functions over the same physical connection, as shown in Fig. 7.2. This

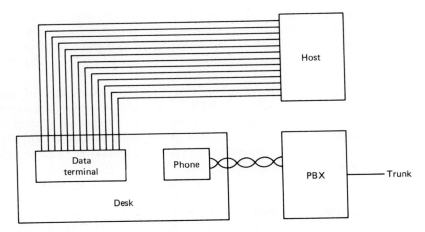

Figure 7.1 The pre-ISDN office.

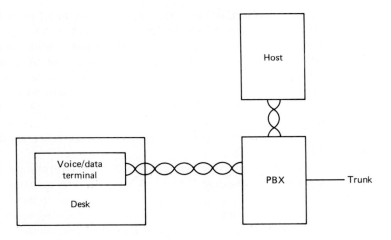

Figure 7.2 The ISDN office.

ability often results in a substantial saving, since office buildings are generally equipped with twisted-pair wiring, but lack special data cables. The agent's integrated voice/data station maintains an open session with the host; that is, the user does not need to log off of the host in order to respond to an incoming call. Even though the terminal is connected to the PBX by a single pair of wires, the two B channels that it carries are used independently. The PBX routes one B channel to the host, while using the other B channel to deliver incoming calls to the agent's terminal.

The financial benefit arising from this application motivates the adoption of a BRI standard capable of two simultaneous conversations. Thus, B channels are like shoes: you can buy them in pairs, but they are not available individually.

One may wonder whether this clerical application should be used as the model for telecommunications in general, to the extent of tailoring the BRI definition to its specific requirements.   The above scenario is not a rare or isolated situation; it is actually pervasive in today's business office.   Insurance agents, bankers, travel agents, stock brokers, ticket agents, personnel agents, and the sales and purchasing departments of most corporations spend much of their time answering calls that request information.   When occupations are grouped into broad categories, such as "farmer" or "factory worker," the group with the largest number of workers in the developed nations is "clerk." We are information manipulators, and the fraction of the population involved with such services is growing.   Therefore, it is reasonable to define the BRI to satisfy this growing need for simultaneous voice and data communication.

Another factor that motivated the formulators of ISDN to address the clerical application, rather than single-line residential service, is the notion that ISDN will be installed first in businesses.   ISDN must be cost effective in the office, to provide a base from which to spread to other applications.

7.2.2 Variations of Basic Telephone Service

Ordinary telephone operation is supported by using one of the two 64-kbps paths of the BRI for digitized voice, with call setup signaling taking place over the BRI signaling channel.   The other 64-kbps channel is unused in this case.   Since the early 1960s, pulse code modulation (PCM) telephone systems have sampled voice at 8000 Hz and encoded each sample into 8 bits, yielding a bit rate of 64 kbps. T1 trunks have been divided into 64-kbps subchannels to carry these PCM bit streams.   Thus, 64 kbps is the fundamental unit upon which the digital carrier system is built.   This rate was carried over as the ISDN B channel, in order to support basic telephone operation.

Certain subsets of the full BRI connectivity provide a range of performance and features that enhances basic telephone service.   High-function telephone sets can be developed that use one B channel and the signaling channel of the BRI to implement additional functions, such as call transfer, speed dialing, and a display screen.   All the special features of pre-ISDN high-function telephones can be easily implemented in the ISDN environment [2].   In addition, the caller's number can be shown on the display screen.   If another incoming call arrives while a call is active, the displayed number of the new caller allows the subscriber to screen the call and decide which call deserves his or her attention.

The availability of intelligence linked to the communication system allows a number of advanced applications.   For example, a directory permits the caller's number to be translated into the caller's name, which is then displayed.   The high-function telephone can access an application processor on the ISDN switch via the D channel to perform directory and other database operations without involving a host computer [2].

It should be noted that the two BRI B channels need not be used for one voice call and one simultaneous data call as described above.   An operator may use one B channel to receive an incoming voice call, while using the other B channel to talk with the person being called to determine whether he or she wishes to accept the call.

A data call can employ one B channel and the signaling channel, leaving the other B channel idle. A terminal adapter is used to convert the user's data rate and code format to the 64-kbps transmission rate. No modems are used, since the BRI extends digital service to the subscriber's facility. The user obtains a substantial advantage in that the transmission time of a given message is greatly reduced by using the 64-kbps rate instead of the usual data rates. For example, a transfer at 1200 bps takes more than 50 times as long as the transfer of the same data at 64 kbps. Connection charges and the user's waiting time are both reduced accordingly.

An extension of this arrangement is shown in Fig. 7.3. It involves using the BRI for two simultaneous data calls. The user of an intelligent terminal can conduct sessions with two different hosts at the same time, perhaps sharing his display screen by a windowing approach. In a fully integrated ISDN environment, single B channels (of a 2B + D configuration) are used to connect each host to the PBX, which combines them into a 2B + D interface to the data terminal.

During the lengthy transition to full ISDN deployment, it is important to allow the subscriber's existing non-ISDN terminal and host equipment to continue in service. The cost of simultaneously replacing the entire system with ISDN equipment would deter many users, delaying the introduction of ISDN. A path has been provided whereby existing systems can migrate to ISDN compatibility. The terminal adapters (TA) shown in Fig. 7.3 perform the necessary conversions. In this application, the terminal adapters are implemented as special line cards of the PBX, rather than as stand-alone devices. One of these sessions could be connected to a low-speed asynchronous computer port and the other to a high-speed synchronous port; the terminal adapter converts these various inputs into BRI format.

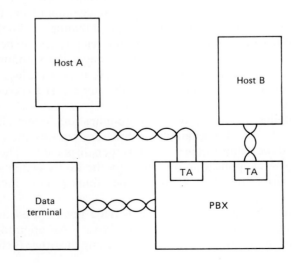

Figure 7.3　Two data calls.

7.2.3 Automatic Call Distribution

As mentioned earlier, numerous features can be built on the transfer of the caller's number (the subscriber identification) to the called party's equipment. Among these features is the ability to automatically route or distribute incoming calls to various agents based on the caller's number. This feature would be performed by an applications processor attached to the PBX. It could look up the subscriber identification as the call is being received to recognize established customers and route them to the particular agent that has been handling their account. Many marketing departments are organized by geographical territories and desire to route incoming calls to regional representatives. If the caller's number is not recognized as belonging to an established customer, distribution can be done on a geographical basis by examining the caller's area code.

7.2.4 Automatic Call Return

Another application depends on the ability of the called terminal to store the number from which it was called. If the call is not answered, the called terminal queues the caller's number on a list of unanswered calls. When the terminal's user returns, he or she can scan the queue and request the terminal to automatically dial selected numbers so as to return these calls. User information elements can be employed to store canned messages, along with the caller's number, in the called terminal.

7.2.5 Call Screening

The automatic call return feature is a step beyond today's answering machine technology; it still requires human interaction and does not provide any immediate response to the caller. Several incremental steps, which may be described as call screening, are available to improve these aspects of the no-answer scenario.

7.2.5.1 Selective messages. An intelligent, programmable terminal can make decisions and select alternate responses based on the calling party's number. This discrimination can be done on a real-time basis so as to deliver a particular response to the calling party selected from a list of canned messages.

To enable this feature, the terminal's user must enter a list of the callers' numbers to be recognized and identify a response for each. In this way, a personal message can be given to designated callers without revealing this information to other callers. For example, the user's home telephone number or travel plans could be disclosed to a restricted audience. On the other hand, noncommittal or discouraging messages can be delivered to frequent nuisance callers. Another possibility is to detect calls from out-of-state area codes and inform them of your WATS number.

Messages can be generated from a voice response unit, or digital messages can be returned via user information elements.

7.2.5.2 Selective forwarding. An alternative to returning a message to the caller is to forward the call. Call screening in this context involves examining the caller's number and making a decision as to the desired destination of the transferred call. When the call is recognized as coming from a co-worker, family member, or important client, the call can be forwarded to the number that was preprogrammed by the terminal's user. Other calls can be forwarded to an attendant or a voice message center, or a canned response can be delivered. The benefit of this feature is that important calls are promptly forwarded, but the subscriber is not subject to interruption by unimportant calls. Another advantage is that the incoming call can be forwarded to the called party's home without revealing the home number to the caller. Of course, these functions can be performed by a human attendant. The advantages of the ISDN solution are (1) lower cost, (2) 24-hour coverage, and (3) higher reliability.

7.2.5.3 Caller authorization. The counterpart of screening a voice call is automatic authorization of a data caller. In the pre-ISDN environment, several techniques are in widespread use to prevent unauthorized callers from accessing a dial-up database. After the connection is established, the user is asked to enter his or her password. In some cases, each user has a unique password. The computer that answered the call looks up the telephone number corresponding to the received password, hangs up, and dials this number. This call-back technique ensures that the call originated at the proper number.

If the caller's number is supplied to the called party by the telephone network, an additional level of authorization can be performed by comparing this number with the number retrieved as a function of the password. In many applications, agreement of these numbers may satisfy the requirement for caller authorization, thereby avoiding the call-back procedure. In addition to saving time and reducing complexity, the single-call system has the advantage that the call is automatically billed to the user who originated the call. In the call-back scenario, the returned call is billed to the host, which must perform the additional steps of obtaining the charges from the carrier and preparing an invoice to reclaim these costs from the user.

Flexibility is an additional benefit. The user may access the host from any one of a number of terminals using the same password. Authorization then involves comparing the subscriber identification with a list of approved calling numbers corresponding to authorized terminal locations. This flexibility would be a welcome convenience. In the case of terminal equipment failure, a substitute terminal and line could be used without physically relocating any equipment. In the pre-ISDN call-back environment, a unique password would be required for each line. The users are burdened with memorizing multiple passwords, since security procedures generally prohibit users from maintaining written lists of passwords.

More sensitive applications may not wish to depend on the integrity of the ISDN switch that originated the call and may insist on more sophisticated authorization procedures.

7.2.5.4 Junk facsimile. The corporate use of facsimile for image and text transmission has been growing explosively. With the widespread deployment of fax receivers has come the possibility of advertising through this medium. An advertiser obtains a directory of telephone numbers of fax receivers and then dials each receiver's number and transmits one or more pages of ads for office supplies or other merchandise. The operator of the fax receiver must sort through this material to find legitimate messages, his supply of fax paper is consumed, and his receiver is unavailable for its intended traffic while the advertisement is being received. For these reasons, such ads impose a cost on their recipient, who describes them as *junk fax*.

The call screening capability of ISDN provides a partial solution to this situation. An ISDN fax receiver can be programmed to accept only calls from designated numbers within his network, or to reject calls from numbers that have subjected him to advertising in the past.

7.2.6 Electronic Funds Transfer

One application that highlights the requirement for security is the transfer of messages that represent capital assets. In addition to communicating the amount and details of the transaction without error, the network must ensure that the end points are certain of the identity of the other end point. In other words, measures must be taken to prevent outsiders from inserting messages that imitate legitimate transfers into the network. Some form of authorization (an electronic signature) is often required for this purpose. Encryption is used to prevent the disclosure of the details of the transfer and the identities of the participants. These functions are not addressed by the ISDN bearer services, so they must be performed by the higher protocol layers, called the teleservices.

7.2.7 Automatic Database Access/Voice Response

There are many cases in which a user wishes to obtain a small quantity of information from a database through his or her voice telephone. Examples include the current balance of the user's checking account, the status of an order, or a price quotation. Instead of speaking with a human agent, as in the applications above, the user can interact with a computer system. Today, the extended 800 service accepts Touch-Tone input digits (such as an account number), and a synthesized voice response is delivered.

In the ISDN environment, short digital queries and replies can be sent through the D channel without requiring that a B channel be set up. The subscriber identification could be checked as a security measure before responding, but this would restrict the caller to a small set of preselected calling numbers.

7.2.8 Automatic Caller Data Retrieval

When a voice caller is served by a human agent, one or more database accesses are generally performed by the agent to obtain the requested information. This process can be speeded by the availability of the caller's number to the agent's host. When an incoming call is received, the caller's number can be transferred from the PBX to the host, where it is used to retrieve and display a considerable amount of information about someone who has called previously from the same number. A database access is made to determine which of the available agents is to handle the call so that customers can be matched with agents they have dealt with in the past. The host directs the PBX to connect the call to the selected agent.

As the voice call is being established, the host displays all relevant information for this particular caller on the agent's data terminal. In addition to the caller's identity, the terminal could display the status of the caller's account, delivery dates of outstanding orders, and recent transactions. If desired, the inventory levels, current prices, and availability dates could be displayed for items that this customer has ordered in the past, in anticipation of a repeat order. Personal information about the caller, such as his or her name, address, age, birthday, hobbies, and names of family members, could be displayed to allow the agent to personalize his remarks. This may impress the caller, until she or he realizes that the information has been "computerized" rather than "personalized."

During the call, the agent may need to make additional accesses to databases. For example, the customer may request delivery dates for items not previously ordered. The agent may record the customer's new order by making database entries. At the conclusion of the call, a summary of the call can be automatically logged in the agent's management information system, which may reside on the host or elsewhere. Facts of interest may include the calling party's number, the identity of the serving agent, the length of time the customer was on hold, and the duration of the call.

The scenario is slightly different when the call connects two people in the same organization. When calling a subordinate, a business executive would like his or her terminal to automatically display the recent memos between the parties, as well as any private notes, reminders, or schedule commitments that the executive has tagged as being relevant to the individual being called. When the employee receives an unexpected call from the boss, a similar display of schedule and status would certainly be most welcome.

7.2.9 Telemarketing

A similar arrangement can be used for outgoing calls to assist a sales representative in contacting customers. In this case, the host computer maintains a list of people to be called. When the agent completes each call, the host directs the PBX to dial the next person's number. If the called party does not answer, the call is dropped and the next number on the list is supplied to the PBX. When a called party answers, the host promptly supplies account status and personal information, if known, along with a call script to the agent's data terminal for display. During the course of the call, the agent may wish to update this material and store it for later use. As in the case of the incoming call, additional information retrieval and database entries may be made, including an automatic management information system log entry. When the agent senses that the call is nearly complete, he or she signals the host to start dialing the next call. In this way, the largest possible number of customers are contacted per hour, and the agent's efficiency is maximized.

In the pre-ISDN environment, some of these functions are performed by an automatic calling unit. Clearly, the ISDN approach to telemarketing replaces this device and substantially extends its capabilities.

7.2.10 Voice Data Applications Interface

The automated retrieval of data as a function of the caller's number, or of the called number in the telemarketing case, is regarded as a fundamental application, which many businesses want to perform. The details differ from industry to industry and from company to company, while the basic nature of the task remains the same. To facilitate the implementation of such simultaneous voice and data applications on intelligent end points connected to ISDN switches, the voice data applications interface (VDAI) was defined. The objective of the VDAI is to allow programmers of value-added applications to access ISDN services in a standardized, high-level manner. These application programs may be developed for a company's own use or for sale to the end user in the form of a software package or turnkey system.

Figure 7.4 illustrates the location of the VDAI within the ISDN protocol stacks, through which the host and switch interact as peers. The VDAI plays the role of layers 4 through 7 of the signaling channel protocol, which have not yet been defined by the CCITT. The following generic capabilities are provided by the VDAI to the user's application program:

Place an outgoing call

Detect an incoming call

Answer an incoming call

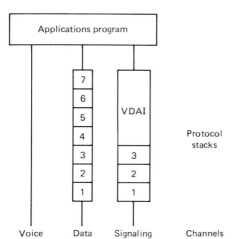

Figure 7.4 The voice data applications interface.

Place a call on hold

Transfer a call

Forward a call

Deflect a call

Add a call to a conference

Request the status of a call

User-to-user data transfer

Clear a call

The VDAI interfaces the user's applications program to layer 3 of the signaling channel protocol by mapping these high-level capabilities into Q.931 messages, relieving the applications programmer of the necessity of mastering the details of the communication process. The availability of these functions at a high level speeds the development of applications software; by standardizing a set of primitive commands, multivendor interworking and software transportability are enhanced.

7.2.11 Electronic Mail

Pre-ISDN electronic mail systems are implemented by storing messages in intelligent terminal equipment, which are connected by memoryless communications paths. ISDN supports the same techniques, while enabling more sophisticated approaches. In particular, the possibility exists of storing messages within the network. If a message is addressed to a terminal that is busy or does not answer, the message can be archived in the network's store and forward equipment for later delivery. A message-waiting lamp on the terminal can be lighted by means of D-channel signaling to alert the subscriber to retrieve the message at her or his convenience [1]. If an electronic mail message is to be sent to multiple destinations, a host may be linked to a network directory to automate this process.

The primary goal of an electronic mail system is to greatly reduce the quantity of paperwork that must be processed by the user [4]. When word processors are allowed to communicate with one another, a document can originate on one system, be sent to a second word processor for editing and proofreading, and then relayed to a third system for approval and distribution to users' terminals for display. All these steps can be performed electronically without producing a hard copy at any stage of the process.

A flexible electronic mail system can serve as a replacement for a wide variety of other communication services. The classical telex function of transporting record traffic in the form of printed text to a remote location is an obvious candidate for replacement and enhancement. Teletex is a system that allows its subscribers to exchange letter-quality messages. Videotex permits images to be retrieved from a central database, while facsimile is used to electronically transmit printed documents, which need not be textual in nature. All these functions can be performed by ISDN networks, assuming channels of adequate bit rate are available.

ISDN is not limited to replacing traditional communications services on a one-for-one basis. The capabilities of these services can be extended by allowing a mixture of types of information to be bundled together and handled as a single message. For example, a text message can be accompanied by vocal notes. This service could be used as a substitute for dictation by an executive to attach his or her comments to a document being reviewed. Another example consists of attaching verbal comments to the images of slides to generate an audiovisual presentation. The mixed-information application differs from separate text, image, and voice messages in that all forms are sent and received in a single operation and are therefore maintained in association with one another for the convenience of their users.

Messages with mixed information types are also differentiated from separate messages in that they may be transmitted simultaneously. If simultaneous presentation is required, special functions must be performed by the network to ensure that one component of the call is not delivered while another component is blocked.

7.2.12 Point of Sale Terminal

When a retail sale is made, the details of the transaction are often entered into a point-of-sale terminal. In addition to a number of local functions, such as calculating the amount of change and printing a receipt, modern terminals communicate with remote devices for several purposes. When a credit card is offered as payment, an enquiry about the purchaser's credit status is made to a centralized database. A similar request for authorization may be made before cashing a check. After a purchase, the financial details may be recorded in a remote computer, and a description of the goods that were sold may be logged for inventory management purposes. Each of these functions may require access to a separate remote host. The point-of-sale terminal may maintain a dedicated path to each host or establish a call whenever a sale is made. In either case, the result is a low efficiency of use of the transmission facilities.

The ISDN contribution in this area is the replacement of slow and expensive communication paths with faster and cheaper counterparts [4]. The terminal uses a BRI path to access multiple hosts as required. Call setup is expedited by the use of the D channel.

7.2.13 PBX to Host Computer Connection

In many installations, data terminals access host computer ports by way of a PBX, which performs contention and queuing functions. As shown in Fig. 7.5, each connection involves a line card on the PBX, a port card on the host, and a cable between them. If a number of these connections can be multiplexed into a single, high-speed interface, as shown in Fig. 7.6, significant economy can be realized. A comparison of Figs. 7.5 and 7.6 shows that the multiplexed approach requires many fewer hardware components, and a single cable replaces the multiplicity of individual cables. Two twisted pairs suffice for the multiplexed cable, while 25-conductor cables are used to support the EIA RS-232 interface. The savings obtained in the areas of cable installation and maintenance go a long way toward paying for the multiplexing and demultiplexing equipment.

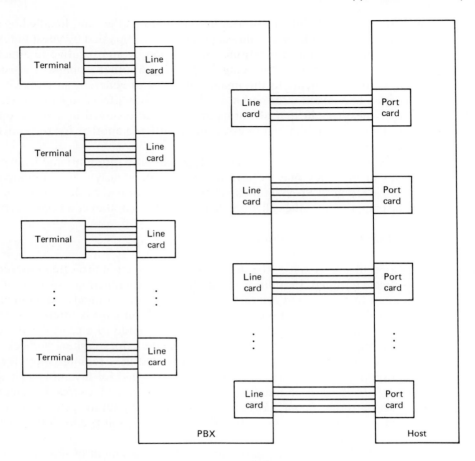

Figure 7.5 Pre-ISDN host access.

One of the earliest uses of the ISDN primary rate interface (PRI) was in this PBX-to-host application. In 1984, AT&T Information Systems defined the digital multiplexed interface (DMI) for this purpose. It employs the 23 B + D or 30 B + D formats and the Q.921 and Q.931 protocols at the link and network layers. DMI has tracked the evolving ISDN standards very closely since its formulation. A public demonstration of interworking between a host and PBX from different vendors was conducted in 1985, and DMI products were delivered in 1986. DMI effectively merged with AT&T's primary rate interface (PRI) in 1987 to become AT&T's ISDN offering.

In the telemarketing application, the host computer interacts with the PBX to place calls on behalf of the agent. In this case, the host is not an end point of the call; rather, it uses the D channel of its interface with the PBX to establish a call between the agent and the called party. This can be done using standard procedures by setting up a call between the host and the called party and then immediately transferring the call to the agent.

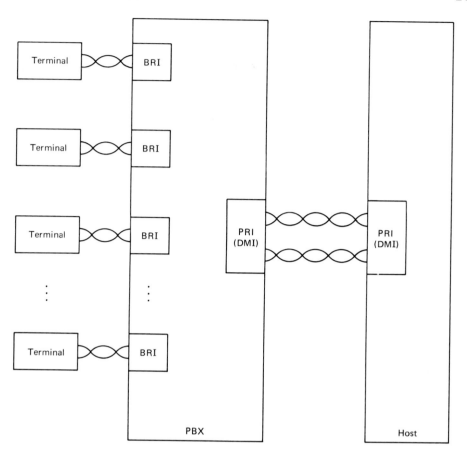

Figure 7.6   ISDN host access.

The host can perform directory and other database operations, replacing the applications processor on the switch.   Alternately, the host can use the D channel to perform integrated applications by accessing the switch's processor.

7.2.14 Workstation

When the processing and storage capabilities of a terminal approach those of a personal computer, it may be termed a workstation.   The integration of intelligence, voice, and data functions enables a number of advanced applications.   For example, the user can customize the handling of incoming calls by providing distinctive ringing patterns for certain callers.   Scripts for logging onto other systems can be stored for recall and transmission by means of a singe keystroke.   Workstations can be connected to a switch or directly to a larger host by the BRI or by an H channel of the PRI if high data rates or graphics are desired.

7.2.15 SNA Terminal Support

Millions of 3270-type terminals are connected to cluster controllers, which use IBM's System Network Architecture (SNA) to communicate with remote front-end processors, which are attached to hosts. Specialized terminal adapters can enhance these networks with ISDN capabilities by serving as protocol converters, translating the SNA protocol to that of the ISDN B channel [2]. Then ISDN switches and networks can be used to allow the terminal's user to select a host, rather than being permanently connected to a single host.

Another possibility is the use of ISDN to connect remote terminals to a controller that is attached to the host's data channel. The remote cluster controller is eliminated, and the terminals appear to be colocated with the host [2].

7.2.16 Configuration Control of Shared T1/T3 Trunks

Corporations are increasingly making use of T1 networks to interconnect their geographically remote plants and offices. An important ingredient of these networks is the digital access and cross-connect system (DACS), a component that routes the 64-kbps constituents of the T1 bit stream, on an individual basis. Thus, a subscriber may economically access the telephone network at the T1 rate without having 24 calls to the same destination; the calls can be individually routed to multiple destinations within the user's network. The subscriber is able to specify the connectivity of this network and to change it on a static basis by sending reconfiguration commands to a customer control center. Presently, reconfiguration is performed every 15 minutes.

This capability allows a corporation with geographically distributed facilities to optimize the use of its communication resources. Figure 7.7 illustrates a hy-

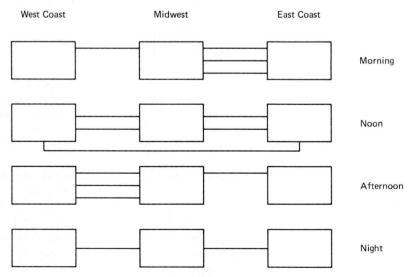

Figure 7.7 Geographical reconfiguration.

pothetical example involving a network with East Coast, Midwest, and West Coast offices. In the morning, the network interconnects the East Coast offices with one another and with the Midwest offices, since the West Coast offices have not yet opened. During the day, the network is reconfigured to connect all the offices. After the East Coast offices close, the network is concentrated on the Midwest and West Coast offices. At night, all offices are again connected to facilitate electronic mail and host–host file transfers. Thus, the network is rolled westward each day, following the sun.

In the ISDN environment, when access to a B channel of a primary rate interface (PRI) trunk is desired, call setup information is placed in the D channel by the calling party. The called party's number and other particulars are thus available to the telephone network, which could dynamically route the call to its destination. A B channel of a PRI trunk could originate or receive voice or data calls to or from any end point, instead of being confined to a particular company's network. In addition, call setup will occur within a few seconds, in contrast to a reconfiguration delay of up to 15 minutes in the pre-ISDN environment.

An even more flexible arrangement is possible. Instead of just allocating and reallocating the elements of a dedicated pool of resources, an ISDN can dynamically add communications paths during busy periods and release them when they are no longer required. In this case, the network is dynamically built to provide the services requested by signaling on the D channels. The enormous benefit to the subscriber is that he is charged only for the time that the facilities are actually used. By contrast, a dedicated network is leased on a 24-hour-a-day basis [2].

Large users of telecommunication services are motivated to use PRI instead of individual trunks by economic considerations. Although tariffs vary from time to time and place to place, short T1 links are generally cheaper than an equivalent number of voice trunks. In addition, intangibles such as maintenance, administration, and provisioning are less costly for the single high-speed connection.

Local and regional telephone operating companies will be highly motivated to provide such ISDN services to their customer base of large corporations. Should attractive features not be available from local carriers, corporations have the alternative of bypassing the local carrier by connecting directly to an interexchange carrier that can provide the desired services. As T3 (44.736 mbps) service is extended to customer premises in the future, similar routing of its constituent T1 subchannels is likely to occur.

7.2.17 Video Teleconferencing

Since pictorial information requires a relatively large number of bits, any service that displays rapidly changing images can be supported only by a high-rate transmission link. Slow-scan video can be sent at arbitrarily low rates, but image motion requires a rate in the neighborhood of the ISDN H0 rate of 384 kbps. The basic video service consists of the picture telephone. Bell Laboratories developed the Picturephone in the 1960s, but the high bit rates that it used limited it to a small number of business conferencing applications. The people who desire a video conference travel to regional centers that are interconnected by high-rate links.

As H0 service becomes available from the ISDN, video telephones can be deployed to individual corporations. They can be used for intracompany conferences and for communication with other firms that also have video service.

In addition to providing a medium for conferences among humans, video facilities can also be used for transmitting images for surveillance purposes and as a substitute for a cable TV system. The equivalent of closed-circuit television can be supported on a broadcast, switched, or interactive basis.

7.2.18 Enhanced Call Progress Monitoring

When a voice call cannot be connected by today's telephone system, different audio tones are returned to the calling party to inform her or him of the reason for the failure, such as (1) the called line was busy, (2) the number rings with no answer, (3) no trunk is available. In addition, recorded messages are played to indicate that the called number is invalid or out of service. Recorded messages also inform the caller of a new number to which the called party has transferred service. When a terminal places a data call, this audio response may not be delivered to a human user, and the information is lost.

The existence of the D channel allows the ISDN to return detailed call status information to the calling party in digital form. The terminal can capture this status for display.

7.2.19 Immediate Call Costing

The D channel could be used to request that the cost of the call be delivered to the end point making the request as the call is being torn down. This capability would allow the subscriber's equipment to monitor the cost of calls, by extension or by department, on a daily basis.

If desired, billing information can be requested periodically during the course of the call to alert the caller that charges are accumulating. In the ISDN environment, various levels of service may be requested as the call progresses, so the cost of the call may vary unpredictably with time. This factor makes the immediate knowledge of the cost of the call more important than in the pre-ISDN environment, in which cost is nearly a linear function of time.

7.2.20 PBX Networks

A private branch exchange (PBX) is a switch located on the subscriber's premises. Its primary function is to share a limited number of trunks (which connect the PBX to the carrier's local office) among a larger number of extensions, or lines. The PBX implements a large number of special services that are not provided by the public telephone network, including call forwarding and conferencing. More advanced switches perform sophisticated services, such as adapting different terminal types for mutual compatibility, providing virtual terminals, and implementing store-and-forward functions.

When a call is made through the PBX of one facility, over the ISDN, and through the PBX of another facility, a network of PBXs is created. In more complex situations, the call may be routed through intermediate PBXs; Fig. 7.8 depicts such a network. In this environment, a desirable goal is to extend the functions that a single PBX provides to the PBX network. Call transfer, forwarding, and conferencing are examples of elementary services that can be provided by means of standardized signaling on the D channel. The implementation of these features is complicated by the desire to accommodate intermediate PBXs that were manufactured by various vendors and that implement ISDN functions to different degrees and in different ways [2].

Examination of a more advanced feature, such as automatic callback, reveals some of the cooperative interactions that must take place. Referring to Fig. 7.8 again, suppose an extension on PBX A calls an extension on PBX B, which is busy at the time of the call. The caller wants to leave a message for the called extension to return the call as soon as it is not busy. If this message resides at PBX A, either an idle B channel must be maintained to PBX B or PBX A must repeatedly try to place the call. Since neither of these alternatives is attractive, the callback message is retained by PBX B. When the called extension is available, PBX B sets up a call between the two extensions. To enable this feature, sophisticated signaling between the PBXs must take place.

7.2.21 Access to Public Networks

By providing uniform interfaces, ISDN facilitates connection of users' terminals to various public networks [3]. In addition to established services such as telex, a number of modern value-added networks have been developed to offer specialized services to their subscribers. Both circuit switching and packet networks are available for data transmission [1].

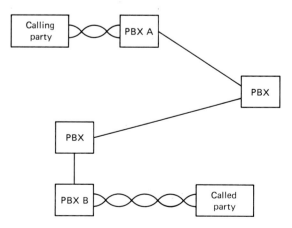

Figure 7.8 A PBX network.

7.2.22 Automated Teller Stations

An automatic teller performs inquiry/response interaction with its host whenever a customer performs a transaction. A unique communication requirement arises when the automated teller is unable to complete the requested transaction by the use of its standard procedures. The automated teller then communicates with a human teller to obtain assistance. Before the human teller initiates a voice conversation with the customer through the automated teller, he or she must review the details of the progress of the transaction as conducted by the automated teller [4]. Thus, a data call to the host is involved, associated with the voice call to the customer. Clearly, one B channel of the BRI can be used for each purpose.

7.2.23 LAN Interconnection

Local area network (LAN) technology has rapidly assumed a major role in the interconnection of local terminals, hosts, and other peripheral devices. The role of the ISDN is to provide a means of interconnection of geographically separated LANs. A gateway or bridge between LANs that comply with various LAN standards and the wide-area telephone network is required. The goal is to allow a terminal connected to one LAN to access resources that are connected to a distant LAN in a transparent manner, that is, in the same way that local resources are used.

The BRI provides a passive bus capability to satisfy this requirement [1]. As shown in Fig. 7.9, a small number of terminals may be connected to the same wire pair, which they use as a connectionless LAN. The D channel is used for contention resolution. The addressing capability may be extended so as to individually access the terminals on the passive bus. The PBX serves as one of the LAN elements, providing access to wide-area networks.

7.2.24 T1 Multiplexer Termination

Time division multiplexers that operate at the T1 aggregate rate have become commonplace. They allow many data and voice users to share a T1 trunk, resulting in substantial savings in many cases when compared to individual lines. A traditional use of such equipment is to connect a number of colocated data terminals to a remote host computer. At the host site, a companion demultiplexer separates

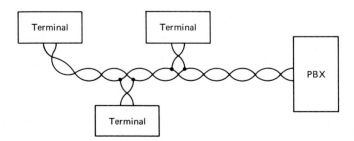

Figure 7.9 The BRI passive bus.

the received aggregate into replicas of the terminals' output bit streams, for connection to individual computer ports or ports of a front-end Processor. Of course, the equipment at the host site also combines the host's outputs for transmission to the terminals.

This configuration is essentially the same as the PBX-to-host interface shown in Fig. 7.5; numerous multiplexer port cards are connected to an equal number of computer port cards by a swarm of cables. Since DMI yielded substantial advantages in the PBX case, it seems reasonable to extend its application to the time division multiplexer. If the multiplexer's aggregate bit stream conforms to the DMI protocol, it is possible to connect the received aggregate directly to a DMI port on the host. The demultiplexer is completely eliminated, along with the individual computer port cards and cables. Figure 7.10 illustrates the connection of the DMI-equipped multiplexer to a DMI port on a host via the ISDN. This application depends on the compatibility between the DMI interfaces of the multiplexer and host and the PRI interface provided by the network.

Multiplexer vendors have been considering the possibility of "software de-multiplexing," or allowing the host to perform the multiplexing/demultiplexing function, for many years. Generally, the advantages have been outweighed by the obstacles of developing hardware and software multiplexing units capable of integration into a wide variety of incompatible hosts and front ends from many vendors. For this reason, host demultiplexing has been done on a very limited scale. With the advent of DMI, the principal obstacle is removed, since DMI capability is available for numerous hosts. In most cases, the DMI modules were developed by the host manufacturer, but several independent firms have developed

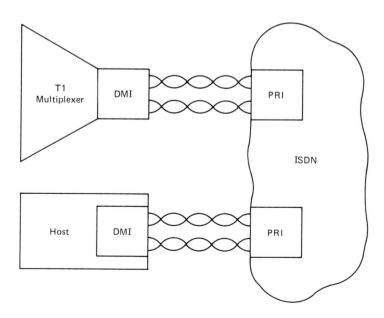

Figure 7.10   T1 multiplexer termination.

DMI interface units for popular hosts whose vendors had delayed their support of this feature.

It might appear that the multiplexer is limited to 23 or 30 user ports, corresponding to the number of B channels provided by DMI. However, each of these B channels can be shared by a large number of users by employing DMI's mode 3. In this mode, packet transmission is used with protocols equivalent to those of X.25. The addressing capability provides up to 8192 virtual channels per B channel; in practice, the number of users that can share one B channel is limited to a much smaller number by the delays that they can tolerate [3].

7.2.25 Maintenance and Administration

In the predivestiture era, the managers of corporate communications networks could turn to The Telephone Company for assistance in the diagnosis of network failures and their restoration. At the present time, such a single source of support is generally unavailable. Due to the 1984 divestiture, a wide-area network is likely to span several local operating companies and one or more interexchange (long distance) carriers. In addition, today's networks are unlikely to be populated entirely with terminal equipment supplied by the carriers; instead, mixtures of components from numerous independent vendors are prevalent. Technicians employed by the carriers cannot be expected to be able to repair terminal equipment made by hundreds of vendors, to carry spare parts for them, or even to tell if a given device is operating properly. For all these reasons, communications managers are increasingly being driven to provide their own dedicated facilities for performing fault isolation and restoral.

The ISDN environment provides some much-needed help in this area. The key facility is the end-to-end digital connectivity of the D channel, which is a substantial asset for maintenance and network administration. In a typical installation, a small computer is used as a network management center. A port of this computer is connected to the network via a PBX, using either the BRI or the PRI, depending on the size of the network. In this way, the computer obtains access to a D channel. Over this channel, the network management center can interact with all the ISDN-compatible switches, cross-connects, and terminal equipment in the entire network.

The network management center can then attempt to make connections to the D channel of each remote device in turn to probe the connectivity of the network. It can retrieve status from these other components and can instruct intelligent components to perform self-diagnostic tests and report their results to the network management center. Diagnostic procedures that interfere with the normal operation of a device can be scheduled for implementation shortly after midnight, when the equipment will be idle. Loopbacks are one such disruptive procedure that are commonly used to verify that communication paths are available and that terminal equipment is operational. To use this technique, the network management center sends a command to a remote component, which causes it to loop back, or return all received data to its sender. Some distinctive test data are then sent to the looped component.   The resulting data returned by this component are compared to the sequence that was sent so as to count errors.

The network management center can automatically perform these status monitoring functions so as to present its operator with an up-to-date, detailed picture of the network's health.   In this way, failed facilities and equipment to be replaced can be reliably identified so that spare units and repair crews can be sent only where needed.

Since diagnostics and detailed status reports are not specified by ISDN, special care must be taken in multivendor networks.   The network management center must keep track of the individual characteristics of each device, since equipment from different vendors will have different characteristics and capabilities and will require distinct data formats.   Nevertheless, ISDN provides a uniform framework in which to access remote devices and communicate with them to conduct maintenance activities [3].

In the pre-ISDN environment, numerous low-level maintenance personnel performed ad hoc troubleshooting procedures to characterize faults and locate the equipment to be repaired or replaced [1].   Frequent voice communication between remote end points was required to coordinate the test procedures.   If the network was not operational, this auxiliary communication had to be achieved by other means.   ISDN's self-contained signaling capabilities reduce the need for end-to-end coordination, while automated diagnostics lead to a reduction in maintenance personnel.   All these considerations cause the ISDN solution to yield a streamlined, efficient, and economical implementation of the maintenance function.

Administration refers to the process of determining the configuration of a network, including selecting values of the variable quantities, called parameters, that "program" intelligent devices to perform the desired function.   An example of configuration administration is the selection of the active components from among a group of spare components of a given type.   An example of parameter administration is the choice of data rate, character structure, and parity for an asynchronous data terminal.   These activities can be performed remotely, in some cases, by means of the D channel.   Parameter values can be adjusted, and some remote circuit patching and selection of the active device from a pool of spares are possible.

Administration also refers to the management of the network.   By making management information more readily available to the users and the network controller, ISDN enables them to optimize the use of the network.   In particular, the timely provision of billing information allows the network manager to respond promptly to changes in the patterns of use or misuse of the network's resources.

Although maintenance and administration are intangible, they are necessary management functions that enhance the availability of network resources to their users.   The capabilities that ISDN enables in these areas are financially significant. By unifying the access mechanism for equipment from various vendors, ISDN allows the network management system to be built into the network.   The alternative method of managing a multivendor network consists of superimposing a separate network management system over the principal communications network. Since the transmission components and terminal equipment from different vendors usually cannot cooperate with one another, specialized monitoring components are added, which communicate with one another via dedicated paths to supervise the performance of the network. The integrated approach permitted by ISDN provides cost savings by eliminating the separate monitoring system. Performance advantages may also be obtained, since a remote device can determine its own internal status more precisely than an external monitoring device can hope to do.

7.3 RESIDENTIAL APPLICATIONS

7.3.1 Extension of Business Services to Homes

The first residential ISDN applications may be the extension of some of the business services to the home. Executives will desire 24-hour access to their employer's communication facilities. They will want to place and receive voice and data mail messages. When an international call traverses a large number of time zones, the corporation's plant may be closed when the foreign party is available. The executive could then conveniently place the call from his or her residence and would desire the availability of the full complement of ISDN features supported by the employer's system.

Another motive for expanding business services to the home is to allow workers to telecommute, or work on corporate projects from their homes. Access to the employer's mail systems, databases, computing resources, and telecommunications facilities would be required. If full services were provided, the home-bound worker could approach the effectiveness of his colleague at the office.

One difficulty with telecommuting in the pre-ISDN environment is that the worker loses the use of his or her residential telephone service while the terminal monopolizes the single telephone line. The BRI solves this problem by providing two independent B channels. One B channel supports the connection of the home terminal to the employer's computer, without blocking incoming calls on the other B channel.

7.3.2 Nationwide Call Forwarding

Individuals could also make use of services such as call forwarding, which are associated with today's PBX environment. To be fully effective, this application would require telephone numbers to be assigned to individuals, rather than to telephone lines. As an example, suppose that the Smith family residence has a single telephone. Normally, the calls to Mr. Smith's personal number and to Mrs. Smith's personal number are directed to their home telephone from their respective offices. When Mrs. Smith goes out of town, she enters her temporary number via a telephone into the network database. When her personal number is dialed, the call is transferred to her at the temporary number. Meanwhile, calls to Mr. Smith's personal number would continue to be routed to his residence.

Other functions that are associated with PBXs or networks of PBXs can similarly be extended to nationwide public networks.

7.3.3 Nuisance Call Tracing

When the caller's number is available to the called party, the tracing of obscene, threatening, false alarm, or nuisance calls will occur immediately and automatically. Repeated calls, a court order, or the assistance of an operator will no longer be required to identify the caller. It is hoped that this exposure of the caller will serve to reduce the incidence of these undesirable activities.

7.3.4 Privacy

The same mechanism that allows undesirable calls to be traced also reduces the privacy of legitimate callers. The area code of the calling number immediately discloses the caller's locality, while the remainder of the number prevents the anonymous call. Some civil rights groups and consumer advocates have objected to this feature, maintaining that it constitutes an improper invasion of the caller's privacy. There is no counterpart of today's unlisted number in the ISDN environment; perhaps special provisions can be made to implement the equivalent of this feature in an ISDN.

7.3.5 Emergency (911) Call Handling

Another aspect of call tracing comes into play in the case of the emergency number. When a person dials 911, the caller's number may be used to access emergency information, such as the caller's name, address, and known medical problems, and the locations of the nearest fire stations, ambulances, and police patrol car routes. Clearly, this capability can reduce the cost and response time for providing emergency services. This is especially true if the caller is unable to speak, since the call tracing procedure is replaced by a database retrieval. Numerous emergency situations may be imagined in which the caller is unable to speak, due to disability, poisoning, intruders, smoke inhalation, or loss of consciousness. In other cases, a speaking caller may be unable to correctly state his location, due to hysteria, youth, or old age.

7.3.6 Home Security

Intruder alarms and smoke detectors may be connected to a central monitoring station by telephone lines, both in business offices and residences. Inclusion of the subscriber identification may simplify the task of determining which alarm or detector has generated the call. Sensor readings may be communicated to the monitoring station to verify that an emergency actually exists and to quantify its scope or magnitude. Medical information may also be telemetered automatically in the event that a disabled person is unable to place the call.

Figure 7.11 shows how various alarm signals may be combined for transmission via a BRI path. Signals from smoke detectors, an intruder alarm, and a medical monitor are treated in this example. Readings from intelligent utility meters can be included; the extra cost of such meters is recovered by avoiding the visits of

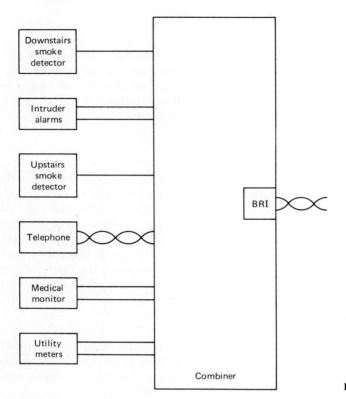

Figure 7.11 Home security telemetry.

human meter readers to the home.   Telephone service is provided on one of the B channels, while the outputs of the sensors share the other B channel.   Packet mode may be used for the sensor data to enable the ISDN network to route the outputs of individual sensors to separate destinations.   Since the actual bit rates from the sensors are quite low, an alternative is to use the D channel for this purpose, instead of the other B channel.

7.3.7 Video Telephone

Video service requires a wideband transmission path if image motion is desired. The expense of providing this service will severely limit its early deployment. Residential video service will have to wait for the advent of ISDN's wideband service to make it economically feasible.   The widespread availability of ISDN video service in the home will not take place until after the year 2000.

The basic video service will consist of the picture telephone.   Initially, it will be valued for providing visual communication among geographically separated family members and friends.

As video penetrates the home, it will be used by advertisers of luxury merchandise, since subscription to video service will be a strong indicator of affluence. Visual display and demonstrations of goods and services will be a powerful selling tool.

7.3.8 Information Retrieval

Video service can be used to retrieve and display items from a remote database. In addition to static displays, such as are now available via teletex, wideband video permits moving images to be recalled. Entertainment and instructional material equivalent to that available from broadcast television are a possibility. This service differs from television in that the program material is selected from a large library for display at the convenience of the viewer. An application for this service is programmed education, in which the viewer progresses from one lesson image to the next at her or his own pace.

7.3.9 Video Transactions

Transactional video is an extension of the concept of video information retrieval. Once interactive home video is a reality, a number of important applications become possible. Many of these are transactional; a subscriber views a menu of choices and then selects one or more items from the menu. The menu may consist of a visual description of articles or services offered for sale, while the subscriber's selections indicate which items are to be purchased. Banking transactions are also facilitated by a visual display of the account status, including recent transactions and the balance. The subscriber may conduct banking activities from home by directing the bank to transfer funds to pay bills or make purchases.

REFERENCES

7.1. Newell, John A., "ISDN Networks for Business Applications," *Proceedings of ISCAS 85*, 1985, pp. 711–14.

7.2. Newell, J. A., and L. D. Landy, "ISDN for MIS Applications," *Conference Proceedings, National Computer Conference*, 1987, 385–96.

7.3. Robin, G., "Customer Installations for the ISDN," *IEEE Communications Magazine*, April 1984, pp. 18–23.

7.4. Schulke, Herbert A., Jr., "User Needs for ISDN as Seen by the Banking Community," *Proceedings of the International Conference on Communications*, 1984, pp. 564–67.

CHAPTER 8

ISDN Multimedia Services

STEPHEN B. WEINSTEIN

Bell Communications Research

What are ISDN services? There are as many answers as there are interests of suppliers, proponents, and even opponents of ISDN. There are formal definitions in the Recommendations of the International Consultative Committee on Telephone and Telegraph (CCITT). From a user's perspective, we believe that no single service can be associated with ISDN and only with ISDN, and in that sense there are no exclusive "ISDN services." But introduction of the core ISDN capabilities into the public network will make advanced services available to large subscriber populations at reasonable cost. The wide availability of digital access and out-of-band signaling, joined with pervasive software control, technical advances in network facilities and terminal equipment, and economies of scale in transport and processing, will create a fertile environment for new communication and information services. The bulk of these services will not be built into the ISDN network, but will be built upon it, using its capabilities in creative ways that are only dimly perceived today.

In this chapter, unlike in current CCITT practice and in other commentaries, a sharp line is not drawn between services and applications. Services as defined here include offerings of network operators, added-value vendors, and information providers of various kinds. This broader view of services is consistent with network evolution. Looking a bit farther into the future than the first years of ISDN access, we can see a blurring of the division of functional responsibility between elements of a communication network and equipment attached to the network. Network intelligence, the processing and database capabilities of the network for call management and services definition, will go beyond simple physical transport to customize communications arrangements over a wide range of protocol levels. It will mediate human–machine interactions that are inseparable parts of many customer applications, and pull together the scattered resources, some belonging to the network and some not, to create communications sessions that might invoke a multiplicity of connections and computer applications. Attached equipment, for its part, will in some cases execute major pieces of call processing and connection services software, participating in distributed network control in an era of open network architecture. Thus the network will do some parts of what today are considered user applications, and user equipment will do some parts of what today are considered network services.

ISDN, in its near-term narrowband version but even more in its future broadband forms, will offer the means to extend advanced *local* communications, information management, educational, and entertainment environments over wide areas and to a great many user locations.   The features available to larger users in high-speed local-area networks (LANs), programmable private branch exchanges (PBXs), centrex systems, and private networks will become available to new populations as well as to "outlyers" of these large users.   Workstations and personal computers, used previously for stand-alone (or locally networked) applications such as computer-aided design, engineering analysis, graphics arts, and desktop publishing, will become communicating terminals as well.   Media integration, higher-speed data communications, and extensive personalization and control will become a feature of dispersed as well as local communications.   Information-based activities will become possible among individuals in distributed, heterogeneous user populations as well as within concentrated and closed user groups.   A communications environment for information retrieval and sharing, collaborative work, and extended social interaction will slowly take shape, part of the infrastructure of the Information Age.   It is this environment and the possibilities it opens, rather than specific network services written into international standards, that is the unique contribution of ISDN.

This chapter emphasizes *multimedia* services because the liberation of the telephone network from its voice orientation is the most prominent services implication of ISDN.   Not only are voice and data given equal billing in ISDN and associated with a single subscriber address, but they may be tightly integrated, as in voice annotation of text and graphics or in "videotex videos" with synchronized animation and music.   In fact, digitally coded and possibly encrypted audio may be thought of as just another kind of data.   The multimedia mix includes digitally coded images and even moving video, although broadband ISDN (BISDN) will be needed for the large-volume information retrieval and high-definition moving video services of the future.   Multimedia communications can be both real-time and deferred, with useful complementary roles.   A few of the many possibilities are described later.

Despite the advantages of the ISDN architecture for large populations of smaller or highly dispersed communications users, and even for cost savings in the concentrated communications environments of larger users, it would be wrong to regard it as a panacea and the only way to realize advanced services.   The rapid evolution of LANs and metropolitan area networks (MANs) to high speeds, efficient interworking, and wider availability, together with advances in software control, is making possible most of the services currently envisioned as supported by ISDN and others beyond the capabilities of narrowband ISDN.   They can often be provided through software-controlled *logical* integration of media and (computer) applications, rather than through the outright *physical* integration that is at the heart of ISDN, at least at the network termination.

It is essential that ISDN, if it is to achieve the ubiquity needed for low cost, interwork with these alternative architectures and exist within them as "virtual ISDN" when appropriate.   It goes without saying that ISDN must also interwork (Fig. 8.1) with existing services on the public switched telephone network (PSTN). In particular, it has to be possible to provide extension telephone service on the same channel as it exists in homes today, to communicate between an ISDN tele-

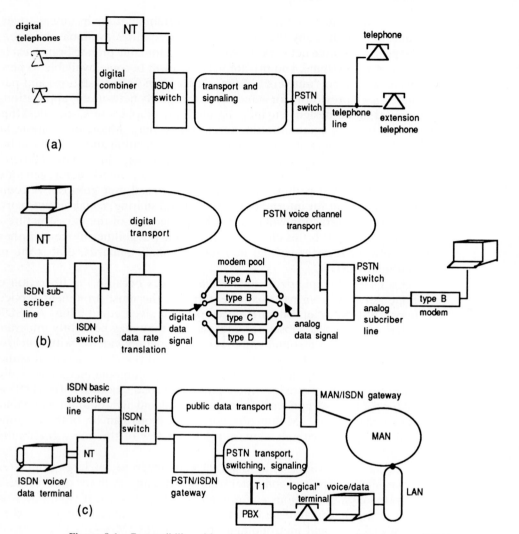

Figure 8.1 Compatibility with existing services and interworking between ISDN terminals and those on the public switched telephone network LANs. (a) ISDN digital telephone (and extension) communicating with ordinary PSTN telephone (and extension). (b) ISDN terminal communicating with PSTN terminal/modem. Network provides "modem pool" to talk with PSTN terminal. (c) Software-integrated "logical" voice/data terminal on LAN/PBX combination interworking with ISDN voice/data terminal.

phone and a PSTN telephone, and to send data between an ISDN terminal, with its direct digital connection to the ISDN, and a terminal–modem combination communicating data through a PSTN voice channel. Many difficult problems must be overcome to realize even these apparently simple services, including working

out compatible numbering schemes, accommodating extensions on digital telephone circuits,* realizing "modem pools" in the network to allow data access to
the ISDN via the voice-channel PSTN, and providing facilities for data rate translation.   ISDN planners and terminal manufacturers must provide for both this
backward compatibility and for forward compatibility in the sense of future upgrading of user equipment to take advantage of new service offerings.

It is also important to maintain compatibility in how services are invoked.
Whatever the possibilities for better user interfaces to manage personal communications environments, the user of an ISDN telephone or terminal must be able
to place a telephone or data call in the same old way as it is placed on the PSTN.
This does not, of course, preclude the parallel availability of new, more flexible
user interfaces.

It is a distinct possibility that narrowband ISDN, with its rigid channelization
and relatively low data rates, will never capture more than a modest share of the
market for business-oriented data services, increasingly served by packet-switched
LANs and MANs.   Its broadband descendants, promising both high-speed packet
switching and a range of switched channel rates extending into the hundreds of
megabits per second, may become more pervasive.   In any case, it is virtually
certain that digital access and out-of-band signaling will sooner or later be made
available to almost all subscribers of the public network, whether or not these
capabilities are called ISDN and whether or not they are delivered through the
standard ISDN interfaces and protocols described briefly next and more extensively
elsewhere in this book.

8.1 ISDN SERVICES ENVIRONMENT

The core ISDN capabilities of integrated digital access and out-of-band signaling
give the user the possibilities of creating multimedia calls, of operating several
computer-supported applications simultaneously, and of controlling calls without
intruding on information channels.   Although the term call is used and adequately
describes the fundamental built-in services, a much broader range of human and
machine information-based activities can be erected on the generic ISDN architecture.   These will be considered after this section's overview of the built-in ISDN
services.

The internationally shared attributes of ISDN, including services, are described in an ongoing series of CCITT documents.   Every four years, a Plenary
Meeting adopts Working Group proposals.   These are summarized in the I-series
recommendations in Table 8.1 [1].   The most recent set of recommendations,
adopted at the 1988 Plenary Meeting, were published as the *Blue Book* in 1989.
Many aspects of technology development and CCITT standards activities have been

---

* A digital extension telephone cannot be simply wired in parallel with the main telephone, as
ordinary analog extension telephones are today.   The digital signals will interfere, not combine.   An
additional digital signal processing function, that of scaling and combining the digital signals individually
wired to the S interface (Fig. 8.1a), must be provided.

TABLE 8.1 CCITT I-SERIES RECOMMENDATIONS [1]

Part 1—General

Section 1: Frame of I-Series Recommendations—Terminology

I.110	General structure of the I-series recommendations
I.111	Relationship with other recommendations relevant to ISDNs
I.112	Vocabulary of terms for ISDNs

Section 2: Description of ISDNs

I.120	Integrated services digital networks (ISDNs)
I.121	Broadband aspects of ISDN

Section 3: General Modeling Methods

I.130	Method for characterization of telecommunication services supported by an ISDN and network capabilities of an ISDN

Part 2—Service Capabilities

Section 1: Service aspects of ISDN'S

I.210	Principles of telecommunication services supported by an ISDN

Section 2: Common Aspects of Services in an ISDN

I.220	Common dynamic description of basic telecommunication services
I.221	Common specific characteristics of services
I.222	Framework for providing additional packet-mode bearer services

Section 3: Bearer Services Supported by an ISDN

I.230	Definition of bearer services
I.231	Circuit-mode bearer services categories
I.232	Packet-mode bearer services

Section 4: Teleservices supported by an ISDN

I.240	Definition of teleservices
I.241	Teleservices supported by an ISDN

Section 5: Supplementary Services in an ISDN

I.250	Definition of suplementary services
I.251	Number identification supplementary services
I.252	Call offering supplementary services
I.253	Call completion supplementary services
I.254	Multiparty supplementary services
I.225	"Community of interest" supplementary services
I.256	Charging supplementary services
I.257	Additional information transfer supplementary services

Part 3—Overall Network Aspects and Functions

Section 1: Network Functional Principles

I.310	ISDN Network functional principles

Section 2: Reference Models

I.320	ISDN protocol reference model
I.324	ISDN network architecture
I.325	Reference configurations for ISDN connection types

Section 3: Numbering, Addressing, and Routing

I.330	ISDN numbering and addressing principles
I.331	Numbering plan for the ISDN era
I.332	Numbering principles for interworking between ISDNs and dedicated networks with different numbering plans
I.333	Terminal selection in ISDN

TABLE 8.1 (*Continued*)

I.334	Principles relating ISDN numbers/subaddresses to OSI reference model network layer addresses
I.335	ISDN routing principles

Section 4: Connection Types

I.340	ISDN connection types

Part 4—ISDN User–Network Interfaces

Section 1: ISDN User–Network Interfaces

I.410	General aspects and principles relating to recommendations on ISDN user–network interfaces
I.411	ISDN user–network interfaces—reference configurations
I.412	ISDN user–network interfaces—interface structures and access capabilities

Section 2: Application of I-Series Recommendations to ISDN User–Network Interfaces

I.420	Basic user–network interface
I.421	Primary rate user–network interface

Section 3: ISDN User–Network Interfaces: Layer 1 Recommendation

I.430	Basic user–network interface—layer 1 specification
I.431	Primary rate user–network interface—layer 1 specification

Section 4: ISDN User–Network Interfaces: Layer 2 Recommendations

I.440 (Q.920)	ISDN user–network interface data link layer—general aspects
I.441 (Q.921)	ISDN user–network interface data link layer specification

Section 5: ISDN User–Network Interfaces: Layer 3 Recommendations

I.450 (Q.930)	ISDN user–network interface layer 3—general aspects
I.451 (Q.931)	ISDN user–network interface layer 3 specification

Section 6: Multiplexing, Rate Adaptation, and Support of Existing Interfaces

I.460	Multiplexing, rate adaptation, and support of existing interfaces
I.461 (X.30)	Support of X.21, X.21 bis, and X.20 bis based data terminal equipments by an ISDN
I.462 (X.31)	Support of packet mode terminal equipment by an ISDN
I.463	Support of data terminal equipments with V-series-type interfaces by an ISDN
I.464	Multiplexing, rate adaptation, and support of existing interfaces for restricted 64-kb/s transfer capability

Part 5—Interworking between Various Networks

I.500	ISDN interworking recommendations
I.510	Definitions and general principles for ISDN interworking
I.511	ISDN to ISDN layer 1
I.515	Parameter exchange for ISDN interworking
I.520	General arrangements for network interworking between ISDNs
I.530	ISDN–PSTN interworking

described in articles in the *IEEE Journal on Selected Areas in Communications* and in *IEEE Communications Magazine*, including [3, 39, 40].

Although only a relatively few sections of the CCITT recommendations describe services directly, the other sections help define the services environment and are highly relevant to services delivery. An effective numbering and addressing plan, for example, is critical to realizing multimedia calls, integrating messaging with real-time communications, and facilitating interworking with other networks. For a variety of different services (telephone, electronic mail, facsimile, and so on), only a unique ISDN number for each service will interwork perfectly with the PSTN. This is because a connection request coming from the PSTN does not carry identification of service type.* But for connection requests within ISDN, a call to a subscriber in *any* mode, be it voice, group 2 or 3 facsimile, electronic mail, or other telematic services, is made to the *same* address (main ISDN number) with an indication, in the subaddress, of the specific terminal desired, as described in Q.931 and I.333. If the subaddress of a specific terminal is not known, there are provisions for higher-level compatibility of terminal classes; for example, we can ask, in the address, for "*any* class 3 facsimile terminal." The reader is referred to other chapters of this book, as well as to the I-series recommendations themselves, for information on addressing, protocols, and other functional issues.

8.1.1 Interfaces

The early chapters of this book describe the ISDN architecture and particularly its sophisticated signaling system. The specification of a limited family of standard digital interfaces is perhaps the outstanding feature of ISDN, opening possibilities for moving and plugging in voice and data terminals with a degree of flexibility comparable to electrical appliances. Many of the services described in this chapter are accessed via the basic interface, with its two 64-kbps B channels for all classes of traffic and one 16-kbps D channel for signaling and some customer data, as illustrated in Fig. 8.2. An ISDN terminal could be a digital telephone, an integrated voice/data terminal, a facsimile machine, a computer, or any equipment or equipments producing one or two digital data streams at 64 kbps and incorporating the proper interface. To avoid obsoleting the vast population of non-ISDN terminals, for example, data terminals with RS-232 interfaces, terminal adapters have been developed and marketed, as suggested in Fig. 8.3 and described in Chapter 7.

The second well-defined ISDN interface is the primary rate interface, offering, within the DS1 channel of the U.S. digital hierarchy, 23 B channels and one 64-kbps D channel. Business users with a multiplicity of local terminations or other forms of aggregated traffic would be the subscribers taking this interface, which could be configured to accomodate 384-kbps H0 channels.

Interfaces at higher rates are also being negotiated by standards-making bodies, especially the BISDN interface (Fig. 8.4). The STS-3C rate, set by the CCITT at 155.520 Mbps, would offer the user a "synchronous payload envelope" of 149.760 Mbps, the maximum payload (including various overheads) for data transfer in the asynchronous transfer mode (ATM), a packet-transmission technique with fixed packet ("cell") sizes [32]. Within this payload envelope, a standard H4 information channel (being defined as this book went to press) with a two-way data rate in the range from 132 to 138.264 Mbps is envisioned in CCITT's I.121 draft recommendation [40]. However, *any* rate up to the capacity of the ATM interface could be

---

* It is possible that future PSTN terminals, designed with interworking in mind, will signal a PSTN/ISDN address translator what type of service, as well as what main address, is desired.

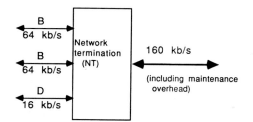

Figure 8.2 Channels and data rates of the ISDN "basic" interface.

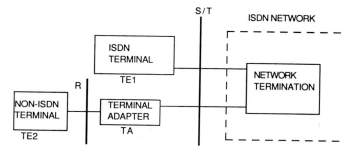

Figure 8.3 Customer access via the basic interface and with Q.931 signaling protocol (and Q.932 for supplementary services) to services supported by an ISDN under CITT Recommendation 1.210. Non-ISDN terminals are supported through terminal adapters.

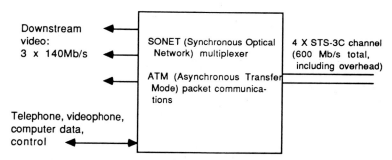

Figure 8.4 Proposed residential subscriber interface for broadband ISDN (BISDN). The user sees three downstream channels, for high-quality video, at a rate in the 132–138 Mbps range each, and one two-way packet-switched channel with a comparable capacity. On the network side, the transmission is entirely packet switched, in fixed-size packets, in a format known as asynchronous transfer mode (ATM).

used, and several STS-3C circuits provided if one were not enough for several channels of video plus interactive traffic, including voice, computer data, and conversational video. A 2B + Big D interim interface (Fig. 8.5), with the Big D channel carrying data at rates above 1.5 Mbps, has been informally discussed [5]. It would facilitate metropolitan area network (MAN) classes of services, interconnecting high-speed local area networks. A description of the evolution of ISDN to high speed and integrated transport is given in Chapter 9.

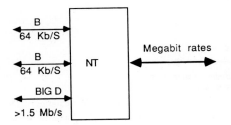

Figure 8.5 Proposed 2B + Big D subscriber interface, extending narrowband ISDN by increasing the D-channel data rate to the megabit range.

8.1.2 Signaling

In describing and forecasting future ISDN services, the capabilities and limitations of the signaling system are of great significance. This system is at least as important as the bandwidths and capabilities of information transport channels for the viability of innovative services. Some observations on ISDN signaling capabilities may be helpful before examining the services they support.

First, as already emphasized, ISDN signaling is *out of band*. A great deal can be accomplished without establishing or disturbing the information channels. For example, a data connection can be added to an ongoing voice conversation with no interruption of voice communications, or vice versa. Multimedia communication of various kinds can be logically integrated even though, in some places and for a long time into the future, traffic may be separately conveyed through dedicated voice, data, and video networks, each optimized for its particular function. Signaling done through the D channel can control the transmission parameters and delivery formats of the various media, whether conveyed together or separately. However, it is questionable whether tight synchronization of different media, for example, lip-synch sound with video, could be guaranteed with such separate transmission. In such cases, the audio and video information would have to be sent end to end in one channel, as with television signals today. Even for less critical synchronization applications, such as voice and hand drawing, variations in transmission delays through the network must be limited to acceptable levels.

Also, the signaling systems presently conceived, designed for call setup in seconds rather than real-time management of an ongoing communications session, may not respond quickly enough to satisfy service requirements. For example, a teleconference that switches the camera view for each participant according to that participant's commands to a distant signal combiner ("bridge"; see Section 8.3.1.2) may not be able to do so in the required fraction of a second through the D-channel ISDN signaling protocol specified in Q.931 (I.451 in Table 8.1) and Q.932. In cases such as this, the control information for session management would have to be sent in band, in one of the permanently established information channels such as one of the B channels in Fig. 8.1. In-band signaling is also necessary when an information medium, such as voice, is used for signaling, as in voice dialing.

One of the most remarkable D-channel capabilities is *user-to-user signaling* (and also user–network database signaling). Before even establishing an ISDN connection in one or more information (B) channels, a brief message (up to 128 octets of user information) can be sent from the terminal of the calling user to the terminals of one or more other users.   Because the "datagram" form of store and forward packet transport is used, passage through the network is much faster than it would be if time (and a considerable number of back and forth messages) were taken to establish a connection.   This is use of a signaling channel and protocol, normally used only for control, for *information* transmission.   Billing questions for such use of the control network will have to be resolved, unlike today's network in which there is no charge for signaling messages.

Some information about the calling party can be conveyed to the called party even without user-to-user signaling, particularly automatic (calling) number identification, or ANI.   As a normal connection is being established, the calling number is delivered to the recipient's terminal, giving the terminal or the recipient personally the opportunity to decide whether or not to answer or take other actions. In this same vein, notice of the number of a "call waiting" can be delivered to a subscriber already engaged in a call.   It should be noted that delivery of calling numbers to ordinary PSTN subscribers is possible in exchange networks that have implemented an out-of-band signaling system among telephone offices and their switching systems.   These calling numbers are delivered *in band* from the end telephone office to the called subscriber before a voice conversation begins.   Many applications can be built on the ANI capability, as described in Section 8.3.1 and in Chapter 7.

Extensions to *personal* identification and information, rather than calling number identification, are envisioned with user-to-user signaling.   During an already established communication session, side information can be conveyed from user to user.   Someone talking on his or her small-screen telephone-terminal may see messages from one or more "call waiting" parties.   These messages could be answered, by keyboard entry, without disturbing the ongoing voice call.

Second, ISDN signaling protocols allow *functional* as well as stimulus signaling.   Stimulus signaling, which from the push-button telephone subscribers' perspective is the use of the switch hook, the 12 push buttons, and the ringing voltage for controlling and indicating the status of a call, is constrained, intrusive, and sometimes confusing.   The user often has to remember the state of the call. Pressing the switchhook can mean hangup, forward a call, or other things depending on what has happened before.

Subscribers are intimidated by the ambiguities, the absence of reminders, and the use of nonintuitive push-button sequences for commands.   There is anecdotal evidence that, as in other multifunctional systems, users call on only a very few of the capabilities provided in centrex and PBX systems.   Improved user interfaces, interpreting stimulus signals and incorporating memory, can go a long way toward overcoming these problems.   But functional signaling, which uses relatively unconstrained data communication between the terminal and the network to convey any kind of information in an unambiguous way, offers a much richer environment for both services and user interfaces to them.   A wide variety of speech, natural-language text, and direct manipulation graphical interfaces can be devised, depending on the sophistication of the terminal, and translated into appropriate signaling messages.   Different combinations of media, transmission formats, and treatments of incoming calls can be requested.   Both the terminal and the network call control system keep track of the state of the call, taking the burden off the user.

Functional signaling will become important for intelligent network communications, explained in more detail later, where a request to establish a communication session may be handled as an inquiry to a database in which instructions reside for how the call is to be treated. The major present-day applications of this kind of database look-up are for translation of 800 calls into delivery numbers and for credit verification on credit-card calls. A call to a particular 800 number of a large retailer may, for example, result in delivery of the call to a nearby service center during the day and to a distant 24-hour service center at night. In the future intelligent network, where a caller will have the option of including his or her personal identity and other relevant information in the call setup request, a much greater range of call treatments will be possible, including such possibilities as answering with a personalized message, forwarding to different parties based on caller identity, or performing format and media translation to accommodate different terminal capabilities of calling and called parties.

The present Q.931 protocol is oriented toward terminal-to-switch or terminal signaling and does not provide an efficient mechanism for negotiation with network intelligence for software-defined call processing [37]. Delays in call (or, more generally, session) setup and unnecessary complexities must be expected until the ISDN signaling protocol evolves to better accommodate terminal-intelligent network interactions. Some progress has been made in recent CCITT recommendations defining separate messages for services control. Thoughtful and far-reaching cooperation between terminal equipment manufacturers and network operators will be needed to realize the potential of functional signaling.

Also, the adequacy of CCITT Signaling System No. 7 (see Chapter 3), the interoffice signaling system referred to earlier, for support of future services can be questioned. If virtually all call attempts are submitted to a network database and negotiations are required to arrange sessions among parties with varying equipment capabilities and media preferences, a signaling system of far higher capability, allowing a vast volume of simultaneous inquiries to network databases, must be developed. Research in distributed databases has suggested possibilities for using some of the vast transmission capacity of future lightwave networks for circulating call treatment information to a large number of widely dispersed query handlers [16]. A signaling/database system of this kind might not only reduce blocking problems, but also reduce the inquiry delays that threaten to make the setup time for intelligent network calls longer than that for ordinary telephone calls today, which are handled by switch-based call processing.

8.1.3 ISDN Service Definitions

It is useful to examine the present specifications of and concepts for ISDN services before exploring the future possibilities for vastly extended multimedia services. As Table 8.1 indicates, services aspects of narrowband ISDNs are described in CCITT Recommendations I.210, I.220, I.230, I.240, and I.250. There are three categories: *bearer* services, *teleservices*, and *supplementary* services.

A *bearer* service is defined as "a type of telecommunication service that provides the capability for the transmission of signals between user–network interfaces." Bearer services are described by attributes, grouped into three categories of information transfer attributes (network capabilities for transfering information from one S/T reference point (Fig. 8.3) to another), access attributes (the means for accessing network functions or facilities as seen from an S/T reference point), and general attributes (dealing with the services in general). Table 8.2 lists the attributes as presented by CCITT Study Group XVIII in January 1988 [41] and explained in Annex B to Recommendation I.210, and Table 8.3 lists possible values for the attributes.

Simply stated, the bearer services are various forms of transport, with attributes defining the capacity, the type of connection, and the data communication protocols to be used. It is sobering to contemplate the complexity, even at this fundamental level, of a public digital network intended to accommodate a very wide range of subscriber formats and practices. Consideration has been made for a number of likely user applications. Audio of three different bandwidths is already written in, aiming for different teleconferencing situations. Bearer channels are to be made available in various degrees of dedication, from on-demand to permanently dedicated to a particular user. Data communications configurations that users today set up with private lines, point-to-point, multipoint (for polling applications), and broadcast are to be offered as bearer services. A number of standard access channel rates are to be accommodated. And as many commonly used computer communication protocols as possible are to be supported, with others, such as IBM's SNA, likely to be included in future CCITT recommendations.

Using these attributes, a number of bearer services have been identified in CCITT Study Group XVIII. They are grouped into two categories:

- Circuit-mode bearer services: User information over one type of channel, and signaling over another type of channel.

TABLE 8.2   BEARER SERVICE ATTRIBUTES

Information transfer attributes

  1. Information transfer mode
  2. Information transfer rate
  3. Information transfer capability
  4. Structure
  5. Establishment of communication
  6. Symmetry
  7. Communication configuration

Access attributes (which may differ at the different network interfaces involved)

  8. Access channel and rate
  9. Access protocol

General attributes

 10. Supplementary services provided
 11. Quality of service
 12. Interworking possibilities
 13. Operational and commercial

TABLE 8.3 POSSIBLE VALUES OF BEARER-SERVICE ATTRIBUTES

Attributes	Possible Values	
1. Information transfer mode	Circuit	Packet
2. Information transfer rate	Bit rate kbps 64 2 × 64 384 1536 1920 (others later)	Throughput (Options being studied)
3. Information transfer capability	Unrestricted speech 3.1 kHz 7 kHz 15 kHz Video (others later) digital information Audio Audio Audio	
4. Structure	8 kHz Service data unit Unstructured TSSI RDTD Integ. Integrity (8) (8)	
5. Establishment of communication	Demand Reserved Permanent	
6. Symmetry	Unidirectional Bidirectional symmetric Bidirectional asymmetric	
7. Communication configuration	Point-to-point Multipoint Broadcast (needs further study)	
8. Access channel and rate	D(16) D(64) B H0 H11 H12 (others for further study)	
9.1. Signaling access	I.430/I.431 I.461 I.462 I.463 V.120 (others for further study)	
9.2. Signaling access protocol layer 2	I.440/I.441 I.462 X.25 (others for further study)	
9.3. Signaling access protocol layer 3	I.450/I.451 I.461 I.462 X.25 I.463 (others for study)	
9.4. Information access protocol layer 1	I.430/I.431 I.460 I.461 I.462 I.463 V.120 G.711 G.722 others	
9.5. Information access	HDLC LAP B X.25 I.462 (others for further study)	
9.6. Information access protocol layer 3	T.70-3 X.25 I.462 (others for further study)	
General attributes (under study)		
10. Supplementary services provided		
11. Quality of service		
12. Interworking possibilities		
13. Operational and commercial		

Example: 64-kbps, 8-kHz structured bearer service for 3.1-kHz audio, with the following attributes:

Information transfer mode: circuit
Information transfer rate: 64 kbps
Information transfer capability: 3.1-kHz audio
Structure: 8-kHz integrity
Establishment of communications: demand/reserved/permanent
Symmetry: Bidirectional symmetric/unidirectional
Communication configuration: Point-to-point/multipoint
Access channel: B for user information, D for signaling and/or operational, administrative, and maintenance messages
Access protocol: G.711 (speech encoding laws) for B channel, I series for D channel
General attributes: Not yet specified.

- Packet-mode bearer services

  Example: Connectionless packet bearer service on a D channel. "Connectionless" implies user-to-user packet transport without the need for and the delays of establishing a call setup between them. The attributes are:

  Information transfer mode: packet
  Information transfer rate: Throughput (for further study)
  Information transfer capability: Unrestricted digital information
  Structure: Service data unit integrity
  Establishment of communications: Demand/permanent
  Symmetric: Unidirectional/bidirectional symmetric/bidirectional asymmetric
  Communication configuration: Point-to-point
  Access channel: D(16), D(64)
  Signaling access protocol: I.441, I.451
  Information access protocol: I.441, I451
  General attributes: Not yet specified.

Even with the definition of standard bearer services, the interconnection or free exchange of terminals on different ISDN exchanges is not automatically possible. There are different realizations of the Q.931 signaling protocol, especially at the third (network) layer of the protocol hierarchy, which are expected to be resolved in 1990 [33]. The question of rate adaptation, between (non-ISDN) terminals operating at different rates, has received much examination and was resolved in November 1988 by CCITT's V.120 protocol for interworking among terminal adapters. Terminal adapters (see Chapter 6) are being defined and developed to match non-ISDN terminals to ISDN interfaces and networks.

As a special case of terminal adapter use, some users are very interested in independent routing of subchannels within a B channel, which would be desirable from locations that have, for example, a number of non-ISDN 9600-bps terminals or non-ISDN 16-kbps compressed voice telephones. One technical solution being considered, ISDN frame relay (Fig. 8.6), facilitates independent connection of multiple lower-rate terminals through one B channel to multiple different destinations. The benefits are greater connectivity and higher bandwidth efficiency. An alternative solution, gamma transfer service [42], offering a connectionless packet-mode access protocol for LAN interconnection at rates below 2 Mbps, includes similar subchannel capabilities.

The example given of 16-kbps voice channels suggests how compression technologies offer new opportunities for ISDN bearer services. At least one manufacturer [29] is developing a videotelephone that combines highly compressed audio with compressed, reduced frame rate video. Compressive coding carries a penalty in coding delay (as well as cost). A 64-kbps codec (coder–decoder) for moving video on a B channel may introduce several hundred milliseconds of end-to-end delay. This limits the utility of high compression in real-time, interactive applications. Reasonable quality moving video might, in the near future, be possible in a 384-kbps H0 channel.

But *messaging*, *broadcasting*, and *information retrieval* applications can sustain

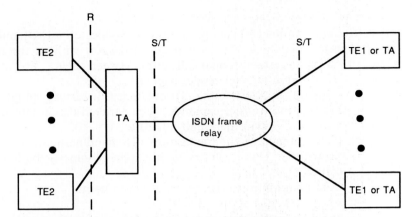

Figure 8.6 ISDN frame relay feature for independent routing of a number of subchannels for lower-rate non-ISDN terminals (TE2). The subchannels are aggregated via a terminal adapter (TA) into a single B access channel, but are later separated and routed to different destinations having either ISDN terminals (TE1) or terminal adapters.

considerable coding/decoding delay without degrading service quality. Such compression is made more attractive by the possibilities for *asymmetric* codings that require expensive, computationally intensive processing for coding but only inexpensive, relatively simple decoders [33]. For still images, *progressive transmission* [4], in which a coarse but usable representation of an entire picture is made available from an initial fraction of the data defining a full-resolution photographic image, can facilitate browsing modes of visual information retrieval on narrowband ISDN.

ISDN trials in the United States have indicated particular business user interest in interworking between ISDN terminals and those on LANs or connected to the PSTN (as suggested in Fig. 8.1), in interconnection of LANs, in primary rate access, in private line access, in telemetry and control, and in certain supplementary services discussed later [33]. In general, users can be expected to demand that ISDN bearer services improve connectivity, support dynamic bandwidth allocation, and enhance services flexibility.

A *teleservice* is a type of telecommunications service that provides the complete capability, *including terminal equipment functions*, for communication between users according to protocols established between telecommunications administrations and/or other administrative entities. Attributes are defined in CCITT Recommendation I.210, Annex C, in tables similar to Tables 8.2 and 8.3. An effort is made here to incorporate, within ISDN networks, services that are already widely used in other networks. Examples of teleservices include:

- Teletex: An office-to-office document transmission system, for example, the interconnection of communicating word processors.
- Telefax: Facsimile transmission of standard pages of textual, graphical, and photographic materials at standardized rates, encodings, and resolutions.

- Videotex: An information retrieval and transactional system with standardized presentation-level protocols.
- Mixed mode: Multimedia communications, for example, simultaneous voice and graphics communication.
- Telex: An international terminal-to-terminal text communications service with standard rates and display characteristics.

Teleservices go beyond the transparency presumed in bearer services and offer specifications for terminal as well as network characteristics. By and large, these services constitute the field known as *telematics*, where definitions of standard textual, graphical, and visual exchange and display formats become important [4]. As new standardization formats evolve, such as architectures for multimedia office documents, standard communication services for their exchange will be added to the list of ISDN teleservices. Popular formats can also be expected to evolve to broader functionality, as in the expected future introduction of store and forward facsimile service, which would give users great flexibility in retrieval, storage, and forwarding to other parties.

Media *conversions* will also be of major interest, such as interworking among voice, e-mail, and facsimile messaging services. Plug-in boards are already available for origination of facsimile from text entered on personal computers, or conversion of e-mail messages, and optical character recognition is being tested for conversion in the other direction, from printed and handwritten characters to ASCII (standard coded) text. Synthesis into machine speech of text messages and conversions among different bit-map rasters for photographic materials are other areas where progress in media conversion can result in new or improved teleservices in the foreseeable future. Repeating an earlier caution, the reader should note that such services do not depend exclusively on ISDN access, although ISDN can make them more widely accessible to the general public.

ISDN *supplementary* services are those in which additional capabilities are provided in conjunction with regular ISDN services. They cannot be provided on a stand-alone basis. A number of useful supplementary services, realizable in the near term and resembling "features" available in centrex and PBX switches, were identified very early: [2]:

- User-to-user messaging (connectionless D-channel communication)
- Call forwarding (and other forms of call diversion)
- Closed user group
- City-wide centrex
- Direct dialing in
- Call waiting
- Call completion to busy subscriber
- Calling line ID presentation
- Line hunting
- Three-party service
- Call transfer

- Conference calling
- Credit card calling
- Call hold

The *identification* of supplementary services is not, of course, sufficient to specify them, and they are gradually being filled in and broadened in scope. For example, conference calling was described in early 1987 by CCITT Working Group XVIII as multiple parties communicating among themselves using the speech bearer capability. Extensive work was done on specifying how a conference is to be controlled (adding and dropping parties, for example), but multimedia conference calls and all higher-level protocol functions were still under discussion. In general, national and international standards have not gotten very far at the upper protocol levels (session, presentation, application). A promising approach is to build supplementary services from supplementary functional components, similar to the intelligent network concepts described later, rather than providing an individual specification for each supplementary service. The supplementary functional components might include hold invocation, retrieve, join, split, and transfer [17].

Directory services are not included in CCITT services descriptions, but support most of the services that are. The data capability of ISDN facilitates automated inquiries, including those, in the future, for which full name and address information are not available. We can conceive of future electronic directories in which subscribers will be able to browse through listings or choose from a number of listings returned in response to a not-too-specific query. A listing can, potentially, include information on the communication capabilities available to the listed party, for example, 3-kHz telephone, 7-kHz telephone, electronic mail, voice mail, and group 3 or 4 facsimile. Dialing from directory, a popular feature today in some local communication environments and terminals, may someday be implemented in ISDN so that selection of a directory listing (including media and parameter choices) automatically makes the connection.

ISDN network designers are concerned about ISDN terminals being able to access not only initially specified teleservices and supplementary services, but also others to be defined later. Efforts are beginning to develop *reference models* for a family of terminals, from simple dumb terminals through personal computers and special multimedia terminals to high-powered integrated workstations, that manufacturers could follow to maximize the flexibility of their products as old network services change and new ones are created. It will be necessary to provide for downloading services software to terminals both off-line and as a call is being made. Evolution of a distributed software environment sophisticated enough to deliver new services to terminals of widely varying capabilities, but that is invisible to users who simply plug in and use terminals, is a high priority for ISDN designers.

8.1.4 Broadband ISDN Services

Broadband ISDN, or BISDN, based on fiber-optic communications all the way to the subscriber, is expected by its developers and many others to usher in a new era in public communications as the twentieth century comes to an end. Audio

TABLE 8.4   CLASSIFICATION OF BROADBAND SERVICES

Interactive Services	Distribution Services
Conversational services Messaging services Retrieval services	Broadcast services (no individual presentation control) Distribution services with individual user presentation control

and visual communications of high quality and large variety, well beyond the passive one-way services of today's broadcast and cable television services, will become economical as well as widely available.   Although it is not necessary to commercially realize narrowband ISDN prior to BISDN, the latter is a natural technical successor to the former and shares many of its most important features [12, 13].

In anticipation of the rapid evolution of ISDN to broadband transport capabilities, a task force of CCITT Study Group XVIII prepared in mid-1986 a list of potential broadband services [10].   They were broken into two categories (Table 8.4) of *interactive* and *distribution* services.   The task force offered the outline for a set of broadband services shown in Table 8.5.

Although this brave early attempt at sketching the broadband future gives some feeling for the scope of future network communications, it does not adequately express the potential already evident for the Information Age.   It reaches out more from existing communications services than from organizational and personal behavioral patterns and needs.   But it does include the important transmission elements of future broadband services, especially transmission of voluminous visual materials, as described in Section 8.3, which would be impossible or impractical without BISDN.

Conferencing is a prime example of a service that blends seamlessly into a vast array of applications and can be described much more expansively than as a set of communications capabilities.   The purpose of establishing communications among the multiple parties participating in a future broadband conference will be to establish group rapport through a feeling of "presence" and to pursue computer-supported applications together, such as editing a "live" multimedia document (containing elements functionally dependent on outside data) and retrieving and sharing information.   The applications, not only the multimedia communications connections, must be supported at higher protocol levels by the directory, format and media conversion, and advisory capabilities of the intelligent network.   The remainder of this chapter, after a brief overview of the intelligent network, is a look at how these complex services–applications of the future are likely to take shape.

8.2 INTELLIGENT NETWORK

Most advanced future services depend more on the concept of an intelligent network [11, 47] than on the ISDN integrated digital interface.   In particular, user and service provider *customization* and *control*, the *logical* integration of media, and

TABLE 8.5   POSSIBLE BROADBAND SERVICES IN ISDN

CONVERSATIONAL SERVICES

Moving pictures (video) and sound:

Broadband videotelephony (including point-to-point videoconferencing)	T
Broadband multipoint videoconference (including sound, moving pictures, and video scanned still images and documents)	T
Video surveillance (building security, traffic monitoring)	T
Video/audio information transmission service	B

Data:

High-speed unrestricted digital information transmission service	B
High-volume file transfer service	T
High-speed teleaction (real-time control, telemetry, alarms)	T

Document:

High-speed telefax	T
Document communication service (transfer of mixed-mode documents)	T

MESSAGING SERVICES

Moving pictures (video) and sound:

Video mail service (electronic mailbox for moving pictures and sound)	T

Document:

Document mail service (electronic mailbox for mixed-mode documents)	T

RETRIEVAL SERVICES

Text, data, graphics, sound, still images, moving pictures:

Broadband videotex (including moving pictures, telesoftware, teleshopping, advertising, news retrieval)	T
Video retrieval (for entertainment and education and training)	T
High-resolution image retrieval (for entertainment, education, training)	T
Document retrieval service (mixed-mode documents from databases)	T

DISTRIBUTION SERVICES WITHOUT USER INDIVIDUAL PRESENTATION CONTROL

Video:

Existing quality TV distribution (TV programs, like cable television service)	T
Extended quality TV distribution (enhanced definition or high quality TV)	T
High definition TV	T
Pay TV (pay per view, pay per channel)	T

Text, graphics, still images:

Document distribution service (electronic publishing, electronic newspaper)	T

Data:

High-speed, unrestricted digital information distribution	B

Moving pictures and sound:

Video information distribution service	B

DISTRIBUTION SERVICES WITH USER INDIVIDUAL PRESENTATION CONTROL

Text, graphics, sound, still images:

Full-channel broadcast videotex	T

T, teleservice: B, bearer service.

personalization independent of location are realized through intelligent network architectures and an efficient out-of-band signaling system. The ISDN D channel and signaling protocols that will develop over time will facilitate the interaction of users and user terminals with network intelligence.

The concept of an intelligent network represents a radically new view of telecommunications. In this view, the telecommunications infrastructure is a vast, distributed, interactive computer system, activated through the execution of computer programs. A communications call is more correctly viewed as a working and/or social session among diverse human and machine participants. Various applications (media, computer-based tools, numerical analysis) can be activated and deactivated during the course of such a session. Computer support is vital for setting up and managing the session, for individual and group access to and manipulation of information resources, for editing and other working capabilities, and for the extensive but easy customization and personalization that will help people and institutions control their environments in an era of information overload.

In the architecture conceived at this time, the intelligent network is defined as a communication system in which services are specified in computer programs (services *scripts*) that invoke relatively "dumb" network *functional components* such as switches, digital cross-connect systems, trunk groups, and billing equipment. *Intelligent peripherals* such as message storage systems and speech synthesizers will also be callable from services scripts. We can think of network intelligence as a cloud of databases and processing capabilities floating above the transport network (Fig. 8.7) and communicating with it through the signaling network, which is, at least initially, CCITT's Signaling System No. 7.

The services scripts utilize elementary subroutines, or *services primitives*, for frequently reused services elements such as trunk seizing, digit collection, directory

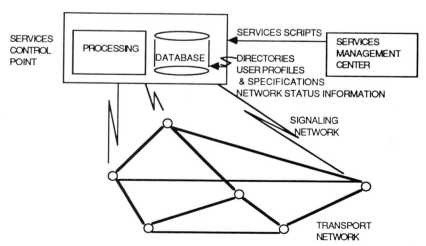

Figure 8.7 The intelligent network concept as software control over functional components in the transport network.

inquiry, and network-to-user signaling. More complex services subroutines can be added to the initial set as services built from primitives, such as point-to-point bearer services in various media, become themselves subsets of other services such as multimedia teleconferencing and messaging. Services subroutines may reside and be executed close to the equipments they control.

Scripts for simpler and frequently used services, such as plain old telephone service (normal dialing to another subscriber telephone number), may continue to reside in switching system software. Other services scripts, dependent on customization data, will be executed in the service control point. The more frequently used scripts for advanced services may be permanently resident in service control point databases. Others may be downloaded from service management centers or user locations.

Customization data, which may be highly dynamic, are placed by subscribers into their personal profiles, which are stored in vast databases that may be broadly distributed. For simplicity, in Figure 8.7 the user profile database is pictured within the service control point.

Many elements of the user profile database are, in fact, also elements of directories. An intelligent network call begins with a database inquiry, seeking instructions for what to do next. For a personalized intelligent network call, the instructions reside in the instruction fields of personal profiles belonging to the called (and sometimes also the calling) party. These instructions in turn invoke services scripts.

The inquiry is thus to the data file of a human being, possibly identified by lifetime number or name plus other descriptors (federal Judge Harold Greene), rather than to a telephone number. The instructions left in the file may be considerably more involved than the simple translation of one telephone number to another described for 800 calls.

Figure 8.8 gives an example of a customized intelligent network call, illustrating the principles of calling an individual rather than a location, selective call forwarding based on personal identification of the calling party, media conversion, messaging complementing real-time communications, and simple user programming of a network service. In this scenario, George, identified by a lifetime number, is in a distant courtroom, where an important decision is about to be handed down. He wants to send the text of this decision from his laptop terminal to his law partner, Steve. Steve is going out of the office, but is anxious to get the decision. So Steve enters an instruction into his personal profile (through a simple and intuitive user interface) that a copy of the text call from George be synthesized into speech and routed to his car telephone. A copy of the original text will also be sent to his electronic mailbox for retrieval through the office's word-processing system.

It is entirely possible, and even probable, that highly customized services scripts, and not only personalization data for existing services scripts, will be generated by future subscribers in personal computers and workstations and executed in a distributed terminal-network processing environment. One could conceive, for example, of a subscriber generating a script for a variety of customized routings, conferencing groups, announcement signals, and calling privileges for a small or-

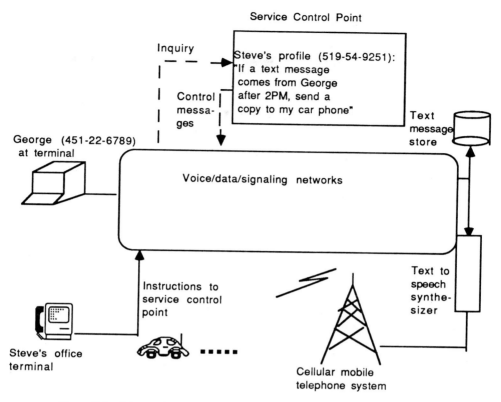

Figure 8.8 A future intelligent network call, illustrating complete software control, communication between individuals (identified by lifetime numbers) rather than locations, media conversion, and the complementary roles of real-time and message communications.

ganization. To make this capability available to a large subscriber population, high-level easy to use programming languages will have to be developed [14], well beyond the capabilities of service creation languages, such as CHILL [15], currently available to network personnel for ISDN and other services environments.

Furthermore, a large and useful collection of services primitives will have to be made available. Services creation from such primitives is an active research area, and clear answers are not yet available to key questions of software architecture and feature interaction, the possible mutual interference of features of different services, and the protection of privacy and software integrity. A major challenge for ISDN, if it is to appeal to tomorrow's customers, is to evolve workable intelligent network principles and structures and offer high-level services creation facilities, in particular services creation languages, specification and verification tools, and comprehensive sets of services primitives, to both network personnel and end users.

Beyond the scenario of Fig. 8.8, the intelligent network has a capability for *logical integration* of media that is not an explicit feature of ISDN, although ISDN's multichannel transport and out-of-band signaling facilitates such intelligent network services.   Voice, text, and visual media can be tightly integrated through software control.   A frequently cited example is annotation of one medium by another, an electronic version of marginal annotation.   We might (say) associate a voice comment with a highlighted word on a screen display of text, or make dynamically related text, voice, and hand-drawing comments on a graphical background (see the example in Section 8.3.1).

Complex applications can be conceived, such as joint editing by separated individuals of a multimedia document [23].   By cross-referencing and time-stamping media components, these components can be separately transmitted and stored according to a service script and retrieved in proper combination.   Early efforts in shared document editing on narrowband ISDN have demonstrated texts or spreadsheets appearing on the screens of terminals at both ends of a B-channel circuit, with cursor and editing control passed from one user to another [31].

Note that ISDN is not necessarily required.   Unified computer control of voice, data, and video networks can achieve media integration without a common physical interface or access line from the subscriber.   In large office or factory environments already equipped with centrex or PBX voice communications and with high-speed local-area networks for data communications, media integration is more likely to be achieved through computer-controlled logical integration than through replacing perfectly good distribution facilities with ISDN wiring, interfaces, and terminal adapters.

The intelligent network concept has many problems to overcome before it becomes a network reality, in ISDN or other networks.   Universal call translation in the public network, such that *every* call made is an inquiry to a database, implies a volume of database queries beyond the capabilities of current database structures. New structures, trading off processing against transmission capacity by circulating databases to a large number of dispersed query handlers, have already been mentioned in Section 8.1.2.   The added delays in call completion that are inevitable if inquiries are to be made outside of switch-based call processing must be kept to acceptable levels.   The integrity of the network must be maintained despite the introduction of software possibly developed by individuals in their homes and offices and the relaxation of central control.   Despite these problems, the metaphor of the communications infrastructure as a large, distributed computer system is already well along to becoming the way things really are.

8.3 END-USER SERVICES AND APPLICATIONS

The revolution of the 1970s and 1980s in personal computer technology, bringing computer power directly to the user for support of thought, creativity, and interaction with other people, has extended human memory, visualization, collaboration, and expressiveness in ways that are just beginning to be recognized [6, 7]. Text processing was the first wave and is still the mainstay of personal computer use.   But concepts of computer support of interpersonal communication, collaboration, and information management are the new wave, realized first in communicating word processors, remotely accessed information services, and electronic mail. Narrowband ISDN will do much to develop and enlarge this whole area of computer-mediated communications.

As the power of personal computer systems has increased, manipulable visual materials of intrinsically high information content, such as high-quality graphics, pictures, and moving sequences, have been recognized as important media for individual thought, personal and group work, and the satisfaction of intellectual and emotional needs. The broadband communications environment of the future holds tremendous promise for much more progress in this direction, removing geographic restrictions from the growing capabilities of office, factory, government, and home information systems [8]. This environment (Fig. 8.9) consists of a large set of distributed resources, provided by a variety of parties, including end users, from which an end-user service is put together under software control. The resources include media and format conversions, machine "agents" to facilitate interaction among human, network, and machine entities with varied interests and capabilities, editors, bridges, storage facilities, processing facilities, information providers, and so on. Distributed computing, file sharing, and shared computer applications are pervasive in this environment.

In the more traditional settings of business and residential communications, such as business terminal-host networks and video programming delivery to residences, ISDN (present or future) offers opportunities for cost savings, easier and better maintenance, media integration, and higher services quality, even without considering added possibilities for choice, customization, and control [9]. These, too, are among the emerging services and applications for ISDN described in this section.

8.3.1 Business and Professional Users

8.3.1.1 Narrowband ISDN services. When business communications users are presented with ISDN proposals, they appear to have three motivations for giving them serious considerations. The first is the prospect of cost savings and revenue enhancements, not so much in initial capital outlays as through lower maintenance expenses and increased business opportunities. The second is the opportunity, at least potential, to extend a local environment, such as a voice/data PBX, centrex system, local area network, or combination, to users who are not at the concentrated locations. The third and last is the future of vastly extended multimedia services, for enhanced human thought and interaction, that inspires ISDN and intelligent network developers. All these potential benefits deserve serious consideration, and the third one most of all, despite the lack of urgent initial interest in the user community.

The nearest-term cost saving is seen in the consolidation of telephone and computer terminal wiring. The coaxial cable used to wire terminals in separate data connections is eliminated. Less cluttered and more easily maintained wiring, with much greater flexibility in relocating terminals and in attaching a variety of synchronous and asynchronous terminals, is a concrete benefit.

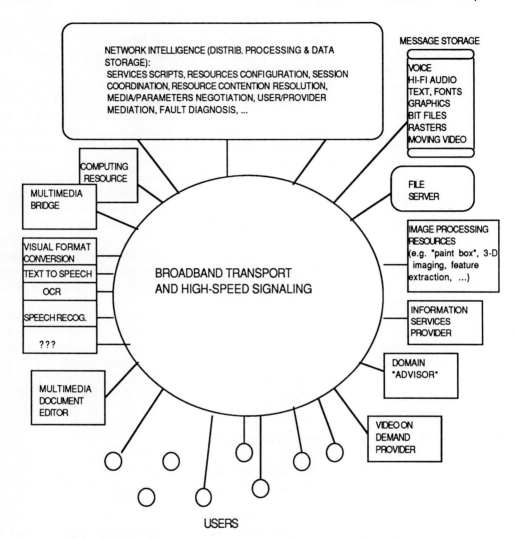

Figure 8.9 The future services and applications environment as a collection of communications and processing resources.

The combination of voice and data in one wiring system encourages interest in integrated voice/data applications. Increased business efficiencies can come through systematic internal use of integrated voice/data capabilities. An example might be an individual in the accounting department discussing an invoice with an individual in the shipping department while both look at it on their visual displays.

Another cost-saving possibility, with side benefits of extension to outlying users and other flexibilities, is in realizing part of a private business voice/data network within the ISDN public network. This could be associated with the coax elimination in the local environment, where twisted-pair telephone company subscriber lines would be used instead of a user-owned local data network, and might be extended over wide areas as ISDN access becomes more widespread. Such *private virtual networks* may eventually become cost effective for interconnecting almost all locations of a large business user, including the low-traffic locations that cannot be economically included in conventional private networks. ISDN protocols make adequate provision for closed user group communications, giving the virtual private network the required privacy and isolation from the public network (with, however, easy voice/data connections into the public network as desired).

Better customer relations and business development opportunities can come through more effective communication with customers. A near-term feature of great interest to credit card issuers and to others receiving calls from customers about their accounts is ANI, the preconnection delivery of the calling number described earlier. This number can be used by a business to immediately call up that customer's record on a screen. By the time the customer's voice is heard, the service representative can see the account history and begin to handle the customer's question. The productivity of service representatives can be significantly improved. ANI does have a serious drawback; it does not distinguish among the several *individuals* who may use a particular terminal and who may have separate accounts. Intelligent network capabilities for *personal* identification, described in the last section, are needed.

In the late 1990s, when many customers will be on the public ISDN network, integrated media capabilities available within a private/virtual private business communication system will be extended to the customer. An airline schedule or credit card bill will be seen while being discussed, and customers will, perhaps more in the broadband era, see sketches, photographs, and moving pictures of products and services.

Protocols being developed now facilitate setting up two-B-channel conferences among a number of parties, but are still largely restricted to transport functions, such as initial connection and adding and dropping parties during the course of a teleconference. These capabilities should be available in the mid 1990s. More sophisticated *broadband* teleconferencing, perhaps commercially significant around the year 2000, is described later in this section.

A number of new ISDN end-user services, such as giving travel directions, have been conceived. At the Telecom '87 symposium in Geneva, the Fujitsu company demonstrated creation and retrieval, on its "Image Terminal" (Fig. 8.10), of an integrated-media message showing a recipient how to get from one location on a street map to another. As a synchronized voice described landmarks and turns, aided by a movable arrow, the route was traced on the map by a hand drawing of the message's author. This application is within the capabilities of narrowband ISDN, using one B channel for voice and the other for all the graphics functions.

A higher level of communications quality is also implicit in ISDN. In addition to higher-speed data communications at subscriber locations with only one or two terminals that cannot afford high-speed digital access lines in today's environment, wide-bandwidth (7 kHz, 64 kbps encoded) voice and secure voice will also be possible. Conversely, as described earlier, a 64-kbps B channel might be subdi-

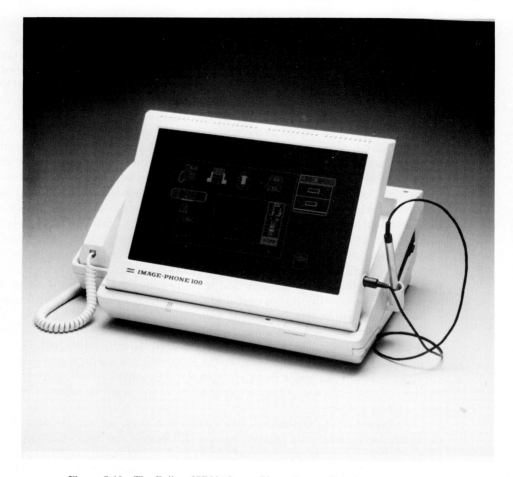

Figure 8.10   The Fujitsu ISDN "Image-Phone," a small desktop terminal with a flat plasma screen. Simultaneous with use of one B channel for 64-kbps digitized speech, the other B channel can be used for a combination of computer graphics, hand drawing, and scanned document visual information. User-to-user messaging, as well as control signaling, goes through the D channel. A document filing system is built in. (Courtesy Fujitsu Corporation.)

vided into several lower-rate voice channels where high quality is not an important factor.   It remains to be seen if this and other "granularity" options (for switched channel capacity at data rates other than the standard channels) can be offered to subscribers without compromising the ubiquity and cost effectiveness of ISDN deployment.

Notwithstanding the granularity questions, bandwidth control is an attractive attribute of ISDN.   Users with primary-rate interfaces will be able to dedicate different numbers of B channels to different users or equipments on a dynamic basis via D-channel control.   This flexibility will accommodate varying combinations of individual terminal communications, bulk file transfers, still picture transmission, and very high speed facsimile (in the future at rates of 384 kbps and above) that would otherwise demand an expensive collection of facilities capable of handling peak loads. D-channel signaling will also facilitate the dynamic reconfiguration of virtual private networks and a vast array of resource allocation possibilities in the open network anticipated for the future.

Secure communications and protecting the privacy of customer data are often cited as growing needs, especially as increased interconnection, more powerful information systems, and intelligent network software control are implemented. On the analog telephone network, the cost of voice security, while retaining high voice quality, has been prohibitive for most users. ISDN, with its integrated digital access, facilitates relatively inexpensive end-to-end encryption of both voice and data signals. It should become possible, sometime in the future, to protect all the media of an integrated-media call with a single-session encryption key. As for protection of customer data (including profiles and personalized services scripts for the intelligent network services that ISDN terminals will access), much still remains to be done by network operators, third-party services providers, and terminal manufacturers. The ISDN D-channel capability for reasonably high speed user– network interaction outside the transport channels will be essential for key distribution and other authentication and security procedures for protection of user information and traffic.

ISDN can also offer the business user better facilities for operations, administration, and management than are currently provided in the public network. Communications users have suffered from a lack of end-to-end service accountability since the AT&T divestiture in January 1984. By providing monitoring and diagnostics capabilities (through the D channel) that allow the user to look into and test public network-provided elements of a connection, as well as the user's own equipment, the user will feel both informed and in control. Problems may in fact occur less frequently as the public network becomes more reliable through end-to-end digital communications, eliminating distortion, noise, and interference problems of analog circuits.

As suggested earlier, the business user, through D-channel signaling with network intelligence, could be given the capability to configure and reconfigure logically dedicated communications facilities on the spur of the moment. Billing functions may also become more streamlined and informative, as the out-of-band signaling system provides opportunities for settling billing questions among communicating parties, reporting a single cost for a multimedia call even if separate transport networks are involved, and monitoring and tracking usage as it occurs.

Business users are understandably anxious that ISDN be compatible with communications arrangements already well-established or on the near-term horizon. X.25 and other data communication protocols used in public and shared networks are already in the ISDN picture. IBM's Systems Network Architecture (SNA) is widely used in corporate data applications and must be accommodated in an ISDN network seeking to attract corporate users. However, even with private virtual network capabilities meeting all user technical expectations, the economics are such that a public ISDN network is unlikely to ever eliminate dedicated private-line networks carrying concentrated traffic [18].

ISDN capabilities for both transport and protocol conversion between business networks operating under different protocols would be very attractive. Business users are also interested in "connectionless" data services for applications characterized by intermittent demand and an intolerance of connection delay, and in high-speed metropolitan area networks (MANs) to carry traffic among equipments on different local area networks. The Big D channel mentioned earlier could play a role here, if it were developed as a standard, but the public network appears to be focusing on an alternative Switched Multi-megabit Data Service [49], which uses ISDN addressing but little else.

In general, ISDN has a significant opportunity to provide a part of the communications infrastructure of the many business information systems being pressed to higher speeds, applications interworking, and multimedia capabilities. An indication of network provider and business user thinking is provided by the ISDN applications studied in the U.S. West ISDN trials in 1987 (Table 8.6).

8.3.1.2 Broadband services.

The most exciting possibilities are in the new or greatly extended services of the late twentieth and early twenty-first centuries, especially those that will link human working communities together and with information and processing resources. In some countries, simple real-time video-telephone services, both desktop and in conference rooms, is seen as a major attraction for business users [38], and more sophisticated conferencing possibilities are described later in this section.

But the potential of nonreal-time communications is sometimes overlooked. Integrating and going far beyond today's electronic mail and voice mail systems, *electronic messaging* in the future will use a single subscriber identifier (or address) for all media. The user at a terminal may see a common message listing, similar to today's electronic mail listings, with indications of the media used as well as the originator and time of arrival (Fig. 8.11).

TABLE 8.6 ISDN SERVICES AND APPLICATIONS BEING ANALYZED IN U.S. WEST TRIALS [19]

Video conferencing	Primary rate to PBX interface
Asynchronous terminal networking	Work at home
Wide-area networking	Security, systems monitoring
LAN interconnection	Integrated voice, data, image
High-speed facsimile	Packet-switching B/D channels
Coax elimination	Private line duplication
SNA emulation	D channel to B channel concentration
Flexible database access	Office automation with ISDN
Network integration	Enhanced ISDN terminals
Wiring simplification	High-speed circuit switched digital traffic
PC networking	Network analysis
VAN/private network interconnection	Videotex
Enhanced call management	PC to facsimile transfer
Facsimile distribution	
High-speed transfer	
Multiple terminal per access line	

INTEGRATED MESSAGING SYSTEM
May 9, 1990

1	voice	Karen	Acquisition figures	5/8/90 19:11
2	text	George	Legal decision	5/9/90 14:25
3	voice, graphics	Albert	Directions to hotel	5/9/90 14:51
4	voice, graphics, video	Akio	New VCR design	5/9/90 15:32
5	voice, text	Linda	Budget spreadsheet	5/9/90 16:45

Figure 8.11 An integrated messaging mailbox as it might appear on a future terminal screen.

By the turn of the century, multimedia messages may be common, ranging from the voice/graphics/hand drawing example given earlier for narrowband ISDN, to BISDN messages with high-resolution animated graphics, full color pictures, high-quality audio, frequent annotation of one medium by another (for example, hand drawing on graphics, voice on text), and moving picture sequences. Executable code and other computer files will be nonvisible (or audible) components of some messages. Execution of this code may, among other possibilities, cause retrieval of additional documents not actually transmitted with the message.

Multimedia messages will be created, sent, retrieved, forwarded, and stored with the same simple commands (and a few more for editing) used today for electronic mail. Messaging will be closely coupled with real-time communications. Pursuing the ideal of "all calls completed," users will have the opportunity, if a real-time communications session cannot be realized, of creating messages in the same media contemplated for the real-time call or in other media.

Part of the potential of multimedia messaging, in this case, message broadcasting to a closed user group, is conveyed in this scenario from an article in *IEEE Specrum* [8] by the present author, reprinted by permission:

It's November 25, 1998, and across the United States car retailers are geared up to receive the first of next year's models. Manager Bob Barnes arrives early at his Fareast Motors showroom in suburban New Jersey. Glancing at the screen of his desk terminal (a standard monochrome voice-data set, $89.95 from the local discount electronics store), Barnes scans its windows for the racing results and his "to-do" items for the day. Suddenly, a cartoon figure appears, blinking and waving at the bottom of the screen, signaling an urgent message. Barnes touches the figure, and the screen dissolves into a message header:

25.11.98 to fremont!dealerlist from tokyo!fareast
URGENT
To all North American dealers:
Front-end suspension modification on 1999 North American
production run "E" sedans.
Fareast Motor Corp.   Design Division

Another touch on the header, and the screen changes again, to a large-type text describing an important safety modification of the suspension on next year's cars. A woman's voice reads the message as it scrolls up the screen, revealing a computer-graphics diagram of the suspension. As the design slowly turns, she discusses its highlights.

The screen then shifts to a movie, with sound, of a mechanic modifying a suspension in Tokyo. The message ends with a display of the Fareast logo and a few cheery bars of the Company song.

Barnes forwards the message to his branch's service department, with a voice cover memo urging immediate attention. He knows the service manager will save the entire message and make sure that every mechanic sees it, in full color, on the department's large-screen projection system.

For personal communication, users may feel more comfortable with video messaging than they have in past trials of real-time videophone. A video message can be edited by the sender until it is satisfactory, can be accompanied by high-fidelity audio, and can include attachments in other media, such as documents and drawings. Company officers might broadcast messages to groups of employees, international banks might use video messaging to help overcome the time-zone problem, and soldiers and college students might send video messages to their families at home.

In many organizations, electronic messaging has found wide acceptance and profoundly affected the way people relate to one another. Its multimedia extensions, controlled through the ISDN and BISDN D channel, are likely to become widely used in the future.

But personalized *real-time* multimedia communications is also going to become prominent. *Desktop teleconferencing* describes a group meeting conducted through desktop communication terminals. The terminals are increasingly coming to be seen as powerful workstations, with the participants sharing computer-supported applications as well as interpersonal communications media. Figure 8.12 is a conceptual rendering of a workstation as it might appear during such a meeting. The workstation has infrared-coupled keyboard and drawing board, a document scanner, and wideband, hands-free audio. Moving pictures of the other participants, like shufflable playing cards, appear as desired in small screen windows. Text and graphical objects, in separate windows, are being edited jointly by the group. A subconference via the drawing board is underway between the user of this terminal and another member of the group. A graphical user control interface (window in the lower right corner of the screen) shows the state of connections in the hand drawing medium, with the dots representing parties to the teleconference and the blank oval representing the combining "bridge." Connection state diagrams for other media and tools can be retrieved from under this one. Connections in various media, subconferences, and access to tools and information can be managed by direct manipulation of the graphical representation. Figure 8.13 illustrates a concept for the user interface of a workstation for the desktop conferencing environment.

A vast array of directory, information, processing capabilities, and machine advisory services can be accessed separately from the ongoing conference and

FINAL REPORT

SUBCONF

PEN

Figure 8.12 Conception of a multimedia teleconferencing terminal of the late 1990s, with wideband hands-free audio, moving pictures of other participants on the screen, subconferencing, and multiple computer-supported applications in different screen windows. A high-resolution color document scanner/printer, wireless keyboard, and thin, wireless display/writing pad are accessories. The terminal has a fiber-optic connector and I/O rates in the hundred of megabits per second.

introduced into the conference as needed. Sophisticated multiuser editing tools support the group interaction. They could be as simple as shared or complementary cursors in a page of text or a spreadsheet or as complex as machine-mediated systems with hierarchical assignment of editing privileges, semantically linked annotation messages, and historical files of past document versions [24]. Multimedia bridging capabilities [20] distributed in the network provide each user a customized display and immediate connection rearrangements. High-level network protocols guarantee the proper sequencing of operations, coordination of the various media, and displays appropriate for each workstation.

A working communication *session* carried on among users at a networked set of such workstations, invoking machine entities that themselves could be considered participants, is very different from a traditional *call* or *connection* [50]. A number of different connections in different media may be invoked from time to time during the session; the connection map is not fixed for the duration. Computational resources are activated and shared, in linked workstation windows (for example, using the evolving X windows management system), and used more or less as they would be in a stand-alone session, except for the protocols of passing control, individually annotating, and otherwise sharing among multiple users.

Very imaginative forms of conferencing are being conceived, some responding to behavioral observations that a great deal of human communication and collaborative work is carried on through informal, chance encounters, rather than through purposeful calls or contacts. For example, we could create an "electronic hallway" allowing members of a distributed group to "cruise" from one office to another,

Figure 8.13 A contemporary prototype workstation for broadband multimedia applications. A user can process data or access a database while using interpersonal audio/visual communications or accessing a video information center. (Courtesy NEC.)

much as we would glance into an office with its door open when walking down the hallway in a local office environment [46, 51].   Other individuals could be bridged into such an informal contact as desired.   Another approach to informal communication is an always-open audiovisual "window" between places where people informally gather, such as lounges and coffee rooms, demonstrated with highly compressed video by the Xerox Palo Alto Research Center and later, in a broadband, life-size version by Bellcore [48].

The geographically unconstrained automated office of the future is most dramatically represented by the examples of multimedia messaging and teleconferencing given above, but other services concepts are also developing.   Some of them may become elements of multimedia messaging and teleconferencing; others will be considered important services on their own.   They include:

- *Dialing from directory:* A user, having located an individual in a textual, iconic, or pictorial directory and having selected the media for the call through similar selection procedures, will be able, by selection of a line of text, an icon, or a picture, to make the connection in the desired media.

It will often be possible, through machine intelligence, to locate parties from personalized descriptions rather than knowledge of their locations.

- *Multimedia document exchange:* Standard interchange formats for office documents in various media are being negotiated in CCITT Study Group XVIII and in the International Standards Organization. They will, in many cases, enable the exchange of materials between dissimilar terminals. Many interesting possibilities are being discussed, such as the "progressive transmission" of images described earlier. In the future, standards may be developed for true multimedia documents, including 'live' documents with elements that are dependent on dynamic externally supplied data.

- *Communicating copiers (very high speed facsimile):* Operating at rates of 384 kbps and above, facsimile transmission may reach the point where a 20-page memorandum can be transmitted in the same few seconds it takes to reproduce it at a modern copying machine. We can imagine a communicating copier, controlled through a terminal, that provides full electronic mail capabilities. A user could create data files from the scanner output, save them, transmit them to other parties, and print them out at distant machines. Full color and gray scale are also future possibilities. Major advances in scanning technologies are needed to achieve these very high speeds.

- *Terminal-host inquiry and polling systems:* Future terminal-host networks may accommodate far larger information bursts than present systems. For example, a bank computer polling automated teller positions may collect photographs of patrons and facsimile records of transactions as well as the transactional information itself. "Connectionless" classes of service, with very small delay between specification of a destination and delivery of a large message, will be demanded. Future versions of broadband ISDN, benefitting from less protocol overhead as a result of extremely reliable lightwave networks and new switching architectures (for example, tunable lasers in wavelength-division multiplexed networks [23]), will meet this growing user demand.

- *Bulk file transfers:* Host-to-host communications, as in transfer of a branch's daily transaction records to a central computer, will remain an important business need. As in terminal to host communications, the volume of data will increase substantially as encoded visual elements become more widely used as elements of archival records. Even narrowband ISDN will facilitate some bulk transfers, but BISDN will be required to replace the large magnetic tape transfers that are done today.

- *Precedence, security, and damage recovery:* In some business applications, but especially in defense communications and information systems, special provisions must be made for priority traffic, for security, and for damage recovery. The end-to-end digital character of ISDN is a great advantage for encrypted security systems, and call precedence is facilitated by out-of-band signaling. The growth of common-channel (out-of-band) signaling stimulated by ISDN is itself an important protection for sensitive, but nonencrypted, traffic in public and government networks. Damage recovery is aided by the multipathed redundancy of the out-of-band signaling network.

- *Remote social interaction:* For working relationships as well as personal ones, multimedia telecommunications may help to overcome the barriers of distance. The casual contacts of halls and coffee rooms can be mimicked, to some extent, with continually open "video windows" joining different work locations and by electronic analogs of walks by offices and through public areas. Casual contact would be enhanced by easy and fast communication of drawings, pictures, and documents. BISDN will offer the capacity, the flexible use of capacity, and the extensive user control required for casual contact.

Information services are implicit in many of the services sketched above, but deserve separate consideration. ISDN, but especially BISDN, opens striking opportunities for multimedia information retrieval and sharing.

Much of the world's wealth derives today from the creation, processing, and distribution of knowledge. It has been estimated that in 1980 34% of the U.S. gross national product was derived from knowledge-based activities and that 43 million workers were involved [24]. As we become even more flooded with information, new and much better means must be devised for people to find what they need in that flood and reject the rest.

What we need is easy and immediate access to widely distributed information sources in many media and techniques for quickly browsing through possibly relevant materials and extracting knowledge that may not have been pinpointed at the beginning of the session. Means must be found to automatically filter out irrelevant or inferior materials. The directed information searches of today, in which the user is presumed to know exactly what he or she wants and to a considerable extent where it is, cannot cope with the information flood. It is the *transparent*, *multimedia*, *automatic filtering*, and *browsing* aspects of future information retrieval that call for much greater bandwidth, network intelligence, media integration, and signaling outside the main transport channels. They also require, on the data storage side, advanced systems with very high capacity and access data rates and very low seek times.

A three-stage information retrieval session model has been described by Irven and others [25]. The first stage is the *query*, from the user, which sets some limits on the scope of the information search. The second stage is *browsing*, in which a possibly large body of information, turned up by the query, is quickly examined, much as we browse along a library shelf or in a magazine. The user filters out uninteresting information and "zooms in" on the detail of the interesting items. It is almost always necessary to have at hand the full bodies of the information items, not merely titles or even abstracts, to browse effectively, and the absence of full bodies has been the major limitation of existing information systems relying on telephone line communications. The final stage is one of *follow-up*, in which actions, including sharing with others, are taken by the user.

An experimental system for transparent, multimedia information retrieval, called "telesophy" (meaning wisdom at a distance), has been investigated at Bell-core [22, 38].   It relies on object-oriented programming to define information units of different types, such as text string, graphics, audio, photographic image, and moving video.   The objects are all retrievable in the same way and contain their own instructions for handling and display, as well as links to other objects.   Widely distributed databases store information in this format, with an information unit server associated with each database.   An index server contains a record for each information unit with a significant volume of descriptive terms and a pointer to the location of the information unit.

As illustrated in Fig. 8.14, a query is sent by the user to the index server. The query may be a combination of words, for example, "lightwave fiber."   The processor in the index server finds those listings that correspond to the query, which in this case might be all listings in which the words "lightwave" and "fiber" occur close to one another in the actual text of the information unit.   It returns citations to the user's terminal, where the first page (10 or 20) of them are displayed in a screen window as "scan lines." The index server simultaneously retrieves and downloads, to a large cache readily accessible to the user, the full contents of the information units referenced by the first page of citations.   A transmission burst at rates of hundreds of megabits per second may be needed for fast downloading. The user can then browse through these full items, viewing them in "browsing windows" on the screen and retaining those of interest, or can move to the next page of citations, stimulating downloading of a second batch of full information units.   An efficient signaling system, huge storage in the index and information servers, and a very high burst transmission rate are required for this imaginative but idealized model of future information retrieval.

More recent experiments explore the potential of information *broadcasting* coupled with personalized information filtering [52]. A future information grazing system might broadcast news bulletins, television news and sports excerpts, movie previews, professional and trade journal articles (including pictures and sound), and company memos to various subscriber populations. With adaptive personalized filtering cutting down drastically on the bulk of material presented to a subscriber, the subscriber could be well informed while avoiding information overload. For follow up, intelligent machine intermediaries, possessing only partial information about users and databases, might facilitate a negotiation process between user and information sources to determine what information the user really wants, where it is, and what arrangements for transfer and payment are to be made.

Broadband ISDN offers the potential of downloading large bodies of information to local caches and of providing fast photographic and motion video transmission for scanning through bodies of visually oriented materials [25].   Visual browsing through, for example, a real estate database consisting of pictures of houses and textual information about them can be easy and fast.   Human–machine interfaces such as hypermedia, linking pieces of information in multiple media in a web of semantic relationships made visible on a terminal screen, can help users navigate, via broadband communications, through a complex information space [43].   The evolution of broadband information services in the future BISDN network is inseparable from progress in human–computer interaction and the devel-

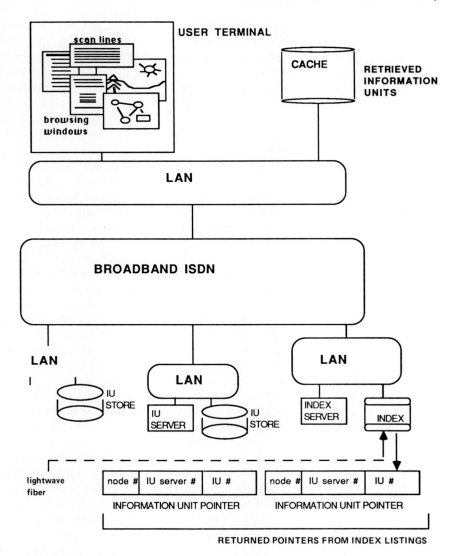

Figure 8.14 A system for transparent browsing through a large, widely distributed collection of databases in different, or multiple, media. Object-oriented programming makes possible a uniform interface for retrieval of information objects of text string, graphical, photographics, and moving video types.

opment of large computerized information systems, but BISDN must additionally resolve questions of directory assistance and of contention for network transmission, processing, and storage resources among multiple users and vendors of information.

8.3.2 Residential and Educational Services

Much of the foregoing discussion relates to residential as well as business and professional communications.   Users may not have high-powered workstations, but many will have increasingly powerful communicating personal computers with workstationlike features.   These terminal capabilities, with easy digital access to the network, will encourage the growth of services.   Students will have access to educational and reference materials, and educational networks among schools, down to the elementary level, will be built.   Airline schedules and arrival information, hours and services of public institutions, electronic banking and ordering will be available on line.   Old, allegedly unsalable information and transactional services such as videotex may, in the mid-1990s, revive with the vastly improved delivery capabilities of ISDN.   Even crude videotelephones may catch on.   Personalized services requiring D-channel messaging may also become attractive to residential customers, assuming the costs have been brought down over a "learning curve" that begins with service to business customers.

At the very least, narrowband ISDN is expected to eventually provide two high-quality telephone circuits (the two B channels) at a lower cost than two analog subscriber lines.   Low-cost digital telephones will also come someday, but network terminations on subscriber premises are likely to have A/D converters and analog jacks to accommodate the large base of analog telephones.

Custom calling services (speed dialing, call waiting, call screening, three-party calling), although widely available now over analog facilities, will have valuable extra features for ISDN subscribers, such as delivery of calling number and distinctive ringing based on the calling number.   As intelligent network capabilities evolve with ISDN, subscribers will have options for specifying additional selective treatments of incoming calls, such as leaving distinctive messages for different callers.

With the advent of low-cost screen telephones, with at least the text display capability of the one described in the multimedia messaging scenario earlier in this chapter, short D-channel messages from services providers and other subscribers could be delivered to the screen before or after initiating a voice connection.   An urgent call might be seen first as a message on the screen, without interrupting an ongoing conversation.   Time savings and fewer mistakes would result from the display of an air travel reservation and its cost on a screen rather than having them spoken by a reservations clerk.   Deaf and hard-of-hearing subscribers will be especially appreciative of this modest data communication capability.

The telegram, a popular form of communication in the past that faded away because it did not fall in price as voice communication did, might well have a modest revival.   For the average telephone subscriber of the future owning a simple screen telephone without a keyboard, a telegram will be sent as it is now, by calling an operator and dictating the message.   This cost will not be reduced, but the cost and delay of delivery (to a screen telephone) will be.   To retain the character of record communications, some screen telephones will have small printers for the contents of the screen.

Voice mail, possible without a screen display, will be greatly simplified when it is combined with a screen display. Visual indicators of voice messages waiting in the "mailbox," readable instructions for sending and retrieving voice messsages, and information on the status of a voice message being edited, retrieved, forwarded, or stored will be shown to the user. More generally, the visual display of D-channel messages will become an invaluable aid to directory assistance, to giving directions to subscribers on how to use network services, and to answering billing questions.

For the residential subscriber with a more powerful terminal, such as a personal computer with a keyboard, a pointing device, a printer, a substantial memory, graphics capabilities, and perhaps electronic pen and document scanning capabilities, much more in the way of multimedia services will become possible. Both voice and text mail will be feasible, separately and as multimedia messages. Fast facsimile, now a popular form of business communication, will penetrate the residential market. Hand drawing, initially embraced for character-based languages such as Chinese and Japanese, will eventually become popular everywhere. Multimedia messages and communication sessions, approaching the scenarios described earlier, will gradually appear in residential contexts.

Information services, as suggested above, will also penetrate the personal computer-based residential market, although not, perhaps, to the extent information providers hope. Videotex at 64 kbps will be far more practical and attractive than the 1.2–2.4 kbps telephone-line services of today, capable of filling screens quickly with text and pictures and delivering sound and animated graphics [26]. Retrieval of directory information, timetables, and market information will become popular if it is fast, easy, and inexpensive. Broadband ISDN will vastly increase the proportion of visual materials in retrieved information and bring in moving video as an additional medium. As in business applications, network-delivered information will complement more permanent information delivered through digital optical or other physical media.

Passive information retrieval may become the predominant mode in the mass consumer market. Users will define the types of materials they would like to have passed by them, and a machine agent will prepare custom delivery packages for them. One application might be a multimedia electronic newspaper or magazine [44, 53]. Another would be an adaptive information service that combines querying and passive "grazing" and follows a user's changing interests [45], as already suggested for business users.

Moving video may appear to a limited extent in narrowband ISDN, as a crude five frames per second videophone or for reduced-rate transmission of video messages and deferred delivery of entertainment and educational materials (presuming availability of the necessary subscriber equipment). Narrowband ISDN will also serve as an adjunct to cable television, facilitating pay-per-view, video shopping, and the coordination of information services with entertainment. For example, someone viewing a football game will be able to call up background information on players for display in a window on the TV screen.

However, the major moving video applications will come only with broadband ISDN. With BISDN, the subscriber will see large improvements along the two axes of choice and quality. *Choice* will be expanded with access to vast libraries of moving video materials, selection of camera views in sports and entertainment broadcasts, multiple picture-in-picture capabilities, and something close to video on demand for entertainment films. Films could be ordered in advance for future downloading to videocassette recorders or for delivery on a schedule decided by videotex voting [28].

It may not be economically feasible, even in the end-to-end optical BISDN network, to provide a subscriber with true video on demand, getting the movie you want at the moment you want it and being able to pause and fast-forward or reverse. It is more likely that a wide broadcast selection, perhaps of several hundred movies, will be offered each evening at fixed times. Popular movies could be broadcast at ten-minute intervals, allowing a granular approximation to video on demand. Out-of-band signaling, as in narrowband ISDN, will support trans-actional communications with video providers to order entertainment and great flexibility in the configuration of services. Sophisticated information services, such as a "movie browser" [25] to aid selection of a movie through descriptions, pho-tographs, and moving video samples, may be provided as adjuncts to entertainment services.

Interactive video services, allowing a user to choose alternative story lines and in some sense participate in a video program, may become the successor to video games. Less dramatically, but perhaps of more practical importance, self-paced learning from an audiovisual system accessed through BISDN, with many options for stopping and replay, branching to side information, and interacting with a machine instructor, could have a significant impact on the way people learn. Applications in language instruction, demonstrated by M.I.T.'s Project Athena, are among the attractive early possibilities.

Video *quality* will be apparent in new video formats, ranging from improved standard NTSC television to high-definition television (HDTV). High-definition television, usually defined as the NHK (Japanese Broadcasting Corporation) studio standard with 1125 lines compared to NTSC's 525 and a 5.33:3 ratio of width to height (aspect ratio) compared with NTSC's 4:3, provides a dramatically enhanced viewing experience. Viewers sitting at a distance from the screen calculated to give the same angular resolution as they now have at standard distances from NTSC television screens will have a 100% wider field of vision, which accounts for much of the effect. Experimental work in a number of countries suggests that com-pressive digital encoding of HDTV signals at rates of 100 to 150 Mbps, accom-modated by an H4 channel, loses very little of the quality and impact of the studio standard signal [28]. Delivery of HDTV is, to many observers, destined to become the driving force behind residential deployment of optical fiber and BISDN.

High-quality audio media will also be part of BISDN. Digital high-fidelity music may become available on demand. Spoken books, from a large library, will similarly become available on demand, a boon for the blind, and could have ad-ditional illustrations for those who can see.

8.4 ISDN EVOLUTION AND THE USER

Narrowband (2B + D) ISDN today, or rather of the near future, is one step in a long evolution of the public network to greater capacity, more flexibility, and digital access.   The multimedia services possible on narrowband ISDN, forms of simultaneous voice and data communication, are only the beginning in an explosion of communications and information capabilities, increasingly oriented toward visual media, that will continue indefinitely.   These early voice-data services may be modest, but they point the way, since they exploit the key ISDN feature of out-of-band signaling and the new capabilities of software-controlled communications networks.

Future services, made practical by advances in both bandwidth and software control, will build on this foundation, adding new and improved media and additional choices for users.   Future ISDNs, or whatever they will be called, will offer increasingly rich services environments.   The extent to which communications users will benefit from the enriched environments will depend not only on the economics of ISDN, but also on the sophistication of user interfaces that make it possible for ordinary people to do fairly complex things in easy and intuitive ways. Matching the user to the services is perhaps the greatest challenge for the designers and developers of ISDN.

REFERENCES

8.1. *CCITT Blue Book*, Vol. III, Fascicle III.5, *Integrated Services Digital Network (ISDN)*, Recommendations of the Series I, IXth Plenary Assembly, issued in Geneva, 1989.

8.2. CCITT Study Group XVIII Report R28(C)-E (Report of Working Party XVIII/1 on Services Aspects, Part C of the Report of the Brasilia Meeting), February 1987.

8.3. IEEE JSAC Issue on Broadband Communications, July 1986.

8.4. Judice, C. N., and D. LeGall, "Telematic services and terminal services: are we ready?", *IEEE Comm. Mag.*, Vol. 25, No. 7, July 1987, pp. 19–29.

8.5. Panel discussions at ISDN '87 Symposium, Monterey, Calif., June 1987.

8.6. Watánabe, H., "Integrated office systems: 1995 and beyond," *IEEE Comm. Mag.* Special Issue on ISDN, Vol. 25, No. 12, Dec. 1987, pp. 74–80.

8.7. Smith, R. M., "A model for human communication," *IEEE Comm. Mag.*, Vol. 26, No. 2, Feb. 1988.

8.8. Weinstein, S. B., "Telecommunications in the coming decades," *IEEE Spectrum*, Vol. 24, No. 11, Nov. 1987, pp. 62–67.

8.9. Felts, W. J., "ISDN end-user applications," address delivered at ISDN '87 Symposium, Monterey, Calif., June 1987.

8.10. CCITT Working Party XVIII/1, Temporary Document 53 (XVIII/1), July 11, 1986.

8.11. Hass, R. J., and R. W. Humes, "Intelligent Network/2: A network architecture concept for the 1990s," *Proc. Internat. Switching Symposium*, Phoenix, Ariz., March 1987, pp. 944–951.

8.12. White, P. E., "The broadband ISDN—the next generation of telecommunications network," *Proc. IEEE Internat. Conf. on Commun.* (ICC), June 1986, pp. 385–390.

8.13. Kahl, P., "The broadband ISDN, an upward-compatible evolution of the 64 kb/s ISDN," *Proc. IEEE Internat. Conf. on Commun.* (ICC), Seattle, June 1987, pp. 609–613.

8.14. Chow, C-H., G. E. Herman, and C. A. Riley, "Coping with complexity: service specification for a network services testbed," *Proc. 1988 Zurich Internat. Seminar on Digital Commun.*, Zurich, Mar. 1988, pp. 13–20.

8.15. CCITT High-Level Language (CHILL), Recommendation Z.220, *Red Book*, Vol. VI-Fascicle VI-12, Oct. 1984.

8.16. Gopal, G., G. E. Herman, and A. Weinrib, "The datacycle architecture for very high throughput database systems," *Proc. Internat. Switching Sympos.*, Vol. 16, No. 3, Dec. 1987, pp. 97–103.

8.17. Kano, S., "ISDN user–network interface layers 2 and 3 protocols: new developments after 1984," *Proc. 1986 IEEE Internat. Conf. on Commun.*, June 1986, pp. 341–345.

8.18. O'Toole, T. J., "ISDN: A large user's perspective," *IEEE Comm. Mag.*, Vol. 25, No. 12, Dec. 1987, pp. 40–43.

8.19. Anderson, C. P., "ISDN market opportunity," *IEEE Comm. Mag.*, Vol. 25, No. 12, Dec. 1987, pp. 55–59.

8.20. Addeo, E. J., A. D. Gelman, and V. F. Massa, "A multi-media multi-point communication services capability for broadband networks,"*Proc. Internat. Switching Symposium*, Phoenix, Ariz., March 1987, pp. 423–428.

8.21. Caplinger, M., "An information system based on distributed objects," *Proc. ACM OOPSLA '87*, Vol. 22, No. 12, Dec. 1987, pp. 126–137.

8.22. Kobrinski, H., and others, "Demonstrations of high capacity in the Lamdanet architecture, a multiwavelength optical network," *Electronics Letters*, Vol. 23, No. 16, July 1987.

8.23. Kraut, R. E., and others, "QUILT, a collaborative tool for cooperative writing," Conf. on Office Infor Syst., Vol. 9, Nos. 2–3, April–July 1988, pp. 30–37.

8.24. Rubin, M. R., and M. T. Huber, *The Knowledge Industries in the United States 1960–1980*, Princeton University Press, Princeton, N.J., 1986.

8.25. Irven, J. H., and others, "Multi-media information services: a laboratory study," *IEEE Comm. Mag.*, Vol. 26, No. 6, June 1988, pp. 27–33, 36–44.

8.26. Sugimoto, S., and others, "Videotex: advancing to higher bandwidth," *IEEE Comm. Mag.*, Vol. 26, No. 2, Feb. 1988, pp. 22–30.

8.27. Judice, C., "Communications in 2001: the third age of video," *Radio-Electronics*, Vol. 58, No. 5, May 1987, pp. 102–105.

8.28. Kishimoto, R., N. Sakurai, and A. Ishikura, "Bit-rate reduction in the transmission of high-definition television signals," *SMPTE J.*, Feb. 1987, pp. 191–197.

8.29. NEC advertisement, *Telephone Engineer & Management*, Feb. 15, 1988, p. 48.

8.30. "RCA Labs' video compression breakthrough gets ovation," *Electronic Engineering Times*, March 9, 1987.

8.31. Chen, C. H., and others, "Integrated services workbench: a testbed for ISDN services," *Proc. Globecom '87*, Tokyo, Nov. 1987.

8.32. Bell Communications Research Special Report on Broadband ISDN, December 1987.

8.33. Felts, Wayne, "ISDN Signaling," *Bellcore Exchange Mag.*, Vol. 4, No. 3, May–June 1988.

8.34. Schatz, B. R., "Telesophy: A system for manipulating the knowledge of a community," *Proc. Globecom '87*, Tokyo, Nov. 1987.

8.35. Minzer, S. E., and D. R. Spears, "New directions in signaling for broadband ISDN," *IEEE Comm. Mag.*, Vol. 27, No. 2, Feb. 1989, pp. 6–14.

8.36. CCITT Recommendation I.121.

8.37. Chow, C-H., M. Adachi, and D. Braun, "An example in interconnecting ISDN with the intelligent network and local-area networks," *Proc. IEEE Globecom '88*, Hollywood, Fla., Dec., 1988.

8.38. Armbruster, H., and G. Arndt, "The evolution of broadband services," *IEEE Comm. Mag.*, Nov. 1987.

8.39. *IEEE J. Selected Areas Comm.*, ISDN Issue, May 1986.

8.40. *IEEE Comm. Mag.*, Special Issue on ISDN, Dec. 1987.

8.41. CCITT Study Group XVIII Report R51, Seoul, Jan. 1988.

8.42. Allen, D., and P. Sanchirico, "Packet transfer services for the LAN environment," *Bellcore Exchange Mag.*, Vol. 4 Issue 3, May/June 1988, pp. 20–24.

8.43. Halasz, F., "Reflections on notecards: seven questions for the next generation of hypermedia systems," *Commun. ACM*, Vol. 31, No. 7, July 1988, pp. 836–852.

8.44. Lippman, A., "News and movies in the 50 megabit living room," *Proc. IEEE Globecom*, Tokyo, Dec. 1988, pp. 1976–1981.

8.45. Patterson, J. F., "Three keys to the broadband future: a view of applications," *Proc. IEEE Infocom*, Ottawa, April 1989.

8.46. Root, R., "Cruiser: A multimedia vehicle for social browsing," *Proc. ACM Conf. Computer-supported Cooperative Work*, Portland, Ore., Sept. 1988.

8.47. Browne, T. E., "The intelligent network," *Proc. IEEE*, 1983.

8.48. *Business Week*, "Developments to watch," Sept. 26, 1988, p. 83.

8.49. Hemrich, C., and J. McRoberts, "Sending high-speed data on the public network," *Telecommunications*, Vol. 23, No. 5, May 1989, pp. 66–68.

8.50. Pate, L., and R. Lake, "A network environment for studying multimedia network architecture and control," *Proc. IEEE Globecom '89* Dallas, Texas, Nov. 1989, pp. 1232–1236.

8.51. Abel, M., "Experiments in an exploratory distributed organization," in *Intellectual Teamwork: Social and Technological Foundations of Cooperative Work*. J. Galagher, R. Kraut, C. Egido, eds., Lawrence Erlbaum Assoc., Hillsdale, N.J., 1990.

8.52. Bussey, H., C. Egido, A. Kaplan, and S. Rohall, "Service architecture, prototype description, and network implications of a personalized information grazing service," *Proc. IEEE Infocom 1990*, San Francisco, June 1990 (to appear).

8.53. Judd, T., and G. Cruz, "Customized electronic magazines: electronic publishing for information grazing," *Proc. Electronic Imaging '89 East Conference*, Boston, October 1989.

CHAPTER 9

Evolution of ISDN

GOTTFRIED W. R. LUDERER

AT&T Bell Laboratories

ABSTRACT

Some speculations about the future evolution of ISDN are presented from the viewpoint of a technologist. We first look at current events and developments that are shaping the evolution of ISDN with an effort to recognize current trends and to imagine future trends. Near-term data communication needs and recent efforts on broadband ISDN standards give important clues. Speculating about the longer-term future, we then consider the telecommunication needs of a futuristic knowledge worker and follow this by a vision of universal information service capabilities to perform various kinds of information movement and management functions. Next we try to find a guiding principle for our speculations and take ideas from the computer field; we use a generalized notion of the network operating system to serve as a model for the evolving network. Finally, we discuss some of the recent relevant technologies, with special attention to fast packet technology, which we think could play a major role in implementing some of the evolving ISDN capabilities.

9.1 INTRODUCTORY REMARKS

9.1.1 Claimers and Disclaimers

How will ISDN evolve? How *should* ISDN evolve? I approach answering the first question with a bit of trepidation, taking, however, consolation from Alexander Graham Bell's historical prediction. Having invented the telephone, he speculated that the most common use of his new invention would be for listening to remote concerts. Hence the reader should take the following speculations more appropriately as an answer to the second question: It is one technologist's view of what *should* happen to ISDN. A word of caution first: ISDN as currently defined has a vast potential that will take considerable time and effort to be exploited. Thus many of the speculations in this paper may not get realized in less than about ten years, if ever.   Furthermore, the reader should take these remarks as my personal view and not as that of my employer or other association.

After these disclaimers, how can I claim more long-range credibility for my predictions?   There are several approaches, and I am going to try a few.   The obvious one might be to look at what is going on right now in standards committees and at conferences and detect some trends, as has been done in the previous chapter. We shall do just this, but we shall not stop there, but try to get a more long-range view on evolution in general.   What do we know about the origin of the species ISDN to take a guess about its evolution?   Does its early history reveal some underlying trend or theme that might lead us in our speculation on its future? There certainly are alternate potential evolution paths, and we shall at least try to find some of them.

The essence of the new ISDN is the creation of a totally digital telecommunication network, with end-to-end digital connectivity.   Even though digitalization of voice is expected to eventually bring about higher-quality service and cost savings, the most important reason for the creation of ISDN is the integration of voice and nonvoice services, such as various kinds of data, including still and live pictures.   In essence we can expect the evolution to proceed in three phases:

- Integrated access (as defined in current standards)
- Integrated transport through a more intelligent network
- Integrated services, with emphasis on higher-level integration.

From these observations, I chose as a guiding idea for my speculations on the evolution of ISDN the merger of data processing and telecommunication, which we at AT&T call *information movement and management*, and which Koji Kobayashi for many years has been calling "*the marriage of computers and communications*" [1].

9.1.2 Plan of Attack

My approach has three steps.   First, I will take clues from some recent events in the area of data networking and computing, and also from current standards activities.   Second, I am going to speculate about the far future, how its user may look, and I will present a visionary network view.   Finally, I am going to speculate about the technologies that might play an important role in the future ISDN.

To give the reader a flavor of things to come, the following sections will address these questions:

- How do we meet the current needs of the computer community?
- What is the impact of the video community on broadband ISDN?
- What are the national and international standards bodies up to?
- What are the needs of the future high-tech telecommunication user?
- How does the visionary concept of universal information services apply?

- Can the computer concept of a network operating system guide our predictions?
- What does the latest technology hold in stock for the future of ISDN?

9.2 INFLUENCE OF DATA COMMUNICATION

9.2.1 Review of Data Networking Evolution

My first conjecture is that the most important influence on the evolution of ISDN will come from the needs of the data communication users rather than from the voice network. ISDN claims integration of data in the new network, and so we have to ask the question of how well the currently defined ISDN* is going to meet the existing needs of the data communication user community.

Certainly, ISDN will go a long way toward meeting current needs; however, a lot more needs to be done to also satisfy the more demanding segment of the market, which may now be rather small but is likely to grow with advancing technology and the appearance of new services. As we will be satisfying a lot of pent-up demand for fast and reliable data communication through ISDN, we ought to look beyond the horizon and think about how to further evolve its capabilities.

Let us take a look at the brief history of data communication to gain some insight on where it might be heading or where we should direct our efforts. The evolution of data communication in the United States in the last 25 years and projecting into the foreseeable future can be broadly characterized by the following modes of operation, in their order of appearance:

1. Asynchronous terminal-to-host communication, typically using modems over switched telephone lines
2. Synchronous terminal-to-host communication, frequently over leased lines and in multidrop arrangements
3. Use of public packet-switching services following the X.25 standard
4. Use of local area networks and data PBXs on customer premises
5. Use of leased lines to create wide-area private networks
6. Integrated access for data and voice services using the emerging ISDN
7. Enhanced ISDN at several megabits per second
8. Broadband ISDN

The major elements of this evolution before the advent of ISDN are schematically depicted in Fig. 9.1. Eventually, ISDN could obviate the need for separate networks and even incorporate the network of private lines (channel network) once

---

* That is, defined by basic and primary rate interface access and bearer services commensurate with these rates as opposed to broadband ISDN. In the following, the use of the term ISDN refers just to this definition.

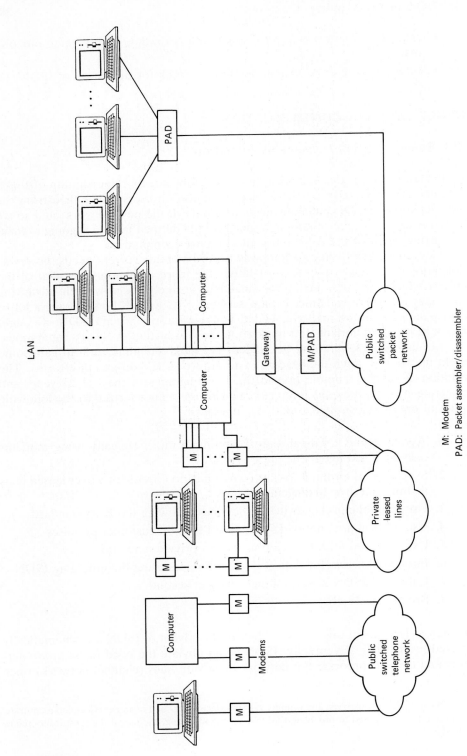

M: Modem
PAD: Packet assembler/disassembler

Figure 9.1 Pre-ISDN Data communication scenario.

network intelligence has increased to a level that permits customers to do their own short-term provisioning.

The last two items of the above list are still in the future and therefore speculative. Item 6 is about now being implemented. I want to use items 4, 5, and 6 as a launching platform for near-term forecasting of ISDN evolution. Notice that local area networks (LANs) have brought economical data communication in the megabit per second access range to end users as long as they stay within the confines of the customer's premises. Contrast these megabit per second interfaces with the tens of kilobits per second that ISDN is now offering: the basic rate interface access (2B + D) and the primary rate interface access (23 or 30 B + D), where the B channels represent 64-kilobits per second that circuits and the D channels hold packet-switched signaling and other traffic at 16 or 64 kbps. It is of interest to the data communication user that ISDN will bring packet-switched service at 16 or 64 kbps to every ISDN subscriber, which is a vast improvement over the current data capability of the switched telephone network, with its limitations to a few kilobits per second. However, neither arrangement offers the delay and bandwidth resources that many users have become used to on their local area networks. Therefore, many data users will be looking forward to ISDN being extended by including channels of higher bandwidth, such as 384 kbps or 1.536 or 1.920 Mbps.

These H channels are currently viewed as wideband circuits, probably to be provisioned using extended signaling on a D channel. These channels and future broadband ISDN circuits will play a significant role in satisfying the more demanding needs of data communication users. I believe it will be essential for the success of ISDN to make local area network (LAN) types of service economically available on a wide-area scale through the new digital network. I define the LAN type of service as offering a virtually dedicated (that is, not shared) access capability of about one-half to a few megabits per second. This is the range at which current and near-future computers, typically workstations or personal computers, are able to communicate given the economic and technical limitations of the hardware and software that make up the network interfaces. (I assume that advanced workstations with communication needs in the 100 Mbps range will remain a very small minority for a long time to come and typically be confined to local area communication.) Thus, I see a need for ISDN to soon evolve toward offering data services in the megabit per second range. In the following, we are going to look at the protocol evolution envisioned in the near future to provide such services in ISDN. Later we will show how this can be done economically by employing fast packet technology within both the existing as well as the future broadband ISDN framework.

Notice that packet technology is used in most current local area networks as well as in public switched packet service networks (X.25). However, the X.25 standard was defined for the network of yesterday, which was characterized by high error rates, expensive and low bandwidths, and relatively long delays. All of these will undergo vast improvements in the new ISDN network, but the X.25 protocol is still the mainstay of ISDN. Again we can take our clues from the LAN environment, where simpler and faster protocols have been in use for some time. The need to introduce protocol standards into ISDN that are more in tune with today's and tomorrow's LAN services has been recognized by the standards community. The CCITT 1988 Standards Recommendations contain the framework for new packet-mode services as explained in the following [2]. These recommendations seem to be the reaction to a lot of experimental work that has been reported, which proves that technology has become available to develop economic solutions for better data communication services. In particular, experimental work has been done in various places with fast packet technology based on a smooth evolution of ISDN to give us a good idea what the new services could look like. We are going to discuss this technology in more detail at the end of this chapter.

The fundamental types of data communication services offered today are based on packet-switching technology: Public switched data networks offer virtual circuit service, whereas local area networks frequently offer a connectionless service, for example, datagram service. We shall discuss each in the following sections and use this as the basis for introducing the next step we expect in the evolution of ISDN, the *frame-relay* service.

There is one other important observation about today's data services that may become decisive for the evolution of ISDN: For their short history, data communication services have been predominantly for closed *private* communities. We shall come back to this point later.

9.2.2 Connectionless Data Communication Service

What is "connectionless service?" In a telephone call, a connection is first set up before the communicating entities can exchange data. Contrast this with telegrams, which contain an address that allows the service to forward the data without the need of setting up a connection first. Both the telephone and the telegraph paradigms have been used for data communication service: they are realized in the examples of *virtual circuits* and *datagrams*. A *datagram* is a data unit that contains its destination address or routing information. Datagram *service* traditionally involves "unreliable" delivery, that is, no acknowledgment is returned to the sender, and datagrams may be delivered out of sequence. In contrast, data units sent through a virtual circuit service are delivered in sequence, and some form of reliable delivery or error control is assumed.

The first local area networks used connectionless service: datagrams were broadcast to all subscribers, and the addressed entity picked up datagrams addressed to it. Thus, the relatively long delay in setting up a connection was avoided, and since the LAN usually involved a relatively small community of subscribers, it was practical to have everybody know everybody's address.

On a larger scale, the idea of using a connectionless wide-area network with advantage originates with the first large packet-switching network, ARPANET [3]. The motivation was how to use a network of leased lines that were designed for voice and hence could be considered unreliable and uncontrollable (in real time). Broadcasting datagrams from origin toward destination required no retention of state information (of virtual circuits) in the network, and if some link in the network became temporarily inoperative, there was still some chance that the datagram would make it on a different path. It was quite practical to leave the end-to-end error control with the end user, that is, outside the network. Thus, every message is labeled with the complete network address, and no call setup is required.

Another aspect of this service is that the terminal has to know all or most of the complete network addresses of all the other subscribers (or even routing information) or must have access to a *name server*, which can provide these addresses. In the latter case, the name inquiry may actually take as long or longer than the circuit setup. However, if we assume a high locality of references and communication within only a small (private) community, this would only rarely occur. Thus, since the typical application area for connectionless service is the LAN, the directory to be maintained in each terminal is small and can be easily kept up to date.

Sometimes confusion arises because no distinction is made between the concept of connectionless service and, quite differently, the use of connectionless technology within a network or switch. The *service* implies some interface agreement (standard) between a customer and the network. The connectionless or connection-oriented mode of the service may actually be implemented in the interface and not necessarily in the network, or, stated differently, it may be a question of where to draw the boundary between customer and network.

The technology inside the network can also be considered as either connectionless or connection oriented. A connectionless network does not maintain state information about connections. It is able to route packets solely based on their label without the need of having to set up a route in a separate activity. It is able to process the logical labels and make appropriate routing decisions.

In looking at a system, it is often possible to take the label processing either out of the network (connectionless) or keep it inside (connection oriented). Again, the distinction between the two types is one of where to draw the boundaries between network and customer interface. We will come back later to this distinction.

Now let us look at successful use of connectionless concepts. The Ethernet* local area network is generally considered as the prototypical example of a connectionless network. In reality, there is often a software interface added to the LAN to provide connection service. For example, one of the most popular communication interfaces used with Ethernet implements the transmission control protocol (TCP), which again makes use of a lower-layer datagram protocol known as internetwork protocol (IP). The combination goes by the name of TCP/IP [4]. Although the lower-level IP implements a (connectionless) datagram protocol, the user software interface is through TCP, which builds a connection protocol on top of IP. We can often see this approach in the design of systems: the most convenient and preferred interface for most applications is a connection-oriented protocol, which may out of necessity reside on top of a connectionless network service.

In general, three reasons are given in favor of connectionless service:

- Avoiding the time and overhead of setting up a connection

---

* Ethernet is a trademark of the Xerox Corporation.

- The ease with which we can do broadcasting
- The embedded software base using this type of service

Broadcasting is usually meant to be directed only at the members of our own group, so a more appropriate term is multicasting or group casting, unless we are talking about emergency announcements, which are very desirable, or junk mail, which is (usually) very undesirable.

A practical example for good use of connectionless service might be the following. Consider a border police that checks each passing car's license plate against the data base in its home town to catch car thieves. Another example is the credit card check in a store. In this case we have many subscribers (store terminals) that are served by a few servers. A convenient way to handle this in a connectionless fashion is to supply the return address with each inquiry. This way the servers do not have to keep very large directories.

In summary, I think it poses a technical challenge to offer high-performance connectionless service in a public network with its virtually unlimited number of subscribers. Stated differently, it seems difficult to achieve the three objectives of public, high performance, connectionless all together, but any subset of two attributes works just fine. Experience has shown high-performance connectionless **private** networks to work very well, and there is every reason to assume the feasibility of public connectionless service with less stringent performance requirements. However, I think it will be most difficult (and hence probably not economical) to provide high-performance **public** connectionless service; hence, I expect public high-performance service to be restricted to connection-oriented offerings.

From the point of view of the provider of public communication service, I think we should approach provision of connectionless service with some caution: whenever a single datagram goes to multiple destinations, there are added responsibilities for the network, such as avoiding unwelcome deliveries and protection of privacy, and hence the service should be appropriately billed. This does not preclude offering connectionless service on "virtual private networks" that exist on public networks.

My conclusion is, barring some technical breakthrough, that the high-performance public network of the future will be offering connection-oriented service, possibly with connectionless service at lower performance.

9.2.3 Fast Virtual Circuit Service

Public virtual circuit service was first offered on public switched service networks, principally following the X.25 Standard Recommendation. The connectionless datagram service was initially included in the X.25 Standard Recommendation. But it was later dropped, and the *fast select* optional capability was added: a call setup including some data, to be answered by a disconnect acknowledgment. It turned out that few public packet switching service providers chose to implement and offer this kind of service, and today it seems to be in very little use.

What is a *virtual circuit*, and where does the concept come from? The telephone service paradigm has been to set up a *circuit*, that is, a connection, by dialing, to use this connection, and eventually take it down again.   Initially, the circuit was a connection with a bandwidth from dc to 3400 Hz; with the advent of the digital age the paradigm was generalized to mean transmission of continuous bit streams between the end points of a call.   The 64-kbps access rate has been adopted as the basic end-user access rate in ISDN, mostly carrying voice encoded with pulse code modulation (PCM, 8-bit values generated at a sampling rate of 8 kHz) as done on most of today's trunk lines.   Packet-switching service has imitated this circuit paradigm by setting up a *virtual circuit* instead of a real circuit.   Since most data communications usually contain a lot of idle or silent time, the virtual circuit does not transmit any bits during the idle periods, but behaves otherwise like a real circuit.   Packets are transmitted only when a data payload is to be sent. Because of statistical sharing and bursty traffic, more virtual circuits can be packed into the same bandwidth than real circuits.   The term virtual has been adopted from computers: the virtual circuit is virtually equivalent to the real circuit in the same way virtual memory on computers fakes a much larger memory than physically available.

One other important aspect of the virtual circuit is the abbreviated labeling of packets with a *logical link number*.   Only the initial call set up request for the virtual circuit uses the complete destination address and arranges with the network some local identifier, said logical link number, on each side of the connection.   All subsequent packets are labeled with this short-hand address that is valid only for the duration of the connection.   The network remembers the mapping from complete (long) address to short, temporary, locally significant link number for the duration of the connections.

With this much processing in place, X.25 has added a lot more protocol features to the link level such as automatic retransmission in case of errors and flow control, which require more processing on the part of the network and hence have added delay.

New network technology in transmission and switching allows us to operate with much lower error rates and much shorter end-to-end delays.   This has the effect of allowing simplification of the link level protocols and moving error detection and control to the end points of communication.   Yet ISDN as currently defined still follows the old X.25 or X.31 standards.   Without abandoning this established standard, in the interest of the advanced data user, we should also offer a simplified, faster packet service option in the evolving ISDN.   There are efforts underway to stay as close as possible to the current link level protocol and yet arrive at a streamlined version enabling LAN-like service quality.

In the standards discussions in Study Group XVIII of the CCITT, we arrived at two different kinds of high-speed packet protocols: an evolutionary step (from X.25) and a revolutionary new concept known as ATM.

As far as the first kind is concerned, it is considered a natural evolution of the current ISDN suitable for data rates of several megabits per second.   Let us look at what simplifications can be applied to the current packet protocol standard to bring it closer to current LAN performance, to move into the direction of protocol simplification to achieve higher speeds.   Two steps are distinguished and are known as *frame relaying* and *frame switching*, respectively.   Table 9.1 shows how the link

TABLE 9.1   REDUCTION OF LINK LAYER PROTOCOL FUNCTIONS

Link Layer Function	X.31	Frame Switching	Frame Relaying
Flag recognition/generation	×	×	×
Transparency	×	×	×
FCS checking/generation	×	×	×
Recognize invalid frames	×	×	×
Discard incorrect frames	×	×	×
Address translation	×	×	×
Fill interframe time	×	×	×
Manage V(S) state variable	×	×	
Manage V(R) state variable	×	×	
Buffer packets awaiting acknowledge	×	×	
Manage timer T1	×	×	
Acknowledge received I frames	×	×	
Check received N(S) against V(R)	×	×	
Generation of REJ	×	×	
Respond to P/F bit	×	×	
Keep track of number of retransmissions	×	×	
Act upon reception of REJ	×	×	
Respond to RNR	×	×	
Respond to RR	×	×	
Multiplexing of logical channels	×		
Management of D bit	×		
Management of M bit	×		
Management of Q bit	×		
Management of P(S)	×		
Management of P(R)	×		
Detection of out-of-sequence packets	×		
Management of network layer RR	×		
management of network layer RNR	×		

layer protocol of X.25 known as LAPB can be simplified.   In the left column, we list all the functions currently performed at the link layer in LAPB, as marked in the second column labeled X.31.   Column 3 eliminates some of the steps to arrive at the frame switching protocol. Further simplification is shown in column 4; the resulting protocol is known as Frame Relaying.   Notice that functional capabilities are not being removed from the protocol as a whole; they are just relegated to higher levels and need to be performed on an end-to-end basis rather than a link-by-link basis.

The essence of the frame relaying protocol is to transmit a variable-length packet with the lowest possible delay from one subscriber to another subscriber. The link layer chain just relays packets from node to node, discarding errored packets, leaving acknowledgment as an end-to-end function to a higher layer.   The link layer protocol (LAPD) allows multiplexing of different data streams (also voice!) in contrast to the X.25 link layer protocol (LAPB), which relegates multiplexing to the network layer (3).   This functionality accommodates a variety of existing higher-level protocols, since packets of different user protocols can be transparent to the network and can be encapsulated and transported with minimum delay and processing; the protocol is even suitable for real-time voice and image transmission. Examples are the SDLC frames of IBM's System Network Architecture (SNA) or the link level frames of the IEEE 802 protocol suite. The IEEE 802 Committee* has defined standards for several local area networks, which are tied together by a common higher-level logical link layer interface definition (802.2) to a variety of different media. These include the carrier sense multiple access/ collision detection (CSMA/CD) medium access based on Ethernet (802.3), the token bus format (802.4), and the token ring protocol based on IBM's token ring product (802.5). There is ongoing work on a metropolitan area network standard in 802.6, which will be discussed later. Another committee, 802.9, is working on a related objective, a LAN access standard that includes voice.

An ISDN protocol that supports frame relaying will go a long way toward improving data networking service and also toward unifying voice, data, and image transport in an integrated network. With a protocol reduced to frame relaying, it is possible to transport packetized voice or image information, which have substantially different error processing and delay requirements. For example, for interactive voice traffic we do not retransmit errored voice packets but prefer to ensure timely delivery of the next (correct) packet within the bounded delay limits. For image information, on the other hand, packets could represent numbered lines in a rastered picture, and errored packets may be displayed showing temporary glitches that could be cleaned up by retransmission after the whole picture has been sent.

A first move in this direction was made when the link level protocol for the D channel of ISDN moved from the X.25 dictated LAPB protocol to LAPD. This change can be viewed as making the link level aware of individual channels with differing requirements, by including a protocol discriminator in the frame format. Thus the LAPB protocol routine remains as an option for those logical links carrying X.25 traffic, but LAPB is not imposed on all the other links. In contrast to this earlier approach, we now recommend using LAPD in each and every case, even on B channels used to access packet service.

Eventually, I see ISDN accommodate the demanding data user through the higher data rate H channels [5]. For advanced data communication I expect to see use of an H channel in the 0.384 to 2-Mbps range with frame relay traffic, that is, using a fast-packet-multiplexed format. Eventually, in broadband ISDN, such traffic can be carried at even higher rates using the evolving asynchronous transfer mode (ATM) format, to be discussed in Section 9.3.2.

One related issue concerns the special problems that need to be addressed if voice signals are packetized, in particular the need for echo canceling as the total transmission delay exceeds certain limits. Even though we can build systems with low enough delays and high enough capacities to handle packetized voice (which will be dealt with at the end of this chapter), there is still the unavoidable pack-

---

* The Institute of Electrical and Electronics Engineers (IEEE) sponsors the 802 Committee on Local Area Networks, which operates as an Accredited Standards Committee under rules established by the American National Standards Institute (ANSI). There are currently nine subcommittees: 802.1– 9.

etization delay, that is, the time needed to collect enough speech signal samples for encoding in one packet. One major objective of the encoding process is to conserve bandwidth; hence we do not want too short a packet because of the constant header overhead associated with each packet. However, if we assume an abundance of bandwidth, certainly a valid assumption in the first leg of the access chain, then voice will be a small fraction of a single user's access bandwidth. We can easily imagine that the clear 64-kbps B channel will be emulated (though with some overhead) by breaking up the bit stream into very short packets, with each encoding containing only a few milliseconds of speech. Hence we would not require the special measures usually associated with packetized voice. In this scenario, we want to give the full bandwidth of multiple megabits minus one voice channel to the bursty data communication activity; the fact that voice may be carried with relatively high overhead is of little concern, since it is still only a small fraction of the channel.

We have seen how the virtual circuit is designed to deal with data communications characterized by two attributes: bursty irregularity of traffic on one hand, and repeated interactions between the same parties in a connection on the other hand. If we still object to the inconvenience or delay of having to set up a connection, there is one other very attractive alternative that gives the equivalent of high-performance connectionless service in a private environment: the permanent virtual circuit.

9.2.4 Permanent Virtual Circuits for Connectionless Service

The permanent virtual circuit is the packet counterpart to the rented circuit or leased line. The virtual circuit identifiers (logical link numbers), which are usually assigned at call setup time, are permanently assigned (provisioned) to define connections that persist beyond network or subscriber failure.

Consider the case of connectionless service. The subscriber has to supply the complete network address with every communication (message or packet). This address, if not frequently used, may have to be acquired from a network name server. It is assumed that the addresses within the local communication area are all known to the subscriber, so that such communications hardly require name service. On the other hand, whenever we leave the local area or communicate with a new subscriber, we can expect to need name service. In other words, the most customary type of use will require a short directory of frequently used destinations. Notice that it is the responsibility of the subscriber to keep this list up to date.

An equivalent service can be provided much simpler using *permanent virtual circuits* (PVC). Just as setting up a virtual circuit involves an agreement between the network and the subscriber about the mapping of a complete network address into a (only locally meaningful) short-hand logical link number, so is the agreement about a permanent virtual circuit. The subscriber keeps a table of destination-to-PVC-link numbers. Packets can be shorter, since they do not carry the complete address. If a destination changes, it is the network's responsibility to map the same link number into the changed address; that is, the subscriber does not have to worry about these changes. Also, if either the terminal or the network facility suffer from an outage, restoration of service automatically involves reestablishment of the permanent virtual circuit, which means that the network has to do more work. Going to new or remote locations could either incur provisioning of a new PVC or alternatively, a PVC to a gateway might be used, just as in case of leaving the local connectionless service area.

A very good example for the power of permanent virtual circuits is a new voice-controlled flight communication system. Voice is packetized, and a PVC exists between flight control and every airplane supervised. No call setup delay is involved, but bandwidth conservation is achieved.

There is still a vocal faction among the data communication experts that is requesting connectionless service extensions to ISDN. The argument of catering to an established base of customers is certainly a valid business reason. To be responsive to customers, I think the future ISDN will have to offer some kind of connectionless service. My speculation is that many such connectionless communications are likely to go over a permanent virtual circuit to a special server, which takes care of getting the packet to its destination. This could by itself occur over a set of PVCs or using call setup or even via a separate connectionless network, the latter being less likely in my opinion. Another sensible approach would be to offer connectionless service on virtual private networks.

Figure 9.2 shows an arrangement where subscribers *A* and *B* of connectionless service have PVCs *m* and *n*, respectively to a connectionless server, where these PVCs appear as *a* and *b*. A datagram from subscriber *A* on his PVC *m* is forwarded by the network to arrive on the server's PVC *a*. The server looks

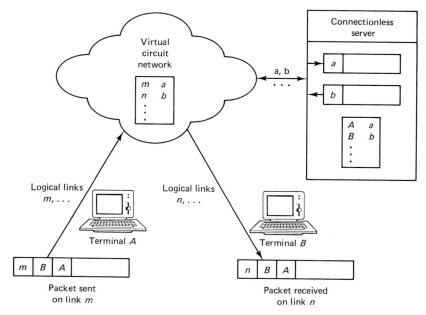

Figure 9.2 Connectionless service via PVCs and a server.

up the address of B from the datagram and forwards it over PVC b to the network, which in turn maps it into PVC n to terminate with subscriber B. The network maintains the definitions of PVCs, and the connectionless server maintains a table of subscriber names associated with PVCs to each of these. Subscribers thus would send and receive datagrams on a dedicated PVC.

The benefit of this arrangement being convenience rather than speed, it would not serve well where low delays are of overriding concern. In these cases I see the PVC solution sketched above as the preferred implementation.

In the near term for ISDN, I see the following configuration as one potentially very useful scenario for digital end-to-end connectivity to the subscriber's desk. We will use one B and the D channel for conventional voice service, and will have at least one additional permanent virtual circuit for fast packet access to a host computer or file server. This takes into account the fact that today most data terminals do not require switched access but rather are mostly associated with one single service system; they are members of a closed user group.

9.2.5 Public Switched Data Services

Today's typical data communication user is different from the user of voice service in one very fundamental aspect: data networking takes place almost exclusively within closed private communities. Even when public switched packet service (X.25) is used, the closed user group service option is very popular. The only indications of breaking out of the privacy is the increasing use of electronic mail and facsimile communication. There has been very little need for public data communication. However, this may change. Already, during certain times of the day, facsimile traffic between the United States and Japan exceeds voice traffic. Such a change is essential for a fast and universal introduction of ISDN. Unless more of a need for public data networking is created, the penetration of ISDN is likely to be slow. Key to increasing the need for public data transport services is the emergence of more and more *information services*. More and more up-to-date databases must be offered for easy access to everybody, and they must provide real added value to their customers. Moreover, ISDN capabilities must play an essential role, by adding substantial benefits to both buyers and sellers of information service, such as speed of access, controlling, billing, advertising for services. There must be enough advantages from ISDN compared to access via dial-up modems through the traditional voice network, which may be offered as a getting-started enticement.

In summary, I hope that the typical future workstation or PC user will overcome the parochialism of private-only data communication and communicate with a larger and larger universe. This should be accelerated as interesting and profitable new services, especially information sources, become available.

9.2.6 Data Outlook

After all these discussions, what are the prospects for the data communication user with regard to ISDN?

In general, I expect an evolution toward fast packet services of increasing speed and sophistication. First, the current ISDN will offer the average data communication user a vast improvement over the currently available services by offering immediate and easy access to public packet-switching networks at 16 or 64 kbps, with today's X.25/X.31 standards. For the demanding data communication users, I expect that ISDN will be extended to offer through the telecommunication network the kind of service that these users are now getting on premises through their local area networks. As the next step, I believe that a frame relay service over the extended ISDN will offer fast packet communication in the megabit range, using a second generation of packet-switch technology. There is also a high probability that some kind of connectionless service will be offered through ISDN, although with lower performance than connection-oriented services. Eventually, we will enjoy the vast capabilities of broadband ISDN as discussed in the next section.

Certain ISDN **circuit mode** services should also serve the data communication user well. We already mentioned access to public or private packet-switching networks through ISDN circuits, which need not be B channels but could be H channels for higher rates. We can also envision computer-to-computer communication through switched high-speed H channels in circuit mode. Even though we expect rapidly decreasing bandwidth costs, I still see a need to exploit the cost advantages offered through packet multiplexing and switching, and I believe that packet-mode communication is the native and hence preferred communication mode for the data user.

Having discussed the influence of current data communication needs on the evolution of ISDN, let us now turn toward yet another force that is likely to influence the future utility of ISDN for the data communication user: the evolving broadband ISDN standard.

9.3 BROADBAND FACTOR

Whereas the range of multimegabit communication is often referred to as *wideband*, we are now entering the domain of *broadband* communications. This is often assumed to refer to bandwidths needed for video signals, and may refer variously to 45 Mbps (or 34 Mbps outside the United States) or the 100-Mbps range and above. Our attention here is primarily concerned with the broadband ISDN (BISDN) efforts of CCITT; a second consideration is the emerging metropolitan area network (MAN) standard, which I expect to have some influence on the evolution of BISDN.

9.3.1 Broadband ISDN for Video Services

With digital end-to-end connectivity in ISDN just beyond the horizon for voice and other services requiring similar bandwidth, the next technological milestone is obviously a digital access rate capable of carrying video signals. Thus, the concept of broadband ISDN has been driven by expectations of future video needs [6]. This raises two major questions: first, what should the signal format for these services be, and, second, what type of video services would be offered? Let's look at these questions one after the other.

It turns out that an uncompressed video signal (PAL, SECAM, or NTSC) takes about 140 Mbps in digital form. Current CCITT standards efforts are aiming at a television standard for broadband ISDN. This would be a component video format; that is, would contain a luminance signal Y sampled at 13.5 MHz in 8-bit PCM and two color difference signals R-Y and B-Y, each sampled at 6.75 MHz and coded in 4-bit DPCM. Transmitting only 720 sample points of 858 points on a line yields a total data rate of

$$720/858 \ (8 \times 13.5 + 4 \times 6.75 + 4 \times 6.75) = 135.95 \text{ Mbps}$$

This is just 3.3 Mbps less than the European fourth level transmission rate of 139.264 Mbps, which can be used for audio, data, and framing information. With additional processing the signal can be encoded without loss of fidelity in a compressed format. Obviously, the more elaborate the processing, the higher the compression ratio. The processing can eventually become quite expensive, in particular since the process of encoding and decoding has to occur in real time. At present, a 5:1 compression ratio (to about 30 Mbps) is within the state of the art, but still expensive. Hence, we might be tempted to select a rate substantially lower than 150 Mbps. For example, current considerations envision packaging three or four television channels into 150 Mbps accepting a degradation equivalent to current broadcast quality, or alternatively, offering enhanced quality television service (EQTV) with the same number of scan lines as NTSC but higher bandwidth. However, in view of plans for a high definition television standard (HDTV, with more scan lines), providing substantially improved resolution and picture quality, we have stuck to the 150 Mbps rate in the hope of easily accommodating a future compressed HDTV signal [7]. Since there is an emerging view of an aggregate access rate of about 600 Mbps, some view this bandwidth to be used for one lightly compressed HDTV channel or four uncompressed regular television channels. For comparison, the current 4-2-2 broadcast studio video standard CCIR 601 uses about 280 Mbps, with

$$8 \times 13.5 + 8 \times 6.75 + 8 \times 6.75 = 216 \text{ Mbps}$$

video bandwidth requirement. Recent broadband experiments in Europe (the Biarritz trial in France [8] and the BIGFON trial and a broadband precursor network in Germany [9] have been using 140 Mbps.

It seems very natural, just as we switch bit streams in B or H channels in the current ISDN, to switch a clear bit channel of about 150 Mbps under the direction of a message-oriented signaling protocol on a D channel, using extensions to Q.931. However, there are good reasons to deviate from the "bit pipe" approach of a clear bit channel.

9.3.2 Which Broadband ISDN Standard Format?

As we enter the world of digital communication, we enter the world of multiplexing. In essence, there are almost no digital communications where we do not have a variety of communications going on at the same time in the same bit stream. At least, besides the basic conversion per se, there is always signaling. Thus, ISDN starts out with defining two fundamental multiplexing formats:

- Basic rate interface with a format of 2B + D
- Primary rate interface with a format of 23(30) B + D

In the analog world of the past, one distinction was between in-band and out-of-band signaling. In ISDN, we have an out-of-band signaling channel (D channel), but we also have rudiments of in-band signaling, when full X.25 is carried on the D channel, as opposed to relying on the initial B circuit being set up through the D channel. Some CCITT standards people prefer to restrict the term out-of-band signaling to circuit mode. In contrast, for packet modes we should talk of logically separate signaling.

The distinction made in CCITT is that connections can be established in three different modes: (1) on demand or switched, (2) permanent or provisioned, and (3) reserved for a limited time in advance.

For the sake of the arguments to follow, I consider the basic rate interface a hybrid format: the D channel is always packetized, whether it carries signaling only, or both signaling and packet data service; the B channel is either a circuit carrying a clear bit stream, or it carries packet traffic to a packet network. Notice that an ISDN connection always includes packet communication; a circuit connection is optional. As we will see repeatedly, we may expect that packet communication will play an increasingly important role in the future of ISDN. As a matter of fact, one of the earlier standards arguments was whether the basic format of the broadband ISDN channel should be packet or circuit mode. This has been settled in favor of a packet format.

For historical reasons, in choosing a format there were basically three alternatives, which are shown in Figure 9.3, which shows the overhead (OH) and the D, B, and H channels packed into a link level frame, under different schemes.

1. A hybrid scheme would define a fixed-length frame with a variable boundary inside, such that STDM and ATM would coexist side by side within the same frame.

2. Synchronous time division multiplexing (STDM): Channels carrying clear bit streams are the base, on which we can put optional packet communications.

3. Asynchronous transfer mode (ATM, also known as pure ATM): packets, now called cells, are the basic format, which can optionally carry synchronous traffic.

The STDM format is essentially an evolution of the DS-1 format introduced for pulse code modulated voice on trunk lines in the 1950s: within a frame, the same slots are allocated to the same connection.

How do we associate a group of bits in a multiplexed stream with a particular conversation? There are two basic methods. In digital circuit switching there is

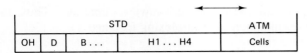

(a) Link sharing between ATM and STD

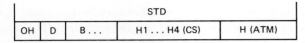

(b) ATM over STD channels

(c) STD over ATM virtual circuits

OH, overhead
CS, circuit switched

Figure 9.3 Basic broadband format alternatives.

association by position of time slots within a frame. In contrast, packet switching like ATM format uses *labeled* data units (packets); that is, there is association by identifier preceding the data. The distinction between synchronous time division multiplexing (by position) and asynchronous time division multiplexing (by label) was first brought to my attention by A. G. Fraser, who used this terminology in his Datakit* packet switch [10]. Asynchronous multiplexing was also called *demand multiplexing*.

More recently, there has been work at CNET in France using the term asynchronous time division multiplexing (ATD) within the context of an experimental broadband packet switch [11]. This work has influenced the CCITT standards Working Group XVIII, and the members decided in February 1987 in Brazil to call the future broadband ISDN packet communication mode which was previously known as new transfer mode, henceforth asynchronous transfer mode (ATM).

There is a range of possibilities on how the ATM format is used to offer end-user services. On one end, we consider ATM a very low level multiplexing format for deterministic allocation of channels on which many other transport services can be put. On the other end, we can view the ATM cell like a frame in a statistically multiplexed packet service offering. I think the choice of a fast packet switching protocol like ATM as the foundation for BISDN will turn out to be fortunate. The reasons are pedagogical, technical, and historical.

9.3.3 New Communication Paradigm

Let's start with the pedagogical aspect. The basic paradigm of the analog voice network has been the 4-kHz bandwidth channel supported by a universally com-

---

* Datakit is a trademark of AT&T.

patible numbering plan. The founders of ISDN have replaced this with the 64-kbps channel accompanied by out-of-band D-channel signaling messages. Of course, we went digital for reasons of supporting all these other nonvoice data services. But what about the bandwidth? Just increasing the bandwidth from a bourgeois 64 kpbs to some stately 384 kbps or 1.5 Mbps does not make the visionary jump the new technology calls for.

The future paradigm of communication is to deliver a group of bits to one or several recipients according to some attached label within a given delay time limit that is characteristic of a service class, such as we know first, second, or third class mail letters. The transmission bit rate is not of importance to the service. This is in contrast to the commodity view of telecommunication — turning on a spigot of a bit pipe to transport a constant stream of bits, which roots in the age when a circuit meant a galvanic connection between the end points. The modern view of communication will be focusing on the rapid shipment of blocks of different types of information, which may well have different transport requirements and hence need different treatment in the network.

The labeled data unit (or packet) transported with a delay time that is specific to the requested class of service will be the future communication paradigm for all sorts of media: voice, data, text image, video. Whenever we want to communicate, we have to think of shipping a set of bits to one or more recipients within a certain bounded time interval; and this is the fundamental operation, not the fixed rate bit channel. So far on pedagogical philosophy. Now let us turn to a technical argument.

9.3.4 Distributed Processing

One of the great recent innovations in computing is the concept of distributed processing. Since processing elements have become less and less expensive, we can easily afford many of them and let them cooperate in the solution of problems. The problem with this approach becomes how to control them to cooperate for doing useful work. A lot of research has been done to find schemes that make such control easy. One increasingly successful approach has been to embed in the data the operational code to be applied to the data when they arrive at a processing element. In its ultimate form, this leads to *data-flow architectures*. At higher levels of protocols, this concept is closely related to transaction processing.

For the purposes of telecommunication, it makes eminent sense to attach to the data unit a label that may be used to request certain operations, say routing, service grade, and error detection. Once we leave the realm of pure voice communication and enter the multimedia world, it becomes very difficult to use out-of-band signaling and yet mix the different types of information within the same stream. Labeling becomes a necessity for differentiating among different services on an instantaneous basis.

At a lower level, we consider the act of switching, that is, deciding on where to move a data unit. We can see that the labeled data unit allows us to distribute the switching decision and hence to build switching fabrics with unlimited growth in the number of terminations. We are talking about the self-routing fast packet switching fabrics exemplified in their simplest form by the banyan network [12]. We will come back to this technology at the end of this chapter.

Here, a packet of bits traversing an intelligent switching fabric can be acted on in an individual atomic node in the fabric solely by considering the address in the packet label, without some higher control authority establishing beforehand a path through the fabric.

Hence, with labeled data units as in ATM, we will be able to do differentiated multimedia communication processing and build arbitrarily large two-dimensional self-routing switching fabrics.

9.3.5 Banking on Technology Advances

Our final argument tries to use a historical perspective. In the course of technological evolution, we have seen conservative voices who warned against taking too large technological steps. The same argument is used to favor an initial approach basing broadband ISDN on the admittedly simpler STDM format. Fiber trunks between central offices are starting to operate in the multigigabit range. At these high rates, the label processing of fast packet switching becomes prohibitive, and STDM techniques have to be used. Thus, some argue, broadband rates may be too fast for packet switching to be done economically. Similar arguments were used to delay the introduction of end-to-end digital technology; at the time the decision was taken, it could be argued (and indeed was) that the final access link could be implemented less expensively in analog technology. We have a tendency to underestimate progress in technology. John S. Mayo of AT&T Bell Laboratories has recently pointed out that in microelectronics we have experienced a doubling of integrated circuit complexity every five years and a doubling of circuit speed every two years. I therefore think that taking a bolder step relying on technology advances is defensible, and I predict that the more advanced ATM philosophy will turn out to be the better choice in the long run.

9.3.6 Embedded ATM

There is yet another aspect to the evolution of a broadband ISDN standard protocol, that of embedding the ATM just discussed inside another network protocol. A U.S. ANSI standard [13] defines a digital transmission format hierarchy known by the name of SONET, synchronous optical network protocol [14]. SONET defines a frame format, based on a 125-μsec period, which includes overhead and payload bits and describes how other transmission rate formats such as DS0, DS1, and DS3 are packed into these SONET frames. CCITT has adopted the term synchronous digital hierarchy (SDH) for the evolving corresponding BISDN standard. Figure 9.4 shows the so-called SDH STS-1 frame format for an effective signaling rate of 51.84 Mbps yielding 155.52 Mbps with triple byte interleaving.

There are 9 rows at 90 octets each; these 810 octets transmitted in 125 μsec (the 8-kHz voice sampling rate) yield the basic SDH building block rate of 51.840 Mbps. The first 3 columns (27 octets) are transport overhead used for network maintenance and the like, 9 as section overhead, and 18 as line overhead, leaving

783 (9∗87) octets as payload. This payload can be mapped into various synchronous transmission rates like DS-0, DS-1, DS-2, DS-3, which would include U.S. and international formats. An open question is how far the SDH framing is carried when coming from the network toward the subscriber. Somewhere in the network termination equipment the SDH framing is removed. Beyond that point, we could carry bare ATM cells with no framing or frames of other protocols in case of terminal adapters.

This issue illustrates the question of how broadband ISDN (ATM) will be used; some view it more as a network-internal protocol that may terminate in a gateway to a subscriber premises network, like a basement multiplexer or a back-yard multiplexer, if one is more concerned with tamper-proofing. Alternatively, ATM may actually terminate in the subscriber's terminal, even though some of us may have a hard time visualizing the use of 150 Mbps bursts, when we consider the current difficulties of getting more than a few megabits per second through the hardware/software interface of a workstation or computer.

9.3.7 What Broadband Services?

The futuristic view of the world has it that every home will be at the end of an optical fiber communication link [15]. Since the cost of this occurring is largely in the labor of installing the cable (digging up the ground), the question becomes mainly one of what valuable services would make this worthwhile? Once the fiber is in place, the transmission rate will not be much of a cost issue, since we can expect that mass-produced transmitters and receivers will easily operate up to several hundred megabits per second.

Considering such a value/cost challenge, it seems much more likely that business terminals will be the first to be fiber-networked. The expensive "last mile"

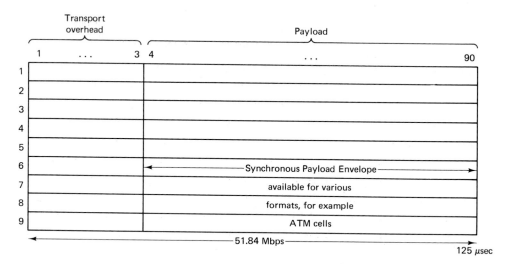

Figure 9.4 SDH STS-1 frame format.

of loop access can be shared for several users, and fibering a building is much less of a cost issue than access across public right-of-ways. Moreover, the "churn" in in-house connections is much higher than in the loop area.

Returning to the private home, the one service that is considered to have the best chance on fibers to the home is something like today's cable television, potentially in form of high-definition television to differentiate it as a more attractive offering than broadcast television. From that point of view, broadband ISDN could supersede and incorporate the distribution system that is used by today's cable television companies. It has been proposed that the access format incorporate four channels at 150 Mbps each [16]. The typical home could receive three television programs in one-way communication and have one channel for all kinds of other broadband and narrowband services (two-way) including voice. Out of the menu of offered programs, the subscriber could select up to three at a remote distribution point. Two-way video for conferencing or two-party video calls would most likely not use a full 150-Mbps channel but be carried in compressed format over a lower rate wideband channel. The typical business would more likely have a need for interactive (two-way) video communication, so it might have one or up to three of the 150-Mbps channels capable of two-way communication.

It is possible and, in certain countries, rather likely that the introduction of broadband ISDN will not be carried by the distribution of entertainment video but rather by emerging new business services, which rely on or benefit greatly from a much larger bandwidth than offered through the current ISDN. Thus we can safely say that the interest of the technologists involved in the broadband ISDN standards work has gradually shifted from a heavy video emphasis to more and more weight on advanced data communication services. There is already an important competitor in this field: the metropolitan area network (MAN).

9.3.8 Metropolitan Area Networks

A new data communication technology known as metropolitan area networks (MANs) extends the scope of local area networks in geographic coverage beyond customer premises and in functionality beyond data only [17]. We can say that MANs provide distributed switching and transport facilities among LANs and PBXs in a limited geographic area. The range covers about a 50-km diameter. At the same time there is an increase in bandwidth from the 1- to 10-Mbps range of LANs to the 50- to 150-Mbps range. Already there is a US ANSI standard [18] proposal for a fiber-distributed data interface (FDDI), which assumes an optical fiber ring operating in a fast packet mode at 100 Mbps [19]. The FDDI standard aims at satisfying the needs of the data communication user, and its sponsors come mainly from the data-processing industry. In this vein, it is well suited for the construction of high-capacity private data networks. Naturally, voice communication is of little concern here.

We mentioned already the other MAN standards effort underway in IEEE 802.6 Committee on MANs, which has been working on various proposals for MAN standards for several years [20].

In my opinion, a promising MAN standard should aim at two major objectives: first, a fast, simple, stable and flexible interface to benefit the user, independent of the network architecture, and second, ease of operation and maintenance for the sake of the service provider. To satisfy the latter objective, if a network topology must be defined, it should be a star-based architecture; a star-based topology is indicated. Figure 9.5 summarizes various chains of reasoning leading to these conclusions.

First, with the extended geographic coverage of MANs, we have to use public right-of-ways, which brings the common carriers into the arena. These service providers could play an essential role by providing a public communication service on MANs.

Since the current FDDI standard proposals do not agree with the evolving broadband ISDN standard (ATM), the 802.6 Committee set itself the objective to harmonize the broadband ISDN and MAN standard efforts. As of this writing, both this committee and the T1S1 committee of the Exchange Carrier Association, which is instrumental in representing the United States in the CCITT working group, have made substantial progress toward this goal. Whereas it seemed for a while that both proposals would converge at a common cell format of 64 octets payload with a 5-octet header, both standard groups have now adopted a proposal for a 48-octet payload and some other changes, so that the ATM format can be seen as representing a subset of the MAN format. The 802.6 MAN architecture is also known as distributed queue dual bus (DQDB) and is based on a system called QPSX [37].

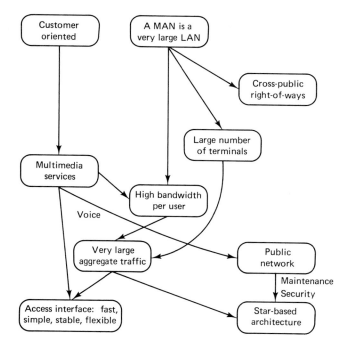

Figure 9.5 Chains of reasoning for MAN objectives.

The current format intended to be common to ATM and DQDB is shown in Figure 9.6. A payload of 48 octets is preceded by a header of 5 octets. The check sequence in the header only applies to the header, to protect against delivery to the wrong party. The access control field supports operation on a shared medium following the IEEE 802 media access control philosophy. Two octets for the virtual circuit identifyer span a space of over 64,000 circuits. The priority bit allows us to mark, for example, signaling messages. The payload type bit allows us to deal more easily with segmentation, that is, multicell messages. Consideration has been given to support connectionless service, although details are still open.

There are many potentially synergistic relationships between broadband ISDN and MANs. Certainly, we like to see MANs interconnected through ISDN to form wide-area networks. Also, we could see ISDN as an access method to MANs or MANs as an access vehicle for broadband ISDN. Alternatively, we could see the MAN as the network that offers broadband ISDN service; that is, the access standard interface for MANs could be the new broadband ISDN standard. Certainly, with MANs focusing on data communication needs, there probably needs to be a way to carry voice to the voice network. It follows that it is very important to bring the signaling methods of MANs into agreement with ISDN.

By LAN tradition and heritage, many proponents of MANs think of MANs as scaled-up versions of LANs, which means that MANs are also viewed as distributed topologies, like buses or rings. In other words, unfortunately (in my view) the standards work extends beyond defining a service interface and tries to include definition of an architecture. This is potentially counterproductive, in that service providers have learned long ago that we should keep these issues separate. Both customers and service providers benefit in the long term if the access interface is kept stable, but the network architecture should be able to be changed, for example, to introduce new cost-saving technology in a user-transparent fashion. This is already manifest in the fact that experience has shown that physically distributed

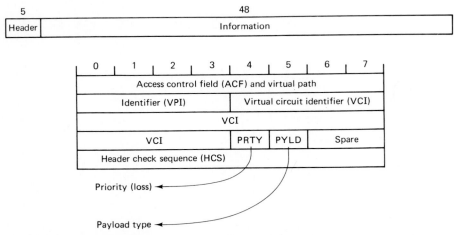

Figure 9.6 Proposal for a common 802.6 MAN (DQDB) and BISDN (ATM) cell format.

systems become difficult to maintain and operate once they exceed a certain size. Hence hierarchical topologies with wire centers (fiber centers) are preferred, which does not mean that a MAN architecture could not be a logical bus or ring, just that the cabling topology should resemble stars.   The fact that we want to handle much larger user communities with much higher individual bandwidth (for example, for multimedia services, certainly including voice) would lead to an aggregate bandwidth that cannot be easily handled by a bus or ring architecture, but provides few problems to modern fast packet switches.

Up to this point in our speculations, our vantage point has been at the leading edge of data communication and broadband/video applications.   I want to leave this relatively safe ground now and move far out into the clouds of a rather speculative future.   Can we imagine the user of the 21st century, and what vision comes up about the network of the future?

9.4 FUTURISTIC VIEWPOINT

9.4.1 Needs of the Knowledge Worker

The sophisticated high-tech telecommunication user of the future is sometimes referred to as an *information worker* or more appropriately as a *knowledge worker*. The term *information movement and management* is being used to describe the way the telecommunication network would serve this user.   What exactly do we mean by these terms?

The basic job of the knowledge worker is to make decisions.   The decision-making process is an input–output process, usually with many iterations.   As input for her or his decisions, our worker needs to have facts and opinions, that is, data that exist in data banks and in the minds of other people.   The network must allow easy access to data banks in many places and to people in various places.   The facts and data need to be presented in the most appropriate way, so we need tools for graphic or animated presentation, for conversion, enhancement, combination, correlation.   Multimedia conferencing with extensive recording capability is another aspect of this environment.

Once our user, through many iterations and in consensus with those who have to agree, arrives at decisions, these decisions have to be communicated to the appropriate people in the most effective and appropriate forms so that they can act on them.   We can, for example, see needs for encryption, authentication, verified acknowledgments, and possibly even legally authorized recording.   Finally, means for helping to follow up on action items may be offered.

Different types of information such as voice, data, text, graphics, and video need to be transported, converted, stored, and retrieved in arrangements that involve many parties.   The future desk top terminal will have a large high-resolution color screen for multiple windows displaying graphical data, facsimile images, video conference pictures, besides the conventional computer text.   A *speakerphone* will be integrated, probably supplemented by a light-weight, tetherless ("hands- off") headset.

The topology of possible arrangements will be a far cry from today's point-

to-point, multidrop or simple conference arrangements. Rather involved multiparty connections with controlled multidirectional information flow for multiparty–
multimedia conferencing will become possible.

A new term has been coined: *information productivity*. The improvement
of information productivity has been chosen as the broadest objective for future
network services. Whereas *manufacturing productivity* has long been understood
to measure the output of goods and services per cost unit, we must not get trapped
to read the inexpensive generation of new information into the term information
productivity. Rather the term should be understood as measuring the improvement of the *whole process* of communication and decision making per effort applied.
However, to come up with some well-defined and meaningful measurement will
at best be very difficult; it may well be impossible. As an analogy, consider the
effort to define *software productivity*; the cost to produce a line of code is often
used, but is a rather deficient measure, since it does not, for example, weigh the
complexity of the function performed. Ease of use is another important aspect.
Even for someone without a telecommunications engineering degree, it should not
be more difficult than learning how to type or how to use a spreadsheet program
to operate the future multifunction terminal. Much human factors work is needed
in the design of ergonomic user interfaces, which may well turn out to be the crucial
factor for the commercial success of ISDN.

The implications for ISDN are that we need multimedia, multiparty protocol
standards, including higher-level languages for application specific functions. Unfortunately, committee efforts have been notoriously bad in generating user-friendly
interfaces. What has worked better is the marketplace; among competing services
the one with the best usability becomes eventually accepted as a de facto standard.

Having created the image of the future knowledge worker and her or his
modus operandi, let us now turn to a visionary description of the future network.

9.4.2 A Vision of Future Information Services

Whereas it is relatively easy to assess today's data communication market needs,
it is quite a different matter to speculate about the markets of tomorrow. Obviously, for the "next century customer," modern technology can bring virtually
unlimited bandwidth and keep delay low and only subject to the laws of physics.
The main question is one of cost benefit: will it be worthwhile to offer such advanced
capabilities? What could these new services be?

Communication service providers such as the Local Exchange Carriers in the
USA and the PTTs in other countries have a vital interest in expanding the telecommunications market, as do, obviously, the vendors of telecommunication equipment. The creation of an advanced telecommunication market is thus a unifying
objective for the whole telecommunication industry. This market must offer products and services that improve the information productivity of the customers.

In 1986, AT&T has made an effort to give momentum to this unifying objective by presenting a vision of the future called *Universal Information Services*
or UIS [21, 22]. Let us look at the attributes of this marketing concept for guidance

of the evolution of ISDN. Certainly, the currently defined ISDN is the first step on the way toward UIS. Progressing further, the UIS concept will guide the natural evolution of ISDN to provide not only integrated access for but also integrated transport of voice, data, and image through a unified network. The following attributes have been declared to characterize UIS:

- Uniform access standards
- Architectural freedom
- Universal ports
- Network resources on demand
- Integrated access and transport
- Adaptive, logically provided services

These attributes have been explained in the following way:

Uniform access standards permit any kind of network and user systems to interwork easily, according to published interfaces. *Architectural freedom* allows us to distribute or concentrate resources anywhere in a network. It means that storage, processing, or customized services for various applications can be located on customer premises, in central offices, in service bureaus, or be distributed across these places, with networks having the speed, responsiveness, and flexibility to facilitate geographic transparency.

Universal ports will provide a common connection mechanism for attaching almost any information appliance to any network. Universal ports will provide consistent physical and logical gateways for voice, data, and image terminals connected at any network location, whether public or private, business or residence, centrex or PBX. *Network resources on demand* imply that transport capacity as well as value-added features can be summoned when needed by network users without cumbersome prearrangements and without paying for capabilities until they are used. Even during a connection, a network user will be able to change the amount of network capacity used from moment to moment in accordance with the user's application.

Integrated access and integrated transport imply a single transport network for voice, data, image, and signaling traffic. A Universal Information Service network will naturally carry all these forms of information, mixed in any combination. The network will provide integration not only on the user access links, but in the internal backbone transport fabrics as well. *Adaptive, logically provided services* require that a general-purpose network can be easily adapted to the varying needs of each user. A diversity of services will be provided through logical rearrangement of the network's resources by software, rather than through physical service-provisioning processes. With Universal Information Services, any customer service desired should be able to be summoned immediately from an ever-capable network.

With the guidance from these general UIS attributes, in the following section I will look for some specific applications, letting my imagination run free and trying to assume a user perspective in a network with (almost) no resource limitations.

9.4.3 Some Advanced Application Scenarios

Before we get carried away speculating about future services requiring an abundance of resources, let us not forget that the currently defined ISDN is capable of delivering a vast menu of mind-boggling services, some of them based on the latest technology. For example, expert system services based on artificial intelligence concepts or transaction processing for conducting business transactions or information retrieval are well within the scope of the currently defined ISDN. However, in this chapter we are not concerned with the current ISDN but with the evolving future ISDN. What applications might become possible, given an abundance of bandwidth, processing power, and storage capacity? I have come up with three examples of type of service that require network resources substantially beyond the reach of today's network. These are:

- Multimedia services
- Classroom teleconference
- High-resolution documents

I would like to briefly explain each of these.

The most general future telecommunication session is a *multimedia teleconference*. Imagine a conference call involving several parties at a number of locations, each with a multimedia service terminal. As mentioned earlier, such a terminal has, besides voice capabilities, a high-resolution color screen with multiple windows. Windows could show as video picture any subset of the teleconference partners, or one window could be for a presentation watched by all. Documents or viewgraphs could be pulled up into windows. Data could be manipulated differently at different sites, and the different presentations could be synopsized in different windows. The facility to store not just data but also voice or video opens up new opportunities [23]. Think of documents with voice annotation, where a marker on the screen indicates that a "voice bubble" exists that can be brought forth from storage and played out. Somebody asked to review a draft of a paper may choose to add voice comments for the author. Or a writer may add voice commands to edit for the typist. We are used to a mixture of pictorial and textual information; why not having sound included? Certainly, the future encyclopedia will store under the entry *robin* the sound of this bird's call. Multimedia service would also include some form of program execution, with transparent geography. Thus, a multimedia document might include a "program" to be invoked. Certainly, exercises could be devised to improve the communication process, for example, through simple quizzes. Or pointing to certain parts of an illustration could invoke a written or spoken response. Eventually, electronic speech recognition will appear and provide yet another human engineered interface opportunity.

The *classroom teleconference* is another scenario of a multimedia application. Students would see the lecturer in one window and the blackboard or projection screen in other windows. If a student wants to ask a question, the lecturer would have a window to see the name of the student and can decide whether to turn voice control over to him or her. Students would be able to get hard copy of the lecture material, store it in their files, and add their own annotations.   For example, during a lecture a listener may take "voice notes" and attach them to certain lines on the screen.

Multiparty game playing is another scenario, be it Bridge, which requires relatively low bandwidth, or be it some variant of Star Wars with real-time controlled graphic animation such as real-world simulations using electronic helmets and gloves.   The matchmaking and organization of tournaments should challenge new enhanced service providing entrepreneurs.

High-resolution documents are another application.   Here we expect quality equivalent to or close to the original, which means letters and memoranda can be carried primarily in electronic form with optional hard copy facility.   Such a capability would allow a variety of applications, for example data banks of all company memoranda, of patents, or collections of illustration.

I am sure there will be uses that we cannot imagine well today.   I see an opportunity to go away from static viewgraphs to dynamic viewgraphs that improve the communication process by animation.   One excellent example I saw a few years ago at Brown University is the illustration by animation of the operation of an electrical backplane bus as a teaching aid for electrical engineering students.

The range and number of potential applications is certainly mind-boggling. What might be holding us back is the definition of appropriate communication standards.   One way out of this dilemma I see is to concentrate early on some kind of program downloading capability.   This by itself would seem a natural extension of the ISDN protocol suite, but it also implies some kind of standard operating system running in the future multimedia terminal.   I hope this problem is addressed early on to accelerate the introduction of advanced integrated services.

Having presented three futuristic examples of the type of service envisioned by UIS, I don't think there will be much of a dispute that the UIS vision does not represent a worthwhile goal.   A much more arguable question is about the best approach; how do we get there from here?

So far we have taken a *user* perspective: first of the current data communication user, then of the broadband or video user, and finally of the "far-out" knowledge worker.   We can take a different position and look at several new technologies as driving forces for the evolution of ISDN.   What are some of the technologies that might help us on the way toward UIS?

9.5 TECHNOLOGICAL FACTORS

9.5.1 Approach: Network Operating System

In my opinion, the overwhelming influence on the evolution of the network has been coming from computer science.   We have already seen digitalization, stored program control, and the introduction of packet switching in signaling and data networking.   More is certain to come.   One particularly useful guiding principle that computer science can offer us is the model of the computer operating system, in particular if we apply two generalizations to adapt it properly to our environment

[24]. The resulting concept I call the *network operating system.** I propose to view the evolving network as one gigantic futuristic general-purpose computing system under control of the network operating system. Let us briefly review the concept of an operating system as it has evolved in this young field of computing science over the last 30 years. The operating system of a computer realizes the system architecture that is visible to the user of the system. It transforms the hardware by performing two major functions:

- It provides a convenient *general-purpose interface* that allows the user to define the tasks to be done in functional terms. This includes a command language and a set of building blocks and tools.
- It implements a *resource management system* that interprets the tasks specified by the user and controls and manages the system resources to perform these tasks.

It is not the operating system as we know it today; rather, for our purposes, we have to generalize and extrapolate the concept into the future by introducing multimedia and geographic distribution. Then we can use it as a guiding model for the evolution of the future network beyond ISDN. Before we elaborate on the generalizations, let us show the analogies to the operating system concept. Just like the computer, the network needs a *user interface* to define the tasks to be done by the network. Message-oriented signaling like in Q.931 or CCS#7 is the basic component, which needs to be extended considerably. This leads eventually to the notion of customer programmability, which we will elaborate on later. Furthermore, the network needs a *control system* that manages the network resources to perform the desired functions. These two basic aspects are just the most general similarities. At lower levels, we will find many more analogies between today's computing systems and the telecommunication system's needs, which will be the subject of the next section. The similarities are no accident. Consider the fact that the most dramatic innovation in today's telephone network has been the introduction of *stored program control*, which has brought with it a wealth of computer concepts.

Now let us return to the two promised generalizations: The first generalization is **geographic transparency**. The network operating system differs from a computer operating system in that it deals not just with a single computing system but with the entire network. The UIS architectural freedom tenet allows transparent access to network resources independent of geographic location.

The second generalization moves us from data-only to **multimedia services**: whereas today's computers deal essentially with data, the network operating system has to deal with voice and images, including video, in addition to classical data. And these media are to be handled not just for interactive use but also for storage, conversion, and so on.

---

* This term has also been used in various other contexts: For example, for the operating system of a multiprocessor system, or for the services provided by the upper layers of the OSI reference model.

9.5.2 Operating System Paradigm

Let us look in more detail at the computer operating system of today and derive some observations for the evolution of the network and ISDN. A large body of knowledge about computer operating systems has been developed over the last 30 years and can serve us as a guide for the network operating system; it can serve as the integrated service system paradigm. There are several aspects that can be transferred from the operating system model to the network operating system model.

At the human interface we can expect to see extensive use of windows, menus, and icons to present a plausible model of the network and its resources to the end user. This model will most certainly appear much simpler than the real network. Graphical representations will show dynamic changes as they appear. As an example, consider a multiparty call setup. A window can show a simplified graph being constructed with icons of telephones depicting ringing and answering events. In most cases, the Touch-Tone pad will be replaced by a keyboard, and we may even see many end users operating a pointing device such as a mouse or a joy stick.

This may lead to the demise of the telephone extension as we know it today. In the infancy of computing, objects could only be accessed by giving their address. This was soon overcome by superimposing a name that was much more convenient than the numerical address. Even though the telephone extensions have lost part of their address significance (except in area codes and, maybe, exchange codes), we are still using cumbersome numeric names, which carry a lot of the baggage of an address. I expect that to change with ISDN. Alphanumeric names should be much more attractive, and computer users have been navigating through hierarchically organized (file) name spaces for many years. Such naming has a local and a global aspect. Locally, a user's telephone directory is a personalized list of names mapped into network numbers. The list can be kept in the user's terminal or in a central file or even in an updatable "smart-card." A global name service must be available to find anybody anywhere. Here a dialogue may be conducted for the modern equivalent of directory assistance. At the end of the dialogue the entry may be added automatically to the user's personal directory. In a time-sharing computing system, users have unique alphanumeric "user ids." It is conceivable that people get a unique alphanumeric form of their name registered (like Social Security Numbers in the United States) instead of today's telephone number, just as has been common for Telex addresses or ticker tape symbols. For this network name, uniqueness would be guaranteed in a local area, be it the town, county, or state, certainly not the local exchange. This is similar to certain 800 services in the United States that use the U.S. dial's mapping of letters to digits, a much too restrictive practice to be satisfactory for future evolution.

In time-sharing systems, when new programs or databases are offered for public use, there is some form of advertisement, or we have access to an on-line directory of services with manual pages, or the like. Similar facilities need to be offered from the network. The network will take on the function of a *broker*. Consider some entrepreneur offering a new information service, say a regularly updated data base with information about some specialty. The network would offer a "yellow page" entry, measure access from customers, and perform the billing task, all functions performed now in advanced time sharing systems. In addition, the credit-worthiness of the customer requesting service could be checked beforehand.

Another function offered by operating systems is a command language with some form of storing and executing sequences of commands, sometimes called scripts. An example is the call forwarding service that is dependent on the time of day and day of the week. Network customers should be offered a similar capability. Such scripts could be triggered by incoming voice or data calls and take different branches dependent on time, origin of call, and type of call. This feature would provide convenient customer programmability of the end-user interface.

Finally, operating system command languages offer connectives to combine programs and data bases. The UNIX system has the "pipe" facility, which allows one program to forward its output as input to another program. This is both a convenient command language notation as it is a powerful operating system service. This feature has proved tremendously useful; not only does it save a lot of repetitive programming by fostering reuse of software, but it is also very helpful for understanding, modifying, and debugging scripts. To use the pipe connective, programs are considered as providing a transformation from some input format to some output format (filters). The same concept can be generalized for multimedia communication, whether it is a noise filtering program, a voice editor, an image enhancement program, or just some data mapping or conversion for better representation. New connectives will allow to split or join information streams. For example, incoming voice could be played out and recorded at the same time, or a voice commentary can be added to a picture sequence or involved multiparty setups can be arranged.

With these remarks, we hope to have shown that the time sharing computing system with its operating system concept provides a plethora of ideas for the evolution of the integrated services digital network. There seems to be universal agreement that more and more intelligence will be associated with the network of the future. But there are different ways of introducing this intelligence into the network.

9.5.3 Integrated Intelligence or Intelligent Integration?

For an investigation of this question, let us take a look at the *broad architecture* of the future network. The notion of architecture has been defined as "the placement of functions" in a system. This view implies, first, a structural definition and, second, definitions of interfaces among the elements of the structure as well as to the outside world.

With regard to different types of network architectures, there are two schools of thought for the network design philosophy: integrate intelligence into the center of the network or attach it as its periphery, ultimately into the terminals. This parallels the evolution of computer operating systems, where we have seen one tendency to offer systems with maximum core functionality and another trend toward a bare-bones system, with a philosophy of putting as many functions as possible outside of the operating system into application programs. What are the factors and how do they weigh in to decide one way or the other? There are subtle implications for either approach.

The integrated intelligence approach wants to create an intelligent network that provides a maximum of useful services to the subscriber, using modules with built-in intelligence that interact with each other. If a customer has special needs, the network should offer basic capabilities to satisfy these needs. The intelligence is an integral, that is, inseparable, part of the network, and some would go as far as to refuse dumb services, that is, such that are very basic. In classical telephone terminology, this corresponds to the centrex approach that tries to maximize revenue for the exchange carrier.

At the other extreme, traditionally employed for computer networking, is the dumb or raw network that provides a minimum of basic services. Enhancements are typically added at the periphery; in telephony this corresponds to the PBX approach. Depending on where we draw the boundary between the network and the customer, we could add an "intelligent crust" to a simple but large and powerful core network and consider this crust part of the network. (The position of the boundary is often an arbitrary or regulatory decision.) Such an architecture might offer the benefits of easier operation, maintenance, and administration for the global core network. An architecture using an intelligent crust with a simple core would show some desirable decoupling of interfaces. For example, the crust would provide the flexibility to offer stable user interfaces on one hand or new nonstandard services in fast response to new market needs on the other hand, independent of changes inside the core network. Furthermore, it would allow to change out internal components of the core network in a way transparent to the end user and in response to advances in technology. This approach might be called *intelligent integration*. This philosophy is best illustrated in a Bellcore proposal for switched multimegabit data service [25].

The standards used for internal interconnection of network components (NNI or network node interface in CCITT parlance) could be quite different from the end user access standards (UNI or user-network interface). The latter should emphasize user convenience and aim for increasing the market. The former should emphasize ease of all aspects of network management and optimize overall cost. In my opinion, this distinction is not being emphasized sufficiently by the standards bodies, possibly because the regulatory forces work in different directions for different participants.

There is a strong movement toward an open network architecture (ONA) that facilitates a free-market multivendor environment. As a part of this movement, the common carriers would like to do custom programming of new services and be less dependent on equipment vendor software. Alternatively, new enhanced services could be provided by third parties connected to the central office switches. In the United States, there is a regulatory request for a comparatively efficient interconnection (CEI) that would ensure such enhanced-service providers access to the network with an efficiency comparable to that enjoyed by the network operator.

In summary, I think from a technological point of view either approach is feasible, but the deciding factor will be one of marketing, that is, of getting to the end user with profitable services in a timely way. Leaving the field of network architecture, let us now turn to some more fundamental technologies.

9.5.4 Killer Technologies

John Mayo has characterized three technologies as "killer technologies" with regard to the evolution of the network: microelectronics, photonics, and software [22]. Certainly all three technologies are increasingly being used in the realization of the network of the future. Let us look at each of them.

Photonics as used for transmission is bringing inexpensive bandwidth everywhere, eventually even to the private home, if and when it can be made cost effective, that is, if the services offered are attractive enough. The near-term challenge is how this abundance of bandwidth can be traded off against currently more expensive technologies. The engineers are challenged to come up with innovative approaches that may fly in the face of conventional technology. For example, the problem of switching entertainment video carried on fibers could be circumvented if we had inexpensive tunable receivers that could pick any one of a large multitude of television programs carried on the same fiber to every home simultaneously. If this problem were solved, it might still be necessary, for business reasons, to remotely control a tamper-proof decryption device in the receiver to enable a pay-per-view service.

It can be expected that technological breakthroughs in photonics will eventually lead to reliable and economical optical read/write storage, to photonic switching, and even to photonic logic allowing photonic computation. In each of these cases the term photonic implies that the detour from the realm of photons to the realm of electrons and back is avoided and that light interacts with light directly. But before we will see the expansion of photonics from transmission into the areas of logic, switching, and storage applications, these fields will be dominated by the enormous progress in microelectronics.

Progress in semiconductor technology and chip fabrication makes it possible to store and process ever more digital information at ever more increasing speeds and at lower and lower cost. The challenge is to find architectures of greatest utility. In the field of computer architecture, there is a debate about the best trade-offs between speed and complexity as evident in the reduced instruction set computer (RISC) architecture. A similar argument exists in the field of communication, as we will see below. In the end, progress in microelectronics may very well have its greatest impact where it achieves the best synergy with photonics and software technology. Integration of photoelectronic converters on the chip is an example of technology evolution. Reducing software complexity through use of new logic designs might be an example of architectural evolution.

The field of communication has seen an explosion of software, to the extent that the success of new public communication systems hinges on their software capabilities for new services, as well as for operation, administration, and maintenance. The problem with large bodies of software in its most general form is a problem of management of complexity. Research in software technology had been addressing this problem for quite some time. I find advances in three areas of significance for the evolution of ISDN.

First, there is *object-oriented programming*. In short, this is a new programming paradigm that holds great promise for building very large complex software systems with less effort than in the past and of higher quality [26]. Under this paradigm, we model the external world with persistent data objects using more precise definitions of operands and operations than conventional programming languages. Flexible classification capabilities (inheritance) ease the management of large numbers of different objects. The introduction of these techniques will bring relief on several fronts, for example, code that is easier to understand and maintain and code that can be produced by relatively independent small teams [27]. Furthermore, there is an inherent element of protection against inadvertent errors as well as intentional malfeasance. A perennial problem with new software technology is that it usually requires a lot more processing and memory resources. Here the challenge is to bring microelectronics to the aid of the new software techniques so that the execution overhead added by more structuralization is compensated.

A second area of software progress is in *user interfaces*, which have progressed to the point that the average person can control quite complex tasks through application-oriented languages. Often such languages are nonprocedural; that is, they do not use an ordered sequence of steps to define an algorithm, but rather allow statements of conditional execution in arbitrary order. The best examples are the interfaces of programs offered on personal computers for word processing and spreadsheets. Similar techniques will have to be introduced so that the ISDN user of the future can easily control multiparty, multimedia communication sessions [28].

The third area of software progress is the field of *artificial intelligence (AI)*. Expert systems with learning capability show promise for the management of the future network. Compared to the traditional networks, the new network has several added degrees of freedom, for example, with regard to multimedia, multiparty, and the time domain, that is, stored versus interactive use. Thus, traffic and failure recovery behavior become less predictable and require more sophisticated control and management. AI technology can also find application in the user interface, for example, for natural (written or spoken) language understanding.

These three technologies, photonics, microelectronics, and software, have been referred to as "killer technologies" because of their expected impact on the old network. Their effect will be even more dramatic when they can work in synergy. I see one such case where the power of microelectronics and software technology, and maybe even photonics, can be combined to aid the evolution of ISDN. This is fast packet switching technology.

9.5.5 Technological Synergy: Fast Packet Technology

Packet switching as a digital data communication technique was invented over 20 years ago.   In spite of its name, it is both a switching and a transmission technique. It is used today in many places as a technology, for example, in local area networks for computers and in the telephone signaling networks (CCS #6, CCS #7).   Contrast use of the *technology*, as just mentioned, from offering a packet switching *service*, on a public (X.25) or private network similar to the voice network.   As we have already seen, ISDN, as initially defined, will take such service out of the esoteric realm of a special service and bring it to every end user, be it over the D channel or connecting a B channel to a service provider.

The advantages of packet service are in two areas.   The obvious one is economy of facility use; due to the statistical nature of data traffic many data streams can be combined and enjoy high peak data rate service.   A second advantage is an improvement in reliability: packets can carry error-detection fields and can be retransmitted in case of error in a fashion transparent to the user.

The obvious disadvantages are more expensive hardware for processing, the traffic dependent variable delay, and the need for some kind of flow control, that is, a means to prevent individual subscribers from flooding the network or the receiver with traffic to the detriment of others.   For some time, it seemed that packet technology was just right for data, and for data only, until recently, when some promising progress in a field called fast packet technology was reported.

Packet switching requires a lot more processing than digital circuit switching. Packets have to be assembled and disassembled, including determination of length and error check sums, and the headers have to be processed to enable routing and switching decisions.   Due to progress in semiconductor technology, this processing has become much faster and less expensive.   In addition, lower error rates on digital transmission facilities allow simplification of protocols, in particular, error correction on an end-to-end basis rather than link by link.   Hence, the new fast packet technology is characterized by:

- Low end-to-end packet delay, in particular just a few milliseconds switch delay in addition to the transmission delay
- High-capacity switches, typically growable to millions of packets per second as an aggregate
- Much wider bandwidth, upward from 1 Mbps soon to reach hundreds of megabits per second

It is the latter aspect that gave rise to the term *wideband packet switching*, also chosen in distinction to another recently introduced concept, called burst switching, which offers statistical multiplexing economies and minimal delay by restricting access to one fixed rate of 64 kbps [29].   Also there is some ambiguity as to the object modified by the term fast: fast data rates, fast response, that is, low packet delay, or fast setup of virtual circuits, a concept explained above. Within the context of switching technology, we can define a spectrum ranging from traditional circuit switching as a deterministic switching method to fast packet switching, considered a statistical switching method [30].

9.5.6 Recent Advances in Switching Technology

Recent years have seen quite a bit of progress in the field of new switching architectures [31], as indicated by two milestones, which have been reached recently in fast packet technology. The first one is packetized voice; the second one, packetized video. While there have been several publications and research reports on packetized voice, the first large-scale field experiment was conducted in 1985/1986 by AT&T in California [32]. Unbeknownst to the telephone and data users (AT&T personnel), several familiar services were offered via an experimental fast packet network. Services included voice and other conventional narrowband services, such as voiceband data, and digital leased lines (9.6 through 56 kbps) for facsimile, compressed video, statistical multiplexers, and LAN interconnection.

The experimental equipment used some new technology. The major result of this 15-month field experiment is that the integration of voice and data services in a network that integrates transport as well as access is feasible and can be offering good (toll) quality voice services. Access to the wideband packet network was via 1.544-Mbps (DS1) facilities, which were used between several adapting multiplexers and a fast packet switch containing a self-routing interconnection matrix. The multiplexer, known as access interface, converted a variety of external formats to a common fast packet protocol, which is very similar to the LAPD protocol proposed for frame relay transport mode. The fast packet switch used a buffered banyan interconnection matrix that belongs to a broad category of self-routing multistage switches. An example of a banyan interconnection network is shown in Fig. 9.7. The switching fabric of such networks is made up of simple two-by-

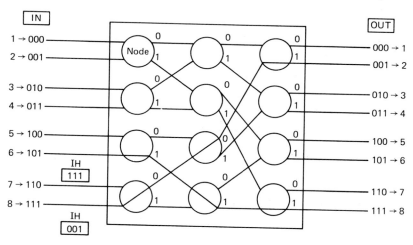

IH, internal header for self-routing

Figure 9.7 Banyan interconnection network.

two switching elements, shown as circles. These nodes operate on subsequent bits of the address in the header, which decides where to route an incoming packet. The figure shows two examples of headers with addresses 111 and 001, and it is left to the reader to prove that this indeed causes them to wind up at the output ports labeled with respective addresses on the right, no matter where the packets entered at the left.

Originating in computer science, where they have been investigated for processor interconnection, multistage self-routing packet switches have enjoyed a remarkable progress in recent years, and quite a few innovative architectures have been proposed and reported on [36].

The banyan is the simplest such network. Internal collisions can be reduced by buffering and by running the network faster than the access lines. Similar effects can be obtained by devising more elaborate topologies. One well publicized such switch is the Starlite switch [33]. Its salient characteristic is the use of a sorting stage (also known as a batcher network) preceding the banyan or omega network to eliminate internal blocking. This type of architecture operates in a packet-synchronous mode to permit the sorting process. There is a continuing race to demonstrate faster and faster packet switches. The technological hurdles to overcome are manifold. For example, at higher speeds the use of the familiar bit-stuffing technique to provide transparency for variable-size packets may be replaced by techniques like 4-in-5-bit coding as used in FDDI, or we resort to fixed frame length. Another challenge is the speed of address translation, which may limit the number of packets per second rather than the bit rate. Figure 9.8 shows throughput as a function of packet size for a hardware packet protocol processor implemented in different VLSI technologies (different clock rates) indicative of what is commercially available today and what we might expect in the near future. Such processing is needed in access interfaces or trunk controllers for fast packet switches.

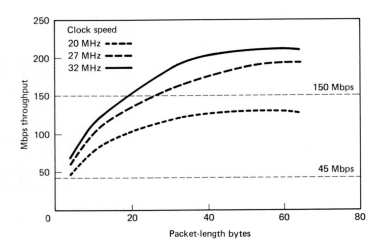

Figure 9.8   Throughput of a packet processor.

We mentioned earlier the first milestone of demonstrating the ability to handle interactive packetized voice. Recent reports indicate that a second milestone has been reached in the laboratory, that of being able to switch uncompressed packetized television signals [34]. In an example, the NTSC video standard was digitized into 15,750 packets/second, each representing a video line at about 700 bytes, which yields a total of 88 Mbps on a single access line. In distinction to conventional banyan switches, the experimental equipment used a multistage alternate routing network that is also capable of broadcasting.

In summary, recent advances in fast packet technology make us believe that it can support services well into the access range of broadband ISDN. The evolving asynchronous transfer mode protocol is another manifestation of the rising power of fast packet technology concepts.

9.5.7 Fast Packet Technology in the Network

Initial proposals for use of fast packet technology focused on the economic benefits of bandwidth compression through statistical multiplexing. The importance of this property will diminish as bandwidth becomes more and more abundant, in particular for transmission. The important power of the technology lies in two other areas.

From a customer access point of view, the intrinsic dynamic management of bandwidth is of prime importance to handle a variety of services, in particular bursty nonvoice applications. In the extreme, burstiness can go so far as to imply some type of connectionless service. For these scenarios, fast packet technology provides the ideal match.

From a network service provider's point of view, there is much appeal in the fact that there could be one unified transport network for all forms of communication. This reduces the complexity of all tasks concerned with operating, administering and maintaining the network. The label on the packet gives an easy handle to differentiate between types of service and thus to offer more customized services than just "plain bit pipes." In other words, better control of the reactions to market changes is provided.

Up to a certain limiting data rate determined by technology, we could use a single uniform network where all information appears in packetized form. At higher data rates we would have to use circuit switching. The intended application would also influence which technology to choose. Figure 9.9 tries to characterize the applicability of circuit and a packet switching for a wide variety of different services.* The abscissa in this figure uses a burstiness measure, where a burstiness of value 1 implies a steady uninterrupted stream of information, whereas a value of 2 indicates that the source is only active half the time, with the active and silent intervals being statistically distributed. The ordinate is the peak transfer rate from the source on a logarithmic scale. The dotted lines around applications indicate expected future trends. The shaded area under the curve on the lower right indicates the domain of packet switching, which seems to be expanding into the

---

* This figure is based on an earlier version created by W. P. Lidinsky of AT&T Bell Labs.

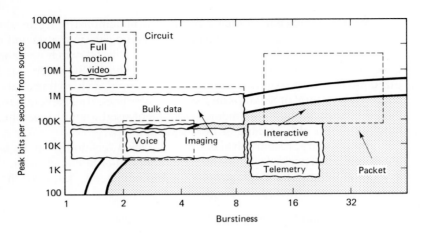

Figure 9.9 Evolution of circuit and packet switching domains.

upper left, the domain of circuit switching. The picture shows that, for applications with high burstiness, packet service dominates, whereas very high data rates are still the domain of circuit service.

We should keep in mind that circuit service at lower speeds can be provided on packet networks. Isochronous schemes have been proposed to emulate a digital circuit interface such as the B and H channels of ISDN in a fast packet network.

Let us conclude our discussion of fast packet technology with a look at its relationship to photonics. There is quite a bit of synergy, in particular when we look at recent advances in photonic switching, a field still in its infancy [35]. The bandwidth offered by light is so enormous that we have yet to grasp its implications—and find good use for it. Notice that a large number of bits are occurring in a very short time interval; hence there is no time to make individual bit-by-bit processing decisions. Instead we have a train of pulsed light, followed by a guard band of silence (darkness) or a pulse train to recapture phase, which gives us time for a switching decision. Rather than bit multiplexing or byte multiplexing (interleaving) at photonic speeds, we are more likely to see such a block multiplexing scheme. This is a situation that we are used to in packet switching, and I see an emerging symbiotic relationship between photonic switching and fast packet switching. The first truly photonic switch may very well be a photonic packet switch.

9.6 CONCLUSION

I have taken the risk of speculating about the future of ISDN. This has been a very personal view, colored by my background as a computer scientist. I must expect that most of my speculations probably won't come true or will evolve quite differently. Yet I am convinced that a grand concept such as the network operating system should prove to be very useful, and, if followed, would result in a network architecture that would survive the test of time as one of the great cultural accomplishments in human history.   I think ISDN has the potential to become an important entry in the history books of future generations.

9.7 ACKNOWLEDGMENTS

I wish to acknowledge that many of the ideas in this chapter evolved from conversations with my colleagues at AT&T Bell Laboratories.   I specifically owe thanks to conversations with W.-H. Francis Leung about operating system concepts, with Andreas Papanicolaou, M. Niel Ransom, and George H. Clapp about standards, with Avinash K. Vaidya on fast packet switching technology, and with R. L.Pawelski and T.S. Rzeszewski on video encoding.   James I. Cochrane, Achilles M. Perdikaris, and Behram H. Bharucha gave me valuable reviews.   Mark A. Pashan provided me with measurements on packet translation.   The opinions expressed in this paper are, however, my own.

REFERENCES

9.1.   Koji Kobayashi, *Computers and Communications, A Vision of C & C*, MIT Press, Cambridge, Mass., 1986.

9.2.   CCITT Recommendation I.122, *Blue Book*, Volume III, Fascicle 3.7, "Framework for providing new packet mode bearer services," IXth Plenary Assembly, Melbourne, 14–25 Nov. 1988; Geneva 1989.

9.3.   Andrew S. Tanenbaum, *Computer Networks*, Prentice- Hall, Englewood Cliffs, N.J., 1981, pp. 22–23.

9.4.   Douglas E. Comer, *Internetworking with TCP/IP: Principles, Protocols, and Architecture*, Prentice-Hall, Englewood Cliffs, N.J., 1988.

9.5.   Wai Sum Lei, "Packet mode services: from X.25 to frame relaying," *IEEE Computer Comm. Mag.*, Feb. 1989, pp. 10–17.

9.6.   P. E. White, "Broadband ISDN—the next generation broadband telecommunications network," *IEEE International Conference Comm. 86*, Toronto, Canada, June 22–25, 1986, pp. 385–387.

9.7.   Ronald K. Jurgen, "High-definition television," *IEEE Spectrum*, Apr. 1988, pp. 56–62.

9.8.   M. Dupire, F. Gering, "BIARRITZ: First French Wide Band Communication Network," *Proc. of ISS '84*, Florence, Italy, May 1984, Session 31C, Paper 2, pp. 1–6.

9.9.   T. Kummerow, "Bild- und Tonuebertragung in Glasfaser- Breitband-Ortsnetzen, Teil 1: Systemkonzept," *NTZ Nachrichtentechnische Zeitschrift*, Bd. 38, H. 3, 1985, pp. 140–144.

9.10.   A. G. Fraser, "Datakit—a modular network for synchronous and asynchronous traffic," *Proc. ICC 1979*, Boston, pp. 20.1.1–20.1.3.

9.11.   A. Thomas, J. P. Coudreuse, and M. Servel, "Asynchronous time-division techniques: an experimental packet network integrating video communication," *Proc. ISS '84*, Florence, Italy, May 1984, Session 32C, Paper 2, pp. 1–7.

9.12. Kai Hwang and Faye A. Briggs, *Computer Architecture and Parallel Processing*, McGraw-Hill, New York, 1984, pp. 494–497.

9.13. Exchange Carriers Standards Association (ECSA), Proposal by T1X1 Committee on Carrier-to-Carrier Interfaces.

9.14. R. J. Boehm and others, "Standard fiber optic transmission systems—a synchronous optical network view," *IEEE J. Selected Areas Comm.*, SAC-4, No. 9, pp. 1424–1431.

9.15. Paul W. Shumate, "Optical lines to homes," *IEEE Spectrum*, Feb. 1989, pp. 43–47.

9.16. C. F. Hemrick, E. J. Isganitis, and R. W. Klessig, "A protocol architecture for access to an ISDN offering broadband services," *Proc. ISS '87*, Phoenix, Ariz., CH2431-5/87/0000-0619.

9.17. William Lidinsky (guest ed.), Special Issue on Metropolitan Area Networks, *IEEE Comm. Mag.*, Apr. 1988, pp. 5–77.

9.18. ANSI Standards Committee X3T9.5, Draft Proposal American National Standards X3.166-198x, American National Standards Institute, 1430 Broadway, New York, NY 10018.

9.19. Floyd E. Ross, "FDDI—a tutorial," *IEEE Comm. Mag.*, Vol. 24, No. 5, May 1986, pp. 10–17.

9.20. James F. Mollenauer, "Standards for metropolitan area networks," *IEEE Comm. Mag.*, Apr. 1988, pp. 15–19.

9.21. S. W. Johnston, "Network services supporting UIS," *Proc. ICCC 87*, Munich, pp. 306–310.

9.22. John S. Mayo, *"The evolution toward universal information services,"* *Telephony*, March 4, 1985, pp. 40–50.

9.23. W. H. Leung and others, "A set of operating system mechanisms to support multi-media applications," *Proc. 1988 International Zurich Seminar Digital Comm.*, Mar. 1988, pp. 140–148.

9.24. W. H. Leung and G. W. R. Luderer, "The network operating system concept for future services," *AT&T Tech. J.*, Mar. 1989, pp. 23–35.

9.25. C. F. Hemrick, R. W. Klessig, and J. M. Roberts, "Switched multi-megabit data service and early availability via MAN technology," *IEEE Comm. Mag.*, Apr. 1988, pp. 9–14.

9.26. Bruce Shriver and Peter Wegner (eds.), *Research Directions in Object-Oriented Programming*, MIT Press, Cambridge, Mass., 1987.

9.27. E. C. Arnold and D. W. Brown, *"Object-oriented software technologies applied to switching system architectures and software development process,"* Proc. of International Switching Symposium, 1990, Stockholm.

9.28. T. L. Hansen and others, "A nonprocedural language for telecommunication call processing applications," *Proc. 1986 International Zurich Seminar on Digital Comm.*, 1986, pp. 100–106.

9.29. Stanford A. Amstutz, "Burst switching—an introduction," *IEEE Comm. Mag.*, Nov. 1983, pp. 36–42.

9.30. J. J. Kulzer and W. A. Montgomery, "Statistical switching architectures for future services, "*Proc. International Switching Symposium*, 1984, Florence, Italy, pp. 43A1–6.

9.31. Jonathan Turner, "New directions in communications," *Proc. 1986 Zurich Seminar on Digital Comm.*, IEEE Cat. No. 86CH2277-2, pp. 25–32.

9.32. R. W. Muise, T. J. Schonfeld, and G. H. Zimmerman III, "Experiments in wideband packet technology," *Proc. 1986 Zurich Seminar Digital Comm.*, IEEE Cat. No. 86CH2277-2), pp. 135–139.

9.33. Allan Huang and Scott Knauer, "STARLITE; a wideband digital switch," *Proc. Globecomm 84*, Nov. 1984, pp. 120–128.

9.34. G. W. R. Luderer and others, "Wideband packet technology for switching systems," *Proc. International Switching Symposium '87*, Phoenix, Ariz., IEEE Cat. No. CH2431–5, pp. 448–454.

9.35. Eric Nussbaum, "Communication network needs and technologies—a place for photonic switching?" *IEEE J. Selected Areas Comm.*, Vol. 6, No. 7, Aug. 1988, pp. 1036–54.

9.36. J. J. Degan, G. W. R. Luderer, A. K. Vaidya, "*Fast packet technology for future switches*," *AT&T Tech. J.*, Mar./Apr. 1989, pp. 36–60.

9.37. R. M. Newman, Z. L. Budrikis, and J. L. Hullett, "The QPSXMAN," *IEEE Comm. Mag.*, Apr. 1988, pp. 20–28.

Index